Hamilton Heights and Sugar Hill

PRAISE FOR *HAMILTON HEIGHTS AND SUGAR HILL*

"Over the years, several books and projects have attempted to capture the essence of Hamilton Heights and Sugar Hill, and thankfully, with Davida Siwisa James, the legendary community has its griot."—**Herb Boyd**, Adjunct Professor, City College of New York

"Harlem is a storied New York City neighborhood that has been recognized as the global capital of the African diaspora for more than a century. Davida Siwisa James's searching and gracefully written *Hamilton Heights and Sugar Hill: Alexander Hamilton's Old Harlem Neighborhood Through the Centuries* . . . a book that is both a history and a meditation on the power of place. The story of Hamilton Grange, during and after Hamilton's life, serves as a binding thread in the book. Hamilton Heights and Sugar Hill are changing, along with Harlem, but there is great value in knowing the past to better navigate the present. Davida Siwisa James's probing, lyrical, and insightful book helps us do both."—**Robert W. Snyder**, author and Professor Emeritus Rutgers University, and Manhattan Borough Historian, *Journal of Urban Affairs*

"*Hamilton Heights and Sugar Hill* traces the transformation of New York's West Harlem community from the ancestral hunting grounds of the Lenape Indians into the cultural mecca of Black America. Davida Siwisa James narrates with pictures one of America's most prolific neighborhoods."—**Dr. Bruce D. Haynes**, author and Professor of Sociology, University of California, Davis

" . . . A sweeping account of the buildings, businesses, and streets that have been affected by modern-day gentrification, and looks at how this has changed Sugar Hill and Hamilton Heights—and Harlem as a whole. James offers an encyclopedic accounting of two of Harlem's historic neighborhoods."—**Karen Juanita Carillo**, *New York Amsterdam News*

"It makes me miss a place I've never been."—**Aldene Fredenburg**, freelance editor

"In *Hamilton Heights and Sugar Hill*, author Davida Siwisa James uses several individual buildings and collections of buildings, the people who built them, and the people who occupied them to describe the centuries-long, rich history of the Upper Manhattan neighborhoods that came to be known as Harlem, Hamilton Heights, and Sugar Hill. The book is an ambitious, comprehensive social and architectural history that provides a chronology that leaves the reader with an appreciation for the people and places that made these Upper Manhattan communities important to New York City and US history."—**Kevin McGruder**, *The Metropole*: The Official Blog of the Urban History Association

HAMILTON HEIGHTS AND SUGAR HILL

Alexander Hamilton's Old Harlem Neighborhood Through the Centuries

Davida Siwisa James

EMPIRE STATE EDITIONS

AN IMPRINT OF FORDHAM UNIVERSITY PRESS

NEW YORK 2025

All photographs attributed as "courtesy D. S. James" are the property of the author.

Cover Photo:
The 400 block of 144th Street in Hamilton Heights, one of the most historic streets in Harlem; part of the original rowhouses built in 1888 by William De Forest and William Mowbray that gave Hamilton Heights and Sugar Hill its distinctive charm. Hamilton's home, the Grange, was still in its original location, across from them, while they were being constructed. Photo courtesy D. S. James.

Copyright © 2024 Davida Siwisa James

All rights reserved. No part of this publication may be reproduced, stored in a retrieval system, or transmitted in any form or by any means—electronic, mechanical, photocopy, recording, or any other—except for brief quotations in printed reviews, without the prior permission of the publisher.

Fordham University Press has no responsibility for the persistence or accuracy of URLs for external or third-party Internet websites referred to in this publication and does not guarantee that any content on such websites is, or will remain, accurate or appropriate.

Fordham University Press also publishes its books in a variety of electronic formats. Some content that appears in print may not be available in electronic books.

Visit us online at www.fordhampress.com/empire-state-editions.

Library of Congress Cataloging-in-Publication Data available online at https://catalog.loc.gov.

Printed in the United States of America

27 26 25   5 4 3 2 1

First paperback edition 2025

To my father,
David "Turk" McNeil
The last of the suave post–Harlem Renaissance gents.
Thank you for giving me Sugar Hill.
I hope this makes you proud.
D.V.

AND

To my grandmother
Drucilla Fitzgerald Porter Maddox
You loved me into being.

CONTENTS

Author's Historical Note ix

Dyckman and Hamilton Maps xi

Note on Spelling xiii

Preface xv

The Neighborhood xxi

1. Dutch Beginnings and Native Americans 1
2. The Making of Harlem Heights 9
3. Harlem Land Grants, Mount Morris, and a Revolution 22
4. Hamilton Grange and the Duel 38
5. The Jumels, the Street Grid, and Audubon 55
6. The Bailey Mansion, St. Luke's, and a Building Boom 76
7. The Great Migration and the Morris Museum 100
8. The Hamilton Museum and the Hamilton Theatre 124
9. The Harlem Renaissance 139

10. The Heights Identity and the Black Mecca   170

11. Jazz Clubs, The Numbers, and Firsts   193

12. The Advent of the Sixties, Generational Changes, and the Arts   212

13. A Neighborhood's Changing Face   236

14. Parlor Jazz and the Great Renovation   253

15. Changing Demographics and a Revived Hamilton Heights   279

16. Bailey House, Jazz, and the Renaissance Remix   302

17. Where It Leads   336

Afterword   345

Addendum A: Excerpted Harlem Ordinances and Land Patents   349

Addendum B: Photos Past and Present   353

Acknowledgments   355

Notes   359

Selected Bibliography   375

Index   383

AUTHOR'S HISTORICAL NOTE:
ON HAERLEM, HAARLEM, AND FINALLY HARLEM

Manhattan, New York City

So named by its original Dutch colonists in honor of the city Haarlem in the Netherlands, situated between The Hague and Amsterdam. Haarlem is renowned in Dutch history for its bravery during a siege.

Historical nonfiction books often contain so many details that it is easy for significant points to be lost 200 pages later, between one fact and another. These are some important points worth highlighting, of which we make early note.

New York, both state and city, had many names. The Indigenous People, the Munsee and Unami, called the city Lenapehoking, meaning "Dwelling-Place of the Lenape," who were of the Algonquin Nation. From Henry Hudson's arrival, the native name was said to be Mannahatta. The Dutch kept the name, with just the slightest change in spelling, to Manhattan.

Part of the western, hilly area in Upper Manhattan was called Penadnic, or Penabnic. Later, it was called Jochem Pieters' Hills, after one of the earliest seventeenth-century Dutch colonists who settled there (Jochem Pietersen Kuyter of Holstein). By the time George Washington won the Battle of Harlem Heights and headquartered in the hilly neighborhood, at the outset of the American Revolution in 1776, it was called Harlem Heights. It was still Harlem Heights when Alexander Hamilton built his home, the Grange, in 1800.

Penadnic. Jochem Pieters' Hills. Harlem Heights. Sugar Hill. Hamilton Heights.

From the original Haarlem land grants, issued by the Dutch West India Company, to the German, French, Dutch, and Belgian colonists who arrived on ships from Holland between 1624 and 1664 to settle in New Amsterdam, Haarlem once covered approximately 60 to 70 percent of Manhattan.

Haarlem was a separate community, incorporated under the Dutch in 1658, and managed by a corporation named *The Town of Haarlem*. The actual "Village" of Haarlem, around 125th Street, was but one small part of the greater Haarlem and its common lands. Haarlem once reached from around 78th Street to the northernmost tip of Manhattan at 220th Street, ending at Spuyten Duyvil, where Jan Dyckman's farm was located. Dyckman was one of the early seventeenth-century Haarlem land grantees. As of this printing, the family's rebuilt nineteenth-century house still stands in Inwood.

The original Haarlem Land Grants were issued to the Dutch colonists, starting in 1646. They were reaffirmed and expanded three times under British rule after they took possession of Manhattan in 1664. The Duke of York renamed Dutch New Amsterdam as *New York*. But when the British tried renaming Haarlem "Lancaster," the residents refused to adhere to that declaration. *Names have power*. Haarlem (which then became Harlem in the British spelling) managed its affairs, land sales, and land grants as a separate township. Harlem was annexed to the City of New York in 1873.

All other neighborhoods created after Haarlem's seventeenth-century Dutch beginnings (Manhattanville, Morningside Heights, Carmansville, Audubon Park, Washington Heights, and Inwood) stem from the original, vast section of Northern Manhattan that was Harlem, settled in the 1600s.

DYCKMAN AND HAMILTON MAPS

Dyckman Property Sales Map

This 1870 map was drawn to show potential buyers the shaded lots to the far right (west) that were for sale by the executors of Isaac Dyckman's property in Washington Heights above 180th Street. It provides a good outline of this section of Harlem and Washington Heights with the newly numbered streets, many of which had not yet been paved.

The infamous 1811 street grid did not reach Alexander Hamilton's home at 141st Street and Amsterdam and Convent avenues until the 1880s.

By the first half of the twentieth century, the neighborhoods of Hamilton Heights and Sugar Hill are roughly defined in this book as about 135th Street and Edgecombe Avenue North to the Hudson River and stretching to approximately 165th Street.

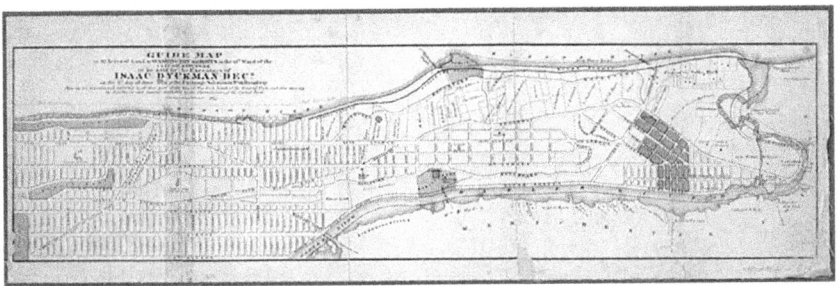

Figure 1. Isaac Dyckman sales map, 1870. Courtesy NY Public Library

Alexander Hamilton's Grange Land Purchase

There is no known existing deed to Alexander Hamilton's land purchase or a surveyor's map from that period. The boundaries of Hamilton's property have been surmised through an educated approximation, given neighboring land holdings, correspondence, and various descriptions of Hamilton's purchase and nearby estates. The map identifying his purchase would show approximately 140th Street to 148th Street, from the Kingsbridge Road (now St. Nicholas Avenue) north between what is now Amsterdam Avenue and the Bloomingdale Road (now Broadway); see Figure 2.

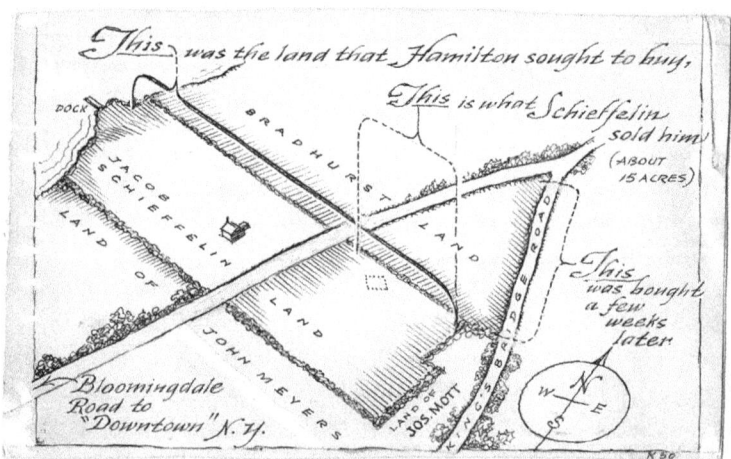

Figure 2. Grange Property Map. Courtesy National Park Service, Manhattan Historic Sites Archive

NOTE ON SPELLING

Research the settling of New York City and one will find that throughout four hundred years of various books, journals, deeds, letters, legal documents (and now websites), there can be several different spellings of the same name for people, places, and things. This reflects the liberty taken by early historians of how they perceived Native American names to be spelled, as well as translations, and variations of the Dutch, British, and then the Americanized versions of spelling. Slight differences throughout this text may vary based on the most common usage and whether we adhered to the spelling within a direct quote.

PREFACE

Names have power. Some words sound and feel better than others. I have always liked the word "Manhattan," as I have the word "Harlem." It is true that we come to associate a name with our personal reality and what it comes to mean to us over time. Yet the sound and feel of certain words can evoke deep-seated emotions. Many cultures have time-honored traditions around naming a person or a place. It carries great significance.

My parents, Ernestine Haggans and David "Turk" McNeil, were both natives of Philadelphia. They were separated by the time I was a toddler, and my father settled in New York City a few years later, in the late 1950s. But in 1961, when I was eight, Dad came back to North Philly to take me to his apartment in Harlem, where I was to spend a summer vacation before starting second grade. Impressed by the sumptuous life that he led with his girlfriend, Mary Mack, in their beautiful apartment, I asked if I could stay. It was the antithesis of the poverty in which my family lived in North Philly. The summer turned into two years.

We lived on West 120th Street, a block from Morningside Park, in a fifth-floor walkup. It was so stylish, beyond any dream I'd ever had, with tasteful furniture, thick drapes, deep carpets, beautiful artwork, hundreds of record albums, and a freezer full of choice cuts of meat that I had never seen before. Who knew there was such a thing as a leg of lamb that people marinated and roasted? Having my own room with a newly built closet stuffed with brand-new clothes seemed like a fairy tale.

Four places were on my tour of Manhattan the day after I arrived. We got in Dad's car, and he drove me past Columbia University on Broadway. He said it was a source of pride that this important university was in Harlem. We kept driving west on Broadway, to about 175th Street, where he took me to Washington Heights and my first visit to a Jewish deli. Dad opened my senses to the smells and tastes of bagels, lox, and cream cheese along with pastrami, coleslaw, and corned beef on rye, smells that would forever comfort me. Because he was greeted warmly by the people behind the counter, I could tell he was a regular. That was my enduring memory of Washington Heights: that it had Jewish delis selling great bread and meat.

After we headed back downtown, my father took me to the most important stop on my first day in New York, our neighborhood library on West 135th Street off Lenox Avenue. He knew that I loved to read. And while I can't remember the names of any of the librarians who were so kind to me in later months, I knew that the library was my favorite place on the tour.

After driving a few more blocks, we parked on 125th Street and walked. He pointed out the Apollo Theater and said that his friend Honi Coles was the manager; it would be decades before I learned he was an acclaimed tap dancer and a fellow Philly native. That was an incredible first day.

In the coming months, Uncle Honi, as I came to call him, would let me sit backstage at the Apollo with his niece while he worked. We played jacks in between watching the singers and musicians do sound checks or rehearse. Later, we went from watching the young singers and seasoned professionals rehearse to seeing them perform on stage. It would be another twenty years before I realized that I had watched the Motown Review that introduced the Miracles, the Supremes, Little Stevie Wonder, and others at their Apollo debut. We didn't realize we were watching history in the making, future legends in their youth. One never does. And I would get tears in my eyes when Uncle Honi appeared as the band leader many decades later in the film *Dirty Dancing*.

I kept devising ways I could hide in the Schomburg library and get locked in there overnight. Recently, I felt a personal sense of pride when I learned that my special childhood "book place" had become a historic landmark, now called the Schomburg Center for Research in Black Culture.

My father was a bartender, handsome, dashing, and he always seemed to be dressed up even when he was home. Women were constantly smiling at him. He worked in almost all the Harlem clubs and bars that have since become legendary. He was also a jazz aficionado, and there was either jazz or Brazilian bossa nova playing twenty-four hours a day in our house. While I liked the younger artists at the Apollo, I was upset that Dad made me go with him to hear Brook Benton, Count Basie, Cab Calloway, and a host of other jazz musicians that I found boring. Though I didn't understand all that she said, I did like the comedienne Moms Mabley.

I was not a latchkey kid. Dad or someone else would pick me up from St. Thomas, the local Catholic elementary school. I would sit in the bar where he was working, at a corner table, drink my Shirley Temple, do my homework, and sometimes listen to the musicians warm up. Occasionally, one of them would stop by to give me a couple of quarters or a dollar because I was "Turk's kid."

I grew to love New York City, as Dad took me to my first Broadway play, the Macy's Thanksgiving Day Parade, and strolls around Greenwich Village and Central Park. But I especially loved Harlem. Even as a child, walking up and down its streets, I was always amazed by the architecture. At eight I doubt if I knew the word "architecture." But I would look up at some incredible design around a window or the entranceway of an apartment building and think, "That took skill and time. Somebody really thought about that." I wondered why the men who constructed it had created that bit of design or chosen a particular type of stone. Without knowing the age of the dwellings, I realized that those craftsmen had left their mark, admired all these years later.

Dad and his friends used to mention a place called Sugar Hill, which turned out to be a section of Harlem just a dozen blocks or so west that one could easily walk to, a dozen blocks and a whole different lifestyle. I liked that name—Sugar Hill—and I assumed they sold a lot of candy there. Yet they spoke of the area as if it were a separate, very special place in New York. And when Dad took me to the apartments of a couple of his friends on Riverside Drive and another on Edgecombe Avenue, I understood why. These places were opulent and spacious.

By the mid-1960s, my father moved to the Paul Robeson Residence at 555 Edgecombe Avenue and 162nd Street, home of countless Harlem luminaries, though I didn't know that at the time. I had already returned to Philly because I missed my mom and my brothers and sisters. I was his only child, but I had siblings that I loved from her two other marriages. I returned to New York regularly during summers and holidays. I recognized immediately that 555 was in a very different part of Harlem than our previous apartment by the park, and everything seemed bigger and better, fancier. We had our own doorman at 555, and I found him exotic in his fancy uniform. I loved that he remembered my name, and Dad seemed to always be slipping him money for some reason.

I knew that Hamilton Heights in Harlem was a special place. Sugar Hill is within Hamilton Heights, and I would learn that the two names would be used interchangeably. But the Hamilton Heights–Sugar Hill neighborhood was from approximately 135th Street and Edgecombe Avenue to 165th or so, stretching to the Hudson River. The neighborhood just had a feeling of elegance about it, even though many people would say that it was well into its declining years by the 1960s. It did not seem so to me.

After returning to New York regularly for holidays for several years, I moved back permanently in 1968, when I was fourteen, having just lost my mother and grandmother. We were now on Convent Avenue, and I would walk the neighborhood with such a sense of joy that you would have thought I owned each building. Even then, I sensed history and stories inside those gorgeous brownstones and Gothic structures.

On one weekend home from boarding school, I still remember coming back from a walk one day to tell Dad, "Believe it or not, there are some Black kids doing ballet down the street." It was not until the 1990s, while skimming the program at a performance of the Dance Theatre of Harlem in California, that I realized that in 1968 I had watched Arthur Mitchell at the studio he had just opened down the street from us.

Our apartment on Convent Avenue had gleaming hardwood floors, a full kitchen with pots hanging from the ceiling, French doors, a separate dining room with bamboo wallpaper, and a working gas fireplace. The streets were spotless, and City College became my happy place where I would sit and watch teachers and students move about the campus. I walked by Alexander Hamilton's former home at 141st and Convent countless times. But while I knew we lived in Hamilton Heights, I don't think I knew that the aging tan wooden building was once his. I doubt I even noticed it.

I love the idea of New York City as a whole, with its very distinct boroughs. But it is Manhattan that makes my heart stir. There is this perfect balance that is hard to describe about the mixture of skyscrapers, fifteen-story apartment buildings, and more-than-a-century-old brownstones. I loved the different feel of the neighborhoods—Greenwich Village, Times Square, Central Park, and especially Harlem, and Washington Heights. There is a harmony in hearing a half-dozen languages on one block and having just as many choices of cuisines. This great, complex, crowded city has so many options for the arts and culture that it would be silly to try to list them. Yet one can still find a quiet place where there is just you and the water upon which to gaze and dream.

All these decades later, since leaving Manhattan in 1976, I finally understand my response when people ask if I would ever move back to New

York. I tell them, "I'd go back tomorrow if I could afford it." The reason I still feel so passionately about the city is in that best cliché: "Once a New Yorker, always a New Yorker." When I left, it was only supposed to be for two years. I always meant to return. Like the accidental tourist, I became an accidental Californian.

The inspiration to write a book on Hamilton Heights and Sugar Hill came to me during the COVID-19 pandemic, which began in early 2020. Partially, I was inspired by Lin-Manuel Miranda's 2015 hit Broadway musical *Hamilton*, which won eleven Tony awards.

The play made me reflect on my old neighborhood. When I first heard about it, I thought it was great that Hamilton was getting his due. I would tell people that I used to live in the Hamilton Heights section of Harlem when I was a teenager. Some folks thought that I was making this up because of the show. But most people were surprised to learn that there was an area of Harlem where Alexander Hamilton once lived. I was pretty sure it looked quite different in his day.

I saw *Hamilton* at the Pantages in Hollywood in 2017, and I agreed with everyone that it was fabulous. But I was disappointed that the only mention of Hamilton's Harlem home were fleeting references to "uptown."

Yet it was the pitying looks and remarks that greeted me whenever I mentioned that I had once lived in Harlem that shocked me. Trying to convince people that Hamilton Heights and Sugar Hill were beautiful neighborhoods, with stunning architecture and mansions, fell on deaf ears. Sadly, I was aware that people tend to have a negative reaction to the name "Harlem" and consider it just a ghetto, even though gentrification had revitalized large sections of it for decades by now.

I could not find an in-depth historical account of the development of this beautiful Harlem neighborhood, where Alexander Hamilton's former home the Grange still stood. There was no historical account of how this particular neighborhood, where George Washington had headquartered in 1776 and Thurgood Marshall had lived, became the Beekman Place or Beverly Hills of Harlem for African Americans.

I thought I would take my idol Toni Morrison's advice. She once said that "if there's a book that you want to read, but it hasn't been written yet, then you must write it." And I firmly believe that my old neighborhood deserves to be written about.

I paid a visit there in 2021 to do research for the book. I was fortunate to get an Airbnb on Convent Avenue. I was overcome with emotion walking those streets again. I had a new appreciation for the beauty of Hamilton

Heights. There were so many changes, and I was shocked at the gentrification throughout Harlem and the dramatic differences of both the people who now called it home and the new construction.

This book shares the history of that special section of Harlem that borders Washington Heights. It is the westernmost part of current-day Harlem. For the purposes of this book, I do not recognize the recent borders of Harlem that end at 155th Street. That dividing line is a false construct that has been repeated and printed so many times that it has come to be considered factual. That happens.

Rather, I use the borders from centuries past, when the original Dutch colonists were issuing new plots in the Harlem common lands that the Town of Harlem corporation owned. These were the Harlem Heights areas where Roger Morris and others bought land from those Dutch descendants and built mansions. The neighborhood history I share of Harlem Heights (which became Hamilton Heights and Sugar Hill) starts at about 135th Street from Edgecombe Avenue north to the Hudson River, stretching to approximately 165th Street.

I use the same borders that George Washington did in reporting to John Hancock and our newly formed Congress that he was camped out with the Continental Army in "Harlem Heights and the Roger Morris House." Harlem's history and those heights are bursting with significant events and people whose stories could have filled another hundred pages beyond what I've written. The John James Audubon estate, Trinity Church Cemetery and Mausoleum, and the Morris-Jumel Mansion are identified in this book as being in Hamilton Heights and Sugar Hill.

For years, as that much anticipated 2001 approached, I would try to get Dad to record some of his memories of his Harlem days tending bar or just clubbing, to no avail. Approaching his nineties, he had started dropping these casual statements: *"I used to work at Minton's. Carmen [McRae] or Nina [Simone] would stop by when they knew I was tending bar. Billie [Holiday] was so sad near the end of her life. Billy Strayhorn was such a nice guy. So and so used to come by the Red Rooster. Did I tell you Thelonious Monk lived on our block?"* Where is a tape recorder when you need one?

There are stories upon stories in those hills that I came to love so much. These are but some of them.

THE NEIGHBORHOOD

In one small section in the heights of West Harlem, so many great things happened, so many extraordinary people lived, died, and socialized there, and so much of New York's most stunning architecture was built, that it is hard to believe one place could contain all that majesty.

On these hills, the Indigenous People walked the ancient trails and hunting grounds they had inhabited for hundreds of years. Jan Dyckman's son built a Dutch stone house in the early 1700s that lasted 150 years. George Washington continued to headquarter there after winning the Battle of Harlem Heights in 1776, his first victory in the American Revolution. Alexander Hamilton built the only home he ever owned. John James Audubon, "the bird man," built his wife a house, died in it, and is buried in nearby Trinity Cemetery and Mausoleum, along with many of the Astors, Charles Dickens' son, and Clement Clarke Moore, who wrote "A Visit from St. Nicholas."

James Bailey of Barnum & Bailey built an 8,200 square-foot Romanesque, castle-like mansion. The oldest residence in Manhattan, the 1765 Morris-Jumel Mansion survives into the twenty-first century. Norman Rockwell played with his friends in open lots by his apartment in 1908 and realized he liked to draw. Albert Einstein delivered his first lecture at a U.S. university about his new theory of relativity. George Gershwin wrote his first big hit, "Swanee." Mary Lou Williams, the woman who helped create bebop, entertained a young Dizzy Gillespie and Miles Davis in her home. Ralph Ellison wrote *Invisible Man*. Almost every single person whose name is known in the Harlem Renaissance would socialize or live there. Madame C. J. Walker's daughter A'Lelia had an apartment in the same building as W. E. B. Du Bois.

Thurgood Marshall and Duke Ellington both called it home.

Queen Elizabeth II and Prince Philip, as well as First Lady Eleanor Roosevelt, visited.

This is *Hamilton Heights* and *Sugar Hill*.

Hamilton Heights and Sugar Hill

Chapter 1

Dutch Beginnings and Native Americans

> The Munsee and Unami called it Lenape Hoking, Dwelling-Place of the Lenape, or E-hen-da-wi-kih-tit, "Where the Ordinary People Dwell." The Mohawk called it Knonoge, or "Place of Reeds." The explorer Giovanni da Verrazzano called it "Angouleme" in honor of King Francis, Count of Angouleme. Later, the Dutch called it New Netherland, and parts of it New Amsterdam. Finally, in 1664, the British called it the colony of New York.
>
> —Evan T. Pritchard
> *Native New Yorkers: The Legacy of the Algonquin People of New York*

Many new lands are discovered by accident, misadventures that involve looking for one passage, island, or continent and coming upon another that gives birth to new frontiers. It is these explorations that have gradually given us a vision of a bigger planet.

The Italian explorer Giovanni da Verrazzano, employed by France, departed from the Madeira Islands off the coast of Portugal in 1524. Of his many efforts to find what was known as the Northwest Passage, a sea route between the world's two great oceans, he came upon the large body of water that would become known as New York Bay. In 1609, the Englishman Henry Hudson sailed up the river extending northward from that body of water, a river that would later bear his name.

Hudson reported his discovery of what the area's earliest inhabitants called the island of Manna-hatta to his employers at the Dutch East India Company. Not until 1624 would the Dutch establish their first permanent settlement at Fort Orange (now Albany). When the ships did start arriving, however, the newcomers settled not just what is now New York State but also New Jersey, Maryland, Connecticut, and Delaware.

In all these many discoveries, including the earlier ones of Amerigo Vespucci and Christopher Columbus, these men did not land upon uninhabited shores. Part of what explorers truly discover, along with the land, wild game, rivers, and lakes, is people. In each of these places, a new discovery for them and their employers meant encounters with the native people whose lands they came upon. These people had families and homes, leaders and social systems, burial grounds and hunting traditions. They had courting and marriage rituals and harmonious or warring relationships with other tribes. The story of those original people after the arrival of the explorers and European colonization is another history that has seldom ended well for indigenous populations. For them, the European discoveries resulted in land grabs, genocide, and diseases to which they had no immunities. The native people were wiped out of their own lands purposely and accidentally by disease.

A vivid account of this early world is provided by Eric W. Sanderson, a senior conservation ecologist for the Wildlife Conservation Society, in his 2009 book *Mannahatta: A Natural History of New York City*. In a *New York Times* article with Michael Kimmelman, Sanderson shares how he reimagined, through old maps, a New York City that was a "cornucopia of hills, beaches, fields and ponds." In approaching New York Harbor, Sanderson said the Dutch described seeing whales, porpoises, and a thickly forested land so beautiful that they could smell the flowers from their ship. The New York into which they sailed would have been populated by otter, beavers, mink, oysters, brook trout, and bears.

"We have historical records of a black bear being shot in the vicinity of Maiden Lane during the 1630s," Sanderson said in a *New York Times* interview. "We know wolves lived on Manhattan until the 1720s."[1]

People leave the land of their birth, the place in which they have lived, or the place they happened to inhabit for any number of reasons. For the early colonists that settled Nieuw Amsterdam and Haarlem, it took a special character to be willing to go to a newly explored, wild land that has more unknowns than knowns to clear its woods, forage for food, and plant the seedlings they have carefully transported with them. Conversely, it takes a unique set of circumstances in the place one is leaving to make a people willing to sail into the abyss on the hope and prayer that it will be better than your debarkation point. After all, if one's home country offers the perfect balance of racial, social, religious, ethnic, and political freedoms, combined with a prosperous economy and low unemployment, there is little reason to emigrate.

Although the Dutch were the earliest colonists and the Dutch West India Company controlled the people and the island, large numbers of those who arrived in 1624 aboard the *Eendracht* and *Nieuw Nederland*, the first ships to make the journey, were not Dutch. Many were French, German, Walloon (from a region in what is now Belgium), and Scandinavian.

The Dutch had embarked on the arduous search for that long-sought passage to the Indies by a western route, which was believed to be quicker than going around the Cape of Good Hope off the coast of what is now formally called the Republic of South Africa. Although Hudson did not find the Northwest Passage, his discovery, while sailing his ship *De Halve Maen* (the *Half Moon*), astonished his employers. Letters and official reports carried on return ships told of the noble river that the natives called Mahicanituk, the Algonquin name for "the river that flows two ways." They told of the land's promising riches in forests full of ship timber and valuable furs, and the rich soil ready to be cultivated.

This discovery led to the formation in 1621 of the Dutch West India Company, an entity created by the Dutch to rule the lands and waterways to which they laid claim. It was the sister company to its already successful Dutch East India Company. Under the direction of the newly formed company, the first thirty or so families of colonists proceeded to the island of Manhattan aboard two ships.

The island was first populated by a combination of Dutch and refugee families who had sought asylum in the free states of Holland. "It was within these far stretching leagues of sea-washed dykes, downs and cliffs that lie the opening scenes of the history of New York's Harlem,"[2] wrote the historian James Riker in his definitive nineteenth-century work *History of Harlem (New York): Its Origins and Early Annals*.

By the late sixteenth century, religious reforms taking place in France and Germany had spread to the Netherlands, but they were met by deadly opposition from the country's civic and ecclesiastical ruling powers. Some of those who would emigrate were members of the De Forest family who had converted to the new Protestant faith, a move that put them in imminent peril. The De Forests had a prominent lineage stretching back hundreds of years in the Belgian provinces, including the city of Avesnes, near the border. The Avesnes area would alternately be part of Belgium, the Netherlands, and eventually France.

Jesse De Forest's father, Jean, was the first of his family to emigrate to

Leiden in 1602. Leiden was called the Garden of Holland and would become famous for its tulips, later introduced to North America. Located in the south, the city is intersected by the Rhine, which flows to the German Ocean (North Sea). The thoroughfares were broad, and the gabled brick dwellings and shops were built in the true Holland style. The architecture was a gradual evolution from Baroque, with unadorned facades and long windows, to a Gothic style of decorative gable tops, big windows, arches, vaulted ceilings, and small stained-glass windows in select areas. Leiden had become a principal haven for the persecuted refugees, having fought bravely in its resistance during the Spanish War. The Pilgrims who sailed on the Mayflower to the New World settled first in Leiden for several years, operating a printing press.

The De Forests were a prominent Walloon family among the refugees. Jesse De Forest, the patriarch of our New Amsterdam descendants, was a master fabric dyer by occupation and was well respected for his skills. His five children who reached maturity were Jean, Henrick, Rachel, Jesse, and Isaac. It was in this spirit of making a home in the new land that large groups of people thought of moving to what was then Dutch America. But it was not to New Amsterdam that one group first considered emigrating.

Jesse De Forest and many others applied to the English ambassador at The Hague about settling in Virginia instead of New Netherland. Jesse's friend and kin Jean de la Montagne, who was an apothecary and student of medicine, had also been among the group that hoped for the Virginia settlement. But the negotiations between the settlers and the Crown's representative failed.

Jesse temporarily gave up his occupation as a master dyer to enlist in a naval expedition to Brazil that the Dutch West India Company sponsored. By the summer of 1624 news reached Jesse's family that he had either fallen at the siege of St. Salvador or had otherwise perished. His widow, five children, and brother Gerard gradually moved on, and the dyeing business continued under Gerard's guidance.

Jean de la Montagne returned to Leiden and resumed his studies in medicine in 1626. He began to lodge with the widow De Forest. Rachel, her only daughter, fell in love with Jean, and the two married that same year.

The De Forests were destined to be one of the leading families to settle Nieuw Netherland. Their descendants would have a profound impact not only on the future Hamilton Heights section of Harlem, but on the cultural life of New York City, populating much of the Eastern Seaboard.

People in the Netherlands had begun to receive letters from the Walloons who had journeyed to Manhattan and Fort Orange aboard the early ships. They spoke in glowing terms of their new home, extolling its handsome rivers, the excellence of its soil, and the abundance of timber, fruits, game, and fish. They urged their friends to come with their families and enjoy the benefits of a country that rivaled the motherland.

Readers of Johannes de Laet's popular book *The History of the New World or Description of the West Indies* learned of the extraordinary advantages of moving to the new country. He wrote of the rich land and its beauty, noting that it was full of noble forest trees and grapevines:

> It is wanting nothing but the labor and industry of man to render it one of the finest and most fruitful regions in that part of the world. Maize or Indian corn, when cultivated, yields a prolific return and so with several kinds of pulse, as beans of various colors, pumpkins, the finest possible, melons, and similar fruits. The soil is also found well adapted to wheat and several kinds of grain.[3]

De Laet also extolled the plentiful number of salmon, sturgeon, and other kinds of fish. Such accounts encouraged several families to make the journey, and many of the new arrivals were among the original prominent families of what would become Nieuw Haarlem.

As to the native population the colonists encountered from the great Algonquin Nation and derived cultures that populated much of the eastern seaboard, the several layers of the Munsee and Unamio became members of the Lenape Confederacy, which was in alliance with the Mohican.

"Together the speakers of the Munsee, Unami, and Renneiu languages (in cooperation with the Mohican sachems, or chiefs, from the north) combined to establish the great population center that became New York City."[4] The predominant group were the Munsee. Yet there is every likelihood that there were smatterings of other native people that moved about the island from neighboring lands, among them the Canarsees and Wickquasgecks.

The Dutch West India Company, which had the exclusive right to property in the New World, would make good on its promise to provide the newcomers with large grants of land. They arrived to find the forested lands with the abundant wildlife of which they had heard, as well as a native population unsettled by the steady arrival of boatloads of strangers. Nonetheless, a town of sorts began to take shape around the New Amsterdam waterfront at the foot of what is now Manhattan. The small county of Bentheim in Westphalia, which would become part of Germany, furnished three colonists—Adolph Meyer, Jan Dyckman, and Arent Harmans Bussing.

Some took that first ship, the *Nieuw Nederland*, with Captain Cornelis

6 · DUTCH BEGINNINGS AND NATIVE AMERICANS

Figure 3. Dutch Sailing Vessel, circa 1677. Public domain

Jacobson Mey, the settlement's first administrator. It was quickly apparent that someone other than Captain Mey was needed to organize the West India Company's claimed lands. A series of administrators and directors followed with varying degrees of aptitude. Willem Verhulst replaced Captain Mey in 1625, followed by Peter Minuit from Westphalia.

Enslaved Africans had been brought to the Virginia colonies in 1619. But it was not until Minuit's arrival in 1626 that Africans arrived in New Amsterdam. The first eleven enslaved Africans were stolen twice: first from their original African homelands and second by pirates who took them as loot from raided Spanish ships. Of the eleven, we found only four names preserved in history: Paul d'Angola, Simon Congo, Anthony Portuguese, and John Francisco, names both Anglicized and suggestive of their original homes or ports while traveling. In 1644, records would show four men with the same names granted freedom and tracts of land.

By the conclusion of Dutch rule in 1664, when the British took possession, a recorded 850 men, women, and children had been torn from their homes and loved ones. Many left their homes as builders, teachers, hunters, artists, healers, students, wise men, storytellers, and midwives. They arrived as stolen people or the bounty of war and forced onto ships to be enslaved.

Minuit's administration did introduce a better sense of order to New

Netherland than his short-term predecessors with the construction of a counting house and meeting room that could hold a good-sized gathering. The somewhat walled enclosure, along with a smattering of other buildings and huts, were shaping up into a rough settlement. The colony worked under a set of Provisional Orders under the strict dictates of the West India Company that everything and everyone was there to support its business purposes. Many of the colonists saw New Netherland as a place to build farms and homes. There was no meeting of the minds among administrators, soldiers, and colonists over whether they were to establish a trading post or build a new homeland.

Then came the folktale that Peter Minuit had bought the island from the native people for $24 and a handful of goods. It is a story debunked several times over by modern historians and Native American scholars. Yet once a yarn has grown to legendary proportions, it is hard to undo it. The roots are too deep and the story too compelling.

The first premise in contracts is that one enters negotiations in good faith. One person makes an offer, and the other can counter or decline until they reach an agreement or not. Since Minuit spoke Dutch and German and the Lenape had three different dialects of their language (Munsee, Unalachtigo, and Unami), it is unlikely that the tribesmen with whom Minuit negotiated understood what this offer of foreign money, beads, and cloth meant. Undoubtedly, the natives' gestures were good enough for the Dutch representatives to assume that the exchange of goods meant they had a deal. Even if there was a fur trader acting as interpreter, is it likely that he spoke all the Lenape languages? Therefore, it is doubtful that Minuit and the native people had the same concept of what was transpiring.

The Smithsonian's Museum of the American Indian clarifies on its website that Native people and the Dutch did not share a common view of land. "For Native people, land couldn't be owned. Sharing land and its resources was a way of building and maintaining relationships. The Dutch viewed land as a commodity that could be bought and sold."[5]

When a Dutch representative named Peter Schaghen sent back the now infamous letter reporting the purchase of Manhattan from the Native Americans, the story took root quickly. His November 7, 1626, letter, shared on the same Smithsonian website, relayed several significant events. Between the facts that some women had given birth and that grain had been sown, he wrote, "They have purchased the Island of Manhattes from the Indians for the value of 60 guilders. It is about 11,000 morgens (about 22,000 acres) in size." This overestimated the size of the island by about 7,000 acres.

The interpretation of what took place on Manhattan between Minuit and the natives in 1626 would continue to cause misunderstandings, sometimes bloody ones. The idea that hapless natives got hoodwinked in a real estate scam is too good a story to refashion with something closer to the truth. Thereafter, "the Schaghen Letter" was and is generally taken as factual by many as to the sale of Manhattan.

The legend is complicated by "the host of meanings attached to the event," starting with the notion smuggled in via the word "purchased" and that the "Island Manhattes" was a piece of property that could be owned and transferred. Recognizing that this idea of land purchase was a European concept, "whatever transpired in 1626 was almost certainly understood by the local side in a profoundly different way."[6] Over time, the natives would gain a sense of the European concept of land ownership and what these exchanges of goods meant to them.

Yet in the Minuit exchange, there appeared to be a presumption that this one small group of Lenape had reached a consensus allowing them to speak for all the natives that inhabited the island.

Many of the colonists who first congregated around the lower tip of Manhattan would become the landed founding generations of the neighborhood that would eventually be known as Hamilton Heights.

Chapter 2

The Making of Harlem Heights

Noble Haerlem! Illustrious example of courage, endurance and sacrifice, ever to live thy memory, and tenderly to be cherished among the proudest and dearest of Dutch Fatherland!

—James Riker
History of Harlem (New York): Its Origins and Early Annals

From the start, New Amsterdam was plagued by bad administrators. Most people blamed Peter Minuit, the colony's third director, for the problems, but his replacement in 1633, Wouter van Twiller, was no more successful than his predecessor. Nonetheless, the New Netherland's colony and its de facto capital of New Amsterdam held great allure for Dutch residents contemplating emigration.

Adriaen Van der Donck's 1655 book *A Description of New Netherland* provides a firsthand account of every aspect of these beautiful new lands, as well as incredible detail about the dress, demeanor, lifestyle, and dwellings of the Native Americans. The university-educated Dutchman came to New Netherland first to work for an "Amsterdam diamond merchant named Kiliaen van Rensselaer who had been granted the right of a patroonship within the colony of New Netherland in 1629. The land extended to both sides of the northern end of the Hudson River along Fort Orange (Albany)."[1]

Van der Donck's map of the northeast coast of North America, including New Netherland, became the standard representation of the area for more than a century and provides an indelible imprint of Dutch placenames on the American landscape.

He describes the new Dutch possession that "in fertility, equable climate, opportunity for trade, seaports, watercourses, fisheries, weather, and wind, and whatever other commendable qualities one may care to mention. It is so similar to the Netherlands or, truth to say, generally superior to it, that for good reasons they named it New Netherland, that is, another and newfound Netherlands."[2]

Yet those rich, fertile lands would begin to develop very differently over the next two centuries. The area around the southern tip of the island would always be more densely populated, more commercial, and the homes closer together, whereas the future northern Harlem lands and its heights, which many of the travelers would inhabit and develop, would during the same period remain more rural.

Although Jesse De Forest died in 1624, his talk about Nieuw Nederland had prompted his family to pursue their patriarch's dream about emigrating to America. In 1636, when Henrick was thirty and Isaac twenty, the brothers resolved to make the journey to Nieuw Nederland themselves.

Jesse's daughter, Rachel, and her husband, Dr. Jean de la Montagne, also agreed to make the journey, but would travel later. The party would include Henrick's new wife, Gertrude, Isaac, and two servants. "Thirteen years after Jesse's death, on March 5, 1637, Henrick and Isaac arrived in New Amsterdam aboard the Rensselaerswyck."[3] The ship was owned jointly by their uncle Gerard and Kiliaen Van Rensselaer, Van der Donck's employer.

Even in the colony's earliest days, small groups of people had moved from the congested settlement around the fort, located on the island's southern tip, to establish homesteads to the north. Such was the case when the De Forest brothers arrived in 1637 and then sailed with their supplies, tools, and foodstuffs toward a two-hundred-acre site to the north that Van Twiller, then the colony's administrator, had made available to them as a land grant. The newcomers settled along what would be called Harlem Creek, in an area the natives referred to as the Muscoota. The land stretched from the flats up a hill to a neighborhood that was the future Morningside Heights, where the rich soil was perfect for farming and grazing cattle.

Dr. Montagne and his family arrived shortly afterward, along with a baby girl named Marie, who had been born at sea off the Canary Islands. The doctor's arrival was a welcome event for the De Forest brothers. Along with preparing the land uptown for planting, they were also building a house, one that was designed in the Dutch style, with a thatched roof, and surrounded by a high picket fence to protect it against the natives. Structures on the property included outbuildings, a house for curing tobacco, and a stockade.

Tragically, however, as Henrick was returning from a brief trip to Virginia, he fell ill, and he died on July 26, 1637. As a longtime family friend and now in-law, Dr. Montagne helped complete the homestead the De Forest brothers had been constructing. And because Henrick and his wife had been childless, it would be Isaac's large family and descendants who helped shape the dramatic landscape that eventually made the future Hamilton Heights a unique part of the city.

Willem Kieft, a learned man from a good Dutch family, arrived as New Amsterdam's newest administrator in 1638. There he was greeted by some ninety structures at the island's southern tip and a population of some four hundred people. The community was home to a mason, blacksmith, carpenter, shoemaker, brewer, and a baker, along with a surgeon, wheelwright, tailor, sailmaker, and a miller. Company lands operated under a feudal-type system in which tenants established farms, producing small crops of beans, barley, maize, and tobacco.

Although slavery was not practiced in the Netherlands, it was an institution in the Dutch colonies, albeit with less of the racial stigma that would later become the norm. Enslaved people could move about town freely, buy their freedom, and own property, which their widows could inherit. Several land grants were issued to Negroes (they were identified by race in Jerrold Seymann's *Colonial Charters, Patents and Grants to the Communities Comprising the City of New York*). These charters identified not only that a particular person was a Negro, but that others had been granted land near the Negroes. Jonathan Gill's book about Harlem indicates that "free Africans frequently appeared in court as plaintiffs, and at one point a group of Blacks traveled to Holland to demand wages equal to that of whites."[4]

Many colonists opposed the institution of slavery and had tried to treat the Africans with some dignity. According to author Lynn Jencks, "The town's minister, the Reverend Everadus Bogardus, had baptized forty-three Africans, married thirteen African couples, and stood as a godparent for a Black child between 1639 and 1647, the eight years of his ministry. About one out of every eight of the marriages and baptisms he performed during his American ministry was performed for Africans."[5]

Such was the complicated history of Black people in New Amsterdam, as the fortunes and social status of their descendants would wax and wane, including in the future neighborhood of Hamilton Heights. Enslaved people that the company owned were given land downtown, where they could cultivate their own farms.

Dutch land records at the New York State archives show that Kieft issued several land grants to Negroes. Among them, on July 13, 1643, at Fort Amsterdam, "Patent GG80 was granted to Domingo Antony, a Negro, land containing 5 morgens, (10 acres) and Grant GG81 issued to Catelina, widow of Jochem Antony, Negro, four morgens (8 acres), a piece of land located north of the wagon road."[6]

But Blacks in New Amsterdam were not equal to free whites. Committing adulterous intercourse with "heathens, Blacks, or other persons" was banned, and "whites convicted of serious crimes were made to work in chains next to the Blacks."[7] To head off any conflict with white laborers, enslaved people could not be employed in skilled trades.

Kieft was the first administrator to ratify property ownership in New Amsterdam when he issued a formal deed on July 20, 1638, to Andreis Hudde, a surveyor and once member of previous administrator Van Twiller's council. Hudde had married Henrick De Forest's widow, Gertrude, through a complicated long-distance engagement that appeared designed to protect the De Forest landholdings. This deed formalized Hudde's ownership of the land. All earlier grants of land to the colonists had been an informal honor system or gentleman's agreement. The formal deed allowed Hudde to possess, inhabit, cultivate, and dispose of his lands north of New Amsterdam township in what would gradually become Haarlem.

Hudde agreed to pay the company a tenth of the products from his property at the end of ten years. He would also make an annual payment for his house and lot to the director of New Amsterdam in the form of two capons. It is hard for a modern mind to grasp how two chickens would cover anyone's annual rent, even more than three centuries ago. In the following decade, Dr. de la Montagne acquired the estate in an auction after suing over what was owed to him for having built on the property and made other improvements.

Meanwhile, back in the Netherlands, a military man named Captain Jochem Pietersen Kuyter, who had previously commanded various operations in the East Indies under commission of King Christian IV, decided to resettle in the new Dutch lands. Knowing of Kuyter's fine reputation, the directors of the Dutch West India Company assured him that he would be given everything needed to set up a home in New Netherland.

In 1639 Kuyter, a Dane born in the district of Ditmarsen in Holstein, engaged a private armed vessel called the *Fire of Troy* and persuaded a friend named Jonas Bronck to accompany him on this adventure. The two men brought with them a large herd of Holstein cattle native to Kuyter's home province, thereby introducing more of the Dutch milk cows, with their distinctive black and white markings, to North America.

Kuyter, upon arriving in New Amsterdam, adopted a shortened version of his name: Jochem Pieters. He was immediately granted a large tract of land, where he found more than enough pasture lands for his handsome cattle along the Great Kill, later named the Harlem River, which extended from approximately 127th Street to 150th Street, to an area that would become the King's Road and later St. Nicholas Avenue. From the heights of Harlem, this made Jochem Pieters the earliest European to own property within what would later be Hamilton Heights and Sugar Hill.

Pieters built a thatched-roofed house and outbuildings and later planted fruit trees. His property encompassed about four hundred acres bordering the narrow waterway. The area where he built his home was commonly referred to as Jochem Pieters Flat. The native name was Schorrakin, but Kuyter called his property Zegendael, or Vale of Blessings. The elevated part of his property on the hill was referred to as Jochem Pieters' Hills.

It is impossible for modern minds to fathom a person being given four hundred acres of land for free. Yet this arrangement was the genesis of the process by which some Americans became what the British called "landed gentry." In New York this generous gift marked the beginning of the accumulation of great generational wealth, established by giving away the hunting lands of Native Americans who were being displaced.

Jonas Bronck wanted to be near his friend. He chose property at Ranachqua, located to the north and on the other side of the Great Kill, a short boat ride away. Bronck came from a distinguished family in Sweden but had lived in Amsterdam. Arriving in the New World with money, he set up his family, farmers, female servants, and cattle on a five-hundred-acre tract of land bought from the Native American Sachem Tackamack and his associates. On this property, which he named Emmaus, he built a walled stone house, a barn, a tobacco house, and barracks. He also leased part of his land, which would gradually evolve from being called "Bronck's land" to "the Bronx."

Riker's *History of Harlem* relays how Pieters quickly became accustomed to the sight of the natives, with which the colonists had generally a good relationship owing to the communal trade that took place. Pieters noted how it was no longer a novelty when traveling about to see "the sight of these savages in their canoes, daily passing and repassing on the streams and rivers, or engaged in their favorite employment of fishing, which excited no apprehensions. The farmers pursue their outdoor labor without interruption, in the woods as well as in the field, and dwell safely, with their wives and children, in their houses, free from any fear of the Indians."[8]

Yet not much later, actions taken by Kieft led to a series of events that would have a butterfly effect, resulting in death and chaos for years to come. In 1639, Kieft began to demand what amounted to protection money from the natives, claiming that the actions of the West India Company were protecting them from rival tribes. That set off a vicious war between the colonists and the Native Americans. While the natives began with just brief harassment forays and killing some animals, Kieft's brutal response, which involved murder and torture, led to even more violence. "The turning point," Gill wrote in his book *Harlem*, "was the murder in 1641 of the elderly Harlemite Claes Cornelissen Swits in his wheel workshop, near what is now Second Avenue and East 47th Street,"[9] by a Wickquasgeck native.

Jochem Pieters, along with Isaac De Forest and some others, formed a new council called the Eight Men to voice opposition to some of the administration's policies. Where they counseled restraint, Kieft moved forcefully ahead. Pieters became a respected leader who was not afraid to speak his mind about injustice and corruption.

Hostilities escalated. In 1643, Kieft and his council sanctioned an ambush and massacre of a sleeping group of Wickquasgecks at Curler's Hook and later slaughtered a band, including children, that had sought refuge across the Hudson at Pavonia. Another group attacked the Wickquasgeck camp on the East River, after which the heads of several of the murdered natives were put on display. An all-out war ensued, with the tribes banding together to attack every settlement outside of the area surrounding the walled New Amsterdam fort. Their target was the farms that were just getting a foothold, including those on the land that would become Haarlem. In the attacks, the natives killed farmers, burned houses, and destroyed animals and crops.

A peace treaty was ratified April 22, 1643, though many doubted its stability. In the midst of this tumultuous period, Pieters was hit with a sad loss in the death of his friend Jonas Bronck, whose property was spared by the fortifications he had built around his home. "Kuyter and Dominie Everadus Bogardus, aided by Bronck's widow and his son Peter Jonassen Bronck, took an inventory of the estate, of which Kuyter and the Dominie had been appointed guardians."[10] Bronck's legacy would live on as the Bronx, but he had lived only four short years in this new version of Amsterdam.

Kieft's war was a disaster all around, one that had sprung from his attempt to get money from people whose lands were already being stolen under the guise of sales. And not surprisingly, Kieft's days as administrator were numbered. Most residents despised him and realized that his actions were destroying relationships with the natives and putting everyone in peril. The consortium of the Eight Men vehemently disagreed with Kieft's policies. De la Montagne had played a vicious role in the atrocities against the natives in Kieft's war, and it would not soon be forgotten. Despite his initial objections, Pieters too found himself involved in the fighting. In 1644, Pieters' farm was burned down by the natives. It would take years for him to recover from the economic injury he suffered.

Tense relations with the natives eased some after the bloody war. Before he was ousted, Kieft made another formal Harlem grant of Papparinamin at Spuyten Duyvil, which would become Inwood on the northern tip of Manhattan. On August 18, 1646, Matthys Jansen van Kuelen obtained a grant of fifty morgen (approximately thirty acres) that covered the meadow land on the island's northern end.

By 1647, it was clear to the directors of the West India Company that Kieft's bloody war had placed New Netherland in serious trouble.

After corrupt or ineffectual administrators, they finally found a better, though stringent leader for the colony in Peter Stuyvesant. "Prior to becoming Director-General, essentially Governor, of New Amsterdam, Stuyvesant had served as a Director of the ABC Islands in the West Indies. The ABC Islands consisted of Aruba, Bonaire and Curaçao."[11] It was there that he lost a leg and thereafter walked on a wooden appendage.

Arriving in New Amsterdam in 1647, Stuyvesant brought a sense of order and a succession of edicts and ordinances. He was not open to sharing power, though. "Stuyvesant was rather authoritarian with his subjects, and he is frequently depicted as despotic. He also tried to control the Dutch Reformed Church. When other religious groups such as Jews, Lutherans and Quakers tried to establish houses of worship he banned them."[12]

Isaac De Forest obtained from the new director, Stuyvesant, a ground brief for a bouwery (farm) previously granted him in 1647, consisting of fifty morgen of surplus land that was between Pieters' lands and the Van Keulen tracts. It bordered the Harlem River, opposite the mouth of Bronck's Kill (the water passage still called "The Kills"), parting Randall's Island from the Westchester shore. Westchester was the name by which much of the Bronx was called at this time, and larger parts would later remain Westchester County.

Unlike what had happened under previous administrators, Stuyvesant's improvement of living conditions in New Amsterdam spurred what was described as "its evolution from a seedy, beleaguered trading post into a well-run Dutch town."¹³ But the system was not perfect. Stuyvesant allowed monopolies, land transfers were unregulated, and a more orderly system of government was still in the future.

To help reestablish himself financially and rebuild, in 1651, Pieters entered into an agreement with Peter Stuyvesant, Lucas Rodenburg, the governor of Curaçao, and Cornelis De Potter, a merchant, which ceded part of his northern estate to them. His attempts thus far to establish his farm had been plagued by the fighting and political upheaval.

The West India Company encouraged their island possessions to use slave labor instead of indentured servants as the growing sugar trade became the dominant crop. From his previous experiences in Curaçao, Stuyvesant immediately realized that New Amsterdam's strategic geographic position enabled it to become a critical shipping crossroads and destination for the slave trade. He was the administrator of an island that needed forests cleared and homes and other buildings erected. Free slave labor seemed the answer.

About this time, a new era of slavery had arrived in New Amsterdam. Previously the island had been home to a modest number of enslaved people who were mixed with free Blacks. Some of them had had their service manumitted or had bought their freedom. At the same time, the population was steadily increasing and immigration was on the rise, from both the Netherlands and other European countries.

Some of Stuyvesant's policies troubled the uptown colonists. Safety concerns became paramount when, in 1654, Pieters' farm, Zegendael, was once again attacked by Native Americans. The roof was set afire, and Pieters and several others were murdered. The northern colonists once more came under attack, with their settlements burned, crops destroyed, and animals slaughtered. Fearing for their lives, they quickly made their way back to Fort Amsterdam.

Peter Stuyvesant eventually realized that the isolation of the various scattered farms farther from town was a continuing problem, as was the constant infringement of the new homesteads on the native population's ancient hunting lands. Establishing a town to the north where a village setting could offer protection for the northern farms seemed to make sense. The town could also provide a warning of any native uprisings for the New Amsterdam residents at the southern tip of the island.

The village was to cover about fifty acres from around an area called Otterspoor (or Otter Track) and Pieters' farm, Zegendael. It would cross the two rivers, the Harlem and the Hudson, and extend from roughly what is

Figure 4. First Slave Auction at New Amsterdam, 1655. Painting by Howard Pyle. Public domain

now 125th Street north to about 150th Street in the flatlands. One group of buildings were already concentrated around 125th Street, but other farms stretched far beyond these boundaries.

Most of the colonists building this community had sailed from the Netherlands, but they were of several nationalities. They chose as its name "Nieuw Haerlem," also spelled Haarlem, in honor of the beautiful Dutch city on the Spaarne, the river that lay between Amsterdam and The Hague.

Haarlem, which was wreathed by groves of leafy elms, had long been famous as the home of Holland's rich and powerful. The city was known for its enclosed courtyard gardens surrounded by almshouses for unmarried women, widows, and the poor. More powerful than its beauty, however, was its history of courage; as Riker noted, "to the Hollander the word Haerlem was the synonym for all that was virtuous and heroic."[14] Its citizens had held off Spanish troops for seven months in a siege in 1573, displaying heroism that would be heralded for centuries.

The name Haarlem and the correlation to bravery paralleled the assaults the New Netherland colonists had endured. They had been burned out of their homes. Many of their friends and family had faced bloody, often fatal, encounters with the natives. The new name might inspire the creation of a glorious city that would remind its people of noble fortitude and heroism.

Stuyvesant formally established the Village of New Haarlem in 1658. The charter, which would be renewed and revised three times, would also be expanded to include all the land in northern Manhattan not yet specifically issued to a named individual. The murder in 1654 of Jochem Pieters meant that he did not live to see the formal establishment of the new town he helped carve out in his Peaceful Valley. Stuyvesant, the last Dutch governor of New Amsterdam, secured the formal establishment of Harlem. Ironically, three hundred years later, his name would be attached to the location of the largest Black population in New York City, bearing the title of Bedford-Stuyvesant in Brooklyn.

It is unknown exactly when Jan Dyckman, who along with his progeny were destined to become leading figures in the development of Harlem, arrived in New Amsterdam. It is possible that he and his two countrymen from Bentheim, Adolph Meyer and Arent Harmans Bussing, arrived at or about the same time. It would appear that Dyckman arrived shortly before the British takeover of Manhattan.

Dorothea H. Romer writes in her book *Jan Dyckman of Harlem and His Descendants* that "in Dyckman's time, Harlem extended from the East River west to the Hudson and from Spuyten Duyvil Creek to a southern boundary that cut clear across Manhattan diagonally from about 75th Street on the East River to the Hudson."[15]

England had long coveted the Dutch lands in North America. The British were envious of the vast trading routes that the Dutch monopolized, particularly the ones that passed through the Spice Islands. At the same time, Great Britain had a vast and powerful navy that was respected and feared. The country also owned the majority of the existing colonies in North America.

The British knew that New Netherland was a vital location from which to control the North American continent. And so, in March of 1664 the Duke of York persuaded his brother, King Charles II, to officially seize the Dutch lands for England. The king in turn gave them all to his brother James, Duke of York, and in so doing gave the duke possession of not only New Netherland but also all the territories along the Connecticut and Delaware rivers and later Delaware, New Jersey, and Pennsylvania.

In August of 1664, the Duke of York sent Colonel Richard Nicolls with nearly two thousand fighting men and four ships to secure the submission and obedience of his new estate. The frigates, which docked off the coast of lower Manhattan, were no doubt an imposing sight.

Stuyvesant was prepared to fight, but it would have been a senseless bloodbath. Many prominent citizens and landholders argued for a peaceful surrender. On September 8, 1664, "the West India Company's colors were struck, and the soldiers of the garrison marched down to the East River shore, drums beating and flags flying" to board ships home.[16]

The Duke of York promptly sent the man he had chosen as administrator and governor of the newly acquired British lands, Richard Nicolls, to allay the fears of residents concerned with land rights and assure them that these rights were secure.

For Haarlem, the first official decree, called the Nicolls Patent, was issued two years later, reaffirming ownership of the previous Dutch land grants. It reads, in part:

> Richard Nicolls, Esqr., Governor under His Royal Highness, James, Duke of York, etc., of all his Territories in America: Whereas, there is a certain Town or Village, commonly called and known by the name of New Harlem, situate and being on the east part of this Island, now in the tenure or occupation of several freeholders and inhabitants, who have been at considerable charge in building, as well as manuring, planting and fencing the said Town and lands thereunto belonging; Now for a confirmation unto the said freeholders and inhabitants, in their enjoyment and possession of their particular lots and estates in the said Town, as also for an encouragement to them in the further improvement of the said lands.
>
> Know ye that, by virtue of the commission and authority unto me given by His Royal Highness the Duke of York, I have thought fit to ratify, confirm and grant, and by these presents do ratify, confirm and grant unto the said freeholders and inhabitants, their heirs, successors and assigns, and to each and every of them, their particular lots and estates in the said Town, or any part thereof. And I do likewise confirm and grant unto the freeholders and inhabitants in general, their heirs, successors and assigns, the privileges of a Town, but immediately depending on this City, as being within the liberties thereof.[17] May, 1666

In the summer of 1673, the Anglo-Dutch wars returned New York to Dutch control. Hostilities ran hot between British and Dutch subjects. The

Dutch tried to quickly undo everything the British had changed. Nonetheless, by fall of the following year, after several land swaps between the British and Dutch, the Brits once again took possession of New York.

The Muscoota, or lowlands, along the Harlem River were further divided, some into plots for the village for building homes and others for use as farms. But the property in the heights that once belonged to Jochem Pieters was not part of this early land division and instead was regarded as common land. Because it had already been decreed that all common lands not assigned or deeded to one party were owned by the Town of Harlem Corporation, the Harlem leaders decided in 1691 to subdivide the common lands of Jochem Pieters Hills, as the area was known, into parcels. It was an important step toward the development of the hilly part of common corporate lands because this area included most of the property between what is now St. Nicholas Avenue and the Hudson River from about 133rd to 162nd Street, as well as some land east of St. Nicholas Avenue.

Many of the original Harlem land patents would be voided and the validity of many titles questioned. Vast forested lands stretched from a small waterway called Sherman's Creek down to the flats, where no families had settled yet. Sherman's Creek was a small waterway on the Harlem River side at the northern tip of the island, close to Spuyten Duyvil Creek.

The grants of the Harlem lands, as reaffirmed by the British, to both individuals and the communities were given on the condition that those receiving the land pay a tribute or tax to the government.

"In 1683, the Duke appointed Colonel Thomas Dongan to govern New York. He was a veteran of the Civil Wars and an Irish Catholic. He was also an experienced imperial functionary who had previously served as the military governor of Tangier. Manhattan's Anglo-Dutch oligarchs liked him at once."[18] The existing members of the gentry also appreciated the fact that while most seats on his council went to prominent English residents, Dongan was savvy enough to seek the advice of leading Dutch merchants like Philipse, Van Cortlandt, and Steenwyck, whom Dongan appointed as mayor.

By the time Dongan instituted a payment system for taxes and tributes, he also made them retroactive to the time the English took possession of New York. A settlement was reached on December 3, 1685, for the various properties. Eighteen bushels of grain, delivered by Adolph Meyer, was payment in full for his land. At Spuyten Duyvil, only partial payment was required. Among the patentees taxed were Jan Nagel, Adolph Meyer, Johannes Verveelen, and Jan Dyckman.

Perhaps one of the most noteworthy passages in the 1686 Dongan

Charter was to reaffirm from the original 1666 Nicolls Patent that the lands were to pass in perpetuity to the heirs. The mandate stated:

> Whereas, the present inhabitants and freeholders of the Town of New Harlem aforesaid have made their application unto me for a more full and ample confirmation of their premises to them, their heirs, successors, and assigns forever, in their quiet and peaceable possession: Now know Ye, that by virtue of the commission and authority to me derived, and power in me residing in consideration of the premises and the Quit Rent hereinafter reserved, I have granted, ratified and confirmed.[19]

When Dongan's patent went into effect, the most western part of Harlem was still all woodland. The commons north of David's Fly (later known as Manhattanville) and from Jochem Pieters' Hills (now Hamilton Heights and Sugar Hill) all the way to Spuyten Duyvil (now Inwood) were practically like the land the earlier colonists had seen when they first arrived.

The community took additional steps to bring order and govern itself, enacting common regulations on fencing, local disputes, and the care of roaming animals. Residents built a new church near the original village, with the old church serving as a schoolhouse. A rhythm of community events and governance began establishing itself, one that would ultimately set the scene for the development of what would become one of the most important parts of the metropolis being born in the New World.

Chapter 3

Harlem Land Grants, Mount Morris, and a Revolution

> We know our lands have now become more valuable. The white people think we do not know their value; but we know that the land is everlasting, and the few goods we receive for it are soon worn out and gone.
> —Canassatego, Chief of the Onondaga Nation, from his speech at the signing of the 1744 Treaty of Lancaster, Pennsylvania; reprinted by Benjamin Franklin

In many respects, a major institution in the history of Hamilton Heights and the person most associated with this history had its roots ten miles to the south. The Episcopal Parish of Trinity Church Wall Street had been a key part of the city's founding and its spiritual growth almost from the very beginning. A group of Anglicans, previously members of the Church of England, had asked New York's royal governor, Benjamin Fletcher, to grant a charter that would give the church legal status in the New World. The charter was granted in 1697, and the first Trinity Church was built in 1698 at the head of Wall Street facing the Hudson River.

Governor Fletcher gave Trinity a six-year lease on a large parcel of land, just north of the church, called the King's Farm. Queen Anne made the land grant permanent in 1705 when she gave the church 215 acres, which would become some of the most valuable property in Manhattan and support its ministry for centuries. In the years to come, Trinity Church would also be inextricably tied to Alexander Hamilton and his family by way of education, baptism, social work, and death. Hence its history would also be part of the history of the neighborhood that would bear Hamilton's name.

At the beginning of the eighteenth century, the land on the heights of Harlem was still mostly virgin woodland, occupied by just a few scattered houses, shanties, and farms. The land previously held by Jochem Pieters had not yet been divided, nor were most of the vast, hilly plots of common lands owned by the Town of Harlem Corporation.

By this time in Manhattan's history, the Native American people were gradually disappearing from the land that they had inhabited for hundreds of years. In his book *Native New Yorkers* Evan T. Pritchard, a descendant of the Mi'kmaq (Algonquin) people, writes of the multiple factors that caused their defeat and disappearance. He shares a quote by historian James D. Folts, head of Researcher Services at the New York State Archives. Folts writes that as to the fate of the Lenape, "Their history was suppressed, their language driven out of them, their New York settlements cartographically submerged."[1]

In time, when people read of the various treaties with the Native Americans throughout the country and their forced placement on reservations, Pritchard writes that:

> Although the Munsee were among the largest holders of what is now New York land at contact, and among the most generous and helpful, the colony of New York never granted or acquired for them a single reservation all their own during its entire history. Instead, New York drove them completely out of the state by every means possible.[2]

The land divisions the town authorized in 1691 began taking place in 1701 and continued over the following decade. They were monumental in shaping Hamilton Heights, Sugar Hill, and points beyond, detailed in Riker's *History of Harlem*. Upon those hills historic events would occur, a war would be fought, and stunning architecture would be built.

The following is an abbreviated summary of resolutions passed in 1691 by the leaders of the Town of Harlem Corporation for the benefit of all its residents:

1. That land lying in the common woods . . . shall be laid out and surveyed into lots or parcels, whereof each inhabitant of this town shall draw a part as his property.
2. That the land lying at the end of the lots named Jochem Pieters shall be laid out behind the high hill on condition that a good and sufficient King's Highway (part of the future St. Nicholas Avenue) shall be left.
3. To lay out a parcel of land at Spuyten Duyvel, between the high hills

by the Round Meadow on condition that there remains a sufficient King's Way (road) where most convenient.

Signed by the authorized men: Adolph Meyer, John Hendricks van Brevoort, Peter van Oblienis, and Samuel Waldron.[3]

Lots were initially drawn around Jochem Pieters' Hills and extended to the unassigned vast Harlem Common Lands. Some of the transfers would also include the original Jean de la Montagne's Flats.

From this 1691 resolution, an Appel Survey was approved and formally adopted on January 4, 1700. Another division of the common lands was sanctioned by an official New York Act, "passed by the Governor, Council, and General Assembly on October 30, 1708, entitled 'An Act for the Easier Partition of the Harlem Freeholders for a more complete division of the common lands.'"[4]

The subsequent drawing of lots after the 1708 Act and land purchases in Harlem Heights covered the Harlem River to the Hudson, from about the southeast corner touching 133rd Street and Ninth Avenue to the northernmost tip of Manhattan at Spuyten Duyvil, now Inwood.

The men involved in these transfers would be well-known leaders of Harlem whose names would live on for centuries, as well as common farmers about whom nothing more would be recorded. The most prominent transactions bore the names of the earliest families from the Netherlands, among them: Arent Bussing to his son Peter, and then his grandson Aaron; Peter and Hendrick van Oblienis; Jan Dyckman; the John Nagel heirs; Lawrence Jansen; John Kiersen; and Bastiaen Kortright.

One of Jan Dyckman's lots around 152nd and St. Nicholas Avenue had been conveyed to his son Gerrit Dyckman. Jan had long before secured a large plot at the very tip of Manhattan at Spuyten Duyvil. Peter van Oblienis sold his common lands to his brother Hendrick, whose previous property was on the Long Hill, another name for the elevated topography of Harlem Heights. Hendrick's house stood at the intersection of what became Twelfth Avenue (Broadway) and 176th Street, now Fort Washington Heights.

Only one lot in this division of the Harlem Common Lands was acquired by someone other than the original colonists and their descendants. It was the assignment to Captain Charles Congreve, an Englishman who came to New York and served under Governor Cornbury, a cousin of Queen Anne. Congreve sold the property to Jonathan Waldron, and it was eventually purchased by the Dyckmans.

It is likely that around 1710, Jan's son Gerrit Dyckman built the Dutch farmhouse, often called the *Old Stone House*, that stood on St. Nicholas Avenue between 151st and 152nd streets until the late nineteenth century.

It would be another fifty years before the actions these men took would lead to a next set of real estate sales and legacy inheritances that would involve Alexander Hamilton, Roger Morris, Eliza Jumel, John Maunsell, and Samuel Bradhurst . . . names that would leave an imprint on Harlem Heights for two more centuries.

Eighty years after these early transactions, the southwest corner at 136th Street and the Hudson River would become the property of a prominent businessman named Jacob Schieffelin, who would develop the property and rename the area Manhattanville. The Dyckman and Nagel heirs purchased lots that would become part of Trinity Church Cemetery and Mausoleum and John J. Audubon's estate. Jan Dyckman, the family patriarch, died in 1715 just a few years after these foundational land transfers and sales on the high hills in Harlem took place.

While downtown New York City was steadily being filled with houses, shops, churches, bars, and people, Harlem remained sparse in terms of both buildings and population. Most residents were the elderly, second-wave arrivals from Netherlands and the first two generations of their descendants. They clung to the culture of their homeland, and their lives in the scattered farmhouses revolved around farming, worship, rearing children, and getting their produce and products to market.

Houses were now built with an eye to style and permanence. Most had low ceilings, roughly hewn oak beams, and sometimes decorative wainscoting, the additional plain or decorative wooden panels around the lower walls. Sleeping chambers were in the loft. If the homeowner could afford it, there would be several small panes of thick green glass, protected by strong shutters. Fireplaces were sometimes faced with glazed earthen tiles from the Netherlands decorated with scenes from biblical stories and other images and would be large enough so that the entire family could gather around the fire.

Life was demanding, often punishing. Farming methods were primitive, dependent on the backbreaking scythe and sickle. Pigs, fowl, sheep, and the thriving Holstein cattle imported by the Dutch populated the farms and meadowlands. Deer, turkeys, and other game still roamed the woods. Sons were invariably taught a trade and given at least a basic education that would have allowed them to conduct business. Daughters were taught to spin cloth, sew, cook, and care for animals so they could maintain a home.

Downtown, in 1754, King's College was formed under a royal charter from King George II. Its first classes, with just eight or ten students, were said to have been held in a small schoolhouse attached to Trinity Church; some reports say they were held in the vestry. It would eventually become Columbia University.

A year later a man who would become one of Columbia's most celebrated alumni was born on the island of Nevis in the West Indies. Although there has been much conjecture about Alexander Hamilton's birth, it is known that his mother, "Rachel Fawcett (Faucette), was born in the island of Nevis, and when a girl of barely sixteen was forced into marriage with a rich Danish Jew, one John Michael Levine (or Lawein), who treated her cruelly."[5] While estranged from her husband, Rachel met James Hamilton, the fourth son of Alexander Hamilton, Laird of The Grange in the Parish of Stevenston, Ayrshire, Scotland. The two fell in love and lived together in a common-law marriage that lasted well over a decade, though Rachel was still legally married to Levine. Their illegitimate son, Alexander Hamilton, was named after a grandfather he would never meet.

A series of land purchases in Harlem Heights in the 1760s would further shape the landscape of the neighborhood that would become Hamilton Heights and Sugar Hill. Three prominent men, Colonel Roger Morris, John Watkins, and General John Maunsell, bought property on sprawling tracts of land in the district. They erected handsome mansions with views stretching from the Harlem River to the Hudson.

Colonel Roger Morris, a British officer who had fought with George Washington in the French and Indian War, bought property bounded on the south by the Kingsbridge Road from about 159th Street to the Hudson River at approximately 174th Street. Morris began building a country estate for his wife, Mary Philipse, a staunch British loyalist who looked with disdain on colonial rumblings against the Crown. Her father, Frederick Philipse III, was a fourth-generation American, Lord of the Manor of Philipsburg in Westchester County.

The couple married in 1758, and their estate, which was completed in 1765, was called Mount Morris. It was a fitting name given its location atop one of the island's highest points. This stately country home would have been elegantly furnished. It was a working farm with cows, sheep, and multiple fruit trees and became renowned for its gardens.

The expansive mansion contained two main living floors, an attic, a basement, and various outbuildings, among them barns, stables, privies, and sheds, on a site that came to include more than a hundred acres of woodlands and orchards. The façade was adorned with a second-story balcony and a two-story portico framed by classical columns. From the widow's walk one could savor uninterrupted 360-degree views: across the

Figure 5. Roger Morris Mansion, circa 1893. Public domain

Harlem River to Bronck's land, the Hudson to the north with New Jersey in the distance, the vast virgin Harlem lands stretching to Spuyten Duyvil, the Harlem Flats, and New York City, which was what lower Manhattan was still called.

Inside, a spacious entry hall led to the dining room, the parlor, and an octagonal drawing room, believed to be the first of its kind in the colonies. On the second floor were family bedrooms and sitting rooms, and in the basement was a large kitchen with a beehive oven that would have been tended to at differing times by paid, indentured, and enslaved servants. Mary Philipse came from a family who had made their fortune in the slave trade, so there is every reason to assume that some of the many slaves on her family's estate may have worked at Mount Morris or helped build it.

In 1767, Jan Dyckman sold his property to Lieutenant General John Maunsell and a British merchant named John Watkins. The sale heralded the last of the Dyckmans's property holdings in this part of Harlem. General Maunsell was a much-admired officer of Anglo-Irish descent who had fought in the French and Indian War. The men were relatives through marriage—Maunsell's wife, Elizabeth, and Watkins's wife, Lydia, were sisters. They wanted to build on neighboring properties. General Maunsell and Elizabeth had both been widowed, and she was from the prominent New York Stillwell family. Another sister, Mary Clarke, lived downtown. Mary's grandson, Clement Clarke Moore, would make his fame as the author of a poem he wrote for his children, "A Visit from St. Nicholas," often referred to as "'Twas the Night Before Christmas."

Figure 6. Maunsell Place/Pinehurst Mansion. Public domain

The Maunsell and Watkins properties began at about 148th and Convent Avenue, almost adjoining Mount Morris. The Maunsells constructed their home around 1768, a time when the rich were retreating from downtown New York to their country estates in Harlem.

Maunsell Place, built in the popular Federal style and approached via a long drive that wound through landscaped gardens, was among the finest of these homes. But Maunsell had little time to enjoy his new estate. Tensions between Britain and its colonies were escalating sharply, and Maunsell, a Loyalist, decided to leave the country. He sold the bulk of his Harlem property to Charles Aitkens, a wealthy merchant from the Danish West Indies island of St. Croix, and sailed to Great Britain in 1770.

There was little mention any longer of the Native American people who occupied Manhattan and these hills before European arrival. We know of the atrocities on both sides in the seventeenth century that resulted in so much bloodshed. There were murders, torture, and the destruction of ancient native hunting grounds that were cleared for stone cottages and farms. It is a story as old as time that when new countries and continents are "discovered," the native people are generally the victims of genocide. According to Evan Pritchard, "The exodus saga of these real Native New Yorkers was one of the greatest tragedies in U.S. history. Descendants of New York City Lenape were removed by treaty at least twenty times and sent to Oklahoma, Ontario, and Wisconsin, where they were subjected to poverty, disease, and death."[6]

The Munsee of New York and neighboring states that included the large contingency of Lenape native to Pennsylvania would intermarry with other tribes over the centuries. They were then known as the Delaware Nation or the Delaware Tribe of Indians. As with the other Lenape originally on the eastern seaboard, they merged into other tribal reservations, mostly in Wisconsin, Oklahoma, and Ontario, Canada. In Pritchard's 2002 book, he writes that the Munsee were never granted U.S. federal recognition, except where they mixed with other Indigenous people.

Harlem and its heights covered a major portion of New York City at this time. As the decades of European colonization turned into a century, there was no more trouble from the Native Americans because they were mostly gone. Those few who remained in the city knew that they had lost the land of their ancestors. They chose the path of least resistance at this point: they blended in and kept to themselves, unable to celebrate their culture, or intermarried as their numbers steadily dwindled.

New York City had become the financial epicenter of the British colonies. But complaints about taxation without representation had been whispered for some time, and as the busiest port in the colonies, New York was especially affected by new British taxes.

The Stamp Act of 1765, under which almost every form of paper used in the colonies was taxed, was an action that hit a commercial center like New York especially hard. It was enacted to help pay British troops. The first public action of a group of young men who would come to be known as the Sons of Liberty was to protest the new legislation. The uprising was in October of 1765, and the Stamp Act was repealed the following year. Hostilities with Britain continued to worsen, especially after passage of the Tea Act of 1773, which granted the ailing British East India Company a monopoly on tea sales in the colonies, thereby ruining the businesses of colonial middlemen.

In 1772, during the growing unrest, an impoverished fifteen-year-old named Alexander Hamilton sailed to North America from the island of St. Croix. At a young age, Hamilton had left his birthplace on the British island of Nevis to live with his mother on St. Croix, who died in 1767. His intellect, skill with a pen, and gift for public speaking had come to the attention of several people who became his sponsors. Because he was adept at numbers, he was employed as a clerk for several ship owners; among the cargo he kept records for were the human beings aboard slave ships.

He arrived first in New Jersey, where "he brought letters which he delivered to the Rev. Hugh Knox and to William Livingston, afterward governor of New Jersey, and stayed with the latter at his house."[7] After a year or so of study with Dr. Barber, Hamilton was set to matriculate to Princeton, but wound up instead at King's College in downtown New York, where Rev. Dr. Myles Cooper served as its second college president. Hamilton did well by his studies but found himself caught up in the fervor of the political unrest with Britain.

Alexander Hamilton's public life began on July 6, 1774, when he attended a rally not far from his college. It was intended to encourage New Yorkers to join the other colonies in opposing British rule, and Hamilton gave a rousing speech that was more moving than those delivered by many of the older men. "It does not appear from the records of the college that he graduated," wrote his grandson Allan M. Hamilton, "but that his career as a soldier and patriot really began in the midst of the curriculum."[8]

Dr. Samuel Bradhurst III, a man who would befriend Hamilton and one day sell him property in Harlem, was descended from a distinguished British lineage of landed gentry dating back several centuries. The Bradhurst family name, along with that of Hamilton, would live on in West Harlem into the twenty-first century.

The history of a city, and even a particular neighborhood, is not fixed on a straight line. It is an ever-changing flow of alliances, stories, conquests, defeats, and the brave and cowardly deeds of major and minor players that forge the happenings upon which histories are built. Such was the case of the Bradhurst family, where century-old events in one borough greatly impacted the development of Hamilton Heights.

The connection between the Pelhams (Pell) and native peoples ran through the Siwanoys, a tribe of Native Americans indigenous to Long Island Sound and Connecticut. Chief Wampage I befriended Thomas Pell, then Indian commissioner in Fairfield, Connecticut. On June 27, 1654, several sagamores [chiefs], including Chief Wampage I, "executed a treaty deeding to Thomas Pell some 9,160 acres of land, including modern day Pelham, New Rochelle, the Pelham Islands, and portions of The Bronx."[9]

Later, Ninham-Wampage inherited his father's title and became Wampage II. His only known child, Anna, married Thomas Pell, thereby sealing the maternal side of Bradhurst's family. The name Pelham would forever be associated with large sections of Westchester County, and many members of the family had properties and business dealings in Hamilton Heights.

Of the large family that Thomas Pell sired, his daughter Ann's marriage to Samuel Bradhurst I of Albany gradually led to Samuel Bradhurst III. It is he who would become part of a large Manhattan extended and intricate web of intermarriages over the next two hundred years. These families became the leaders of New York society, many with properties and business dealings that shaped Hamilton Heights and Sugar Hill. Yet Samuel the Third, who would befriend Alexander Hamilton, came into his inheritance in an unusual way.

In April of 1762, when Samuel Bradhurst II died of smallpox at the age of thirty-five, he left four surviving children: twelve-year-old Samuel III, his brother, and two sisters. In a strange set of circumstances, the father had been adopted by a childless and wealthy woman named Meliora Lewis of New York, who took it upon herself to care for the four orphaned children. When she died three years later, her sister, Cornelia Norwood, became the children's guardian.

Young Samuel Bradhurst received a sound education and "next devoted himself to the study of medicine, and thus acquired that skill which rendered his services so valuable in the Revolutionary War to come."[10] When Bradhurst received his medical license in 1774, he was already a young man of considerable property and heir of one of the state's oldest colonial families.

Britain's American colonies were headed toward seeking independence. A strong leader was needed to organize the various militias from thirteen different colonies. George Washington was appointed commander-in-chief of the Continental Army on June 15, 1775. By April 14, 1776, he was camped with his troops in New York City. He headquartered for a time at Richmond Hill on the Hudson, not far from Greenwich Village. From there, events moved quickly.

On July 2, 1776, the Continental Congress voted in favor of independence from Britain. Two days later the document that became known as the Declaration of Independence opened with the memorable words, "When in the course of human events it becomes necessary for one people to dissolve the political bands which have connected them with another...."

The Roger Morris House in Harlem Heights, which would prove of major importance to both the Americans and the British during the conflict that quickly followed, was first occupied for military purposes starting that August. According to historian and author William Henry Shelton's 1916 book about the mansion, "For a short time before the arrival of General Washington, the Morris house was used by General Heath as a station where the officers of his picket made their quarters. On the

5th of September, nine days before the house was occupied by General Washington, he established four hundred and fifty men along the East River."[11]

Shelton also wrote that General Washington ordered the arrest of Frederick Philipse, the brother of Mary Philipse Morris, at his house in Yonkers. He was sent to Middletown, Connecticut, as a prisoner. It is probable that if Mrs. Morris occupied her house at all in the early summer of 1776, she left it when her brother was arrested, and joined her sister in the old manor house at Yonkers. Colonel Morris had left for England the previous year.

Howe attacked Long Island on August 27, and the American lines retreated in disarray. The Continental Army held several high-ground positions in Harlem, and opposite them was a large contingent of British soldiers. On September 15, Howe's army attacked Manhattan at Kip's Bay, where a Connecticut militia unit fled in fear and confusion.

That same day General Washington moved his headquarters to Roger Morris's house on Harlem Heights. The stately Georgian mansion stood atop the bluff at the corner of what is now West 160th Street and Edgecombe Avenue. It was an ideal spot for viewing the enemy's advance.

On September 16, an encounter with Knowlton's Rangers and British light infantry turned into a running fight. The British had the American troops back through the woods toward Washington's position on Harlem Heights. In his planning, Washington had three parallel east-west lines of resistance mapped for north of the rim of the plateau, one at what is now 147th Street, where the colonials had some entrenchments. According to a Revolutionary War website, "The overconfident British, having advanced too far from their lines without support, had exposed themselves to counter-attack. General George Washington ordered a flanking maneuver which failed to cut off the British force but, combined with pressure from troops arriving from the Harlem Heights position, succeeded in driving them back."[12]

The colonial forces under Washington consisted of about 2,000 men. The British forces commanded by General William Howe were closer to 5,000 soldiers. The Americans rallied, and an exchange of fire ensued.

What became known as the Battle of Harlem Heights, Washington's first success of the war, proved pivotal. It was estimated that thirty Americans were killed and a hundred wounded. The British casualties were somewhat higher—about ninety killed and three hundred wounded.

With almost 360-degree vistas, Roger Morris's Georgian mansion had provided a good vantage point. Two days after this first victory, Washington

HARLEM LAND GRANTS, MOUNT MORRIS, AND A REVOLUTION · 33

Figure 7. Battle of Harlem Heights, 1776. Public domain

wrote to John Hancock providing a detailed account of the battle, listing the number of men injured, dead, and deserters. Washington expressed his pride in the action of his troops, having redeemed themselves from a rout the day before the battle. An excerpt from the letter reads:

> Head Qrs at Colo. Roger Morris's House
> Septr 18th 1776
> To John Hancock
>   Sir
>   My letter of the 16th contained intelligence of an important nature, such as might lead Congress to expect the evacuation of New York and retreat to the Heights of Harlem. I beg leave to inform them, that as yet nothing has been attempted upon a large and general plan of attack.
>   ... On the appearance of our party in front, they (the enemy) immediately ran down the hill, took possession of some fences and bushes and a smart firing began, but at too great a distance to do much execution on either side. . . . Their men (Knowlton & Leach) however persevered and continued the engagement with the greatest resolution.

This affair I am in hopes will be attended with many salutary consequences, as it seems to have greatly inspirited the whole of our troops. The Serjeant further adds, that a considerable body of men are now encamped from the East to the North River, between the Seven & Eight mile Stones under the command of Genl Clinton. I have the honor to be with sentiments of the highest regard & esteem sir,
Yr Most Obedt Servt.[13]
G. Washington

Whether one calls it a battle or a skirmish, most historians agree that this successful encounter against the British Army, one of the most powerful empires on earth, by a ragtag group of Continental regulars undoubtedly gave the men hope that they could triumph on the battlefield. Many years later, Hamilton's son John wrote that it was "at Harlem Heights that Washington first recognized Hamilton's unique organizational gifts, as he watched him supervise the building of an earthwork. It was also at Harlem Heights that Hamilton's company first came under the direct command of Washington."[14] And it was during this time that the young Alexander Hamilton began forging a bond with George Washington that would have a profound effect on his life and career in the years to come.

Shelton's book on the Morris Mansion provides personal accounts of the transition of the house from George Washington to the British Army. The Continental Army's position was compromised by the advance of the growing British troops. By October 13, 1776, Washington and his officers were aware of the buildup and movement of enemy forces, and the next morning Washington journeyed to Westchester to see how matters stood.

On October 18, in the waning days of Washington's occupation of his army's headquarters at the Morris House, a war council was held at General Lee's headquarters above King's Bridge. According to a clerk named Charles Knowles, "All our regiment was employed in getting cannon and mortars over to the Jerseys and getting other things off the island."[15] He was left in charge of packing up the Morris House.

As Shelton described what followed, "General Washington separated himself so far from his troops that night as to return to the Morris House. Saturday, the 19th of October, was certainly moving day for headquarters. No papers were issued on that day, and no letters written."[16] By evening, Washington had established his new headquarters in his tent near King's Bridge. Unable to hold New York, he ordered his men to retreat. New York City was lost to the British.

Perhaps the most eventful day in the history of the Morris House was November 16, 1776. On that day more than 14,000 British and Hessian troops captured Harlem Heights, including Fort Washington. Captain Alexander Graydon of the Continental Army was one of the straggling Continentals captured by the British. The Hessian (or German) troops were analogous to mercenaries, as the British had hired thousands of them to help fight the war. Hundreds of them chose to stay in New York at its conclusion, while others would return later with their families, thereby establishing an early German ancestry for future generations. The money Britain paid for the hired army went directly to the government, which, in turn, paid the Hessian troops and their families well, lowered taxes in general, and filled the treasury.

Graydon had been with General Mifflin's brigade in Harlem Heights. On November 16, he learned that enemy soldiers were heading down the Harlem River to land at his rear. He and his men returned to the fort, and the advancing enemy took possession of the area surrounding the Morris House. Graydon and several others were captured and moved to the barn on the Morris property. There were nearly two hundred colonial officers, regulars, and militia troops in various garb. The barn became the guardhouse of the new British headquarters. Graydon heard one smartly dressed British officer say he believed that the Morris grounds were such a strong location that 10,000 of their men could defend it against the world.

At the time, an avenue of trees lined the carriageway, which stretched from the barn to the house. Behind the house stood another double row of trees that led to the great gate on the King's Bridge Road. The shaded lane from the barn extended from what is now 162nd Street and St. Nicholas Avenue nearly to Edgecombe Avenue and the driveway along what is now Sylvan Terrace.

After its capture by the British, the house was used as a summer headquarters by British and Hessian generals. The British would occupy Mount Morris and Manhattan for the remainder of the war.

Ron Chernow writes in his 2004 definitive biography, *Alexander Hamilton*, that the man who would give his name to this section of the city came to George Washington's attention when "he had occasion to marvel anew at Hamilton's prowess during the retreat, when posted with guns high on a riverbank, Hamilton ably provided cover for the retreating patriots."[17] On January 20, 1777, Washington invited Hamilton to join his staff as an aide-de-camp despite the fact that many more seasoned officers were troubled by the quick rise to such an important position of a green twenty-year-old. Aaron Burr, with whom Hamilton had often had encounters that alternated between being friendly and tense, was stunned by the sudden promotion.

Shortly after getting his medical license, Dr. Samuel Bradhurst, who would befriend Hamilton, had joined the New Jersey militia as an officer. Bradhurst was wounded and taken prisoner at the Battle of Brandywine in 1777, but sometime after providing medical care to a British officer, he secured his release. During the war he had met and fallen in love with a woman named Mary Smith, who came from the prominent Stilwell and Maunsell families. The two married as the war still raged, and their second son, named John Maunsell Bradhurst, was born at Paramus, New Jersey, on August 14, 1782. Dr. Bradhurst became "one of the leading men of New York in his day, taking not only an active part in the stirring events which he survived, but, when peace was concluded, devoting a great portion of his time and fortune to the advancement of local matters, and the endowment and management of charitable institutions."[18]

After the British defeat at Yorktown, Virginia, in October 1781, the peace talks began in Paris in April 1782, between Great Britain's representative, Richard Oswald, and the American peace commissioners Benjamin Franklin, John Jay, and John Adams. Sporadic fighting continued during this time. As fate would have it, the Netherlands would be one of the first countries to acknowledge American Independence in many of the lands over which they once held claim.

On April 18, 1783, while the Treaty of Paris was being finalized, Washington announced the cessation of hostilities between the United States of America and the king of Great Britain. He congratulated the army and said, "Nothing now remains but for the actors of this mighty scene to preserve a perfect, unvarying consistency of character through the very last act; to close the drama with applause; and to retire from the Military Theatre with the same approbation of Angels and men which have crowned all their former vertuous Actions."[19]

On November 25, 1783, the last of the British troops were rowed out to waiting ships, evacuating New York City and the country. Bands of citizens, a motley group of jubilant Continental servicemen, officers, and several Sons of Liberty escorted the triumphant George Washington and Governor Clinton into town. Later that evening, Clinton hosted a grand banquet at Fraunces Tavern for Washington and his officers with thirteen distinctive toasts. Located on the corner of Pearl and Broad streets in lower Manhattan, Fraunces Tavern opened in 1762 first as the "Queen's Head Tavern" under the proprietorship of Samuel Fraunces, a patriot born in the French West Indies whose heritage as mixed-race African and French would be debated for centuries.

The war was over, a new country begun.

The U.S. Library of Congress notes that the next week, on December 4, 1783, General Washington received the officers of the Continental Army to salute their victory and say farewell. Once again, they gathered in the Long Room of Fraunces Tavern. It was located across the Bowling Green from the Whitehall Ferry landing. A waiting barge carried George Washington across the Hudson to New Jersey and then to Annapolis, where he resigned his commission. Fraunces would later serve as Washington's steward when the latter became president and was acknowledged by both the Congress and President Washington for his patriotism.

Fraunces Tavern would become one of New York City's most storied landmarks well into the twenty-first century. Its history included being the founding home of the New York Chamber of Commerce in 1768 and a regular meeting-place for the Sons of Liberty as early plans for a revolution were formulated. Two of those sons, Burr and Hamilton, would meet there a week before their fateful duel.

The Treaty of Paris officially ended the Revolutionary War between Great Britain and the United States. It recognized American independence and established borders for the new nation. Many of the same men who participated in the war would find themselves in Harlem Heights in the coming decades as the work of building the new nation continued.

Chapter 4

Hamilton Grange and the Duel

> One of the deepest impulses in man is the impulse to record, to scratch a drawing on a tusk or keep a diary.... The enduring value of the past is, one might say, the very basis of civilization.
> —John Jay Chapman, American author (1862–1933)

There was a tumultuous period after the Revolutionary War as the United States learned to be its own nation. At its center was a mix of old British laws by which the colonies had been ruled for a century. Add to that a populace that included a mix of races, foreigners and locals, enslaved and freed people of African descent, and socioeconomic layers from paupers to the very wealthy. The people and property transactions during this era cemented some of what would make Hamilton Heights and Sugar Hill legendary. Several northern states addressed the burning issue of slavery within a year of the war's end, either abolishing it or making plans for gradual abolition. New York and New Jersey were the only two northern states that did not immediately adopt such a plan, though New York had already agreed to free enslaved persons who had fought against the British.

Very notably, there was considerable confusion and disarray involved in the ownership of property after the British departed American shores. As Richard Howe described the period in an article about the street grid that would soon bring order to Manhattan thoroughfares, "So many properties had been abandoned, reclaimed, and abandoned again over the preceding eight and a half years that chief among the doubts and disorder were the frequent uncertainties as to who could legitimately claim to own a given property."[1]

These problems were compounded by murky boundary lines and the fact that many landmarks had been lost or destroyed. This was the shambles of a city that the British troops left when they departed. Confiscated lands that had belonged to British Loyalists went up for sale, were bought for bargain prices, then were divided quickly into smaller lots and resold at huge profits. Trinity Church and King's College (whose name would soon be changed to Columbia College) narrowly survived attempts to confiscate their lands.

A short time after the Revolution ended, many Loyalist estates became the property of the new government. The commissioners of forfeiture for the Southern District of New York, Isaac Stoutenburgh and Philip Van Cortlandt, sold the 115-acre Roger Morris estate, or Mount Morris, as it was called, to John Berrian and Isaac Ledyard on July 9, 1784, for £2,250. It underwent a quick succession of owners and uses. Three years later, shortly after the beginning of stagecoach service between New York and Albany, Mount Morris was renamed Calumet Hall, owned by a man named Talmage Hall. It was used as a roadhouse tavern where stagecoach operators could change horses en route to their destination. The property was put on sale in 1788 with an advertisement in the *New-York Packet*, a short-lived newspaper that published the first of the Federalist Papers:

> To be sold or let, that very pleasant Seat, late the property of Roger Morris, Esq., situated on Haerlem Heights, containing upwards of 130 acres of meadow and arrable land, the mansion house and outbuildings are perhaps not exceeded in this state for elegance and spaciousness, and the prospect from the house is the most commanding on the island.[2]

The wealthy landowner Cornelia Norwood, who had been a devoted guardian to Dr. Samuel Bradhurst and his siblings when they were orphaned, died in 1787. She bequeathed her entire property, including her land in Harlem Heights, to Dr. Bradhurst and his brother and sisters. Dr. Bradhurst was already a wealthy man, but only after his inheritance from Miss Norwood did he become aware of the extent of her real estate holdings throughout Manhattan.

Charles Aitkens, who had bought General Maunsell's Harlem Heights estate in 1770, died in 1784. He was survived by his wife, the former Cornelia Beekman, whose family had massive holdings downtown. Samuel Bradhurst negotiated the purchase of some of Aitkens' property from his brother. Thus began Bradhurst's acquisition of the Maunsell estate, which eventually became his through both purchase and inheritance.

In Augustus Maunsell Bradhurst's book about his family's history, he gives a detailed description of the family's Harlem property. It bordered the Roger Morris estate, stretched between the East (Harlem) and Hudson rivers, and would eventually become part of Convent Avenue and the outer border of Alexander Hamilton's land. The Maunsell estate totaled 110 acres and included the mansion built in the popular Federalist style and several smaller buildings. The first parcel is said to have been laid out in 1691 by Order of the Patentees of the Township of New Haarlem out of the common land divisions. Dr. Bradhurst renamed the estate Pinehurst.

As to social reform relating to the Black population, in 1785 a group formed the New York Manumission Society. "Among those present were Governor George Clinton, Alexander Hamilton, Mayor James Duane, John Jay, and a large contingent of Quakers."[3] About half of the members owned enslaved persons, which presented an interesting paradox. While the society's stated purpose was to abolish slavery in New York, it would be decades before that happened.

However, in 1787 Hamilton, John Jay, and the society founded the African Free School in Lower Manhattan on Cliff Street, believed to be the first school in America specifically for Black people. Although their numbers were small, African Americans had always had a presence in Harlem. A 1790 census tally of "the Harlem division found 115 slaves working upper Manhattan's farms and estates, roughly one-third the population."[4]

At the conclusion of the war, heated debates were raging about establishing laws, property claims, and states' rights over a strong federal government (which Hamilton favored). Having married Elizabeth Schuyler in 1780, one of General Philip Schuyler's daughters, Hamilton had taken up country life in Albany after the war. But he continued to put his natural intellect and writing skills to good use. He took a crash course in the law, then hung up his shingle and resettled himself and his family in downtown Manhattan, where he established a thriving law practice.

Hamilton and Washington had maintained a close friendship, writing to each other frequently. On September 11, 1789, when the new President Washington submitted to the Senate several nominations for the Treasury Department, key among them was Alexander Hamilton as secretary. The appointment was approved by the Senate that day.

When the president appointed Hamilton as the nation's first secretary of the treasury, Gouverneur Morris warned Hamilton of the scrutiny and criticism he would face. Hamilton's goal, as Ron Chernow, explains, would be "to transform America into a powerful, modern nation-state by creating a central bank, a mint, a customs service, and manufacturing subsidies."[5] Hamilton knew this was where he could do the most good and prove that the U.S. was not imitating the British model, but becoming its own nation and a power with which to be reckoned.

To the surprise of many legislators, Hamilton insisted upon federal assumption and dollar-for-dollar repayment of the country's war debt of $75 million in order to revitalize the public credit: "The debt of the United States was the price of liberty. The faith of America has been repeatedly pledged for it, and with solemnities that give peculiar force to the obligation."[6]

On July 10, 1790, a year after becoming the nation's first president, George Washington gave a dinner at the Morris Mansion for the members of his new Cabinet, along with other gentlemen and their wives. As Washington later noted in his diary,

> Having formed a party consisting of the Vice President, his lady, son and Miss Smith, the Secretaries of State, Treasury, and War, and the ladies of the two latter, with all the gentlemen of my family, Mrs. Lear and the two children, we visited the old position of Fort Washington, and afterwards dined on a dinner provided by a Mr. Marriner at the house, lately of Colonel Roger Morris, but confiscated, and now in the possession of a common farmer.[7]

Abigail Adams and her husband, Vice President John Adams, Elizabeth Schuyler Hamilton, and Secretary Alexander Hamilton were joined with the country's first president and others to make a stately party in the great parlor, heavy with the symbolism of having been the place Washington headquartered in the previous decade to write accounts of his first victory in the Revolutionary War.

General Maunsell decided to sell the balance of his land in Harlem Heights between the Morris and Watkins places, which eventually came into the possession of the Bradhurst family. Maunsell's widow survived him by twenty years and built a smaller house at the corner of 157th and St. Nicholas Avenue. Bradhurst and Samuel Watkins had been in business together but dissolved their partnership in 1796. Watkins left the city for his other country home, which would develop into the small village of Watkins Glen and later become a state park of the same name. There was a tangle of family in-law relationships among many of the wealthy and landed families with properties in Harlem Heights and downtown. Bradhurst's wife was John Maunsell's niece, and Aaron Burr's first wife, Theodosia, was also related to Mrs. Bradhurst.

After several successful years establishing a firm basis for the country's financial security, Hamilton resigned as treasury secretary in 1795. Over the course of 1796–97, Alexander Hamilton's life was upended by his own behavior. In 1796, he wrote a ninety-five-page document referred to as the Reynolds Pamphlet, in which he admitted to adultery with Maria Reynolds. He did so to clear accusations that had been made against him of embezzling public funds. "Hamilton's strategy was simple: he was prepared to sacrifice his private reputation to preserve his public honor. He knew this would be the most exquisite torture for Eliza."[8]

Loyal friend that he was, Washington sent the Hamiltons a set of silver wine coolers, along with a note saying that he and Mrs. Washington held Hamilton in the highest regard and that he remained Hamilton's "sincere friend and affectionate and honorable servant." The gift became a treasured family heirloom. The two men had continued to communicate, including on government matters, even after Hamilton's resignation and the Reynolds scandal.

Even as late as the 1790s, nearly a decade after the end of the war, New York had no real downtown and uptown, though downtown was referred to as New York City and uptown as Harlem. Much of the city was still heavily damaged, and there were not yet rows of fashionable streets or a clear separation between residential and business areas. Even doctors, lawyers, and merchants generally lived over their offices just as shopkeepers lived above their shops.

At the same time, Lower Manhattan was becoming increasingly dirty and crowded, and by 1795 the yellow fever outbreak that had begun in Philadelphia in 1793 was racing through New York City. The pastureland of Harlem looked increasingly safe and inviting and encouraged more people to move uptown, on the theory that fresh country air was better than the soot and odors of downtown.

Among their number were Hamilton and his family. In addition to his familiarity with the area during the war, Hamilton had spent some leisure time in Harlem and had visited some of its stately residences. When deciding to build a country home in its wooded hills, he may have also been thinking about the natural beauty of his native Caribbean.

For Hamilton the ideal home was far removed from the bustle of the commerce and crowded conditions of the city. During the summer and fall of 1798 the Hamiltons, along with Alexander's brother-in-law

John B. Church, leased a country house in Harlem. Hamilton's friend Jacob Schieffelin, a pharmacist and businessman, had a handsome summer home in Harlem Heights, and while fishing on the Hudson Hamilton had sometimes docked his boat at Schieffelin's pier.

That year, Hamilton wrote a letter to his wife from Philadelphia containing what is believed to be the first hint of his plans to build a house: "I have formed a sweet project, of which I will make you my confident when I come to New York, and in which I rely that you will cooperate with me chearfully. You may guess and guess and guess again. Your guessing will be still in vain. But you will not be the less pleased when you come to understand and realize the scheme."[9]

Hamilton found land he liked at about 141st Street, extending from the Hudson to almost the Kingsbridge Road (now St. Nicholas Avenue). The boundaries are generally agreed upon as extending to about 147th Street. The property was, his grandson Allan McLane Hamilton wrote, "formerly much larger in extent with the western limit being the Hudson River. The Albany or Bloomingdale Road which passed diagonally through it has, of course, now entirely disappeared, but undoubtedly divided the part upon which the house stood from the farm on the easterly side."[10] Despite his grandson's description, other accounts make clear that though Hamilton wanted the land reaching to the river, he did not actually acquire it.

In an October 25, 1799, letter to General Ebenezer Stevens, a prosperous merchant with a nearby country place, Hamilton made clear his interest in purchasing the land.

> If the owner of the ground adjoining you will take £800 for sixteen acres including a parcel of the woodland, and lying on the water the whole breadth you will oblige me by concluding the bargain with him, and I will pay the money as soon as a good title shall appear. If he will not sell a part at this rate, I request you to ascertain whether he will take thirty pounds an acre for the whole tract and let me know.
>
> If I like it, after another view of the premises, I shall probably take the whole at this price. But I can only pay one half down, a quarter in six months and the remaining quarter in a twelve month. He shall be satisfied on the score of security if he desires.
>
> Yrs with Regard, A. Hamilton[11]

Hamilton's reference to the part "lying on the water" makes clear that he was negotiating for property that reached the Hudson. The majestic views of woods, flowers, and rivers, with streams running through the property, convinced him to choose this site. And as it turned out, the land was owned by his friend Jacob Schieffelin, who sold Hamilton fifteen acres of his property, but not reaching to the river by all accounts.

On December 14, 1799, a sad day for the new nation, former president George Washington died. "Samuel Bradhurst deeply mourned the loss of the General under whom he had served, and who had so generously recognized his services in the grant of a Virginian estate. About this time Bradhurst withdrew to his country place on Harlem Heights, making it his chief abode, and devoting much of his time to its improvement."[12]

Hamilton's friend Jacob Schieffelin was of German descent, born in Philadelphia in 1757. An astute businessman, he proved himself successful in commerce and real estate speculation in multiple locales, including Canada and Detroit, Michigan, still very much a frontier town in the late 1700s. He had served with the British forces during the Revolutionary War, but his marriage to Hannah Lawrence, an anti-British Quaker, caused him to shift loyalties. By 1794, he and his family had resettled in New York City. Along with his brother-in-law John, they took over a pharmaceutical business.

The following year Schieffelin had bought the property bordering the Hudson in Harlem Heights. On a portion of land adjacent to Hamilton's purchase, Schieffelin built a mansion that he called Rooka Hall. In 1806, Schieffelin and other businessmen would incorporate a section of Harlem located some twenty blocks east as Manhattanville. His great-grandson, Ed Schieffelin, founded the town of Tombstone, Arizona, in 1877.

Hamilton bought an additional twenty acres from his friend Dr. Samuel Bradhurst, whose hundred-acre farm adjoined Schieffelin's. According to most historical accounts, by the time the various pieces were assembled, Hamilton's property was thirty-five acres. In later centuries, it would commonly be said to encompass thirty-two acres. There are no known existing surveys or deeds of the purchase. Hamilton named his estate the Grange, after his father's ancestral home in Scotland, though he would never visit the latter.

Alexander Hamilton chose the noted architect John McComb Jr. to design the Grange and a man named Ezra Weeks as the builder. McComb was a highly respected and prolific architect and builder. He would also design New York City's new City Hall and several other important structures. The design of the Grange was in keeping with the Federalist style popular at the time, similar to the Morris Mansion and Pinehurst. The Federalist style did not contain many ornate designs; rather, it emphasized balance and symmetry. The arrangement of windows, chimneys, doors, porches, and balustrades was usually square or rectangle-shaped, with a sturdy hipped roof that points downward. The interior rooms were often shaped octagonally.

Hamilton likely contributed to the plans, and he often consulted with his father-in-law, General Schulyer. In support of the home that Hamilton was building for his daughter and grandchildren, Schulyer provided the timber from his Saratoga estate.

By 1800 construction was underway, and on August 25 of that year General Schuyler wrote to his son-in-law about specific details regarding the building. He explained how the clapboards should be filled with brick, described the steps necessary to keep out water and rodents, and told him how to treat the wood. "As soon as Cornelia is brought to bed," he continued, referring to Hamilton's pregnant sister-in-law, "[I will] go up and contract for the timber and purchase the boards and planks, and if possible I will cause the boards and planks to be put into water for two months and then piled up with decks between them that they may be seasoned before they are worked up."[13]

Even in the earliest stages of building his home, Hamilton was engaged with his fellow landowners to better the neighborhood that would carry his name. He drafted a letter dated August 26, 1800, that he and thirty-five of his fellow Haerlem Heights neighbors sent to the "Honarble Mayor & Corporation of the City of New York" about the inconvenience they suffered from the dangerous Bloomingdale Road. He noted that "the public road as it now runs between the nine and ten Mile Stones, through the land of Doctor Samuel Bradhurst, ascending that very difficult and dangerous hill, being the only direct way of communication for the state at large to the city and that something ought to be done."[14] The street commissioner recommended that a new section of the road be laid out in Haerlem Heights to alleviate the problem.

As work proceeded on the Grange, General Schuyler continued to support his son-in-law's efforts. He sent horses to replace some that had drowned while en route to the Hamilton home. He provided the paint for the house, which had been lost in the same accident. On June 22, 1801, as construction was moving forward, the architect made a list of the final stages of work to be completed on the house. They included:

> two stacks of chimneys to contain eight fire-places; to plaster the interior walls which separate the Octagon Rooms in both stories, to be finished white, or as General Hamilton may chose; to plaster the side walls of kitchen, drawing room, hall and passage; the rooms, hall,

and passage of the first story to have neat stucco cornices, those of Octagon Rooms of best kind (but not inriched); to put up the two sets of Italian Marble in the Octagon Rooms, such as General Hamilton may chose, and six sets of stone chimney pieces for the other rooms. To lay the foundations for eight piers for the Piazza.[15]

Hamilton was heavily involved with the creation and design of the gardens, and he had several experienced botanists as friendly associates. In one memorandum discovered in family papers after his death, he asked that English raspberry bushes be planted, as well as tulips, lilies, hyacinth, and wild roses, with laurel at the foot. He also suggested adding dogwood trees and had a question mark as to whether they could acquire some potatoes from the Bradhursts. And, of course, there were the thirteen sweet

Figure 8. Hamilton Grange, Miriam and Ira D. Wallach Div. Henry Duff engraver. Courtesy NYPL

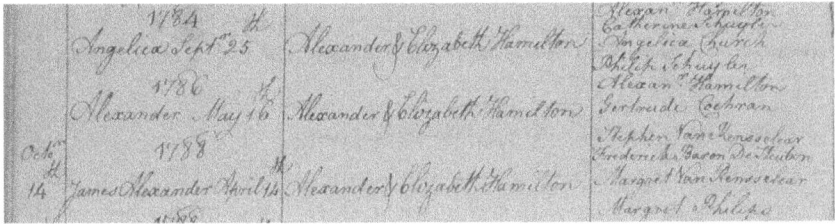

Figure 9. Hamilton Family Baptism Records. Courtesy Trinity Church Wall Street

gum trees planted next to the house to represent the original thirteen colonies, sometimes attributed as a gift from George Washington's Virginia estate.

When the Grange was completed in 1802, the estate consisted of the main home, the gardens, a duck pond, orchard, and several outbuildings, among them sheds, barns, and stables. Hamilton was often seen wandering through the nearby woods, where he hunted woodcock and other game, and he fished in the clear waters of the Hudson. He and Eliza went to the theater downtown, and he continued to work with the Manumission Society. He also provided free legal services at Trinity Church, where the Hamiltons kept a pew and where the couple's children were baptized.

Hamilton corresponded regularly with his wife during his frequent travels and the long carriage rides to downtown Manhattan for his law practice. Their new home would still undergo various refinements. In a letter dated October 14, 1803, sent from Claverack, in upstate New York, he wrote:

> My Dear Eliza,
> There are some things necessary to be done which I omitted mentioning to you. I wish the Carpenters to make and insert two Chimnies for ventilating the Ice-House. . . . I hope the apple trees will have been planted so as to profit by this moderate and wet weather. If not done, a temporary fence is to be put up along the declivity of the Hill from the Kingsbridge Road. . . . You see I do not forget the Grange. No, that I do not; nor any one that inhabits it. Accept yourself my tenderest affection. Give my love to your Children. . . . Adieu my darling A H[16]

The Kingsbridge Road, where Hamilton considered building a temporary fence, was also the place where wealthy landowners held horse races along the Harlem Lane.

In April of 1804, a few months before Hamilton's duel with Aaron Burr, visitors included Judge James Kent, a great admirer of Hamilton's courtroom skills. There are few accounts of visitors to the Grange, and in a letter to his wife Kent wrote:

> I went out with General Hamilton on Saturday, the 21st, and stayed till Sunday evening. There was a furious and dreadful storm on Saturday night. It blew almost a hurricane. His house stands high, and was much exposed, and I am certain that in the second story, where I slept, it rocked like a cradle. He never appeared before so friendly and amiable. I was alone, and he treated me with a minute attention that I did not suppose he knew how to bestow. His manners were also very delicate and chaste. His daughter, who is nineteen years old, has a very uncommon simplicity and modesty of deportment, and he appeared in his domestic state the plain, modest, and affectionate father and husband.[17]

The Hamiltons entertained other friends often at the Grange, though it was a much more modest home than some of the larger estates in Harlem Heights like Pinehurst, which belonged to his friend Dr. Bradhurst. He wrote to his wife about one upcoming gathering:

> To Elizabeth Hamilton
> [New York, May 7–11, 1804]
> My Dear Eliza
> On Sunday Bonaparte & wife with the Judges will dine with you. We shall be 16 in number if Morris will come. Send him the enclosed note on horseback, this Evening, that James may bring me an answer in the morning. He is promised the little horse to return.
> If not prevented by the cleaning of your house I hope the pleasure of seeing you tomorrow. Let the waggon as well as the Coaches come in on Saturday. I mention this now, lest you should not come to Town yourself. I have particular reasons for this request.
> It is my intention to get out Gentis & perhaps Contoix.
> Yrs. Affecty
> A H[18]

Gentis was Hamilton's cook and Contoix another man who did work for them. The Bonaparte to whom he refers was Napoleon Bonaparte's younger brother.

Hamilton's professional income was about $12,000 annually, but building the house had extended his finances. Early in 1804, to meet his obligations, his friend and client Louis LeGuen loaned him $5,000 on bond and mortgage against the property.

The tense and often hostile relationship between Alexander Hamilton and Aaron Burr had never fully dissipated. At a dinner in Albany in March 1804 at the home of Judge John Tayler, Hamilton had spoken disparagingly about the possibility that Burr would become the state's governor.

One of the men at the dinner was Dr. Charles D. Cooper, Tayler's son-in-law, and no friend to Burr. He listened as the two men spoke openly in what they assumed was a private conversation about the low opinion they had of Burr. Cooper's letter to a friend that shared the gist of the discussion somehow became public, portions of which were published in the *New York Evening Post*. Cooper embraced his brief moment of fame, assuring people of the conversation's accuracy.

Burr understandably took offense. Letters flew back and forth between Burr and Hamilton, with Burr demanding a printed retraction. Hamilton refused, and by June 27 the duel to which Burr challenged him was inevitable. Hamilton only had two years to enjoy his new home, take long walks through his property, relax with his children, and admire his handiwork while he continued to finesse small things in the gardens. The duel was set for July 11, 1804.

Alexander Hamilton was president general of the Society of the Cincinnati, the order of retired Revolutionary War officers. Despite knowing that Burr would be present, "Hamilton could not skip the group's festivities without drawing notice, and he and Burr shared a banquet table at Fraunces Tavern."[19]

Hamilton wrote what would be his final letter to his wife dated the same day, July 4.

> This letter, my very dear Eliza, will not be delivered to you, unless I shall first have terminated my earthly career; to begin, as I humbly hope from redeeming grace and divine mercy, a happy immortality.
>
> If it had been possible for me to have avoided the interview, my love for you and my precious children would have been alone a decisive motive. But it was not possible, without sacrifices which would have rendered me unworthy of your esteem.
>
> The consolations of Religion, my beloved, can alone support you; and these you have a right to enjoy. Fly to the bosom of your God and be comforted. With my last idea; I shall cherish the sweet hope of meeting you in a better world.

> Adieu best of wives and best of women. Embrace all my darling children for me.
> Ever yours   A H[20]

Dr. Samuel Bradhurst, when hearing rumors of the impending duel, inserted himself into the dispute to try to save his friend. After failing to reason with Burr, Bradhurst challenged him to a duel with swords in an effort to waylay or stop the encounter with Hamilton. The duel took place almost entirely in secret. The ruse failed as Burr escaped unharmed, and Bradhurst was left nursing a sword wound to his arm and shoulder.

Hamilton left from his downtown house on Cedar Street the morning of the duel to head to Weehawken, New Jersey, the agreed-upon site. Dueling was outlawed in New York and New Jersey, but New Jersey was more lenient about it. Hamilton had borrowed a set of dueling pistols from his friend and brother-in-law, John Barker Church, Angelica's husband. Philip Hamilton and George Eacker had reportedly used the same pistols three years before in the duel that had cost Alexander Hamilton the firstborn of his eight children.

Hamilton did as he said he would and what many gentlemen fighting duels of honor do. He famously fired in the air, deliberately missing his target and assumed, erroneously, that Burr would do the same. But Burr's aim was true, and the bullet headed straight toward Hamilton's stomach. Hamilton's friend and second, Nathaniel Pendleton, came to his aid immediately and propped his limp body against a boulder, as Dr. David Hosack rushed to his side.

"His countenance of death I shall never forget," Dr. Hosack later wrote in a letter describing those agonizing moments. "He had at that instant just strength to say, 'This is a mortal wound, Doctor,' when he sunk away, and became to all appearance lifeless. I immediately stripped up his clothes, and soon, alas! ascertained that the direction of the ball must have been through some vital part."[21]

Hamilton was taken right away across the river to the home of his friend William Bayard Jr. at 80–82 Jane Street, which was near Greenwich Street. Eliza Hamilton arrived to find her husband mortally wounded. Hosack wrote that during the night Hamilton slept little, but by the next morning his symptoms were worse, though his mind remained sharp. "The great source of his anxiety seemed to be in his sympathy with his half-distracted wife and children. He spoke to her frequently of them. 'My beloved wife and children' were always his expressions."[22] In his last moments, he reminded Eliza that she was a Christian, perhaps a wish that she forgive Burr.

Figure 10. Dueling pistols used by Hamilton and Burr. Courtesy National Park Service, Manhattan Historic Sites Archive

Hamilton died the day after the duel on July 12, 1804, in an upper room of his friend William Bayard's home, which has long since been demolished.

At the news of his death, the New York Supreme Court placed black fabric across its benches, and New Yorkers wore black arm bands.

The funeral was held two days later. To the sounds of ringing bells, military drums, and firing guns from the Battery, the mourners began their journey north. Two Black children wearing white turbans led the eight pallbearers carrying Hamilton's coffin, atop of which were his hat and sword. Hamilton's four oldest bereft sons followed, along with other family members. New York society turned out in full force to honor the man who had fought in the American Revolution and had done so much to help establish the country. Doctors, attorneys, military officers, bankers, students and professors from Columbia College, business owners, and ships' captains escorted Hamilton's funeral procession.

Keeping one another's company uptown were Eliza's sister Angelica Church and the two youngest Hamilton children, five-year-old Eliza and two-year-old Philip, the baby named in honor of his lost brother. Also at the

Figure 11. Trinity Church Wall Street, circa 1800. Courtesy Trinity Church Wall Street

Grange was the couple's nineteen-year-old daughter, Angelica, whose mind had been fractured after the tragic death of her beloved older brother, Philip, who had also died in a duel just three years earlier. She so loved her father that Angelica succumbed to a nervous breakdown and a depression from which she would never recover, requiring constant care.

Gouverneur Morris, who had dined at the Grange just two months earlier, delivered the eulogy, as he had done for George Washington five years before.

Not until her husband's death did Eliza learn of the family's dire financial situation. The Grange had been heavily mortgaged, and little of the principal had been paid. John B. Church and Nathaniel Pendleton, the executors of his estate, joined with others of Hamilton's friends and business associates to devise a way to keep Eliza and her children from being turned out of their home and reduced to poverty.

In settling the estate, there was a question answered that would not have been the least controversial at the time: that the last of Hamilton's assets left to his family included the value of enslaved servants.

Alexander Hamilton kept meticulous records of his expenditures, such as coach fees, rent, and bills for the ladies' hairdresser. His accounts show purchases of enslaved people dating back to the 1780s. In a 1797 entry into his accounts, he lists, "May 29. John B. Church paid for a negro woman & child £225."[23] It is jolting to see such an entry for the purchase of two human beings below that for thirty skins of parchment for £21.88 and above a tax and stable bill for £43.40. Despite the contradiction of Hamilton being one of the founders of the manumission society, some would argue that a true abolitionist would not take any part in the sale of human beings. This entry and Hamilton's various writings make clear that slavery was a complicated part of his life, but that he did facilitate such sales. Eliza Hamilton had grown up in a family who generally held a dozen or so slaves. There would have been nothing uncommon for her to have one or two in her married household.

In a 2020 article from the Schuyler Mansion State Historic Site, Jessie Serfilippi's documentation in family letters, the national archives, and Alexander Hamilton's own ledgers make it clear that "the enslavement of men, women, and children of African descent was part of both Hamilton's professional and personal life."[24]

This issue is a contentious subject, and one most Hamilton biographers would later want to either ignore or minimize. In the 1864 biography of his father, John C. Hamilton insists that he never owned a slave. Alexander Hamilton's grandson Allan McLane Hamilton's 1910 book acknowledged his grandfather's involvement in enslaving people. The unassailable facts in his own writing that Hamilton acted on behalf of family members and others purchasing human beings does not lessen that he was a great man who was essential in building the United States of America. Humans are complex creatures and can act in conflicting manners. Look only to Hamilton's defense of his own honor with the public acknowledgment of the Reynolds affair and the duel with Burr.

In the final tally of debits and credits after Hamilton's death, "The auditor, possibly Church, then calculates the value of Hamilton's estate, which he estimates as follows: House: £2,200; Furniture & library £300 and Servants £400."²⁵ This same information in a handwritten entry is listed in the Library of Congress. And one does not place a monetary value on free people.

It would have been impolitic, even cruel, for Hamilton's creditors or the executors of his estate to have evicted Eliza Hamilton from the Grange. Instead, they bought the home from her for $30,000 and sold it back to her for half the price, one of many generous acts. In this way, Eliza and her children could remain there indefinitely. Yet Eliza still needed money to sustain her household and care for the seven remaining children.

On August 2, 1804, Oliver Wolcott wrote to James McHenry about raising monetary aid for the family, but they did not want the Hamiltons to feel they were the objects of charity. To that end, Wolcott suggested that "Mr. Govr. Morris, Genl. Clarkson, Mr. Gracie, Mr. Bayard and a number of gentlemen of fortune should come forward and pay Hamilton's debts and provide handsomely for the family."²⁶

Gouverneur Morris and others subsequently organized the secret fund to which more than a hundred subscribers contributed a total of about $80,000.

Chapter 5

The Jumels, the Street Grid, and Audubon

History is not the past but a map of the past, drawn from a particular point of view, to be useful to the modern traveler.
—Henry Glassie, U.S. Historian and Folklorist

The validity of land titles was still in question several decades after the American Revolution ended. The Roger Morris family had long since returned to England, but the courts there held that the act of attainder for treason against Colonel and Mrs. Morris would not prevent their children from inheriting their American properties. While this was an accepted decision in America, it served to cause doubt about legal title to former properties owned by British loyalists.

The ruling impacted the Morris property in Harlem Heights that George Washington and then British troops had occupied during the war. Additionally, before Mary Philipse and Roger Morris married, an indenture binding the parties to certain obligations had been placed on the Harlem acreage. The indenture was recorded and signed on January 31, 1758, by Mary Philipse, her two sisters, Johanna Philipse and Beverly Robinson, and Major Roger Morris and held in the Office of the Secretary of State. John Jacob Astor claimed to hold the title to their lands by virtue of this indenture. The property was conveyed for the use of Mary Philipse and Roger Morris for their lives, with the remainder in fee simple to their children.

British subjects who lost their estates by forfeiture put in claims against Great Britain for reimbursement, for which the parties received large sums. In 1809, the Morrises' son, Captain Henry Gage Morris, sold their interest to John Jacob Astor for the sum of £20,000 sterling on behalf of himself and his two sisters, thereby transferring their inheritance to Astor.

What would prove to be one of the most significant real estate transactions ever to take place in Harlem Heights occurred in 1810, when Stephen and Eliza Jumel bought the Morris Mansion, located on a site that once covered 135 acres, from a British merchant named Leonard Parkinson. After acquiring the house and all its property, the couple promptly started making alterations. Among other things, they added stained-glass windows and imported furniture from France, some of which Eliza claimed was given to her by Napoleon Bonaparte. Eliza also played a vital role in her husband's business interests and helped him double his fortune. But she had a complicated and, in many respects, mysterious past.

"She began life as Betsey Bowen, and her origins are clouded in myth and historical fiction. Records indicate she moved to New York as a young woman and became an actress, and perhaps a courtesan to wealthy and influential men of the day."[1]

Elizabeth "Betsey" Bowen had been born illegitimately in Providence, Rhode Island, and would go on to lead a colorful if complicated life that included being raised for a time in a brothel and the workhouse. Shelton writes that in 1794, "Betsy Bowen was brought to bed of a son in the old gambrel-roofed house by the canal, on Mill Street. Freelove Ballou, a doctor and trained nurse, was in charge of both mother and infant, and she may have known who the father was."[2] Since there was no family Bible in the Ballou household to record the birth, her husband, Reuben Ballou, wrote what had taken place under his roof in a rare old book. "George Washington Bowen, born of Eliza Bowen, at my house in town, Providence, R.I., this 9th October 1794." He also signed his name.

An eight-year-old boy named David Hull who was making his rounds delivering water crackers for his baker father was among the first to see the infant. When Betsey heard David's voice, she called him into her room and asked him if he wanted to see "her little fat baby," whom she then held up for inspection. That fleeting moment of maternal pride and Ballou's entry in the book would prove important seventy-eight years later in Harlem, the significance of which would be presented before the U.S. Supreme Court. After a few weeks, Betsey abandoned her son to the care of Major Reuben Ballou and his wife, Freelove, while she headed for New York. The infant grew up in their home until Major Ballou's death, when the boy was about eight, at which point he was sent out to make his own way in the world.

THE JUMELS, THE STREET GRID, AND AUDUBON · 57

After their marriage in 1804, Eliza and Stephen Jumel lived for six years in Lower Manhattan. Eliza was part of what was considered the nouveau riche and was generally considered a lower-class person because of her sudden wealth, rumors of her illegitimate birth, and questionable past. New York society was controlled by families with old money or distinguished lineages, those who could still trace their heritage and wealth from two centuries earlier to the first Dutch settlers of New York or to the Mayflower. Eliza would yearn her entire life for their acceptance.

Frenchman Stephen Jumel's "purchase of the Roger Morris house, in 1810, its lavish refitting and furnishing, making it the most elegant and luxurious country seat in the vicinity of New York, and at the same time announcing it a munificent gift to his wife, was a last supreme effort to force social recognition for her."[3]

Jumel was a rich French wine merchant, apparently a man of cultivated taste, and, like most Frenchmen of the time, an admirer of George Washington. He undertook the restoration of the house that had been Washington's headquarters, maintaining the purity of the colonial interior and exterior. He sent a sample of the old colonial wallpaper in the room where Washington had held court-martials to Paris for reproduction; it would remain in place for seventy years. No expense was spared, and the Jumels settled down in their sumptuous home. The couple had no children, but they had already adopted Mary Bowen, the nine-year-old daughter of Eliza's stepsister Polly Clarke.

The couple visited Paris several times, and on a trip in 1826 Stephen Jumel decided to remain in France. He gave his wife the authority to manage his affairs and granted her broad control over his money and properties. Among her attorneys and advisors was Alexander Hamilton Jr., her closest neighbor. She proceeded to make a series of transactions that increased their wealth and secured stronger titles for her to her husband's lands, encouraging him not to sell the property.

New York City in those years was made up largely of shanties and warehouses, with some government buildings, churches, and lovely homes mixed in. But the city was growing haphazardly. Expansion continued moving north. Streets were given names on a whim as people began to grab land and construct new buildings on their property in an era before formal building permits or standards were in place.

In 1811, seven years after Alexander Hamilton's death, New York City planners laid out what would become the signature feature of the metropolis, an organized plan for the streets. The population had doubled since the war, and with former Loyalists and patriots still coming and going there were endless claims as to who owned what. Nearly three decades after the war's end, the city's streets were still chaotic.

In 1807 a bold plan was put in place when a state commission was formed to make sense of New York City's streets, with a four-year deadline to complete it. Appointed to the commission were Hamilton's old friend Gouverneur Morris, a surveyor named General Simeon DeWitt, and John Rutherfurd, a wealthy landowner who was the only one born in Manhattan. He was also related to Gov. Morris by marriage. The three men proposed a grid of symmetrical blocks, streets, avenues, and boulevards that stretched from Wall Street north twelve miles to one point in Harlem. Yet there were country estates and modest houses already located beyond the point to which they planned to pave, including in Spuyten Duyvil at the tip of the island.

What would become historically and socially significant for Harlem, even into the twenty-first century, is that the 155 blocks that the commissioners initially planned as the end of the mapped streets was an arbitrary number based on the topography of the land and projected population growth. The 1811 plan mapped out by the surveyor drawing 155 parallel streets held no special significance as to the Harlem boundaries, except that in 1811 it was as far as they thought the City of New York would eventually expand. Their formal comments acknowledged that they knew some people would be surprised that they had not laid out the whole island as a city, formalizing plans to pave more of it. To some extent, they also recognized that the topography of parts of the island were a challenge to these plans. The commissioners thought it would be centuries before the rest of Haerlem would become a thriving city, and their comments of March 22, 1811, explain this:

> It is not improbable that considerable numbers may be collected at [the village of] Haerlem before the high hills to the southwestward of it shall be built upon as a city; and it is improbable that (for centuries to come) the grounds north of Haerlem Flat will be covered with houses. To have come short of the extent laid out might therefore have defeated just expectation, and to have gone further might have furnished materials to the pernicious spirit of speculation.[4]

This was 1811, and one hundred fifty years later 155th Street would start to become an erroneous line of demarcation in terms of where Harlem ended and Washington Heights began. The three commissioners were also trying to discourage real estate speculators from buying up land in the hilly Haerlem common lands. "The commissioners placed their streets, from 1st to 155th, roughly two hundred feet apart and commanded that they all be made sixty-feet wide, except fifteen that would be one hundred feet wide, at (mostly) regular intervals," wrote Koeppel.[5] It would take decades before the paving was complete, by which time many adjustments would be made along the way, including significant ones impacting historic homes in Haerlem Heights.

The work was long and time-consuming, as well as noisy and dirty. Questions arose almost immediately as to why the city commissioners chose to lay out the city as they did. Yet their own remarks were simple: "A city is to be composed principally of the habitations of men, and straight-sided and right-angled houses are the cheapest to build and the most convenient to live in."[6] Therefore, Manhattan became the city it did, on a straight-lined grid, because it was the simplest and cheapest thing to do.

There had been some ordering of the streets up to this point, of course. Bloomingdale Road, which began as the Native American Wickquasgeck Trail, had portions of it widened and straightened. In 1795, the roadway was extended to join the Kingsbridge Road near what would become 147th Street and St. Nicholas Avenue in the future Hamilton Heights. If ever there was a street that epitomized the winding nature of some of the island's topography, it was the Bloomingdale Road. Eventually, successive sections would be forever renamed Broadway. It would gradually touch parts of Hamilton Heights in what is now Hamilton Place.

The impact of the Hamilton family on Manhattan did not end with Alexander Hamilton's death in 1804. Harlem Heights was still an isolated area with a mix of modest to luxurious homes. There were no public schools in the area, and few if any of the poorer families could afford private school tuition. Eliza Hamilton, eager to fill that void, found a small house two miles from the Grange, at the corner of Fort Washington Avenue and 183rd Street, that could be repurposed as a schoolhouse. It became the neighborhood's first free public school and was known as the Hamilton Free School.

The number of students quickly grew, and soon about fifty children were enrolled. In March of 1818, with the help of other wealthy women in the area, Eliza Hamilton petitioned the state legislature to incorporate a free public school for the neighborhood. The group received $400 to build the school, along with a modest annual stipend. The one-room, thousand-square-foot building, located in the area that is now Broadway near 187th Street, could accommodate forty to fifty students.

Meanwhile, the population in the area around Hamilton's house continued to grow slowly in the first half of the nineteenth century. Small farms, a few scattered houses, and larger estates still dotted the heights. Although the largest populated area, the Village of Harlem, had long since been rebuilt after the British burned it down during the war, records indicate that "in 1820 just ninety-one families lived in Harlem."[7]

African Americans had gone through many stages of liberty and restrictions in New York since scholars say the first enslaved persons arrived 1626. Later Dutch historians attribute their arrival on a ship named the Bruynvisch in 1627. Some of these enslaved people made their way to the hills of Harlem as servants or farm workers. During some periods, Black people had the right to legally marry, to own and transfer property, and to purchase their own freedom. Then came a period when the city instituted a gradual manumission. In 1827, thirty-six years before the Emancipation Proclamation but decades after other states had done so, slavery was officially abolished in New York.

Harlem continued to be seen as a beautiful and bucolic place for wealthy New Yorkers to live. When a cholera epidemic hit the city in 1832, taking the lives of more than 3,500 New Yorkers in just two months, those who could headed up to Harlem in search of the cleaner air, just as people had during an outbreak of yellow fever in 1795.

Freed Blacks who were still working uptown had begun to form pockets of communities. "But as the farming economy waned, and Irish immigrant squatters moved into abandoned plots on which they tended pigs and grew vegetables, Blacks began to diminish as a percentage of the total. Nothing happened fast, though, and sleepy Harlem remained disconnected from distant dynamic downtown."[8]

As to the Roger Morris lands, Astor made a compromise with the state of New York in 1828, by which he received $500,000, the equivalent of $15 million in 2023, for the rights he had purchased in the Morris estate and other properties. "The terms of the arrangement required that within a specified time he should execute a deed of conveyance in fee simple against the claims of the Morrises, their heirs, and all persons claiming ownership under them, and that he should also obtain the judgment of the Supreme Court of the United States affirming the validity and perfectibility of his title."[9]

Upon meeting all these conditions, title was confirmed of all the land sales that had taken place since the properties were sold by the commissioners of forfeiture after the Revolution. John Jacob Astor made an unprecedented windfall through all these machinations. He would refer to it as a favorite deal. The country's first millionaire, the butcher's son, turned fur and opium trader, was establishing a legacy for his family that would cement the Astors as one of the preeminent names of the coming Gilded Age and American aristocracy.

Harlem was still so rural that horseback, private carriage, the infrequent stagecoach ride, and boat trips up the Hudson or Harlem Rivers were the most frequent modes of travel. "But that changed in the 1830s when service on the New York and Harlem Railroad began, what we know as Metro-North."[10]

Having a private horse-drawn carriage was fairly common for those with means, and carriages were, in all likelihood, shared with other friends and neighbors. But twenty years after Hamilton's death, transportation to the area around the Harlem Heights neighborhood of the Grange was still somewhat limited. If one did not own a private coach and buggy, the twice-weekly stagecoach was still the norm. Enterprising men who could afford to purchase or build their own coaches, or hackneys, transported individuals or small groups around the city for a fee.

There was no mass city transit system yet, so private companies managed transit routes and surface lines. Businessman John Mason, president of Chemical Bank, was one of the founders of the New York and Harlem Railroad. It began operations in 1832 and was one of the first railroads in the U.S. Horses pulled streetcars with metal wheels along a metal track, a revolutionary early mass transit system for the city. It would take several years before the tracks actually reached Harlem. These early forms of transportation served the city well, growing in stages with new technological advancements.

Yet it did not serve everyone equally. Despite the fact that New York had abolished slavery in 1827, Black people were still subject to restrictive laws and policies, including in transportation. When schoolteacher Elizabeth Jennings [Graham] tried to board a horse-drawn streetcar in lower Manhattan on July 16, 1854, she and her friend were denied access by the conductor. Jennings insisted she had a right to ride, but both Black women were tossed from the car. In an act of defiance that would still scare some people of color a hundred years later, Jennings jumped back onto the streetcar and insisted on her right to ride the public transport. The conductor, driver, and a police officer beat her brutally.

"Outraged, the African American community rose to her defense. Led by her abolitionist father, Thomas L. Jennings, the Black Legal Rights Association was formed to battle discrimination. It was the first case for Chester A. Arthur, an attorney from the firm of Culver, Parker, and Arthur."[11] Arthur would go on to become the twenty-first president of the United States in 1881, succeeding President James Garfield after his assassination.

Judge William Rockwell presided over the trial, Jennings v. Third Ave. Railroad Co., held in Brooklyn Supreme Court. A new law made railway companies responsible for the actions of its employees, and Jennings sued the rail company for $500. Against all odds, in 1855 an all-white male jury awarded Elizabeth Jennings $250 in damages. Judge Rockwell declared, "Colored persons if sober, well-behaved and free from disease, have the same rights as others."[12] Jennings' victory led to the end of segregation on New York City transportation.

Twenty-two years after the Jumels bought Mount Morris in Harlem Heights, Stephen Jumel died there in 1832. His widow, Eliza, proceeded to run a thriving real estate business that would eventually make her one of the city's richest women. Her mourning period was brief, however, because the following year the very wealthy fifty-nine-year-old widow married Aaron Burr in the parlor of Mount Morris, perhaps as a last attempt to be accepted into polite society. At the time Burr was seventy-eight years old, practically destitute, and had never recovered socially from murdering Alexander Hamilton. Yet because he had been vice president, his name still carried a certain level of distinction.

The marriage created little fanfare, with barely a notice in the local papers. The *Evening Post* of July 4, 1833, noted, "On Monday evening last, at Harlaem Heights, by the Rev. Dr. Bogart, Col. Aaron Burr to Mrs. Eliza Jumel."[13] Once again, the social invitations failed to appear. It was a short-lived, tumultuous union, a marriage of convenience rather than a romantic liaison. The two separated within a year, and Eliza Jumel sued for divorce. Ironically, her lawyer was Alexander Hamilton Jr. The divorce was finalized on September 14, 1836, the day Aaron Burr died.

Meanwhile, as crowded conditions in the city made the idea of expanding farther north more appealing, speculators began taking a closer look at rural Harlem real estate. An investor named Richard Carman bought several tracts of woodlands and built modest houses on the property with the hope of creating a legacy in the form of a housing village. The area, which he called Carmansville, would later be described as "a working-class village being developed between 152nd Street and 155th Street."[14] The parcels he bought were from the same Watkins-Maunsell-Bradhurst Harlem estate that had sold some of its acreage to Alexander Hamilton.

Carmansville boasted its own church and a 125-bed hotel called the Riverside. He built several modest houses on the property, intending to make it an attractive place for middle-class residents.

Harlem Heights seemed to attract people from the Caribbean, from Alexander Hamilton and Charles Aitkens in the eighteenth century to an escalating trend by the twentieth century. In the late 1830s, after most of his travels in America and abroad, the celebrated naturalist John James Audubon returned to New York to establish a home in the city. Audubon, who had been born in 1785 in Haiti (then St. Domingo), shared more than Caribbean roots with Alexander Hamilton. They were both illegitimate and subject to questions as to whether they were of mixed race.

Audubon's seminal work *Birds of America* was published and updated in several printings from 1827 to 1838. It had earned him considerable money and great fame, and Audubon would become the world's leading artist and authority when it came to ornithology. In 1839, he and his family were living in downtown New York at 86 White Street. But it was hardly the setting for a man who loved nature, and in 1841 he bought property in Harlem Heights adjacent to the home of his friend Richard Carman. It was a fourteen-acre stretch bordered by what is now approximately 153rd to 158th streets, bridging a little north of Amsterdam Avenue to the Hudson River. The property became a compound for the Audubons, with his sons also building homes for their families. The father called the compound Minnie's Land, Minnie being both a nickname for his beloved wife, Lucy, and a Scottish term of endearment for one's mother.

The Audubons entertained frequently at Minnie's Land. Samuel F. B. Morse, who had invented the telegraph and the Morse Code method of communication, was friends with Audubon. While a guest at his Harlem home in 1843, Morse had erected a mast along the Hudson River to transmit the first messages between New Jersey and New York. He received the first telegraphic message from Philadelphia while at Audubon's estate.

Almost three decades after Hamilton's death, it became apparent that Eliza Hamilton could no longer maintain the Grange. Except for her daughter Angelica, who would forever be fragile mentally, her children were grown and on their own. Eliza never wrote a memoir, though she was a prolific letter writer, as we are aware from archived records. And she destroyed almost all her husband's love letters to her after the publicity of his affair with Maria Reynolds.

John Church Hamilton, the Hamiltons' fifth child, wrote extensively about his father's life as well as compiling Hamilton's voluminous writing. The fourth child, James, penned a memoir in 1843, at age fifty five, the only one of Hamilton's children we are aware did so. While it focused primarily on his life, he did share several anecdotes of private family moments: of his travels from the Grange to town with his father on visits to friends and for business, relaying moments that spoke to his father's principled character. In helping to manage his mother's business matters, James wrote of his own affairs as well as staying with his mother as often as possible. "I remained at the Grange with her as long as she remained there, attending to the cultivation and household, and after her father's death I became useful in collecting her rents and selling such parts of her property as her needs required. She was a most earnest, energetic, and intelligent woman."[15]

He praised his mother's tireless work for the New York Orphan Asylum Society, which she helped found, and her continued skills as a homemaker. It was 1833 before a buyer was found, when Theodore Davis and Isaac Pearson, a pair of real estate speculators, bought the Grange for $25,000. Shortly before they sold the house, James removed the Italian statuary marble mantels. He would install them in the Greek Revival style country home named "Nevis"—a tribute to his father's birthplace—that he built in 1835 in Irvington, New York.

Eliza moved to the newly built 4 St. Marks Place in Greenwich Village, where she lived for nine years with two of her children, Alexander Hamilton Jr. and Eliza Hamilton Holly, and their spouses. In 1848, she moved to Washington, D.C., where she lived with her widowed daughter Eliza until her death in 1854 at the age of ninety-seven. Once again, James shared in his memoir how his sister Eliza notified him of their mother's declining health just in time for him to arrive on November 9, 1854, the day she died. He remarked that she was sharp mentally until the very end.

At about nine that night, as his sister took a break from their mother's sickbed, he wrote that "I took my seat at the bedside with my face to my mother's, holding the pulse of her right wrist with my right hand, and so continued about two hours, the pulse growing more feeble all the time. At length, about eleven o'clock, mother in a clear voice asked me to change the bedclothes at her feet, which I did. I bowed my head down to see if there was any change in her countenance. She put her arm around my neck, pressed me to her, kissed me most affectionately and said, *God bless you, you have been a good son*,"[16] and she died moments later.

Now orphaned, Eliza and Alexander Hamilton's many children and their descendants would create new histories of their own in the centuries to come.

It had been clear for some time that the city had to take steps to supply its burgeoning population with access to clean water. The first infrastructure change to have a real impact on Harlem Heights, and a profound one on the rest of the city, was the Croton Aqueduct that was built between 1837 and 1842. It brought fresh water to the city from the Croton River in northern Westchester County via gravity-fed aqueducts. "The idea was simple, pipe clean water from the relatively unspoiled Croton River through gravity-fed aqueducts to New York City."[17]

In December of 1835, after the Great Fire of New York wiped out a huge portion of New York City, which was to say "downtown," plans for an aqueduct took firmer shape. The fires bankrupted most of the fire insurance companies. It also prompted city officials to ban wooden buildings in future construction. No doubt, a ready supply of water would have saved more structures. On August 22, 1838, the *Vermont Telegraph* published a detailed description of the construction:

> The Aqueduct which is to bring Croton river water into the city of New York, will be 40 miles long. It will have an unvarying ascent from the starting point, eight miles above Sing Sing to Harlem Heights, where it comes out at 114 feet above high water mark. A great army of men are now at work along the line, and at many points the aqueduct is completed. The bottom is an inverted arch of brick; the sides are laid with hewn stone in cement. . . . It will stand for ages a monument of the enterprise of the present generation.[18]

By 1842 the aqueduct was operational and able to carry water across the Harlem River. The route of the aqueduct from Westchester, once it reached Manhattan, was through Harlem Heights over the High Bridge at 174th Street. In his historical report of Hamilton Heights, Andrew S. Dolkart writes that "the aqueduct then ran south through what is now Highbridge Park until about 158th Street, not far from the Morris-Jumel Mansion. It crossed beneath the current Edgecombe Avenue, continued south, and turned southwest beneath St. Nicholas Avenue at around 154th Street. The aqueduct route traverses St. Nicholas and Amsterdam Avenues at 153rd and 154th streets. It continues south towards the receiving reservoir in Central Park."[19]

There can be few changes to a metropolis as monumental as providing clean water to its residents. The route the aqueduct took through its landed point in Harlem Heights would cause odd-shaped structures in the neighborhood for a century to come.

The High Bridge was still under construction when the aqueduct became functional and was not completed until 1848. The pedestrian walkway above the pipes carrying the water was completed in 1864. The bridge quickly became both a popular spot for New Yorkers to promenade in pleasant weather and a favorite subject for artists and photographers. "The walkway's popularity led to the construction of hotels, restaurants, and

Figure 12. The High Bridge, circa 1849. Public domain

amusement parks nearby. Boat cruises up and down the river, and racing competitions for crew boats were also popular."[20]

Other changes were afoot. As the century reached its midway point, Trinity Church Cemetery on Broadway and Wall Street needed room to grow. After two centuries of interments of people whose numbers included famed engineer Robert Fulton, inventor of the first steamboat, Alexander and Eliza Hamilton, and their son Philip, it had reached its capacity. In 1842, Richard Carman sold the church a twenty-four-acre site bounded by Riverside Drive, Amsterdam Avenue, and 153rd and 155th streets for use as a cemetery and mausoleum. James Renwick Jr., the architect of St. Patrick's Cathedral on Fifth Avenue, was hired to design the landscaping and proposed a layout that featured sweeping flower-lined walkways and pathways with graceful trees. The cemetery was located partially on land once owned by Jan Dyckman, just a few blocks west of Hamilton's original estate, in the neighborhood that some eight decades later would be known as Sugar Hill.

Author David Fiske writes of how a free Black woman named Anne Northup came to live at the Morris-Jumel Mansion around 1841. That summer Anne had met Madame Jumel at the Pavilion Hotel in Saratoga

Springs, in upstate New York, where Anne had worked in various hotels and was known as a fine cook. Anne, who had three children, Elizabeth, Margaret, and Alonzo, was undoubtedly in considerable distress because her husband, Solomon, also a free person, had mysteriously disappeared from their home. "At summer's end, Elizabeth went to New York City with Madame Jumel to work as her servant."[21]

Anne would not learn for a decade that her husband had been kidnapped in Washington, D.C., and sold into slavery in Louisiana. During some of those years, she worked at the Morris-Jumel Mansion with Elizabeth and Alonzo performing various chores. The youngest Northup daughter, eight-year-old Margaret, was sent to Hoboken, New Jersey, to live with Eliza's now grown married daughter, Mary Bowen Chase, whom she had adopted as a child.

Within a few years, the Northups returned to Saratoga, and a decade later Solomon was rescued from slavery in Louisiana and reunited with his family. He would describe his harrowing experiences in a book titled *Twelve Years a Slave*, a powerful memoir and slave narrative published in 1853.

Around this time, the issue of a more formal method of education for all the poor children of New York emerged again. By 1842, fifteen years after New York had abolished slavery, the African Free School system founded in 1787 had grown to encompass seven locations in Greenwich Village. If a Black child in Harlem wanted a formal education, their families would have had to make their way downtown unless they could afford private tutors. One of the most important things about these schools, and a benefit that would be lost in future years, was that most of the teachers were Black and thus provided children with needed support and empathy.

The Association of Women Friends for the Relief of the Poor had established the Free School in 1802, but it admitted only poor white children. In 1842, the Board of Education was formed, and it was composed of thirty-four popularly elected commissioners. The African Free School was eventually incorporated into the Public School Society, which in 1853 merged with the Board of Education. This series of mergers essentially meant that two smaller educational organizations were subsumed by a much larger bureaucracy and lost their autonomy.

The beginnings of the racism and unequal funding that would plague the city's public school system well into the twenty-first century started right after the merger. The African Free School structures were allowed to deteriorate, many Black teachers were fired, and white teachers were often openly hostile to both Black parents and their children.

In 1845 a financier named William G. Ward bought Hamilton Grange.

The Wards would be the longest private occupants of the house, using it as their summer home and weekend retreat for more than thirty years. It is likely that they also installed indoor plumbing, since by then the Croton Aqueduct was supplying running water to most of the city.

In the decades to come, the neighborhood that surrounded Hamilton's original thirty-two acres would become home to a cluster of educational institutions, among them the City College of New York, the Teachers Training College, and the College of the Sacred Heart. It began with the Academy of the Sacred Heart, founded in 1841 by the Society of the Sacred Heart, a Catholic order of nuns. In 1847 they moved their small female school to a site in Harlem between 131st and 135th streets and what would soon become Convent Avenue. The school would continue to grow and morph into an undergraduate college named the College of the Sacred Heart in 1917. The neighborhood would further develop with the influx of houses of worship with St. Luke's Episcopal, Lenox Presbyterian, and Washington Heights Baptist Church, all constructed within blocks of the Grange.

Other significant changes happened when in December of 1847 the Audubons and other residents deeded their riverfront property to the Hudson River Railroad Company. Less than two years later trains were running daily along the West Side of Manhattan between the city and Peekskill, some thirty miles north of the Harlem stop, which was at 152nd Street. The new service shortened the trip from the Grange to Lower Manhattan to less than an hour and was among the improvements that would catapult Hamilton Heights into the modern era and encourage more people to move there.

More infrastructure changes were inevitable when "explosive growth in the early 1800s forced New York to finally confront its sanitation problems," wrote Michael Markowitz in the *Gotham Gazette*. "In 1849, after years of haphazard planning and a series of deadly cholera outbreaks, the city started systematically building sewers. Between 1850 and 1855, New York laid 70 miles of sewers."[22]

By the 1850s, the former estate of John James Audubon was struggling financially, and its owner was losing his memory as a result of dementia. Audubon died at his Harlem estate in 1851 and was buried right up the hill in Trinity Cemetery. Part of the land he owned came to be called Audubon Park, although just a few decades later the once idyllic woodland with a river view, flowers, and forest animals would give way to paved roads and new construction.

By the 1850s, with the family heavily in debt, Audubon's widow, Lucy, expanded what started out just teaching her grandchildren into a school to earn extra money for the family. George Bird Grinnell, one of their students, would himself go on to become a leading naturalist, founding the Audubon Society and encouraging President Theodore Roosevelt to preserve vast tracts of America's open lands as national parks.

During this same period, the packed Hamilton school building was now in poor condition, and it burned down in 1857. The destruction of the old Hamilton Free School coincided with the opening of P.S. 46 at 156th Street near the Hudson River. Although the school would serve children in varying demographic groups, segregation would have likely kept out Black children. New York City would continue to sustain the generic identification numbering system of schools so that the name for all public schools was shortened to "P.S." and then the ensuing number corresponding to that school.

New York State had abolished slavery in 1827, several decades before the start of the Civil War. Nonetheless, many restrictive laws still affected the quality of life for the city's Black residents. While the Underground Railroad was helping people in slavery make their way to the North, it was nonetheless a perilous time. Manumission societies were springing up across the country. Harriet Beecher Stowe's novel, *Uncle Tom's Cabin*, which was published in 1852, would have a major influence on the Anti-Slavery Movement.

Thanks to Lincoln's Emancipation Proclamation, delivered on January 1, 1863, two years after the start of the Civil War, millions of formerly enslaved men, women, and children across the country were set free, but their economic conditions had changed little. There were pockets of successful Black communities in Manhattan and Brooklyn. But generally, descendants of Africans in New York were still confined to the worst jobs, earned the lowest salaries, and faced competition from a constant influx of newly arriving immigrants. Regardless of how destitute or uneducated they were, the new arrivals quickly embraced the socially accepted belief that the poorest white person still stood above a Black person. The Irish saw Negroes as competition for jobs and ignored the reality that these people of color had a 150-year history in New York that preceded their recent arrival.

The New York City Draft Riots of 1863, during which Irish immigrants launched a five-day assault on Blacks in lower Manhattan, forced some African Americans to move uptown. The federal government had announced that it would draft men to serve in the Union Army, and while rich men could avoid the draft by paying $300 or hiring someone to take their place, the average man did not have that option. Certainly, some of the draftees would have noted the irony that Black men were not eligible for the draft, since they were not considered citizens.

As Isabel Wilkerson wrote in her brilliant 2010 book *The Warmth of Other Suns: The Epic Story of America's Great Migration*, "In five days of rioting, anti-war mobs lynched eleven Black men and drove the colony of former slaves in lower Manhattan into a continual search for housing. Black residents moved steadily north from one unsavory neighborhood to the next . . . and finally to pockets of upper Manhattan, in the emerging district north of Central Park known as Harlem."[23]

Still other changes were in motion during these tumultuous years. In 1864, for example, Lucy Audubon finally sold the last of the Audubon property. "At the end of May, Jesse Benedict bought the homestead, its thirty-six lots, and the well lot at the top of the hill for $24,000."[24] Benedict was a wealthy and philanthropic businessman.

Harlem was being divided into sections that would later be termed East, Central, and West Harlem. The neighborhoods would be home to a mix of Jewish, German, Irish, Italian, African, West Indian, and other immigrants, along with a growing African American populace. A natural evolution happened where the Harlem neighborhoods began to define themselves by the ways in which different immigrant and racial groups began to congregate and establish their sense of self and home in this new place.

Starting in the 1870s, the eastern section of Harlem became an Italian enclave that replicated the South Italy homeland they had left. The neighborhood was bounded by 96th Street to 125th Street, from the Harlem River to Fifth Avenue. It would be known at various periods as Little Italy, East Harlem, Spanish Harlem, and El Barrio. A parallel Italian neighborhood would develop in lower Manhattan around Mulberry Street.

Thousands of Italians had left the poverty of Southern Italy for the promise of America's better economic opportunities. They crowded into dilapidated, overcrowded tenements and began to build a close-knit Italian neighborhood through their cultural traditions, music, food, festivals, and deep-seated religious convictions, with a strong Catholic base. An estimated 100,000 Italians would occupy East Harlem by the 1920s, the largest Italian American community in the U.S. The residents built social clubs, banks, restaurants, and churches in celebration of their heritage.

Many of the other European residents gradually moved more toward Central Harlem around Lenox, Seventh, and Eighth avenues. A strong Jewish presence developed that shaped the area's economic, cultural, and entertainment character. One man in particular, Oscar Hammerstein, would leave an indelible imprint with real estate acquisitions and the arts, building his first theater, the Harlem Opera House, on 125th Street in 1889. The slower growth in the population of the western neighborhood of Harlem Heights on the hilly areas of Edgecombe, St. Nicholas, and north to the Hudson would blossom in a few decades.

Meanwhile, transportation uptown had steadily improved. The June 3, 1867, schedule for the Hudson River Railway listed among its Manhattan stops Manhattanville, 152nd Street, Fort Washington, Inwood, and Spuyten Duyvil.

In addition, the fields of medicine and health care were being transformed. The medical profession was still in its primitive stages in many respects. Doctors had not yet totally embraced the notion of how germs were spread and their impact on patient care. Vaccines were still fairly new. In 1862, during the Civil War, the Manhattan Dispensary was founded to serve as a temporary medical facility for returning Union Army invalids, although it was little more than tents. After the war, the dispensary opened as Manhattan Hospital at Convent Avenue at West 131st Street, its mission to provide medical care primarily for immigrants and the poor.

The *New York Times* praised the institution's rebirth in 1885 as the fully equipped Manhattan Hospital, "the only general hospital north of Ninety-ninth street." It established the city's most extensive twenty-four-hour ambulance service, which served an area bounded by West 76th Street, West 145th Street, St. Nicholas Avenue, and the Hudson. For decades it was relied upon to transport patients to other hospitals. Not surprisingly, the hospital had a strict policy not to admit or treat Negroes in a neighborhood soon to be home to an influx of them. Eventually, the institution would change its name to Knickerbocker Hospital, often referred to as "the Knick."

The name "Knickerbocker" was part pseudonym and part fictional character Diedrich Knickerbocker, created by Washington Irving in his 1809 mock epic book *A History of New York*. Surprisingly, the name "Knickerbocker" became representative of elite New York society. The name was adopted by a school of writers, a magazine, the Manhattan hospital, a baseball and basketball team, a hotel, and, in the twenty-first century, a TV show called "the Knick." Harlem Hospital, which would open in 1887 on East 120th Street, would move two decades later to Lenox Avenue between 135th and 137th streets. Despite the historic significance of what the hospital and its location would come to mean to the city's Black population, it was unwelcoming to them at that time. It would be 1920 before Harlem Hospital hired its first two Black doctors.

Eliza Jumel died in 1865 at the age of ninety-two. "The poor demented lady breathed her last in the chamber of the old house known as the Washington Bedroom," wrote historian William Shelton. "She may be said to have died in state decked in all her jewels and powdered and rouged to the end."[25] After Madame Jumel's death and the reading of her will, a twenty-year battle would ensue over her estate, a battle that eventually reached the United States Supreme Court. During some of this time, the many distant relatives contesting the will were living in the house, most of them not speaking to one another. Jewelry, silver, clothing, and other valuable items mysteriously disappeared.

Two years before her death and already suffering from dementia, Eliza Jumel had made a will, leaving the bulk of her property to charitable societies and churches. A generous sum was to go to her favorite pastor, John Howard Smith, rector of the Church of the Intercession, who had been her advisor. It took a year for the will to be set aside on the grounds that Eliza Jumel had not been of sound mind when she wrote it. Ironically, those contesting the will had little or no blood relationship to her; they were the children and grandchildren of her estranged stepsister, Polly.

The life-size family portrait painted by Alcide Ercole would be moved from room to room but continue to hang somewhere in the Morris-Jumel Mansion.

In the midst of all the claims, George Washington Bowen, the son to whom Eliza had given birth in 1794, reemerged as an interested party to the estate. Bowen had successfully made his way in the world. He had worked in the rubber business, as a lottery agent, and in the grocery business, establishing his own companies, marrying twice, and gradually leaving his business to his son. For thirty years George Bowen had spent part of his summers at Saratoga, where Madame Jumel was a familiar figure. Reportedly, she never publicly acknowledged his existence except in her advanced years or when she had too much to drink. Bowen said that a few months before she died, Freelove Ballou, the woman who raised him, told him the identity of his mother. He was twenty-nine at the time.

Shelton's meticulous account of the estate dispute and trials indicate that, "in 1867, two years after Madame Jumel's death, GW Bowen was informed by Judge Edmonds that, by a law then in force in the State of New York, an illegitimate son could inherit from his mother when there were no legitimate children, and steps were immediately taken to bring an action to dispossess the resident heirs, which resulted in the famous case of George Washington Bowen vs. Nelson Chase."[26] Bowen was seventy-eight at the time of the trial.

In 1872, when the case went to court, ample evidence was offered to

Figure 13. Eliza Jumel and Her Grandchildren, by Alcide Ercole, 1854. Public domain. Photo by D. S. James

establish that George Washington Bowen was Eliza Jumel's natural-born son. Among the many people who testified was David Hull, now an old man, to whom Eliza had shown off the infant. "An old colored woman, Elizabeth Freeman, who had sometime been in the service of Madame Jumel, and was in charge of the house on Circular Street in Saratoga in 1869"[27] was sought out as to her knowledge of his maternity. So it was that Anne Northup, the free Black woman who had worked for Eliza in

1841 after her husband Solomon's disappearance, returned to New York City. She and her daughters, Elizabeth Northup Freeman and Margaret, all gave evidence in the court case asserting their awareness that Bowen was Madam Jumel's son by her own account.

The prosecution read into the record from the King Henry Book, the notation written by Reuben Ballou that on October 9, 1794, a male child, George Washington Bowen, was born of Eliza Bowen at his house in town, Providence, Rhode Island. He then admitted into the record that Eliza B. Jumel died on the 16th day of July, 1865, and rested his case. It would seem he felt those two statements were a sufficient argument.

However, the evidence also supported the fact that Mary Bowen Chase, by then deceased, had been the adopted daughter of the Jumels and that Eliza Jumel had intended the property to be passed on to Mary and her children, who had always lived on the estate.

Shelton wrote that, in his opinion, it was a case "where justice lay on one side and a hard and strict interpretation of the law lay on the other side. No jury could have the hardihood to oust the claimants in possession, who had been born, lived, and died on the estate, and whose possession was the will and desire of the deceased owners."[28] George Bowen was Madam Jumel's natural-born child that she abandoned and never publicly acknowledged. It was to her adopted daughter Mary Bowen Chase, whom she had raised in the mansion, and her heirs that Eliza intended to leave the estate.

It took the jury only a few hours to find for the defendant. Eliza Jumel's son appealed the decision, and seven years later, in 1879, the United States Supreme Court upheld the lower court's decision, ruling that George Washington Bowen could not inherit his mother's property. He died in Providence in 1885 at the age of ninety.

At the conclusion of the case, the property was subdivided, and a large estate sale took place in November of 1882, after which several apartment buildings were constructed on parts of the property, among them Sylvan Terrace, a string of wooden rowhouses. Mary's husband, Nelson Chase, became the owner of the mansion.

Neighbors just to the east were feeling the effects of the street grid. "Rather than blast through a steep ridge in the area, Andrew H. Green closed Ninth Avenue between 126th and 145th streets and laid out three new roads that curved around the contours of the land between Eighth and Tenth avenues: St. Nicholas Avenue, St. Nicholas Terrace, and Convent Avenue."[29] These became key streets in Hamilton Heights.

In 1867 the commissioners of Central Park prepared a map of new streets that included St. Nicholas Avenue, which they first called Avenue

St. Nicholas. The street honors New Amsterdam's patron saint, whose image often adorned the masthead of ships from Netherlands, as he was also the patron saint of sailors. St. Nicholas was the inspiration for Santa Claus in many fables. Convent Avenue, another addition to the 1811 grid plan, named as an homage to the convent of nuns that founded the Academy of the Sacred Heart at the far end of the street, originally ended at 145th Street. Seven more blocks would be added in the years to come.

The developer, Richard Carman, died in 1867. He may not have left behind the lasting village of Carmansville that he had planned, but another look for Harlem Heights developed during his time that became standard in other neighborhoods of the city. Carman had made a great deal of money constructing buildings on Amsterdam Avenue. Although some variation of this style of building had almost always existed, with shopkeepers and businessmen often living in an apartment above their businesses, it became a hallmark of Harlem Heights' commercial boulevards and avenues starting in the mid-1850s.

At some point during these years, people began calling parts of the Harlem Heights neighborhood Washington Heights to honor the nation's first president. In the coming century, the definition of where that new neighborhood designation began would shift again and again, with some people calling the areas above 175th Street as such and others starting to call areas around 155th Street Washington Heights. The start, the finish, which avenue and which boulevard was the true marker would keep changing and be debated, too often complicated by demographic changes and an ever-evolving racial makeup of the area.

Chapter 6

The Bailey Mansion, St. Luke's, and a Building Boom

> History is an aggregate of half-truths, semi-truths, fables, myths, rumors, prejudices, personal narratives, gossip and official prevarications. It is a canvas upon which thousands of artists throughout the ages have splashed their conceptions and interpretations of a day and an era.
>
> —Philip D. Jordan, American historian

Ever since the early nineteenth century it had been apparent that public transportation had not kept pace with New York City's growing population, which by the mid-1860s was close to 900,000 people. City officials agreed that the most practical solution was to build an elevated train line that would solve the congestion problems in Manhattan. But not until the mid-nineteenth century would progress on such a project begin.

"On April 20, 1866, the West Side and Yonkers Patent Railway Company was formed by Charles T. Harvey and eventually got awarded the approval to begin construction of his elevated line up Greenwich Street, then Ninth Avenue from Battery Place to 30th Street."[1] Harvey received a patent for an elevated train the following year and lived to see it built and operational.

The appeal of the new system was that "elevated trains were fast, predictable, and cheap: five cents during rush hour, compared to five dollars for a private carriage, and ten cents for horse-drawn railways or omnibuses."[2]

The move uptown to Harlem was not quick. The city was still deeply in the middle of digging up land and tearing out trees and flowers to build the smooth streets and sidewalks that would make the public's journey cleaner and quicker. Modern advances come at a cost, and the radical new elevated system was met with incredible criticism and mechanical problems, as well as legal and financial challenges. So, the shift was neither simple nor easy.

Most power in the city was concentrated in the hands of a political operator named William Magear Tweed, arguably one of the most corrupt figures in New York's history. "Boss" Tweed, as he was universally known, ran Tammany Hall, the unchallenged machine of the Democratic Party, and during the 1860s and 1870s he and his minions had a firm grip on politics in the city, especially in the areas of real estate and construction contracts.

"Tweed realized early that some of the most tempting opportunities for plunder were in Harlem. Gas lighting had been in use downtown since the 1820s, but it wasn't until the supposedly civic-minded efforts of Tweed, a director of the Harlem Gas and Light Company, that it came uptown."[3] Although seemingly untouchable, in 1874 Tweed was convicted of embezzling millions of dollars from the city and state, and he was sentenced to twelve years in prison on Blackwell's Island.

The appeal of moving huge numbers of people more quickly than was possible with horse-drawn carriages was powerful. And so, "on February 9, 1871, the Transit Commissioners granted permission for the elevated railway company to proceed with their plan to discard all previous equipment and replace it with steam locomotives."[4] Necessity being the mother of invention and reinvention, the existing structures were strengthened to withstand the extra weight, and steam operation began on April 20, 1871. A key stop would be in Sugar Hill at 155th Street.

It was a new era for the city, and expanded service would eventually make its way even farther uptown as the world's first successful elevated railway went into operation. The city would use steam power throughout the system until the switch to electrical power in 1902.

There were other pivotal changes in the making. "Harlem was annexed to New York City in 1873. From about this time on, it experienced phenomenal growth due to the building of railroads to and through the area. Around this time, some 1,350 acres of marshlands were filled once disputes and misunderstandings over rights to ownership of the Harlem patents, which included tidal creeks and marshes were resolved."[5]

The corporate and governmental bodies of New York City had always proceeded with development and infrastructure improvements to Harlem over the centuries. The separation of downtown Manhattan from the northern Harlem community had long evaporated. The annexation formally ended any ghostly vestiges of control that the now defunct Township of Harlem Corporation had over Harlem's fate. Because of the modern-day fluid relationship among the five boroughs, it may seem surprising that they were not all formally annexed to create the interconnected City of New York until 1898.

In the Panic of 1873 the Ward family, which had purchased the Grange in 1845, lost the Hamilton estate through foreclosure to the Emigrant Savings Bank. In 1879 the bank sold Hamilton's former home to Anthony Mowbray, an architect and real estate speculator, who promptly sold the property to his business associate, a silk merchant named William H. De Forest.

The Harlem Heights property was thus placed in the hands of a descendant of the seventeenth-century Dutch colonist Isaac De Forest, brother of Henry and son of Jesse the dyer from Leiden in the Netherlands. Isaac's numerous offspring and their descendants had populated multiple continents and states—among them Canada, New Jersey, Connecticut, and Oswego County in upstate New York, yet there remained a New York City contingent that still had history to make. And William H. De Forest and his son were destined to provide Hamilton Heights with its signature architectural style.

De Forest moved forward with his plan to subdivide his thirty-two-acre parcel into three hundred individual lots and offer them for sale at a public auction in 1887. But because he had inflated the asking price, sales were disappointing, and he was forced to sell many of the lots at a loss.

There was yet another sign of development in Hamilton Heights, during the same period when so many of the handsome buildings on Hamilton's former estate were being erected. A February 16, 1886, article in the *New York Times* reported on the opening of the Washington Heights Athenaeum, developed by local property owners on 157th Street near 11th Avenue (now Broadway). The building was constructed in the Queen Anne style, and the opening program included vocalists, readings, and a performance by the Columbia College Glee Club. Structures like this one helped transform the once rural outpost into an urban environment, and the name made the theater one of the earliest structures in West Harlem to use the name Washington Heights.

In these years, Harlem farmland was poised to give way to townhouses, apartment buildings, and what were known as French flats, apartment buildings for the middle and upper middle class. Thanks to the building boom and newly paved streets in Harlem Heights, between 1881 and 1898 some sixty-two rowhouses were built, structures designed in various late nineteenth-century styles, including neo-Greco, Queen Anne, neo-Renaissance, and Beaux-Arts. Some of the materials were brick, brownstone, and limestone, and they were trimmed with terracotta, stained glass, and cast and wrought iron.

The unrealistic prices that William H. De Forest had set would be his downfall and lead eventually to madness and bankruptcy. But before that, De Forest defined what would become the most unique architectural and design feature of the Hamilton Heights neighborhood. While restrictive covenants have often been used for racist or exclusionary purposes, De Forest placed a two-decade restrictive covenant that future construction in the area be limited to brick or stone two- or three-story-high dwelling houses.

William De Forest Jr. commissioned architect Harvey L. Page to design four townhouses and an adjoining apartment building in the Queen Anne style at the southwest corner of Tenth (now Amsterdam) Avenue and West 144th Street, almost directly across from the Grange. A similar pattern was maintained throughout the neighborhood, with mostly three-story residences along the numbered streets, Convent Avenue, and Hamilton Terrace.

William De Forest Jr. was the natural-born son of Col. Othniel De Forest, who died in the Civil War. The senior William and his brother Othniel were part of the Connecticut branch of the extensive legacy of seventeenth-century patriarch Isaac De Forest's eleven children. "In September 1866, [Othniel's] widow Fanny married William Henry De Forest, his brother, who was eleven years his junior. William adopted the three children—Rebecca, William, and Othniel Jr. Both sons joined their adopted father, technically their uncle, in a prosperous import business."[6]

William E. Mowbray completed a group of the Hamilton Grange houses at 455–467 West 144th Street in 1888. As Michael Henry Adams writes in his book *Harlem: Lost and Found*, the town houses were reminiscent of those built in the Netherlands by early wealthy Dutch settlers in the 1600s, and they were a tribute to the West Harlem area's rich heritage. "Far more ambitious than the typical dwellings colonists erected in New Netherland, they nevertheless embodied Mowbray's vision of what colonists might have built had they been able, grand houses like those of the original Haarlem."[7]

De Forest and his son continued to develop the former Hamilton estate until 1893, and they spared no expense to make it have a semi-suburban ambience. Each house was set fifteen feet from the curb with a flower garden and shrubbery or trees, some with ornamental ivy climbing the front.

"The Mowbray row is configured so that every chimney and gable contribute to a pyramidal composition. The houses vary a great deal

Figures 14 and 15. LEFT: William Kaupe House, 459 West 144th Street, William E. Mowbray (architect), circa 1904. RIGHT: Figure 15. William Kaupe Family, 459 West 144th Street. Photos courtesy of the collection of Amiaga Photographers, Inc.

individually . . . and stone bases alternate in color; some employ bits of schist rubble removed during the excavation, while others feature sandstone."[8] Each of the houses had unique whimsical designs and carvings on the exteriors, some of red and gold terra-cotta: dragons, garlands, lions' heads, and sunbursts with stuck-out tongues.

This 400 block of 144th Street would later become one of the most photographed streets in Hamilton Heights as a stunning example of postcolonial Dutch architecture. It was also the street on which both the De Forest and Mowbray families secured homes for themselves.

Hamilton Heights retained its characteristic smaller homes until the early twentieth century, when De Forest's restrictive covenants expired. At that point, a new era of urbanization would arrive as taller apartment buildings were constructed along Convent Avenue, St. Nicholas, and Edgecombe. But there was one patch of land that was outside of the developed areas.

New Amsterdam's Dutch beginnings and the men and women who carved homes and businesses out of its wilderness can have no finer example of legacy than the De Forest family. The fullness of their history in America has been told in other books. But the powerful contributions of the descendants of Jesse from Leiden in the Netherlands are not just that one of them is an original founder of Harlem, but also that another descendant is a founder of the cultural heart of New York City.

At the exact time in the late 1880s that William H. De Forest was shaping the overarching character of the Hamilton Heights neighborhood and his son William De Forest Jr. was engaging architects to create a unique vision of the style of the houses, another branch of their family was making his mark on the newly opened Metropolitan Museum of Art downtown on Fifth Avenue. Having married the daughter of one of the museum's founders, in 1889 Robert W. De Forest became one of its trustees and eventually its fifth director. His contributions to the museum's development would be monumental. His family had a two-hundred-year-old heritage of seeing New Amsterdam transition into New York.

Along with the concurrent development of his kin uptown in Hamilton Heights, the De Forests were proof that a city and its people can have ever-shifting, yet interconnected threads that help shape it. Artwork and collections involving the Indigenous People of New York, George Washington, Alexander Hamilton, and an acclaimed African American artist not yet born who would grace Hamilton Heights—Romare Bearden—would find its way to the Met and the American Wing that Robert and Emily De Forest would donate for Americana art.

It had been many decades since New Yorkers from downtown had escaped to the woodlands of Harlem in search of cleaner air and wide vistas. Now their country homes were making way for the grid as numbered streets and avenues became the norm. As buildings rose, many river views disappeared, as did the wild animals and small game that once roamed the hills. The Native Americans who had lived on this land for centuries had long since vanished. Small clusters of them lived quietly in the city, in all but obscurity. Most had long since moved to other parts of the state or country, and the majority were living on reservations, having lost their New York City ancestral lands by unscrupulous land sales and the spoils of war.

De Forest held onto the Grange and the remaining property directly around the house while the new buildings were being constructed all around it. It was reported in the local press that he was the one who had carefully fenced in the famous thirteen gum trees that Hamilton had planted around 1801. But in lieu of some entity buying the trees and replanting them, they were doomed. In 1889, De Forest sold the Grange to a wealthy New York banker named Amos Cotting.

On August 13, 1888, down the street from the Grange, a fire had spread throughout the main building of the College of the Sacred Heart. Miraculously, all 190 students and teachers escaped uninjured. The sisters rebuilt on the same foundation, and one year later, on June 2, 1889, they held commencement in the new building.

"Population growth had expanded dramatically in the area, necessitating the imposition of the gridiron over the entire Hamilton Grange district. The rectangular grid pattern, however, often could not accommodate private land ownership boundaries, including the diagonal orientation of The Grange."[9] It was destined for demolition.

A mile from Hamilton's former home, at the Morris-Jumel Mansion, the settlement of the estate by the various surviving heirs left only a small plot of land around the house itself. From the original 132 acres there was now less than a city block of green space, only enough for some walkways and a modest garden.

The last private owners of the mansion were Lillie Earle and her husband, General Ferdinand Earle, who claimed a family relationship to Col. Roger Morris. Despite their respect for its history, the Earle family made the most major physical changes to the mansion since its construction in 1765. It is also believed that they added indoor plumbing. Carol Ward writes how they "completely changed the Octagon to create a two-story studio, with a skylight for one of their sons who was a painter. They broke into the garret on the right to create the north light. A dormer window was removed, and a railing with an English hob-gate was brought up from the parlor to decorate the studio itself."[10] There were no historic landmark protections established yet. But in 1898, after just four years in residence, the Earles put the house up for sale, with no takers.

None of the mansions that had belonged to the Maunsell/Bradhurst families survived the paving of Harlem Heights and the rush to erect rows of apartment buildings. Pinehurst Mansion, the Bradhurst former estate, had become Koch's New Mount St. Vincent Hotel and was eventually bulldozed to make room for part of the expanded Convent Avenue. The home of Hamilton's old friend Dr. Samuel Bradhurst, a man whose lineage included the Pelhams of Britain and Native Americans in Westchester, would disappear, although the name Bradhurst would continue to live on in West Harlem.

As the grid reached the area around the Grange, Hamilton's old home was in the way of what would become 143rd Street. Stunning brownstones and apartment blocks were now facing it. The land where the Grange rested would soon be readied for paving and subject to the designs for dwellings that were bigger and newer.

Even in the late 1800s, people of means continued to view Harlem as a haven from crowded downtown Manhattan. Mansions were still being

BAILEY MANSION, ST. LUKE'S, AND A BUILDING BOOM · 83

built in the district with the assumption that Harlem would remain mostly pastoral and be defined by sprawling estates, despite the grand row houses that had begun to replace the larger private homes.

In 1885 descendants of the Bradhurst family, whose roots ran deep in this section of Harlem Heights, built a stunning mansion known as the Van Rensselaer House at 22–24 St. Nicholas Avenue. As the Maunsells had no children, Mrs. Maunsell had left the property to her grandnieces; Maunsell Van Rensselaer was the grandson of one of them, Anna Dunkin. It was the intermarriage among the Bradhursts, Watkins, Schieffelins, and Maunsells that kept this circle of families forever entwined, all with a connection to Hamilton as friends and former landowners.

The Van Rensselaer House was next door to an adjoining pair of shingled and stone villas at 14–16 St. Nicholas Avenue that William Milne Grinnell had designed for James Montieth. The double houses presented a unique style compared to the more familiar lime or brownstone.

If ever a building deserved a book of its own, it would perhaps be the magnificent Manhattan mansion: the James A. Bailey House at 10 St. Nicholas Place at 150th Street. The house's namesake, Barnum & Bailey circus magnate James A. Bailey, was the shy half of the legendary pair, who were reinventing what it meant to go to the circus. And like the wealthy landowners who had settled in the area a century earlier, Bailey anticipated that Harlem, with its vistas of the rivers and open tracts of land, would continue to be an exclusive residential district.

In 1886, after buying the lot at St. Nicholas Place, Bailey hired the architect Samuel B. Reed to design the house. An 8,250-square-foot limestone structure with a sixty-nine-foot-high tower, the house is built in the Romanesque Revival style and resembles a small castle. It contains thirty rooms and is adorned with arches, gables, and tiled porches topped with spires. An article published in *Scientific American* in 1890 "catalogued the different woods in various rooms, hazel in the parlor, quartered oak in the main hall, sycamore in the library and black walnut in Bailey's office, and noted that the house had a billiard room and art gallery on the third floor."[11]

Especially notable are the sixty-four stained-glass windows, which had been designed by Henry F. Belcher and changed color during the course of a day, using a technique the designer perfected and patented. Belcher's method involved leaving a space between each pane of glass, into which molten lead was poured, binding the sheets of glass together. The two layers created a solid panel of glass and metal that concentrated the light and threw it into the room, causing brilliant reflections that shifted during the

Figure 16. James A. Bailey House, circa 1890. Public domain

day according to changes in the natural light. The final cost of the mansion was estimated at $160,000, equal to well over five million dollars in the twenty-first century.

Although these intricately decorative windows seemed to be fixed, they open like any other window. Not surprisingly, the house quickly became the showplace of the neighborhood.

The Nicholas C. and Agnes Benziger House, at 345 Edgecombe Avenue, was built in 1890–91 by a successful publisher, manufacturer, and importer of religious books. The Benziger House was directly behind the Bailey House on another lot that might have given them more space for gardens had Bailey purchased it.

The late nineteenth century brought a profound change in the way New York City's African Americans communicated with one another when T. Thomas Fortune, born in the South in slavery and freed as a child with the Emancipation Proclamation, moved to New York City and entered the newspaper business. Fortune had worked in print shops when he was young and spent a short period of time at Howard University before coming to the city. In 1881 he established a publication he called the *New York*

Figure 17. Stained Glass James Bailey initials. Courtesy D. S. James, © 2021

Globe and changed its name twice, first to the *New York Freeman*, then to what became its permanent name, the *New York Age*. Although Fortune's major concern was the condition of Black people in the South, the paper became a vital source of general information for Black New Yorkers.

As Walter Greason wrote in an article summing up Fortune's achievements, "By 1887, he had established himself as the most prominent Black journalist of the time," and the *New York Age* "became one of the most influential Black newspapers in the nation."[12] The *New York Age* would also become an invaluable source of information as the Great Migration brought millions of Black Americans from the South to the North, thousands of which would find their way to New York City.

The streets we walk upon become part of the fabric of a place after a couple of generations. Eventually, no one alive would remember the inconvenience faced during the creation of the master plan of sidewalks, streetways, and modern plumbing that adds to our standard of living. Pavements and cement mean less nature but more of what is convenient. People forget that there was earth surrounded by trees, grass, flowers, and wildlife before the pavements. As an architectural historian, Gregory

Wessner made a study of the grid of Manhattan that aptly described what Harlemites, and indeed most New Yorkers, were experiencing as the mostly rural landscape gave way to modernity. Wessner wrote that:

> Our 19th Century forebears, resident in the city during the decades it took to fully realize the street grid, had to live through the blasting of Manhattan rocks and the clearing of soil, the laying out of streets and the endless building required to fill these new blocks with their first houses, shops and schools.[13]

Meanwhile, huge changes were poised to take place at Hamilton's Grange. In many ways it is a miracle that the Grange survived demolition. Cities and states had not yet fully embraced the fact that it was important to save historic buildings. During these years many country estates were bulldozed to make way for businesses, schools, private homes, and nondescript apartment buildings.

At the same time, changes were taking place downtown that would have a ripple effect on structures uptown. In 1820 homeowners in the West Village had established St. Luke's Episcopal Church, located on Hudson Street. It was built to serve the growing Greenwich Village neighborhood, and there were direct links between the downtown congregation and West Harlem.

Trinity Church Wall Street, which had extensive land holdings in downtown Manhattan as well as its new cemetery in Hamilton Heights, informed St. Luke's in 1887 that it planned to build a new complex on land it owned surrounding the St. Luke's building. Certain that such a project would threaten its existence at the same location, St. Luke's felt compelled to find another place to worship.

When Trinity Church offered to pay St. Luke's for its property, they accepted, whereupon they needed to find a site to build a new church. They decided on the wide-open spaces of Harlem, despite the ongoing construction of a few apartment buildings and new streets courtesy of the grid. The church wardens selected a plot of land on the newly paved Convent Avenue where gaslights were also being installed.

We know about the history of Hamilton Grange between 1889 and the early 1920s thanks to a book titled *The History of St. Luke's Church in the City of New York 1820–1920*, written in 1926 by a woman named Penelope T. Sturges Cook Tuttle. It was published under the name of Mrs. H. Croswell Tuttle in an era when women were referred to by their husband's names. Her incredible contribution to the history of both St. Luke's and the Grange during this period bore only her husband's name.

In 1914, the author would be living at 10 Hamilton Terrace, the new street lined with handsome brownstones and apartment buildings. Her husband, Henry Croswell Tuttle, was the son of the Reverend Dr. Isaac Tuttle, St. Luke's rector of forty-two years. Penelope and Henry had one son, Charles H. Tuttle, who would become a lawyer and trustee of City College. Penelope was a historian and a member of several boards and organizations, including the Washington Heights Chapter of the Daughters of the American Revolution.

When he was near death, Dr. Isaac Tuttle begged his daughter-in-law to write a history of the church and his time as rector. The church wardens also asked Penelope to write the history of the church's first one hundred years. The resulting book would become the sole record of how Alexander Hamilton's home was saved from destruction, its various uses, and its structural changes.

Dr. Tuttle was searching for a property where he could hold services while the church's new building at 141st Street and Convent Avenue was under construction. When he saw what he described as the "large, old-fashioned frame dwelling that had the appearance of former glory and elegance," he was surprised to learn that it had been built by the nation's first secretary of the treasury."[14]

The church had bought three lots from William De Forest and another five from Jacob Butler, who arranged a meeting with Dr. Tuttle and Amos Cotting, the owner of Hamilton Grange. The banker agreed to transfer the house to St. Luke's for use as an interim chapel while the new church was being built.

Mr. Butler had promised the church a $5,000 donation, so he assumed the expense of a new foundation for the house once it was moved. The Grange was lifted off its original foundation and drawn by horses 250 feet, about a block, to the new church property on Convent Avenue.

Ironically, "on the day of the opening services of the chapel in the Grange the weather proved rainy, and Dr. Tuttle stayed at home with a cold. Mr. Cotting, expecting to meet the rector, ventured to be present and was seized with a chill. Pneumonia ensued, and he expired in less than a week."[15]

On April 28, 1889, services were held for the first time at the church's new location. Despite the bad weather, the house was filled to capacity. The church wardens noted that the Sunday before the Centennial of George Washington's inauguration was a good time "for the opening Church Services in the historic building which was the house of Washington's trusted friend."[16] More than just President Washington's friend, Alexander

Figure 18. Hamilton Grange as Chapel. From *History of Saint Luke's Church in the City of New York*

Hamilton had shaped the young country, which was still becoming a united nation in a myriad of critical ways. And when the Reverend John T. Patey chose as the message for his sermon "Except the Lord build the house, their labor is but lost that build it," he gave Hamilton Grange its next breath of life.

Mid-nineteenth-century photographs and correspondence between McComb and Hamilton during the planning and building of the Grange show a carved wood balustrade surrounding the perimeter of the main roof and the porch roofs. The balustrade was removed at a later period. The original front door, which was centered on the south elevation and led to a columned porch, was lost in the 1889 move. The architect hired by St. Luke's, Alexander McMillan Welch, altered the entrance and made other changes to accommodate the move.

The staircase originally stood where the front door is now, but it was shifted as well. The ceiling between the upper hall and the entrance hall was removed to make it a two-story stair hall. And, of course, the side porches were taken off. The original basement kitchen was also lost in the move. The two bathrooms in the basement were adjacent to one another. The one under the first-floor north hall was put in when the floor was built during the relocation.

The church's needs and Mr. Cotting's generosity had come together at an ideal time, since the Grange needed to be either moved or demolished to accommodate the street grid and new housing. Now Hamilton's old

Figure 19. Grange First Floor Staircase. Courtesy of National Park Service, Manhattan Historic Sites Archive

Figure 20. Grange Second Floor Hall. Courtesy of National Park Service, Manhattan Historic Sites Archive

home would be used for church services, special events, as a school, and as the rector's home.

On November 10, 1891, at three in the afternoon, the clergy left Hamilton Grange and walked the few feet to the appointed location for the laying of the cornerstone of their new church. Dr. Tuttle, who had donated $20,000 for the building of the new church, closed his address by saying, "We hope and pray that the new Saint Luke's, whose walls are now rising, will be highly blessed of God, that prayers and alms, as well pleasing sacrifices, will ever come upon his altar."[17]

A few months later, after four decades as pastor, on March 18, 1892, Dr. Tuttle submitted his letter of resignation.

When the Richardsonian Romanesque church building erected on the Convent Avenue location was completed in 1892, it wrapped snugly around Hamilton's old home. The opening service was held on December 18, and at Dr. Tuttle's invitation, "the Reverend Doctor Schuyler Hamilton, a great-grandson of Alexander Hamilton, read the prayers and litany."[18] Schuyler's father had served in the Civil War, once acting as a liaison for Abraham Lincoln. One can only assume he would have gone next door to the Grange to visit the Hamilton family's former home.

With the opening of the new church, the Grange became the home of the reverend emeritus, the Reverend Tuttle. The sign at the entrance of the Grange read, "St. Luke's Church."

Convent Avenue had been extended, pushing it farther north, and it angled slightly northeast at 152nd Street to terminate when it joined St. Nicholas Avenue. During this period, "some wealthy city residents raced their prized trotters through the neighborhood en route to the Harlem Speedway, while others enjoyed quieter pleasures at the New York Tennis Club, near 148th Street and Tenth Avenue, or at the Atheneum, a building devoted to dancing and other social amusements."[19]

A more advanced form of mass transportation was still a serious concern for the city. By 1891, the rebuilding project of elevated trains expanded into Harlem north to 116th Street. The name of Ninth Avenue changes at various parts of the city; in the area of Harlem Heights it would become St. Nicholas Place, and the Ninth Avenue El would extend to 155th Street in Sugar Hill, ending next to the southern terminal of the New York and Northern Railroad. This would become a critical transfer junction and allow commuters to switch for points in downtown Manhattan. Eventually, the baseball stadium named the Polo Grounds would be built at that location. Behind the Polo Grounds would be the 159th Street Elevated Yard, the largest one of the Manhattan Elevated Railroad Company.

Figure 21. St. Luke's Church and the Grange, c. 1894. Courtesy of National Park Service, Manhattan Historic Sites Archive

In April of 1893 Dr. Tuttle offered to give Hamilton House to the vestry of St. Luke's. He also forfeited part of his salary and suggested that some of the money be used to paint the house a color that would blend with the stone of the church. The house then reverted to become the home of the current rector who, the following year, opted to live elsewhere and returned use of Hamilton House to the church.

By this time, the Grange was in poor condition. A new roof and other costly repairs were badly needed, and some people felt that the building was not worth preserving. Rev. Tuttle, aware of the sound construction and the quality of the hand-hewn white oak that had been transported down the Hudson River from Albany, was convinced that the Grange would serve the church for many years once it was repaired. The vestry then passed a resolution stating, "In consideration of Dr. Tuttle's generous offer to repair the Hamilton House at his own expense, said house shall for a period of five years be under the sole control of Dr. Tuttle, and during said period he shall enjoy all the rents and profits thereof."[20]

Dr. Tuttle promptly had a new roof installed and began making repairs to the interior. His care of Hamilton's former home allowed for several church functions and two successive pastors to enjoy the house. Four children were born there. Left to the resources of St. Luke's, the house would have fallen into disrepair, and interior decay from the damaged roof could have made it uninhabitable. In every real sense, Dr. Isaac Tuttle's respect for Alexander Hamilton's contributions to the country extended to the home he built in 1802. In short, Dr. Tuttle saved the ninety-two-year-old house from falling into ruin and being destroyed.

In 1895, Central Park Commissioner Andrew Haswell Green founded the American Scenic and Historic Preservation Society, a national organization whose goal was to protect historical sites and the first organization that began nurturing an appreciation for the care of historic buildings. Green was also particularly motivated to safeguard the natural landscape of northern Manhattan, as he noted in his 1901 address.

> It is the highest, boldest, and most diversified section of our ancient city, and it commands a combined view of land and water, of city and country, unsurpassed in the United States. It is the only portion of Manhattan Island where the shore-line of our beautiful American Rhine has been left in its native picturesqueness, and it is the only portion where any trace of its pristine beauty remains undesecrated and unraised by the leveling march of so-called *public improvements.*[21]

Green's organization and other like-minded civic groups lobbied the city to preserve the natural portions of the island's northern landscape that had not already been destroyed by dynamite and repaving. His work as commissioner influenced the creation and/or expansion of Central Park, Morningside, Riverside, and Fort Tryon parks, as well as Highbridge and Inwood Hill parks. He was the driving force behind the merging of New York's five boroughs into one city.

The natural, rocky topography of one area adjacent to Hamilton's former home would not succumb to the street grid. It was left to be developed as a park and to allow for some needed green space. The area was "bounded by 148th and 155th Streets, Bradhurst and Edgecombe Avenues, and in 1894 land was acquired by condemnation between 145th and 150th Streets. It was developed and named in 1899."[22] It would take another decade for Colonial Park to open, to be renamed Jackie Robinson Park in 1978.

Although Harlem's population was modest even at the end of the nineteenth century, the neighborhood has long been home to a mix of races and socioeconomic groups. There was an ever-increasing Italian population in East Harlem. The area around Hamilton Heights may have been where rich landowners built large estates, but it was also where small farms struggled or flourished and where squatters eked out an existence. Aside from the Village of Harlem around 125th Street and scattered farms, the greater Harlem population at the brink of the twentieth century still had a sprinkling of Native Americans and a growing contingent of immigrants from Great Britain and Ireland, along with Jews from Russia, Poland, and Germany. But the African American population uptown was still small. It would be years before racial tensions and other issues forced large numbers of African Americans to move north from their homes in Midtown and Greenwich Village.

Troger's Hotel at 92 St. Nicholas Place, near 155th Street, was a popular dining place for five decades, largely because of its proximity to both the Polo Grounds' grandstand and the Harlem Speedway. Sportsmen and their ladies often found their way here after a game or buggy race. And the hotel would also become home to a popular jazz club called Bowman's Cafe and Grill when the area later became the African American elite residences of Sugar Hill.

When St. Luke's was notified in December 1894 that a new church, St. Anne's, planned to move from downtown to 148th Street and Amsterdam Avenue, the church leaders immediately objected, given that its new church was just two years old. They gave an insightful description of the

Figure 22. Troger's Hotel, circa 1900. Courtesy New York Public Library

sparsity of the neighborhood, which was on the cusp of major changes, concerned about competing for parishioners.

> That south of Saint Luke's Church there are no dwelling houses except two or three wooden cabins or shanties until the Convent of the Sacred Heart is reached situated at West 130th St. That west of Saint Luke's church there are few buildings, and that in all probability there will not at a near date be a large population in that section. To the east, on St. Nicholas between 135th Street and 145th Street, there is not one dwelling house.[23]

They expressed their certainty that even from a population farther east they did not expect many to attend St. Luke's because of the proximity of other parishes. And noting the elevation and steep grade of both 141st and 145th streets, in particular, in winter it made getting to St. Luke's challenging. The church wardens said that even with the advent of rapid transportation, it was likely that between St. Luke's and the Church of the Intercession at 155th Street they could more than care for an increased population. The ensuing small edifice that was built instead became a specialized church for the deaf and services held in sign language.

The new owner of the Jumel Mansion, General Earle, offered his home as a place where a colonial lawn party might be held to raise funds for St. Luke's. On June 17, 1895, tents were erected at the Jumel Mansion. Many of the women dressed in colonial attire, and people paid a fee to tour the interior of the house. The colonial outfits became a mainstay of Morris-Jumel celebrations.

Doctor Isaac Tuttle, the man who had secured the Grange for the church and who was the home's chief champion, died on November 20, 1896. It was just a year after all the repairs he had paid for at Hamilton Grange were completed. The house reverted to the church for use by the current rector and his family. St. Luke's paid great tribute to Dr. Tuttle for his leadership as rector for over forty years and for his financial generosity.

Toward the end of the nineteenth century, Alexander Hamilton's alma mater wanted more room to expand its campus. Columbia University had been founded in 1754 as King's College, and as the city had grown and changed, it solidified its place as the oldest institution of higher learning in the State of New York. In 1897, Columbia moved from 49th Street and Madison Avenue, where it had stood since 1857, to the Morningside Heights section of Harlem at 116th Street and Broadway. It was just a little over a mile from Hamilton's former home.

The population shifts that created Black Harlem were not just a product of the Great Migration, which began in the early twentieth century. African Americans had started moving North in the early 1800s when they began to populate Five Points in Lower Manhattan, then considered one of the city's roughest and dirtiest neighborhoods. In later years, Black people moved to Greenwich Village, creating thriving neighborhoods, then to the Tenderloin District on Manhattan's West Side, and also to San Juan Hill, which was a small enclave of tenements and factories. It is now the Lincoln Center area. These were neighborhoods where Black families were creating a middle-class lifestyle for themselves, though they were often displaced. One strip of Seventh Avenue came to be called the African Broadway.

In 1903, the City of New York bought the Morris-Jumel Mansion from the Earle family. The official city minutes note that as to "Roger Morris Park, the Board of Estimate is in favour of buying the block bounded by 160th and 162nd Sts., Edgecomb Ave. and Jumel Terrace, 1903 May 29. City takes title to, and Jumel Mansion."[24] The following year, Lillie Earle worked with the Daughters of the American Revolution to assume management of the house as a museum to honor George Washington and the American Revolution.

By the turn of the century, phones were starting to be installed in rooming houses and the quickly rising apartment buildings in Harlem Heights. Doormen, private bathrooms, dumbwaiters, and elevators became selling features. The phone numbers in this district began with the first two letters of the exchange, and Harlem recognized its history with numbers that began with Audubon 4-3893 (284-3893) or Bradhurst 4-3252 (274-3252).

On February 3, 1894, in a building at 206 West 103rd Street near Amsterdam Avenue, a woman named Anne Mary Rockwell gave birth to a son she named Norman. The family moved to Harlem Heights two years later.

"My family moved to a railroad apartment on 147th Street and St. Nicholas Avenue when I was two years old," wrote Norman Rockwell, who would become one of America's most celebrated artists. He further shared in his autobiography that it was "narrow and gloomy . . . only the parlor, which faced St. Nicholas Avenue, and the dining room, which looked out on a bleak backyard, had windows."[25] His father, Jarvis, would carry coal up four flights from the basement.

Rockwell described the neighborhood on the cusp of the twentieth century as pitifully genteel, home mostly to apartment buildings with a grocery store or saloon on every corner. Children played on vacant lots scattered with debris. Rockwell recalled that he and his friends "went over to Amsterdam Avenue to look under the swinging doors of saloons (it gave us a terrible thrill to see the feet of the men standing at the bar)."[26]

Like other families, the Rockwells would sit on the stoop in the evenings as the light faded and watch as the lamplighter climbed his ladder to light the gas streetlamps. "Ours wasn't a slum neighborhood, just lower-middle-class with a smattering of poorer families," Rockwell wrote. "The tough slum districts were east of us toward Third Avenue."[27] The family would have moved to St. Nicholas Avenue just as work was beginning on the nearby Harlem River Speedway, which would eventually stretch from the Macomb's Dam Bridge at 155th Street to Dyckman Street in Inwood. Construction started the year Rockwell was born, and the roadway officially opened in 1898 with successive sections opening over decades. Wealthy men raced their one-horse rigs along the Speedway, giving people strolling on the High Bridge an opportunity to look down and observe the scene.

After the death of Norman's grandmother a few years later, the Rockwells moved up the street to his grandfather's house at 152nd Street and St. Nicholas Avenue. It was the start of a new century, and six-year-old Norman had begun drawing battleships for his older brother Jarvis.

"There was (I hope it's changed; it's a nasty stupid business) a lot of racial prejudice in New York City in those days,"[28] Rockwell wrote. He mentioned the demeaning names that children called Italians and Jews. (There was no mention of what they called Black people, probably because St. Nicholas and Convent Avenues were two decades away from being integrated.) Rockwell grew into a man whose spirit of tolerance and a belief in civil rights was admirable. That may be why, when writing his autobiography, he expressed his hope that racial prejudice had changed in the city. It may also have been a precursor to the character of this man who would create the iconic painting of a little Black girl being escorted into her all-white school by U.S. Marshals.

The class distinctions the young Norman observed and later wrote about would prevail for some time. There were fathers who were white-collar workers and fathers who worked with their hands. The Rockwells were well-regarded members of the middle class. Norman's father was the manager of a textile firm downtown, the family had a house full of books, and they owned two Caruso records.

In his writing, Rockwell offered a vivid portrait of what it felt like to live in the Hamilton Heights neighborhood in those days.

"On summer evenings as the first cool breath of the sunset wind rustled in the dusty leaves of the two scrawny elms across the street, my family used to walk to Amsterdam Avenue to catch the trolley for our evening airing."[29]

He described the trolley making its way up the hill and rattling to a stop, the wheel connecting with the wires and activating the lights. The ride progressed through the outskirts of the city, then back to where the homes began to crowd each other again, with streetlamps lighting each corner. Rockwell detailed how the street would become crowded with carriages and wagons, and then his family would arrive back home, the ride on the trolley having served as modest entertainment.

It was during these years that Norman's love of drawing became evident. In the evenings when his father gathered the family and read from the novels of Dickens, Norman drew pictures showing how he envisioned the different characters. He later considered his early sketches of Samuel Pickwick, Oliver Twist, and Uriah Heep crude, but his desire to imagine people to life on paper was sparked during this youthful period.

Rockwell did what so many other children of religious families did. He was a choir boy at St. Luke's on 141st and Convent Avenue, which was brand new at the time. And from their apartment, the young boy would have had a clear view across the street to the Bailey Mansion during the brief time the Baileys were in residence. The family spent summers in the country until Norman was about ten. In 1906, the Rockwells left Harlem Heights and moved to Mamaroneck, New York, in Westchester County.

Harlem Heights in those years was home to several private schools. Around 1899 the Barnard School for Boys, a college preparatory founded in 1886, moved to 721 St. Nicholas Avenue at 146th Street, then two decades later moved to the Bronx. The ground floor of the St. Nicholas building would eventually become a nightclub and then a speakeasy. Its sister school, the Barnard School for Girls, on West 148th Street at Convent Avenue, was built in 1895 and prepared the daughters of well-to-do families for college. The building was sold in 1934 when the school moved to Fort Washington Avenue.

A few blocks away, James Bailey and his family were finally in residence at their home at 10 St. Nicholas Place. But the neighborhood had changed dramatically since Bailey had started building the house in 1886. More streets were being paved, and the occupants of the new apartment buildings were very different from the wealthy estate owners. Bailey put the house up for sale, and a series of quick real estate exchanges occurred, with short-lived ownerships.

The increasingly large apartment buildings that were rising throughout Harlem made it clear that the era of private mansions and grand estates

98 · BAILEY MANSION, ST. LUKE'S, AND A BUILDING BOOM

Figure 23. Former Barnard School for Boys, circa 1942. Courtesy Municipal Archives, City of New York

was waning. If you were going to build in Harlem, a new kind of structure was required.

The house of George W. Backer at 51 Hamilton Terrace, constructed in 1909, is almost a hybrid between house and private apartment building. The Backers were German-Jewish immigrants, and the patriarch had morphed from being a mantelpiece salesman to a successful contractor. According to historian Michael Henry Adams, there were parts of 51 Hamilton Terrace that were twenty-five feet wide by eight feet deep. "There are four levels, including the basement, which contains a large billiard room and office, laundry, kitchen, storage rooms, bathroom, servants' rooms, and walk-in safe."[30]

The apartment on the top floor, minus a kitchen, was planned for Mrs.

Backer's brother and his wife. It included three bedrooms, a parlor, a dining room, and a private bath, along with a butler's pantry and a dumbwaiter. The drawing room was outfitted with plaster cherubs, mirrors, and cut-glass lighting fixtures, and the library contained an intricately designed fireplace. It was, by all accounts, a luxurious home.

Despite the obvious changes in the area, with rows of apartment buildings going up in record time, many rich people seemed to hold on to the illusory belief that the neighborhood was staying much the same. But the most discerning among them could not have predicted how profoundly its appearance and demographics would be transformed in the next decade or those to come. For many of the wealthy, just the notion that buildings were being erected without servants' quarters was a sign the area was in decline. But the real changes on the horizon would impact both Harlem and the city as a whole.

Chapter 7

The Great Migration and the Morris Museum

> A blue haze descended at night and, with it, strings of fairy lights on the broad avenues.... What a city! What a world!... The first danger I recognized was that Harlem would be too wonderful for words. Unless I was careful, I would be thrilled into silence.
>
> —*Arna Bontemps,* American Poet (1902–73)
> "The Two Harlems," *American Scholar,* 1945

A new century had dawned on Jochem Pieters' old hills in Harlem Heights. The original 1811 grid had been changed a half-dozen or more times in the decades since its creation, and, as planners had discovered with Central Park years earlier, some topography would not bend to the plan for straight, even streets. For this reason, adjustments had to be made along the way.

This was evident in 1906 when work began on St. Nicholas Park, which runs along the west side of St. Nicholas Avenue between 127th and 141st streets crossing sections of Manhattanville, Central Harlem, and Hamilton Heights. The site is long and narrow, and the rugged landscape and rock outcroppings date back thousands of years. The park was designed by Samuel Parsons Jr., a horticulturist by family tradition and a founding member of the American Society of Landscape Architects.

Parsons, who also oversaw designs for Central, Riverside and Morningside parks, believed that St. Nicholas Park could be a place to which people might escape from the noise and bustle of the city. He blasted some

Figure 24. World Series Game Polo Grounds, New York City, October 1905. Photo Library of Congress

areas to retain the hilly topography, and he filled in others to provide level places for lawns and paths.

The residents in the new apartment buildings in the heights got to glance down from their windows at history in the making. Figure 24 shows Coogan's Bluff, a ridge of Harlem Heights above the Polo Grounds with a view to the baseball field, newly constructed apartment buildings on Edgecombe Avenue, and the Morris-Jumel Mansion at 160th Street almost in the center, with a flag flying over it.

It was also in the early twentieth century that a major chapter of baseball history unfolded on these streets. In 1889 the Giants had moved to the Polo Grounds on Coogan's Hollow, the huge meadow that led up to Coogan's Bluff almost at Edgecombe Avenue. The hollow was located at 155th and 157th streets, along the start of Eighth Avenue, and stretched almost to the top of what would soon be called Sugar Hill. The team played their first game at the new Polo Grounds on April 22, 1891. At the time of its opening, the stadium could seat 16,000 people, and by 1911 it would expand to accommodate 31,000 spectators, making it the nation's largest baseball stadium at the time.

In 1913, a rival ball team arrived: the New York Yankees. After the Yankees acquired Babe Ruth in 1920, the team easily drew more crowds than the Giants, which did not sit well with owner John McGraw. For a time, the Babe lived within walking distance of the ballpark at 409 Edgecombe Avenue in an apartment house that overlooked the Polo Grounds. Once the building was integrated in 1927, it would become the home of many luminaries of the Harlem Renaissance, along with the future United States Supreme Court Justice Thurgood Marshall.

After Giants owner John McGraw evicted the Yankees from the Polo Grounds in 1922, the team went on to build what quickly became one of the most hallowed stadiums in sports history. Yankee Stadium, which opened in 1923, was located a short distance from the Polo Grounds, across the Macomb's Bridge in the Bronx.

The Polo Grounds would also become the home of the New York Giants football team and the New York Jets. It was the site of many celebrated boxing matches, including the 1923 heavyweight championship match between Jack Dempsey and Luis Firpo. The celebrated 500th home run of the Giants' Mel Ott took place there on August 1, 1945. And in 1954, Giants center fielder Willie Mays made a phenomenal catch that would be talked about for decades,

A few blocks up the hill on Broadway, the multi-millionaire art collector and historian Archer Milton Huntington had begun buying large tracts of the former Audubon Park, and in 1904 he founded a complex of cultural institutions called Audubon Terrace (now known as the Audubon Terrace Historic District). On a site bordered by Broadway, Riverside Drive, and 155th and 156th streets, Huntington built a stately complex of five museums. The granite and limestone structures, designed by his cousin Charles Pratt Huntington, were in the Beaux Arts/American Renaissance style and shared a common courtyard.

Archer was the son of the railroad tycoon Collis Huntington and his wife, Arabella, once known as one of the richest women in early-twentieth-century America, who filled their mansion on East 57th Street with important artworks. Archer accompanied his mother when she traveled throughout Europe touring museums and galleries, and the deep appreciation he developed for art and architecture would prompt him to build great libraries and museums around the country, some of which would bear his name. The Audubon Terrace museums are an example of his philanthropy.

Originally, the complex included the American Academy and Institute of Arts and Letters, the American Geographical Society, the Hispanic Society Museum & Library, the American Numismatic Society, and the Museum of the American Indian/Heye Foundation, as well as the Church of Our Lady of Esperanza. Eventually, both the Museum of the American Indian and the American Geographical Society would move to different locations.

The twentieth century would witness one of the most profound transformations in American life, one that remade the nation and led to the creation of modern-day Harlem. Starting around 1916 and continuing until approximately 1970, great waves of Black people from the rural South made their way to the cities of the North, seeking not only to escape the shackles of racism—the beating, the lynchings, the degradation—but also

Figure 25. Audubon Terrace Museums, c. 1926. NY Public Library

to make a better life for themselves and their children. What became known as the Great Migration would ultimately lead to the relocation of an estimated six million people, many of them formerly enslaved or their first-generation descendants.

As Isabel Wilkerson wrote, "When the migration began, 90 percent of all African-Americans were living in the South. By the time it was over, in the 1970s, 47 percent of all African-Americans were living in the North and West. A rural people had become urban, and a Southern people had spread themselves all over the nation."[1] What began as a trickle had become a flood. Of all the words written about what is now commonly known as the Great Migration, perhaps the most important point is that no one knew there was such a movement happening as it occurred. It is one of the greatest examples in history of a grassroots, word-of-mouth social movement that would reshape the United States.

Imagine it. There was no TV show, radio station, newspaper, or magazine that was providing consistent accurate information to Black people across the South about why they should leave, how to make the move, where to go, and what opportunities or challenges awaited them. People whispered to each other what they had heard rumors about; what was possible in the

Figure 26. Great Migration Series, Jacob Lawrence. Courtesy National Archives and Records Administration

North. Letters from those who had made the journey, those early pioneers, became like gold. It described a land, within these United States, whose description was not like anything Black Southerners could fathom. Sometimes, tales from the North would be shared in churches. People spoke softly, or sometimes with feigned confidence, debating whether they should gamble on a move northward. The few who ventured back to the South on visits encouraged others to make the journey. They shared tales of prosperity that often left out some of the more glaring struggles faced in the North: the more subtle and sometimes blatant racism, the competition for jobs, and often inferior housing. Leaving the South was not easy, as every possible obstacle was placed in the way of those trying to buck a system designed to keep them as sharecroppers or cheap labor in other occupations.

Despite the racism and discrimination that the newcomers faced, they continued a slow and steady move out of the South with the promise of better-paying jobs in stores and factories. The "North" came to represent every place that was not the South, with its suffocation, lynchings, and stifling Jim Crow laws.

The newcomers would in turn reshape the social, racial, economic, and political landscape of the places in which they settled. With 50,000 Black residents in 1914 and nearly 165,000 by 1930, Harlem would be transformed. And while the Great Migration was largely responsible for what became Black Harlem, further divisions would occur, creating internal social rifts between the people who lived in Central Harlem and those who lived in Hamilton Heights and Sugar Hill. Sadly, there would also be divisions by skin color.

John Mollenkopf's article "The Evolution of New York City's Black Neighborhoods" makes clear that while Harlem may have initially been the primary destination, it did not remain the only one in the coming decades. "After the Depression, the city's Black population grew more quickly in other neighborhoods than it did in Harlem. The opening of the A train in the 1930s and the magnet of wartime shipbuilding jobs in Brooklyn drew Harlem residents to Fort Greene and Bedford-Stuyvesant in Brooklyn."[2]

The urban environment was deeply unfamiliar to these newcomers, and they adjusted to it uneasily. Nor did life in the cities of the North prove to be the paradise that was heralded; quite the contrary. In Harlem and other urban neighborhoods, the new arrivals were initially forced into cramped and dirty tenements because few places would rent to Blacks. There were too many people per block, too many per apartment.

"Human hives, honeycombed with little rooms thick with human beings," is how Mary White Ovington, a white journalist and cofounder of the NAACP, described the filthy tenements that Black New Yorkers were relegated to at the turn of the twentieth century.[3]

Just as when immigrants from other countries arrive with their offspring, these southerners running from Jim Crow brought babies and children who simply went where their parents took them. The list of their accomplishments, big and small, changed the country. Conversely, there were some people who returned to the South, unable to acclimate to northern lifestyles in box-like apartments. Their spirits could not adapt to concrete pavements and the absence of green fields with the sun on their faces.

Nonetheless, the city offered vastly more opportunities than did the rural South. Perhaps even more important, places like New York and especially Harlem came to represent a new world, one in which beatings and lynchings were not a common part of life. The freedom formally granted to enslaved persons in 1863 was more real here, versus the illusory version in the South, where their existence was only a step above slavery.

In this new place, bordering on a fragile Utopia not without its thorns, a Black person could walk down the sidewalk without having to step into the street to make way for a white person. They could look a white person in the face with less fear of being called uppity or constant admonitions to stay in their place. For many, this would become the first time that they were experiencing large numbers of Black people gathering publicly to dance, sing, gossip, march, voice political opinions, and sit down in a restaurant to enjoy a meal. Black people were letting out a collective long-held-in breath. And in few neighborhoods was the change as profound as it was in Harlem.

In addition to the Great Migration, another change helped transform Harlem from a middle- and upper-class white neighborhood into a working-class Black neighborhood. This change had its roots in the boom-and-bust cycle of the late 1800s: overconfident construction of apartment buildings, followed by a depression—the Panic of 1873, as it was known.

As the city began draining ditches and mapping more streets, speculators started buying large plots of land. Most of the initial building took place in Central Harlem on Lenox, Seventh, and Eighth avenues, where "apartment buildings and row houses flowered, in architectural varieties ranging from Italianate and Greek Revival, to Gothic or Second Empire to Romanesque and neo-Renaissance."[4] But the Panic of 1893 destroyed so many fortunes that fewer white families could afford to live in the gorgeous new buildings.

Wilkerson wrote about not only the discriminatory rental policies and covenants, but the redlining that solidified a system with housing and banks seldom approving mortgages in the neighborhoods where Black people lived, thus denying them a chance to be homeowners. "These policies became the pillars of a residential caste system in the North that calcified segregation and wealth inequality over generations, denying African-Americans the chance accorded other Americans to improve their lot."[5]

City College of New York, which moved to Harlem Heights in the early twentieth century, had been founded in 1847 by Townsend Harris, president of the Board of Education. Originally known as the Free Academy of the City of New York, the school was established to provide access to higher education for poor students and the children of immigrants. Admission was free and based solely on academic merit.

The college was originally located at 23rd Street and Lexington Avenue. But by the end of the nineteenth century, with a student population that had more than doubled, the school had begun to outgrow its downtown space. And the design for its new location would help transform the nature of college architecture.

"In 1898, George B. Post garnered the commission to construct a new campus," wrote Sydney Van Nort in her book on the history of the college. "The trustees and alumni on the competition jury found themselves led by the belief that the kinship of Post's Collegiate Gothic design was associated with the medieval images of Oxford and Cambridge."[6] Post's vision would come to define the college, and the buildings would rival those of any campus in the nation.

In 1900, the newly paved Convent Avenue was mostly vacant and had but a few lampposts. An open swatch of land looked south to the female Academy of the Sacred Heart and the Croton Aqueduct System pumping station, on 135th Street. "Six undeveloped parcels of land, which included this area, were purchased by New York City with appropriations from the state legislature for the development of the new campus."[7] It was in stark contrast to how full it would become in just a few short decades with townhouses and City College's expanding construction.

The initial parcels were bounded by 138th Street to 140th street, St. Nicholas Terrace, and Amsterdam Avenue. The groundbreaking ceremony was held on March 10, 1903, and the first phase of construction would last until 1907, when City College officially moved to its Harlem campus and the neighborhood that would soon be called Hamilton Heights.

Shepard Hall, in Figure 27, was the original Main Building, meant to be the focal point of the campus. "The Gothic Great Hall, sitting along the central axis, included seating for 2,200 members of the community gathering for ceremonial occasions. The two curving wings for classrooms

Figure 27. CCNY Shepherd Hall, circa 1910. Courtesy New York Public Library

attached just behind the eastern face of the building. The structure housed the administrative offices, the library, and the classrooms for those disciplines not taught in the other four buildings."[8]

Work on the campus would continue for decades as the college continued to acquire other property in the neighborhood, until it came to cover thirty-six acres. Several stunning arched gates would grace the campus, including the "Hamilton Gate" at the main entrance on 141st Street and Convent Avenue, one block from Hamilton Grange, part of Alexander Hamilton's old estate.

Of the white people who had settled in Harlem at this time, there was a large and very affluent Jewish population, though highly focused in Central Harlem around Fifth and Lenox Avenues bordering 125th Street, as well as Morningside Park. Later, they would make huge enclaves in former sections of Harlem in the burgeoning neighborhood of Washington Heights.

In the area of Hamilton's former estate, Jewish newspaper publisher "Oswald Ottendorfer was the most noticeable. Having made a fortune as president of the *New Yorker Staats Zeitung*, the most important German-language weekly in town, he transformed a property on West 136th Street near Broadway into a huge and ostentatious pagoda and a Moorish pavilion with a Jewish star in the dome in the garden."[9]

As the City College campus was taking shape, newcomers to Harlem included a Massachusetts man named Philip A. Payton Jr., an individual who, though long forgotten, would have a profound impact on the neighborhood and be instrumental in the evolution of Black people renting, buying, and eventually becoming a majority in Harlem. A college dropout whose siblings were all college graduates, Payton made his way to New York and entered the real estate business almost on a dare. The Panic of 1893 had led to a high vacancy rate in the many newly built brownstones and apartment blocks. Racism was very real throughout the city in terms of its Black citizens. The beautiful structures were clearly intended for white people, and landlords held out as long as possible when it came to renting to Blacks. Then they eventually found a strategy to their benefit by charging Black people inflated prices far above those they would have charged white tenants.

Adeel Hassan's *New York Times* article about Payton's legacy shares that his "first opportunity came as a result of a dispute between two landlords in West 134th Street," as Payton told the *New York Age* in 1911, still a leading Black paper at the time. The one landlord wanted to get even with his competitor and so "turned his house over to me to fill with colored tenants.

Figure 28. Philip Payton. Public domain

I was successful in renting and managing this house and after a time I was able to induce other landlords to give me their houses to manage."[10]

Payton knew that the planned expansion of the subway to Harlem, slated for 1904 or 1905, would result in far greater access to both uptown and downtown. He ran ads promoting himself as a colored man who made a specialty of managing buildings that rented to colored tenants. "In the years that followed, Payton steered Black New Yorkers to the area where the subway opened up. Harlem was white and home to wide boulevards, brownstones, and rowhouses. It would become the nexus of a community whose cultural output helped shape 20th-century America."[11]

The steady arrival of more Black people in Harlem caused whites to flee, in what was possibly one of the earliest examples of white flight. Property values plunged, ironically helping to create more rental opportunities for African Americans. Payton began to snap up properties and vowed to go into business for himself to combat rumors of white landlords threatening to evict Black tenants.

By 1904 he had incorporated the Afro-American Realty Company. Between his initial work managing the properties of white landlords and his own company, Payton was almost single-handedly responsible for helping to reshape Harlem as a home for Black people who faced constant discrimination in housing.

Hassan wrote that Payton told Black investors, "Today is the time to buy, if you want to be numbered among those of the race who are doing something toward trying to solve the so-called Race Problem." The company's brochure stated that "race prejudice is a luxury, and like all other luxuries can be made very expensive in New York City. The very prejudice which has heretofore worked against us can be turned and used to our profit."[12]

Nevertheless, problems lay ahead. Despite his success, Payton's Afro-American Realty Company was shaken because stockholders doubted some of Payton's high-risk speculations and oppressive management style. "In 1906, stockholders sued Payton on the grounds that he ran the company without any input from the board of directors, which made him responsible for any losses the company might accrue."[13]

The courts found the company guilty of misrepresentation in some of its business claims. Nevertheless, by 1907 the Afro-American Realty Company controlled twenty apartment houses in New York, valued at almost $700,000, and the company's stock was worth a half million dollars. Payton used his position and growing wealth to help promote other black-owned businesses. He founded an organization to protest police brutality and a coalition of other Black real estate agents and businessmen to encourage the expansion of Black businesses in Harlem. Two of Payton's salesmen, John E. Nail and Henry C. Parker, opened their own real estate firm. They would handle the early sales and rentals of the handsome townhouses on 138th and 139th streets that would come to be known as the historic Strivers' Row.

The homes on Strivers' Row were originally named the King Model Houses, built from 1892 in Georgian, Colonial, and Italian Renaissance Revival styles. The elegant buildings were intended, as was all the early Harlem construction, for middle- to upper-class whites. Famed contractor David H. King Jr. was the developer of Madison Square Garden, the Washington Arch, and the Equitable Building. Developers had overbuilt, especially in Central Harlem, and most of the foreclosed properties that never sold sat empty for almost two decades, while some were rented. The bankers resisted selling to Black residents as long as they could.

Those that finally did start buying were mostly the upwardly mobile Black Americans, artists and professionals, those "striving" to make a better life for themselves or enjoying the fruits of their labors—thus, the two streets were nicknamed "strivers' row." The earliest residents include legendary entertainers Bojangles, Fletcher Henderson, and Eubie Blake. In later decades, after its 1967 landmark designation, other famous musicians and finally just people of means would populate the two streets. The alleyways designed for deliveries and stabling horses still have signs that read, "Walk your horses." In all the urban decay that would occur around these two streets, Strivers' Row often seemed by mutual agreement as the place one left unmarked.

Payton's company went under in 1908. But his methods of promotion and expansion became a model for other Realtors. In 1917, a few months before his death, he bought six apartment buildings valued at $1.5 million, a purchase that was the highlight of his career. Because of his pivotal role in transforming Harlem into a safe haven for African Americans, Payton has been called the "father of Harlem." While his name would slip into oblivion, his legacy endures.

Though transportation had slowly improved uptown, most people from the modern age have little frame of mind for how people traveled great distances in past centuries. Procuring everything you needed close to home would negate the need to travel to another part of the city. People walked long distances if they did not have a horse. Varying forms of stagecoaches were still in use, as were ferries that ran along the Hudson and Harlem rivers. Horse-drawn carts did a huge business in transporting goods around the city. Carriages of every description, according to one's financial means, would have been in use. And then, of course, horse-drawn trolleys and elevated trains were developed.

Harlem Heights and all of New York City changed forever on October 27, 1904, the day that years of work on an underground transportation system came to fruition in Manhattan. Mayor George McClellan took the controls for the inaugural run of the city's revolutionary new rapid transit system, called "the subway."

Although in 1879 Boston had built the first subway in the United States, New York City's subway system soon became the nation's largest. That first line, operated by the Interborough Rapid Transit Company, soon to be known as the IRT, traveled nine miles through twenty-eight stations, running north downtown from City Hall past Times Square before making its way to 145th Street and Broadway in Harlem Heights.

The IRT subway stopped just six blocks from Alexander Hamilton's former home. Later that historic October evening, the subway line was opened to the public. Hamilton Heights and all of Harlem were now connected to Downtown by a few minutes' ride on the subway. In the twenty-first century, the IND line at 145th and St. Nicholas would have several entrances, including an exit at 147th Street, almost in front of Norman Rockwell's old address and a block from where Ralph Ellison wrote *Invisible Man*.

The Hamilton Bank at 213–15 West 125th Street off Seventh Avenue opened in 1893. It was the result of a merger with the Bank of Harlem the year before. The branch at 1707–9 Amsterdam Avenue between 144th and 145th streets opened on April 7, 1899, situated on Hamilton's former estate. It marked the first bank in Harlem above 125th Street, and it served the needs of a rapidly growing upper west side. Both buildings would survive into the twenty-first century. As with other banks, it was also taking advantage of a new law permitting state banks to have branches. By 1926, Hamilton Bank had plans to open a third branch at 110th Street and Broadway and in Washington Heights, while expanding its quarters at 130 West 42nd Street.

Farther north from the new subway station on 145th Street, the Hamilton Grange Branch of the New York Public Library opened in 1907. It was designed by the architectural firm of McKim, Mead & White and constructed between 1905 and 1906. It was one of sixty-five branches built by the New York Public Library, more than half with funds provided by the philanthropist Andrew Carnegie. It is a three-story-high, rusticated gray limestone building with large bay windows designed in an Italian Renaissance style. McKim, Mead & White were one of the leading architectural firms of the period. They designed eleven other city libraries, as well as the original Penn Station, which was under construction at the same time and opened in 1910. The Hamilton Branch was destined to become a city landmark and an essential addition to the community.

A Carnegie library is one underwritten by funds from Scottish-American philanthropist Andrew Carnegie, who became an incredible example of the lasting good one can do with one's wealth. Of the 2,509 libraries he built around the world, 1,689 Carnegie libraries were constructed in the United States. They included community libraries as well as those in K–12 schools and in universities.

The city's parks department had managed the Morris-Jumel Mansion since 1903, and a Civil War veteran named William Henry Shelton was named as its first curator in 1908, a year after it formally opened as a museum. Shelton would write an in-depth book about the mansion, published in 1916, pulling no punches when it came to describing Eliza Jumel's past, her less than generous acts toward her husband, and the eccentricities that bordered on madness toward the end of her life. The book describes Madame Jumel's ostracism from respectable society in New York, her abandonment of her natural-born son, and the long court battles over her estate. Within the mansion, she created a world in which a demented woman always craved social recognition that never came.

If those walls could talk, and those stairs could whisper, the rooftop widow's walk shout, and the basement kitchen fireplace gossip, they would, individually and collectively, have stories like no other to tell of the Morris-Jumel Mansion. The house and its occupants had endured every possible high and low as the residence of both free and enslaved people, the wartime occupation by American and foreign troops, the presence of legendary individuals, farmers, and weary travelers, and finally as a museum for visitors to imagine all that had come before.

"Under its roof a British Admiral was born, the first president of the United States of America entertained his Cabinet, a former Vice-President of the United States was married, and a woman died," Shelton wrote.[14] And, of course, the mansion's rich and colorful history had begun with its first owners, the British Loyalists Mary Philipse Morris and her husband, Colonel Roger Morris, who had built the house. The couple had four children, two daughters and two sons. So, first the house would speak of love, the laughter and antics of young children, dinners with friends, and hopes for a long life.

Lillie Earle, its last private owner, was heavily invested in getting the Daughters of the American Revolution (DAR) involved in the upkeep of the mansion and in the initial ways in which the historical artifacts were displayed. As Carol Ward writes, the Washington Heights Association "officially took control of the mansion and held a formal opening of the house as a museum in May, 1907. The grand reopening of the mansion in 1907 was and still is one of the largest events in its history."[15]

Under the influence of the DAR, the house exhibits showcased American history through the lens of the American Revolution, but also reflected displays that had nothing to do with the period. In bringing Shelton on as director, the ladies must have sensed that a more organized approach was needed. They also wanted the mansion to be held to the same standards as other museums. Shelton was able to curb the enthusiasm with which DAR members kept purchasing and donating miscellaneous historic items that were not at all reflective of the mansion's history. "Shelton worked extensively on researching the history of the mansion. He was instrumental in persuading the city to appoint a committee to assist with the restoration of the house itself."[16]

But what later became known as the Roger Morris House had undergone several changes over the centuries. During the World War I period, Shelton officially changed the name to Washington's Headquarters, and the entire house was opened to the public. Because the neighborhood and its residents had grown up around the house, with many of the surrounding buildings constructed on former Roger Morris lands, to many people the grounds of Roger Morris Park seemed like an extension of their backyards. In 1916, Shelton decided to have a public auction. While the goal was to consolidate some of the collections, the unintended result was that many original artifacts were sold.

In 1912, just a few blocks north of the Morris-Jumel Mansion, construction started on the Church of the Intercession. There had been a smaller version of the church nearby. At completion, its Gothic Revival sanctuary at 155th and Broadway, adjacent to Trinity Church Cemetery and Mausoleum, would be a stunning structure. Designed by Bertram Grosvenor Goodhue, it includes a cloister, vestry, vicarage, parish building, and a crypt. It would remain a chapel of Trinity Church for several decades and was known as the Chapel of the Intercession before becoming its own official church in 1976.

Figure 29. Church of the Intercession. Public domain

During these years the demographics on Harlem Heights were slowly shifting. Although most residents were rich homeowners, working-class families were starting to occupy the new apartment buildings rising along its streets.

One of the most notable buildings was at 555 Edgecombe Avenue at 160th Street, across from the Morris-Jumel Mansion. The building opened in 1916, after two years of construction, and was fittingly named the Roger Morris Apartments, to be known years later as the Paul Robeson Residence. Designed by Schwartz & Gross, one of the city's leading architectural firms, it would become one of Sugar Hill's most famous buildings, home to scores of very talented and celebrated figures of the twentieth century. At thirteen stories, it was also one of the neighborhood's tallest buildings and among the first to break the old construction covenant on building height.

Buildings are made of stone, concrete, wood, and steel. It is anyone's guess whether its occupants will be world heavyweight champions, hairdressers, mailmen, salesgirls, Tony and Oscar winners, civil rights leaders, award-winning authors, or future Supreme Court justices. So, it is particularly fascinating when a neighborhood grows to contain some of the most famous and talented people of the twentieth century in several buildings within a half-mile radius of each other. Tenants in the building that was once part of the vast Roger Morris estate could look over at the Morris Mansion where George Washington had headquartered.

The exterior of the thirteen-story building was not particularly exceptional, unlike many of those a few blocks away on Riverside Drive, St. Nicholas, Convent Avenue, or Hamilton Place that have unique floral or cherubic stonework on the edifices.

But it was the richness of the vast, tan marble-lined lobby that gave the building its reputation. A uniformed doorman standing outside of the canopied entrance added to the charm. The walls were painted with Greek mythological scenes of cherubs playing flutes atop dancing goats, and the space was topped by a spectacular circular stained-glass window on the ceiling.

When the building opened in 1916, each of the 105 apartments had one bathroom, although by this time other buildings had started adding a second bath. There were no servants' rooms, which for owners of private homes was one of the most distressing things about this and other apartment buildings starting to dot the landscape. To the wealthy, the lack of a servant's room, usually adjacent to the kitchen, spoke to a lower class of resident who could not afford live-in help. Instead, the "triple nickel," as

Figure 30. Roger Morris Apartments, 555 Edgecombe Ave. Courtesy NYC Landmarks Preservation Commission

it came to be called, had twenty-one very small penthouse rooms available for live-in servants.

All in all, it was one of the neighborhood's largest and most impressive apartment buildings. And like all these structures at this time, the Roger Morris Apartments initially housed only white tenants. "The 1915 New York State census shows that the vast majority of the residents of 555 Edgecombe Avenue were American born, although their names seem to indicate that there were people of German, Irish, English, and Jewish backgrounds living in the building."[17]

GREAT MIGRATION AND THE MORRIS MUSEUM · 117

Figures 31 and 32. TOP: Ornate Cover over the Stained-Glass Ceiling. Public domain. BOTTOM: Lobby Marble Wall Cherubs on Dancing Goats. Courtesy D. S. James

The thirteen-story apartment house just a few blocks away at 409 Edgecombe Avenue was also designed by Schwartz & Gross. Originally named the Colonial Parkway Apartments, it was built in 1916–17. The design gave the appearance of three interconnected buildings and included penthouses. The apartments, most of which had three to five rooms, featured dumbwaiters, gas stoves, and decorative interior finishes. There were two passenger elevators with uniformed operators as well as one service elevator.

Figure 33. 409 Edgecombe Avenue (Colonial Parkway Apartments). Courtesy NYC Landmarks Preservation Commission

While other buildings in the area kept to the five-story code height limit, 409 and 555 towered above that. Later, a New York City Preservation Landmark Report would note that its location on the dramatic rocky ridge Coogan's Bluff above the Harlem River added to "409's appeal as a desirable place to live [which] was augmented by both its natural surroundings and by an unobstructed river view from Sugar Hill's tallest building. The site also commands a perspective of the Macomb's Dam Bridge, the Harlem Speedway (now Harlem River Drive), and what once was the Polo Grounds."[18] It would only take another decade for the color barrier to be broken.

Other changes were coming to the neighborhood when, in 1909, the wardens of St. Luke's Church on Convent Avenue installed electricity in the church. They also made updates to Hamilton Grange so it could once again be used both for church services and as living space. Both interior and exterior were freshly painted and decorated. The rector boasted in the church bulletin that "not only have we now a building that is a credit both to the Church and community, but we also have a charming and spacious home rich with its historic associations."[19] He was pleased that the Grange could be used for parish activities, offices, and housing for the rector and curate, along with guild meetings and social events. More than a century after its construction, Hamilton's former home was full of life and activity.

Yet in the summer of 1913 several changes were then made to Hamilton Grange so that it was no longer used as a parish house. There were two small rooms on the north side that had served as offices and were now converted into a kitchen and maid's room. The parish offices were moved to a space on the south side of the Sunday School room and partitioned off by doors with glass windows. The basement of the rectory was arranged for the convenience of the sexton's family, "while the two floors above were renovated and appropriated for the exclusive benefit of the rector. The two large rooms on the entrance floor would no longer exist for organization meetings, but would serve as a parlor and dining room. The four sides of the exterior were painted white, the blinds green, and the grounds in front and rear put in orderly condition."[20]

As to the city's growing Black population during the early twentieth century, it was not surprising that New York City's newspapers offered little or nothing positive to report. In the city and elsewhere, a flurry of Black newspapers emerged to fill this void. The *Amsterdam News*, started when there were only fifty Black newspapers in the country, would become the gold standard when it came to describing and celebrating Black life in New York City.

James H. Anderson, the publisher, lived in New York's San Juan Hill section, now the home of Lincoln Center, and named the paper after Amsterdam Avenue, the street near his house. The first edition appeared on December 4, 1909, and Anderson sold copies for two cents each from his house at 132 West 65th Street. By 1910 its sales would start to increase in the early stages of African Americans moving north as part of the Great Migration, and many would populate Harlem. By 1920, Anderson moved the paper's offices uptown to 135th Street.

Whites were still protesting the growing numbers of Black people moving into Harlem. Among their number was a retired Irish police officer named John G. Taylor, who had moved from Waverly Place in Greenwich Village to West 136th Street in 1903. Taylor had waged several campaigns to keep Blacks from moving further north. In 1913, when it was apparent that his efforts were in vain, he reportedly asked his fellow white association members, "When will the people of Harlem wake up to the fact that they must organize and maintain a powerful anti-invasion movement if they want to check the progress of the Black hordes that are gradually eating through the very heart of Harlem?"[21] Taylor voiced that it was a matter of whether Harlem would be ruled by whites or the Negro. Despite his efforts, the hordes, as he called them, continued to arrive for decades.

The author and civil rights activist James Weldon Johnson also wrote about this unease, bordering on hysteria, recognizing that "in the eyes of the whites who were antagonistic, the whole movement took on the aspect of an 'invasion' . . . an invasion of both their economic and their social rights. They felt that Negroes as neighbours not only lowered the values of their property, but also lowered their social status."[22]

Prompted by this anxiety, whites fled Harlem in a panic-stricken fright. It was as if they could catch something by the mere presence of a Negro family on the block. It did not matter, as Johnson wrote in his book *Black Manhattan*, that some of their Negro neighbors "might be well-bred people, with sufficient means to buy their new home. . . . The stampeded whites actually deserted house after house and block after block."[23]

Property values dropped and then dropped even lower. Negroes who could afford to took advantage of the prices and bought property. Hence, a first generation of Black homeowners was created, many of whose parents and grandparents had been enslaved.

The union of Elizabeth Ross Haynes and George Edmund Haynes in 1910 and the story of the beautiful home they would purchase in Sugar Hill is an unsung slice of Black history. As with several other houses in the area, there is no marker to indicate either the significance of the building on Convent Avenue or its residents. Nonetheless, the couple's legacy lives on in the many firsts with which they can be credited: the groundbreaking sociological studies, the organizations they founded and fostered, and their contributions to the Harlem Renaissance. It also lives on in their grandson Dr. Bruce Haynes, a sociology professor at the University of California, Davis.

Elizabeth Haynes had been born in 1883 in Lowndes County, Alabama, the daughter of prosperous farmers. She received a bachelor's degree from Fisk University, a Historically Black College in Nashville, Tennessee, and a master's degree in sociology from Columbia University in 1923. It is notable the roster of accomplished African Americans who received degrees at NYU and Columbia in the early twentieth century at a time when most U.S. schools were still fighting to keep Blacks out, particularly in the South. Her master's thesis, titled "Two Million Negro Women at Work," was praised for decades as the most comprehensive study of Black women in the United States.

Her husband, Dr. George Edmund Haynes, who was born in 1880 in Pine Bluff, Arkansas, was by most accounts an unassuming man who nonetheless accomplished great things as a social worker, civil rights activist, and educator. Notably, he was the cofounder and first executive director of the National Urban League. The founding goal of the league was to help African Americans arriving from the South acclimate to urban life through education, job training, and housing, among other things.

Dr. Haynes attended the State Agricultural and Mechanical College for Negroes in Normal, Alabama, then transferred to Fisk University in Nashville, Tennessee, where he met his longtime idol, W. E. B. Du Bois. The Fisk alumnus, Du Bois, delivered the commencement address and would become Haynes' mentor and advocate for his selection to some of the highest offices in the world of social sciences.

Author, sociologist, and Civil Rights advocate William Edward Burghardt Du Bois was more widely known as W. E. B. Du Bois. In 1899, he authored "The Philadelphia Negro," the first critical study of an American city, conducted under the auspices of the University of Pennsylvania. His later seminal work on race and the work for which he is best known, *The Souls of Black Folk*, was published in 1903. Du Bois was highly critical of the accommodationist stance on segregation of Booker T. Washington, a former slave who grew to be one of the most powerful leaders in the post–Civil War fight for Negro civil rights and the need for education and economic empowerment.

After earning his bachelor's degree at Fisk, Haynes received a scholarship from Yale, where he earned his master's degree in 1904. His further studies at the University of Chicago sparked his interest in social problems affecting Black migrants from the South, and he graduated in 1910 from the New York School of Philanthropy, the precursor to Columbia University's School of Social Work.

Dr. Haynes served as director of Negro Economics in the United States Department of Labor and as a special assistant to the secretary of labor, focusing on issues affecting Black people that had to do with racial conflict in employment, housing, and recreation. This was a powerful position for an African American in the early twentieth century, especially since under President Woodrow Wilson formal segregation was introduced in the federal government.

Decades before other historians identified the true impact of the Great Migration, Haynes would recognize the patterns of the growing movement of Blacks from the South and how this movement affected cities in the North. The Haynes couple would leave an indelible mark on the history of Sugar Hill.

The Hamilton Heights neighborhood on the cusp of coming to life

Figure 34. Audubon Ballroom. Public domain

would become much more than just the celebrated figures who would live there, the drugs that would one day invade the streets, or the crime that would escalate. The neighborhood's legacy had long since become more than the history behind the house that Alexander Hamilton had built in 1802, a house that had fallen into disrepair, been on the verge of demolition, and sat in obscurity several times since the last Hamilton lived there in the 1830s.

The neighborhood would become a point of pride for African Americans: a place where hard-working people raised their children; where jazz clubs were sprouting on the avenues; and perhaps most important, where a cultural movement known as the Harlem Renaissance would flourish. It would also become an esteemed hub for education and the arts. An address in Hamilton Heights made it clear that one had moved up in the social order.

Three years before he became famous for founding the Fox Film Corporation, which became 20th Century Fox, the Hungarian-born movie producer William Fox embarked on a project to develop an entertainment venue in Uptown Manhattan. Fox hired the noted theater architect Thomas W. Lamb and built the Audubon Ballroom, which opened to the public on November 28, 1912. Located at 3940 Broadway, the palatial structure filled the block on Broadway between 165th and 166th streets. It had two distinct uses, with a 2,368-seat theater on the first floor and a "ballroom" on the second floor that also had a room that seated 200 people.

The stylized façade was heavy on mythological imagery and Roman-inspired motifs, with colorful terra cotta that featured griffins in the arches and an immense head of Poseidon, god of the sea, above the entrance. There was no end to the various ways it would be used in the coming century. For the most part it was a place of celebration. Yet it is because of one violent act decades in the future that it is most remembered, after which the name Malcolm X would forever be associated with the Audubon Ballroom.

Chapter 8

The Hamilton Museum and the Hamilton Theatre

> Is it not cruel to let our city die by degrees, stripped of all her proud monuments, until there will be nothing left of all her history and beauty to inspire our children? If they are not inspired by the past of our city, where will they find the strength to fight for her future? This is the time to take a stand, to reverse the tide, so that we won't all end up in a uniform world of steel and glass boxes.
> —Jacqueline Kennedy Onassis
> New York Preservation Archive Project
> Committee to Save Grand Central Station

George Edmund Haynes, the pioneering turn-of-the-century sociologist whose work would provide the nation with a greater understanding of what it meant to be Black in America, was determined to study the economic conditions of Black people in New York City.

His research showed that for both whites and Blacks the Great Migration had been part of a transformation in which the United States shifted from being an agricultural economy to an industrial one. But as his grandson would note decades later in his own analysis of his grandfather's work, Haynes identified factors that negatively affected only Black people, such as segregation, discrimination, the harsh sharecropping system that was akin to slavery, and the constant threat of mob violence. George Haynes was a man far ahead of his time in recognizing this profound shift that was decades away from being formally recognized as the Great Migration.

Many of the new arrivals ended up in New York, and more and more headed to Harlem, where they would occupy the brand-new apartment buildings, some of which were being abandoned by whites. And because the landlords had increased rents beyond market price, quite often there were too many people sharing one apartment so they could split the rent.

Some of the new arrivals would become part of the Harlem Renaissance, while others would revolutionize musical standards in the growing new jazz scene and the birth of bebop. They and their descendants would make history on stage, in film, the sciences, literature, and in sports. Many more would contribute to society and the growth of the city in more obscure ways, yet just as importantly.

The words that would be written by Langston Hughes and Zora Neale Hurston, the music of Thelonious Monk and Duke Ellington, would inspire future generations. The Great Migration produced a father and son who made their way to New York City and the stage separately. Robert Earl Jones left his wife and son in Mississippi and pursued a stage career in New York that would include starring in a Langston Hughes play in 1938: "Don't You Want to Be Free?" His young son would migrate first from Mississippi to Michigan, shocked into being mute for years by the violence he witnessed and a debilitating stutter, before finally making his way to New York City. He grew into the man, James Earl Jones, whose contributions to stage and screen would be legendary.

Most of these southerners would be average people whose names would never become famous. Yet they would be an integral part of changing the country.

As more and more African Americans left the South and resettled in Northern cities, Haynes realized that there was a great need to help them make the transition to a new and often punishing world. They needed support, education, and training for the jobs they hoped to get in their new homes. To address this need, in 1910 he and Ruth Standish Baldwin, the widow of railroad tycoon William Henry Baldwin Jr., founded the National League on Urban Conditions Among Negroes, one of the nation's oldest and largest organizations devoted to empowering African Americans and helping them succeed.

In 1912, Haynes became the first Black person to receive a Ph.D. from Columbia University. The university press published his dissertation, which was titled *The Negro at Work in New York City: A Study in Economic Progress*. In 1919, the organization Haynes cofounded was renamed the National Urban League. By the twenty-first century it would have more than a hundred local affiliates around the country and serve millions of minorities and underrepresented people nationwide through programs, advocacy, and research.

As with the white philanthropists who had helped support and establish HBCUs in the nineteenth century, John D. Rockefeller Jr. and Alfred T. White, as well as Julius Rosenwald, the Sears, Roebuck and Company president, provided the much-needed financial connections. Haynes came to see his theoretical studies come alive, with economic empowerment and education as a model for social change.

As serendipity would have it, Oscar Hammerstein II, of Rodgers and Hammerstein fame, was just entering Columbia in 1912 as Haynes was graduating with his Ph.D. Both Rodgers and Hammerstein were Harlem natives and attended Columbia University, drawn to the musical theater program. Richard Rodgers was connected to Hamilton Heights as well, having attended Townsend Harris Hall. This was a three-year feeder high school on the City College campus. Oscar Hammerstein II was from a musical theater family and the grandson of the famous Oscar Hammerstein. Rodgers & Hammerstein would come to transform Broadway musicals in the 1940s and 1950s, with Rodgers composing and Hammerstein writing the lyrics. Among their hits were *Oklahoma, Carousel, South Pacific, The King and I*, and *The Sound of Music*.

The American Scenic and Historic Preservation Society wrote a letter on January 12, 1912, to the rector of St. Luke's. They were hoping the church would deed the Grange to the city, which did not happen. The house was still in use by the church for various activities at this date. Even in 1912, the Scenic Society's suggestion was that the Grange be moved to St. Nicholas Park, as it would still be on Hamilton's former estate lands. Considering a relocation to the park would be a point of contention and debate for the next eighty years.

Hamilton Heights had never been famous for being a center of entertainment in Harlem; the renowned dance halls and nightclubs like the Savoy and the Cotton Club were located a couple of miles away in Central Harlem on Lenox and Seventh avenues. Yet the neighborhood had a unique distinction in terms of "firsts" in both vaudeville and movie hall history, thanks to the Hamilton Theatre. Between 1910 and 1915 the Real Estate Record and Guide described this period as one of the greatest theater building booms in New York's history, many the work of noted movie theater architect Thomas W. Lamb.

"Thirty-six theater projects were underway in 1912, eleven of which had been designed by Lamb, including the Hamilton."[1] In Hamilton Heights, there was also the Washington Theatre at 1801 Amsterdam Avenue at 149th Street, built in 1910–11. In Central Harlem, architect Victor Hugo

Koehler's Lafayette Theater was constructed at 2225 Seventh Avenue and 132nd Street.

Seamon's Music Hall at 253 West 125th Street, designed by the architect George Keister and built in a neo-Classical style, opened in 1913 as Hurtig & Seamon's New Burlesque. As was the case in nearly all of the nation's theaters in the early twentieth century, African Americans were banned from attending or even performing. This would prove ironic by the 1930s, when the name changed to the Apollo and African American performers began to create the theater's lasting legacy.

Moss and Brill's Hamilton Theatre, on Broadway and 146th Street, opened on January 23, 1913, with a lineup the first night that included "performances by the theatre's resident orchestra, a series of short dramas, several comedians, an acrobatic act, and short motion pictures."[2]

The theatre had been commissioned by the vaudeville operator Benjamin S. Moss and the theater developer Solomon Brill and had been designed by theater architect Thomas W. Lamb. His plans called for a 2,500-seat theater in the Renaissance Revival style with a terracotta façade, a polished granite base, and a roof garden. The elaborate entryway featured an arch topped by an outstretched eagle flanked by angels. The new theater was to be named the Lafayette, perhaps a tip of the hat to

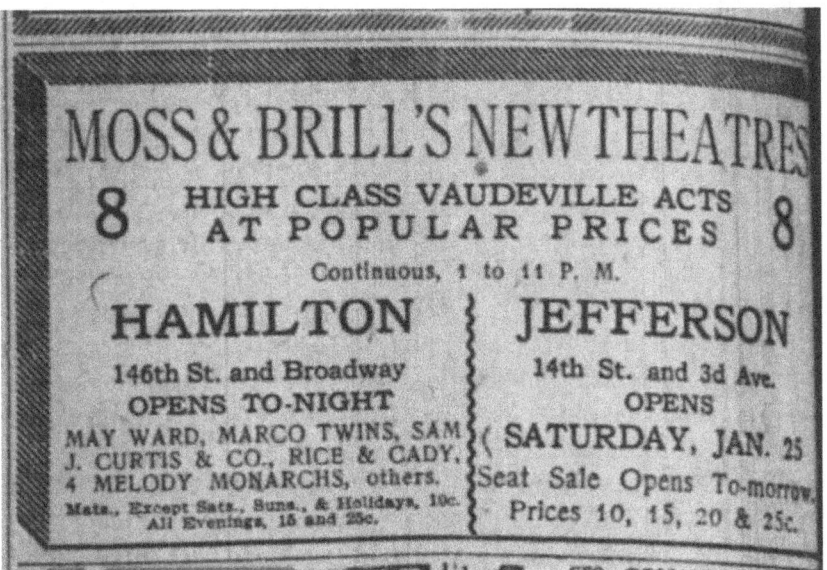

Figure 35. Moss & Brill's Advertisement. Public Domain

Figure 36. Hamilton Theatre, 3560–3568 Broadway, c. 1928. Courtesy Billy Rose Theater Collection, NY Public Library of the Performing Arts

its location along the stretch of Broadway called the Boulevard Lafayette until 1899.

"The new institution is a handsome building, seating about two thousand persons, and will be devoted to vaudeville at popular prices," one article noted in describing opening night. "Friends of those interested in the new enterprise expressed their feelings by sending numerous large bouquets."[3] Before its completion, however, it was renamed Moss & Brill's Hamilton Theatre, possibly to avoid confusion with the theater in Central Harlem, the Lafayette, that was under construction at the same time. The opening-night lineup included Ethel Barrymore in her second silent film titled *The Final Judgement*, her first as a player for the new Metro Pictures, later part of MGM.

In 1915, when Brill ended his association with the Hamilton, the theatre was renamed the B. S. Moss Hamilton Theatre. Five years later, Moss and E. F. Albee of the Keith & Proctor vaudeville chain combined their business interests, assumed management of the Hamilton, and renamed it B. F. Keith's Hamilton Theatre.

In another change to the neighborhood's identification, in 1921 the corner of Amsterdam Avenue and Hamilton Place was renamed Alexander Hamilton Square, and the street from which the Grange had been moved in 1888 was now called Hamilton Terrace. It was clear that Hamilton's old neighborhood had not forgotten him.

In 1924, the American Scenic and Historic Preservation Society bought the Grange from St. Luke's Church for $50,000. The society was formed in March 1895 by then parks commissioner Andrew H. Green. A gift of "$100,000 for purchase and maintenance by J. P. Morgan and George F. Baker, Jr. was set up as a trust fund, the income of which was to be used for maintenance."[4] The society had gotten relics relating to Hamilton from his grand-niece, Louisa Lee Schuyler Hamilton, and they hoped to receive more items, including some from the Schuyler Museum in Albany, Elizabeth Hamilton's childhood home. The Scenic Society pamphlet of 1933 noted that the gum trees Hamilton planted had "stood until the centennial of his death in 1904, though then dead or dying," and added, "They were cut down in 1908. Pieces of the wood or bark are kept by old residents of the neighborhood, and more are preserved in the Grange."[5]

The chairs and table pictured in Figures 37 and 38 are original to the Hamiltons' time at the Grange. The furniture is listed as part of the National Park Service's archival furniture. There is another original chair, one of a pair of English mahogany armchairs in the Chinese manner, given to Alexander Hamilton by Gen. Philip Schuyler for use at the Grange.

Hamilton's personal travel desk, shown in Figure 39, as well as other original pieces, are at the Smithsonian National Museum of American History. They are part of the collection donated by Allan McLane Hamilton (Alexander Hamilton's grandson and biographer).

Figures 37 and 38. Original Grange furniture. LEFT: Pair of Side Chairs. RIGHT: Pier Side Table. Courtesy of National Park Service, Manhattan Historic Sites Archive

Figure 39. Hamilton's Travel Desk. Gift of Allan McLane Hamilton to Library of Congress; Item # PL016507

The Scenic Society was very critical of the lack of care that the city and state had paid to preserving significant sites impacting Hamilton's life, noting that:

> The statues in Central Park, at Columbia University and the Hamilton Club in Brooklyn, were all constructed with private funds. His law office at 31–33 Wall Street was on a site now covered by the building of J. P. Morgan & Company. The dueling ground in Weehawken where he fell is obliterated by railroad tracks, although there is a bust of Hamilton on the summit of the Palisades above. The house of William Bayard, at Nos. 80–82 Jane Street where he died, has long gone.[6]

The society now saw its role as preserving the most lasting physical reminder of Hamilton's life in New York. They were determined that the house he built, the place where he planted trees and flowers, and where he lived in harmony with his wife and children for such a short time be preserved and protected for future generations.

NPS records show a small bath in the very back of the first-floor north hall at this time. It seems that in 1933 the first-floor bathroom was removed and a basement bathroom added a little later. In 1933, after an extensive renovation, the Grange opened as the Hamilton Museum, and it was around this time that the area began to be called Hamilton Heights. This was also the year when electricity was finally installed.

The Hamilton Club of Brooklyn Heights donated a life-sized bronze statue of Hamilton, which had sat at the entrance to its headquarters since 1892. It was placed on the front lawn facing Convent Avenue. The memory of Hamilton's intellectual, oratory, and writing skills had been revered by

Figure 40. Alexander Hamilton Statue, 1892 (Photo 1968). Courtesy National Register of Historic Places and National Historic Landmarks Program Records

the Hamilton Literary Association, a prominent nineteenth-century Brooklyn debating society that had merged with the Hamilton Club in 1883.

Hamilton Gate, one of the three gates at City College, is located at 141st Street and Convent Avenue, less than a block from the Grange.

On April 7, 1921, City College hosted Dr. Albert Einstein, who attended a lecture on campus during his "first visit to any American academic institution, and the first of five visits to City College."[7] Dr. Rheinhard A. Wetzel of the Physics Department was well acquainted with Dr. Einstein, as they had communicated for several years.

Columbia University professor Edward Kasner gave a lecture on the General Relativity Theory. Dr. Einstein spoke for twenty minutes at the conclusion of the lecture. Sydney Van Nort reported in a college news article that "on Monday, April 18, 1921, Dr. Einstein gave the first in a series of four consecutive afternoon lectures concerning the theory of relativity for faculty members of the scientific departments of City College and other colleges in the vicinity."[8] Dr. Einstein's remarks were in German, and Professor Morris R. Cohen translated.

Figure 41. Albert Einstein at City College. Courtesy Leo Baeck Institute, F5343J. Circa 1921.

The climax of Einstein's visit before his lecture on April 21 in the Great Hall was after former City College president Sidney E. Mezes introduced him, citing the distinguished and honorable guest's accomplishments. Einstein thanked everyone for his warm welcome and said, "It gives me the greatest pleasure, on this my first visit to America, to have this opportunity of meeting the student body of this great university. I appreciate very much your friendly reception and applause and extend to you all my heartiest good wishes."[9]

In the late nineteenth and early twentieth centuries, the farmland of Harlem had increasingly become home to great numbers of immigrants from eastern and southern Europe, who were occupying the growing number of apartment rows that lined the boulevards. Some of the single-family brownstones were converted to boarding houses as well. A great social change was in progress when, "as a stream of colored people trudged north from other parts of Manhattan and from the countryside of the American South, the Italians and Jews ceded much of Harlem to the new arrivals in the early decades of the twentieth century."[10]

Three years later, on Thanksgiving morning, November 27, 1924, a police escort started at 145th Street and Convent Avenue to lead the first "Macy's Christmas Parade" six miles from Hamilton Heights, weaving its way through Harlem downtown to Herald Square. It would quickly be renamed the "Macy's Thanksgiving Day Parade." The parade itself was just two blocks long that first year, but the excitement over this novel event was such that thousands of people joined in along the way. It included nursery-rhyme-themed floats, Macy's employees dressed as clowns, and a menagerie of animals, including bears, elephants, and camels on loan from the Central Park Zoo. Santa Claus brought up the rear and exited his sleigh down a ladder at the store's new 34th Street entrance near Seventh Avenue. Its unanticipated success prompted Macy's to announce the next day that it would be an annual event, though with a much-shortened route in the years that followed, and the signature huge balloons introduced in 1927, with cartoon character Felix the Cat as its first.

The massive influx of Blacks during the era of World War I essentially altered Harlem's residential and racial balances. The shifting tides took a little longer in Hamilton Heights than in Central Harlem. As Jeffrey Gurock wrote in *The Jews of Harlem*, the very predominant Jewish population especially felt the demographic change.

> The artificially inflated rental costs persisted throughout the 1920s, and the vast majority of the neighborhood's Jews chose to move elsewhere. And as each Jewish family exited, one or more African American families replaced them, which furthered the predominance of Black families, which promoted in turn the further departure of Jewish families. By 1930, the era of Jewish residential life in Harlem was well-nigh over.[11]

Among those who would make Sugar Hill his longtime home was a Washington, D.C., native named Edward Kennedy "Duke" Ellington. Duke's mother played piano, and he was raised in a cultured environment. As a teenager, he began to listen to ragtime pianists performing around Washington and during the summer in Philadelphia and Atlantic City. "While vacationing in Asbury Park, Duke heard a hot pianist named Harvey Brooks. At the end of his vacation, Duke sought him out in Philadelphia where Harvey showed him some pianistic tricks and shortcuts."[12]

A PBS Masters feature on Ellington shared that "Brooks' early guidance sparked something in Ellington that made him embrace music and suddenly want to play piano. By the time he was seventeen, he began playing professionally. Making his name as a piano player in Washington, Ellington started to compose his own music."[13] In this he was guided by two musicians, Oliver "Doc" Perry and Louis Brown, who taught him how to read music. He improved his piano playing skills and started finding gigs throughout the D.C. area.

Shortly before his high school graduation in 1917, Duke dropped out and formed his first band, the Duke's Serenaders. One booking led to another, and over the next two years the group built a reputation playing in and near Washington for society balls and embassy parties.

In 1923, Ellington, by now married and the father of a son he named Mercer, moved to New York City. He was already known to local audiences because of the radio, and his newly renamed band, the Washingtonians, made their first recording that year. It was the Prohibition era where speakeasies, private house parties, and legitimate clubs all still found a way to make money selling illegal liquor. His band played at Harlem clubs and cabarets like Connie's Inn and the Hollywood Club. The Duke had elegance, refinement, and movie-star looks, and in 1927, despite a "whites only" policy for audiences, Duke's Washingtonians started a four-year run as the house band at the famed Cotton Club at 142nd Street and Lenox Avenue.

The club got national attention after CBS began broadcasting the performances. And although Duke had been composing his own music for several years, the radio show "Live from the Cotton Club" meant that his music was heard around the country. His reputation was cemented.

As musicians like Duke Ellington were helping to reshape Harlem's cultural scene, less glamourous changes were taking place that would nonetheless have a major effect on Hamilton Heights, among them the opening in 1930 of the IND subway line. Plans for the new line had been approved in 1924, and of the five new routes, several ran beneath St. Nicholas Avenue. In 1932 work was completed on the "A" train express, about which a song would be written.

Figure 42 shows construction of what would be the 147th Street exit of the IND subway line. The structure with the onion dome is 14–16 St. Nicholas Place, designed by William Grinnell. He would also build the famous apartment complex, the Grinnell, on Riverside Drive. Farther down the street are the Bailey House and the John W. Fink House, with the corner turret. The taller Jacob P. Baiter House would become the Dawn Hotel.

In 1926, with the encouragement of Head Librarian Ernestine Rose and the National Urban League, the Carnegie Corporation funded the New York Public Library's purchase of Arturo Schomburg's private library collection for $10,000. It included three eighteenth-century trailblazers: poems by Phillis Wheatley, the first published African American poet and second woman (after Anne Bradstreet); correspondence from Toussaint L'Ouverture, who led the 1793 slave revolt in Haiti; and music composed by Frenchman Chevalier de Saint-Georges.

These items became part of the huge collection that the library had

Figure 42. St. Nicholas Ave Subway Construction, circa 1928. Courtesy New York Transit Museum and NY Historical Society

already accumulated and proved the catalyst for the eventual transformation of the 135th Street branch into the Schomburg Center for Research in Black Culture. Schomburg's library consisted of approximately 10,000 items, including 2,932 books, 1,124 pamphlets, and many valuable prints and manuscripts. It was delivered in 104 crates to the Central Research Library on 42nd Street in May of 1926 for cataloging before it was deposited at the 135th Street branch.

The branch's namesake, Arturo Alfonso Schomburg, had been born in Puerto Rico in 1874. His mother was a Black woman from St. Croix and his father a Puerto Rican of German descent. In 1891 he moved to New York City, living in Harlem and then Brooklyn. Schomburg was a lover of the printed word, committed to collecting books about Black history from his travels around the world.

He was involved in several organizations devoted to promoting African American research and scholarship, and he would move in the same circle of Harlem Renaissance greats that would make this period so significant. In 1929, Schomburg's reputation encouraged Charles S. Johnson to recruit him to curate Fisk's library. After having transformed it and multiplied its library holdings, Schomburg would return to New York's 135th Street branch library in 1932. He would serve as curator of his collection until his death in 1938.

Harlem was full of music during these years, whether down the hill in the Harlem flats, in East Harlem (later called Spanish Harlem), or on the hills of Hamilton Heights and Sugar Hill. In these places white and Black musicians found a camaraderie in music that was far less common in the general society.

Among those who were part of this world was the composer George Gershwin. Born in Brooklyn in 1898, he and his family lived in more than twenty different apartments, as his father often changed jobs. By February of 1915, the Gershwins were living at 108 West 111th Street, and at the time their father, Morris, owned the St. Nicholas Baths on 111th Street and Lenox Avenue.

George and his brother Ira became a powerful team as composer and lyricist. By 1919 the family was living at 520 West 144th Street, just two blocks from the original location of Hamilton's Grange. It was here that George wrote his first hit song, "Swanee." In 1920, Al Jolson's recording of the song became a huge hit, going on to sell millions of records and copies of the sheet music. Gershwin's reputation and fortune were made.

The arrival of the Gershwins in Hamilton Heights coincided with the steady influx of more African Americans in Harlem. World War I was just ending. The music he composed in his all-too-short life is still celebrated a hundred years later. Gershwin's "Rhapsody in Blue" and operatic masterpiece *Porgy and Bess* were soon to come.

By the 1920s, the Gershwin brothers were moving in an integrated crowd of musicians and artists in Harlem that were a key part of both the arts scene of the Harlem Renaissance and the Civil Rights Movement. It was in an apartment at 501 West 110th Street on Harlem's Cathedral Parkway in 1924 that George Gershwin wrote his legendary "Rhapsody in Blue." Just as poets test their early drafts on friends, George played the composition for a gathering at the home of the civil rights activist Walter White in Sugar Hill. On July 20, 1925, he made the cover of *Time* magazine. The influence of Black culture on Gershwin's work and the associations he made in Harlem were evidenced in his music, particularly in his friendship with the famed stride pianist James P. Johnson, composer of "the Charleston."

In 1928, with the decline of vaudeville, the Hamilton Theatre was sold to the newly formed Radio-Keith-Orpheum, known as RKO Pictures.

RKO was founded by a combination of business circumstances and new film mediums that brought together the interests of Radio Corporation of America (RCA) president David Sarnoff and Boston financier Joseph Kennedy, father of eleven-year-old John F. Kennedy. The previous year *The Jazz Singer*, starring Al Jolson, had ignited the talkies boom in the movie industry, which had previously been silent save for the music. RKO promptly eliminated all vaudeville from the Hamilton, installed a sound system, and converted the theater into one of the city's, and indeed the country's, first playhouses to show "talking pictures." In so doing, the theatre became a part of movie history.

During this period, Hamilton Heights had witnessed Alexander Hamilton's home becoming a museum, Albert Einstein speaking at City College, George Gershwin creating music that would be heralded a century later, and a palatial vaudeville house becoming one of New York's first talking picture movie theaters, a revolutionary change. It was the dawning of a modern era.

Though there is no definitive documentation we could find about

Figure 43. Hamilton Theatre interior, circa 1935. Public domain

whether these films debuted at the Hamilton, there is every likelihood that they were shown there, since they were RKO's films and its theater. During the time that the Hamilton was still exclusively a movie theater company, RKO studios produced several future classics, including *King Kong* (1933), *Bringing Up Baby*, starring Cary Grant (1938), and *Citizen Kane* (1941). At the Hamilton, the RKO logo was visible above the second set of private boxes.

Chapter 9

The Harlem Renaissance

> How was the creativity of the Black woman kept alive, ... when for most of the years Black people have been in America, it was a punishable crime for a Black person to read or write? And the freedom to paint, to sculpt, to expand the mind with action did not exist.
>
> —Alice Walker, *In Search of our Mothers' Gardens*

If ever there was a moment in history where lightning was caught in the proverbial bottle, it was the Harlem Renaissance of the 1920s and 1930s. In that brief, intense, and magical period in African American and literary history, a confluence of events brought together a remarkable collection of brilliant and gifted African American artists, writers, actors, musicians, singers, civil rights activists, scholars, and legal minds.

It would be another forty years before Lorraine Hansberry left her sickbed to provide encouragement to a group of teenage writing contest winners by telling them that they were "young, gifted and Black." Four years later her husband would create a play and book, and then Nina Simone would memorialize the phrase in song. Yet in this beginning group of artists of the Harlem Renaissance it was the heart of who they were: young, gifted, Black talent making history.

Harlem was just emerging as the Black mecca it would become when this period began. Shortly after the end of World War I people from around the country, but primarily the South and even the Caribbean, had been

Figure 44. Edgecombe Ave. at the top, looking down on Colonial Park and Bradhurst Avenue. Courtesy NY Public Library

converging on this place they had heard about, read about, and dreamt about. This was the promised land of hope and possibilities, a land where Black people were gathering. And Sugar Hill was the ultimate destination.

Sugar Hill is the elevated area of Harlem in both a literal and metaphorical sense, making it one of the highest peaks in Manhattan. The steep incline seen in Figure 44 is indicative of why the hilly neighborhood was referred to first as Jochem Pieters Hills and then in the eighteenth century as Harlem Heights. Its physical hilltop elevation above the adjacent Fifth through Eighth Avenue dwellings allows one to look down on the valley to Central Harlem, once called the Harlem Flats, or for the people in the flats to look up. The grand apartment complexes in Sugar Hill had stunning architectural features and liveried doormen, stately mansions and luxurious brownstones. It became the place to which one aspired to rise—to a cleaner, safer, more graciously designed elegant neighborhood where the rents were higher and the residents, presumably, of a better class.

It began to attract professionals like doctors, lawyers, teachers, judges, and a sophisticated group of the new Negro intelligentsia. Sugar Hill, whose physical parameters would morph over the years, roughly included 135th to about 165th streets, from Edgecombe Avenue to the Hudson River. It encompassed Edgecombe, St. Nicholas, Convent, Amsterdam,

Broadway, and Riverside Drive. Its metaphorical mapping was and would remain a state of mind: reaching Sugar Hill meant you had arrived in a special place and were living the sweet life, the good life on the hill, elevated in every sense of the word.

In many ways, the very term "Harlem Renaissance" is a misnomer, since the definition of a renaissance is the revival of, or renewed interest in, something. This inimitable period in the historical evolution of literature, Harlem and African American culture and sociology, was the origin of something, rather than a renewed interest in it. By the 1930s, just a decade after the Harlem Renaissance blossomed, people were already questioning what it all meant as it began so quickly to fade.

During the time it was happening, it was not called the Harlem Renaissance but the Negro Renaissance. Langston Hughes and others living through the period referred to it as such for decades. It is unclear when someone renamed it the Harlem Renaissance, perhaps to be more politically correct or sensitive to growing Black Power and African American history sentiments.

Starting around 1910 and continuing until about 1970, some estimated six million African Americans from the South relocated to Northern cities like Chicago, Detroit, Milwaukee, and New York. Whether unskilled laborers or educated members of the small elite Black middle class, they or someone they knew shared common experiences of slavery, emancipation, and racial oppression. During the Great Migration, Harlem attracted an estimated 175,000 to 200,000 African Americans, among the largest concentration in the country.

Across the world, in every culture, there is a history of storytellers, wise men and women, griots who held the histories of their people or village in their heads. Minstrels traveled the land and entertained while they shared the news. They told stories of small and great deeds by the obscure and famous. Such is the case with so much of Harlem's history during this period. Those who traveled north were not recording every moment of their day, keeping a record for future generations. Yet they told stories of this era as rumors and tall tales, in letters to friends, and in interviews, many of which were recorded by the federal Works Project Administration (WPA). Some stories were told via the joy or agony of music or disguised in fiction and poetry. Some were told through the lenses of the white people who had become embedded into the Negro party circuit.

Members of this storied group of individuals would be credited with a series of firsts in African American history. They would be the first to integrate certain streets and buildings, the first to hold prestigious positions in various organizations and government agencies, the first to be elected to certain offices, and the first to receive awards, prizes, and medals that had previously been bestowed only on white people.

Yet stories can also be told in pictures. And if they can take the place of a thousand words, then Harlem's story during its unique time as the Black mecca was captured for perpetuity by the thousands of photographs taken by Massachusetts native James Van Der Zee. He arrived in Harlem sometime around 1906 with dreams of becoming a professional musician. After several jobs to make ends meet, he made a profession from his love of photography. His initial studio, Guarantee Photo, was at 109 West 135th Street and opened in 1916. He became the most famous Harlem photographer ever, specializing in both commercial photos and family portraits. Not only did he capture social clubs, athletic teams, and church groups, but family events, both joyous and sad. He came to alternately be called "The Rembrandt of Harlem" and "Mr. Picture Takin' Man" and photographed regular working folks where he set up his elaborate backdrops. In addition, there were the wealthy clients, legendary musicians, famed actors of both stage and screen, and those making a name for themselves during the Harlem Renaissance. The accessibility of personal cameras in later decades eventually negated the dependence on studio pictures and was one thing that led to financial troubles and some difficult years.

Many decades later a rebirth of sorts would happen after his photos were shown as part of an exhibit in 1969 at the Met. In the decades that followed Van der Zee would be made a "Fellow for Life" at the Metropolitan Museum of Art and receive the Pierre Toussaint Award from the Archdiocese of New York and the Living Legacy Award at the White House. His photographs would be seen at several museums, including the National Art Gallery in Washington, D.C.

The other veteran photographer who so stunningly captured Harlem life and architecture for six decades was Austin Hansen, a Virgin Islands native who moved to the city in 1928. His vast collection is now part of the Schomburg.

James Weldon Johnson wrote in 1930, "The fact that within New York, the greatest city of the New World, there is found the greatest single community anywhere of people descended from age-old Africa appears at a thoughtless glance to be the climax of the incongruous."[1]

Although the figures who came to represent the Harlem Renaissance disagreed about many things, they knew that they were living through a remarkable period because they had gathered together in this place called Harlem. Many of these legendary figures had very different views about the way forward for the Negro, about whether one should be an activist or try to fit in and bide one's time, about the images to present, the tone of the stories one should write, and the hills on which human rights were to be fought for or died upon.

What was critical about the movement they formed was that they built a safe place in Harlem in each other's homes, libraries, church basements, and other public spaces. They found a place to express themselves, create, and challenge one another with discussions about who they were and who they could become. In doing so, they laid the foundation for the generations of extraordinary talent that would follow. They came to Harlem because they had heard that Black poets and writers and social activists were walking proudly on these streets and in the process changing the world. They were creating paintings and sculptures and displaying and selling their work.

Many of the important gatherings of the time took place in Hamilton Heights and especially in Sugar Hill, where the Black intelligentsia surrounded themselves with up-and-coming artists, thinkers, and literary figures. But even for those who never set foot in New York City, this transformative period of Black social thought and creative energy was the birthing ground of so much that would follow.

And the question remains: has there ever been, or will there ever be, another gathering of that kind of Black excellence living, working, and socializing in one place again? As for the role of the neighborhood in which this unprecedented cultural and intellectual moment occurred, the Pulitzer Prize–winning historian David Levering Lewis wrote in his book *When Harlem Was in Vogue*, "It was the existence of Harlem above all else, the translation into brick and asphalt of the New Negro's own special, cartwheeling nationalism, that made the Golden Age possible. Almost everything seemed possible above 125th Street in the early twenties for these Americans who were determined to thrive separately to better proclaim the ideals of integration."[2]

W. E. B. Du Bois was central to this singular moment in history, a resident at differing times of both Sugar Hill and Central Harlem. He envisioned an American society that was unencumbered by race, and he believed that a small minority of educated, upper-class African Americans, the "Talented Tenth," as he called them, could uplift the masses out of poverty. One of Du Bois' most enduring legacies was as cofounder, in 1909, of the National Association for the Advancement of Colored People (NAACP). "Today he is recognized as one of the founding fathers of American sociology and the first to establish it as a scientific discipline.

He produced the first generation of Black social scientists, including Richard R. Wright, Monroe Work, and George E. Haynes."[3]

Also essential to this movement were three important magazines that appeared in Harlem at this time. The *Messenger* was published by Chandler Owen and the great labor organizer A. Philip Randolph; the *Crisis* by the NAACP, and *Opportunity* (in full: *Opportunity: Journal of Negro Life*) by the National Urban League. Both the *Crisis* and *Opportunity* would have as their main focus civil rights, political and social issues affecting African Americans. The *Crisis* and *Opportunity* would be notable for being the first to publish the work of many of the era's celebrated poets and novelists, among them Langston Hughes, Zora Neale Hurston, and Countee Cullen.

George Edmund Haynes had been working for the federal government in Washington, D.C., in the Division of Negro Economics, but returned to New York City in 1921. Some religious leaders who were members of the Federal Council of Churches had begun to realize the hypocrisy of espousing Christian values while at the same time displaying blatant racism toward Blacks. These leaders sought to improve cooperation between Blacks and whites, and Haynes was selected to head the Council's new Commission on Negro Churches and Race Relations.

In seeking support, he immediately tapped into his network of organizations and philanthropists, among them the real estate magnate William E. Harmon and Julius Rosenwald, co-owner of Sears, Roebuck & Company. Rosenwald had long been a supporter of Black education. Deeply moved by the writings of Booker T. Washington, with whom he had been friends for many years, he built schools for Negro children throughout the South in a time when Black schools were routinely being burned down by the Ku Klux Klan. By the time he died in 1932, the fund that bears his name had built nearly 5,000 "Rosenwald Schools" throughout the South for kindergarteners through high school students, and he had supported several Historically Black Colleges and Universities (HBCUs).

Haynes worked to "establish the Harmon Foundation Awards, an organization that gave generous cash prizes in the areas of literature, music, the fine arts, business, science, religion, education, and race relations."[4] He was in touch with the most noted writers and artists of the Harlem Renaissance, all of whom would proudly list being a recipient of the Harmon Award as a pivotal experience in their lives.

At the same time, Haynes' wife, Elizabeth Ross Haynes, broke ground early in the Harlem Renaissance, though her name is seldom mentioned with the other writers of the era. She distinguished herself in 1921 by writing the first book geared to Negro children, *Unsung Heroes*. African Americans

Figure 45. Dr. George Edmund Haynes. Public domain

were so accustomed to seeing the negative images of Black people in advertising and media that the idea of creating something that would instill racial pride in Black children was major. "In games, books, and children's ditties, in postcards and advertisements, in every form of popular culture, Negro children were depicted as naked, wild, unkempt creatures with bulging white eyes and exaggerated lips."[5]

Elizabeth Ross Haynes created a collection of short story biographies about accomplished Black poets, leaders, and scientists who had gone mostly unrecognized. It was published by W. E. B. Du Bois and Augustus Granville Dill. A century later, *Unsung Heroes* would be classified by scholars as being so culturally important that it is part of the knowledge base of civilization as we know it.

In addition to Du Bois' groundbreaking work, the year 1921 brought another historic publication. Its author was James Mercer Langston Hughes, born in Joplin, Missouri, in 1902. He came from a distinguished, educated family: Hughes's great-uncle, John Mercer Langston, had been the first dean of Howard University Law School. Young Langston showed literary promise early on; he had written his first poem when he was in elementary

Figure 46. Elizabeth Ross Haynes and Her Son George Haynes Jr. Courtesy Dr. Bruce Haynes

school and been elected class poet. His interest continued while writing for his high school newspaper.

Hughes was mostly estranged from his father, who lived in Mexico. In 1919, just after graduating from high school in Cleveland, he received a letter from his father inviting him to come south and spend the summer with him. In Hughes' first autobiography, *The Big Sea*, published in 1940, the author described an experience he had around sunset when the train he was taking to Mexico in 1920 was crossing a bridge over the Mississippi:

"I looked out the window of the Pullman at the great muddy river flowing down toward the heart of the South, and I began to think about what that river, the old Mississippi, had meant to Negroes in the past—how to be sold down the river was the worst fate that could overtake a slave in times of bondage."[6]

He had also read about Lincoln's trip on a raft down the Mississippi to New Orleans and learned that Lincoln, seeing the brutality of slavery, had made a commitment to himself that it should end. "Then I began to think about other rivers in our past, the Congo, and the Niger, and the Nile in Africa," he wrote, "and the thought came to me: I've known rivers."[7] It was from these reflections that in the space of fifteen minutes he wrote the poem "The Negro Speaks of Rivers," the first draft of which he scribbled on the back of an envelope, the only paper he had in hand.

Although a number of events, publications, and meetings during this period would signal the start of the Harlem Renaissance, it is generally agreed that the writer and social scientist Charles S. Johnson, the editor of *Opportunity*, was instrumental in encouraging and shaping the careers of a great many aspiring young Black writers during the 1920s.

Langston Hughes would later identify Jessie Redmon Fauset at the *Crisis*, Charles Johnson at *Opportunity*, and Alain Locke in Washington as the three people who, as he put it, "midwifed the so-called New Negro literature into being."[8] Hughes and his fellow writers, among them Countee Cullen, Zora Neale Hurston, Arna Bontemps, Rudolph Fisher, Wallace Thurman, Jean Toomer, and Nella Larsen, all benefited from the guidance these visionaries provided them. And at some point, almost all these people either lived or socialized on Edgecombe and St. Nicholas avenues in the elegant apartment buildings in Sugar Hill.

These were the brand-new stately buildings in Hamilton Heights and Sugar Hill that had been erected for white middle-class families during the Harlem building boom from the late 1880s through about 1925 on the heel of developers like William De Forest. Yet they would quickly become the home of well-to-do African Americans making their way in this new Harlem. Along with the stunning brownstones with fireplaces, marble features, servants' quarters, distinct woodworking, and hardwood floors were the rowhouses that offered more modest yet modern accommodations.

While some buildings would have elegant facades, not all had noteworthy architectural designs. They were modern and innovative in that these were the decades of new construction that included elements that were still a marvel. Along with some that had elevators and doormen, they had electricity throughout, running hot and cold water, functioning indoor toilets, and central heating.

Jessie Fauset, who as an editor would be a positive force in the lives of so many of these authors, was also one of the most prolific writers of the Harlem Renaissance. She grew up in a proud New Jersey family of modest means that had been free for several generations, unlike the vast majority of African Americans, who were mostly the descendants of enslaved people. Fauset attended Cornell, where she studied the classics. "For the four years," she once remarked, "I was the only colored girl in a college community of over 3,000 students."[9] It is hard to fathom the emotional strain all these early achievers in mostly white institutions endured as they broke color boundaries.

In 1903, eager to know more about her people and to teach in the South, Fauset wrote to Du Bois, then a professor at Atlanta University, seeking his assistance in getting a summer job. He helped her get a position teaching English at Fisk, and the two would develop a decades-long friendship as Du Bois became a teacher, mentor, and friend. By 1912 Fauset was contributing articles to his NAACP magazine, the *Crisis*.

After extensive travels and studying at the Sorbonne in Paris, Fauset returned to America to complete a master's degree in Romance languages at the University of Pennsylvania. Having published several articles in the *Crisis* and having kept in contact with Du Bois, she moved to New York to become the magazine's literary editor, a role in which she would have a profound influence on the careers of many other Black writers.

While in Mexico, Langston Hughes had sent some of his writings to Du Bois. The magazine accepted the pieces, and encouraging letters came back from Fauset. In response Hughes sent her the poem he had written on the train, "The Negro Speaks of Rivers," which in June of 1921 appeared in the *Crisis*. It was the first Langston Hughes poem published in something other than his high school newspaper. "For the next few years my poems appeared often (and solely) in the *Crisis*," he wrote in his autobiography. "And to that magazine, certainly, I owe my literary beginnings, insofar as publication is concerned."[10]

Among the millions of people migrating from the South in those years were Richard Howard Bearden and his wife, Bessye, who in 1914 moved from North Carolina to Harlem with their toddler son, Romare. Howard worked as a sanitation inspector, but his love was music, and he was an accomplished pianist. Bessye became the New York editor of the *Chicago Defender*. The Beardens enrolled their son in school at P.S. 5 in 1917, on 141st Street and Edgecombe Avenue in Sugar Hill. He was destined to become a world-renowned artist.

The family lived on West 131st Street, not far from the Savoy Ballroom and other clubs, a location that allowed them to become deeply immersed in Harlem's jazz and blues scenes. In the early days of the Harlem Renaissance, the Bearden apartment was a popular gathering place for the Black literati, artists, and members of the intelligentsia, with many of the familiar names from the Du Bois' "talented tenth" in attendance.

Romare graduated from DeWitt Clinton High School in 1927 and headed off to Lincoln University in Pennsylvania. As he became an increasingly celebrated artist, it would be clear that his early immersion into jazz and the blues greatly influenced his work. His paintings and collages combined vibrant colors and mixed media, often depicting the fullness of Black life in various cultural settings. Bearden's work would eventually be on display at the Metropolitan Museum of Art in New York, the Museum of Fine Arts in Boston, the Art Institute of Chicago, and the Philadelphia Museum of Art.

As demographics shifted, both members of the African American upper crust and ordinary working men and women would occupy many of the stunning apartment buildings in Hamilton Heights. Members of this early generation were often the first Blacks to live in a building. The higher rents created a new phenomenon—the Harlem "rent" party where tenants would host regular gatherings with music, food, and liquor for sale to help augment their rent. And while it may have been more common in Central Harlem, Sugar Hill had its share of these gatherings, as well, where accomplished musicians entertained while people danced, laughed, ate, and drank.

And for a brief yet historic moment, 580 St. Nicholas Avenue came to signify the very essence of this charmed period in Harlem's literary history. During the height of the Harlem Renaissance, writers, artists, and civil rights pioneers frequented the apartment of librarian Regina Anderson, Ethel Nance, and Louella Tucker.

Regina Anderson (Andrews) became a key figure during this period who would help shape these years in subtle and profound ways. Ironically, the prejudice she experienced when she applied for a job at the New York Public Library's main branch on Fifth Avenue and 42nd Street set in motion events that proved a catalyst for many historic meetings of members of the Harlem Renaissance.

As Ethelene Whitmire writes in her biography, *Regina Anderson Andrews: Harlem Renaissance Librarian*, Regina's sense of racial identity was based on her own family's mixed-race heritage. Her mother was an artist from the Midwest. Her New Orleans–born father was an accomplished lawyer. She had family members of African, Swedish, and Jewish descent and, despite her light complexion, identified as a Black woman. In 1919 Regina briefly attended Wilberforce University, an HBCU where she worked as an assistant at the school's Carnegie Library. She returned to Chicago and then enrolled in the Chicago Public Library's apprentice training program, where she obtained a job as a library assistant. Chicago's library system was based on the civil service exam, which saved African Americans from being subject to some of the blatant racism in most library systems, where it was up to the senior staff who was hired.

In 1922 Regina visited New York and liked it so much that she decided to stay. A few days after filling out an application for the New York Public Library, she was granted an interview. Some places become such a fixture that it is hard to imagine when they were new, but the 42nd Street branch, with its regal, imposing lions standing guard, had just opened a decade before, in 1911. The interviewer, skipping over Regina's education, training, and previous library positions, instead focused on her race. What did she mean when she indicated under race and religion that she was "American"? he asked.

"Well, I always considered myself an American," Regina replied. "I don't know what else I could be."[11]

In response, he questioned whether she was in fact an American because she wasn't white, and he decided that because of her color she would have to work at the library's Harlem branch on West 135th Street.

In being assigned to this branch in 1923, Regina was sent to a place where she would meet and befriend nearly every influential writer, social scientist, artist, and philanthropist of the Harlem Renaissance. During its height, she and her roommates would host legendary literary salons attended by those who were up and coming and others established in their fields.

Regina would prove to be lucky in terms of her boss, Ernestine Rose, the head librarian of the 135th Street Branch. Like all the city's head librarians at the time, Rose was white. Her outspoken support for the people of color who came to work for her and who represented the neighborhood's shifting demographics raised eyebrows among her peers. Nonetheless, she persisted.

"Rose protested the designation of her branch as the colored one," Whitmire wrote. "She believed that African American librarians should be able to work at any of the NYPL branches."[12]

Regina promptly accepted the position of junior clerk at the 135th Street branch, and within a few months she was promoted. Her monthly salary of $102.41 represented a sizeable increase over what she had earned in Chicago.

What Ernestine Rose established at the 135th Street branch was the foundation of its landmark role during the Harlem Renaissance. As the director of the city's public library system wrote in his 1924 report, he heralded the positive relations between branch libraries and the several communities they served. But he was especially effusive about those developed over several years at the 135th Street Branch in Harlem as being particularly interesting and effective.

> The Branch Librarian belongs to many neighborhood social groups. She has arranged monthly Book Evenings attracting a large number of people to hear literary personages; she has arranged a weekly Forum for the discussion of current topics, and has been closely

Figure 47. Ernestine Rose, 135th Street Branch, circa 1930. Courtesy NYPL

associated with what promises to be a valuable Community Theater Movement, which originated with meetings held in the branch.[13]

One of the most praised poets of the Harlem Renaissance, the Jamaican-born Claude McKay, arrived in New York in 1917. Already a published author, McKay was highly critical of middle-class values; he believed that it was the common man who was worthy of the attentions of the African American writer. His 1919 poem *If We Must Die* had spoken to that horrible summer of rioting and murder termed "the red summer," during which hundreds of Black people had been killed in race riots across the country.

"McKay had become co-editor of the nation's outstanding avant-garde literary and political publication, *the Liberator* (Max Eastman, its debonair socialist founder, having retired to the sidelines). McKay did his job well. He published some of E. E. Cummings' early poetry, after Max Eastman adjudicated a sharp office spat in McKay's and Cummings' favor."[14]

McKay's book of poetry, *Spring in New Hampshire*, later retitled *Harlem Shadows*, was published in 1922. But that same year, disenchanted with the elitism of the Harlem Movement and race relations in America generally, he went to Russia and traveled Europe for over a decade. He did not return permanently until the 1930s.

In 1923, author Jean Toomer's novel *Cane* was published. It was considered the era's first major work of fiction and described as a "collection of finely written and poetically evocative studies of Black rural life in Georgia."[15] Toomer, a native of Washington, D.C., was a light-skinned man of mixed race who resisted being labeled either Negro or white, although he identified as a Negro. In 1930, respected author James Weldon Johnson wrote of the book, "It is still often referred to as one of the finest pieces of modern American prose."[16]

Ethel Ray (Nance), the young woman who would become one of Regina's two roommates, had been blessed with a father, William H. Ray, who had encouraged her educational pursuits and took her traveling with him across the country to meet the leading Negro thinkers of the day. Ray, who was president of his local NAACP chapter, invited W. E. B. Du Bois to speak there. The two began to correspond and became lifelong friends, a friendship that extended to Ray's daughter, Ethel.

Ethel met Charles S. Johnson, the editor of *Opportunity* magazine, at a National Urban League conference in Kansas City, and the meeting led to her getting a job at the Urban League's Kansas City offices. Johnson then asked Ethel to come to New York to work on the magazine. She would become both Johnson's secretary and his confidant, working closely with the magazine's editors to seek out and identify new literary talent.

Once in New York, Ethel met Regina, with whom she became friends, and by chance both young women needed a roommate to afford the rent on a nice apartment. The friendship proved fortuitous. Ethel's position at the Urban League working directly for Charles Johnson and his magazine and Regina's position at the library made them a formidable pair in terms of the connections they fostered among new young and talented artists.

Along with a third young woman, Louella Tucker, Regina and Ethel moved into an apartment at 580 St. Nicholas Avenue, a building at 139th Street that faced St. Nicholas Park and the expanding towering campus of City College. Number 580 was one of Sugar Hill's fanciest apartment buildings, completed in 1914 and increasingly home to affluent and prominent African Americans. Across the hall was Ethel Waters, already a well-known jazz and blues singer as well as a budding actress. Waters would boast a string of career-defining roles: the first African American woman to integrate Broadway in Irving Berlin's 1933 musical *As Thousands Cheer*; the second nominated for an Academy Award for her role in Elia Kazan's 1949 film *Pinky*; the first to star in her own television show, *Beulah*, in 1950;

and the first Black woman nominated for an Emmy Award in 1962 for an episode of the classic television show *Route 66*. Her recordings of "Stormy Weather" and "Am I Blue?" are listed in the National Recording Registry maintained by the Library of Congress.

Regina's job at the library and the literary gatherings there gave her a chance to meet and interact with a host of writers. She set up a private space in the library where they could write. And the apartment at 580 became a place where groups of writers stopped by to relax, read some of their work, give one another feedback, and chat with both their peers and new arrivals.

Between the events at the library that Regina helped oversee and Ethel's connection to the writers, poets, and artists published in *Opportunity* magazine, a remarkable group of people were part of their social circle.

The legendary salons at 580 St. Nicholas were attended by nearly all the names that would become historic examples of the period: the painter Aaron Douglas; the writers Langston Hughes, Jean Toomer, and Eric Waldron; the actor and singer Paul Robeson; James Weldon Johnson; and Charles Johnson, Ethel's boss at *Opportunity*. Another frequent visitor was the white philanthropist and writer Carl Van Vechten, the former music critic of the *New York Times*. He was popular in Harlem as a supporter of the growing Negro arts movement and helped make valuable connections for the artists with publishers and patrons. Van Vechten was a regular at the salons held by Regina and others, moving effortlessly among Black people at the many Harlem parties and homes. Some would say this was done for selfish reasons when he later published his controversial novel *Nigger Heaven*, as he had immersed himself into these inner circles, becoming a voyeur who could later write about his encounters under the guise of fiction.

It was through this group of friends and acquaintances that Regina met the man she would spend her life with, a graduate of Howard University and Columbia Law School named William T. Andrews Jr., who was one of Harlem's most eligible bachelors.

And there were others, among them author Countee Cullen, who used to drop by on his way home from City College. Sometimes, the writers wanted to share a new poem or a brief reading from a new story on which they might be working. "He [Cullen] was always so unassuming and charming, a fine young man," Regina said, "and we were only too happy to have him come, whatever we were doing we would stop and listen to it."[17] Cullen in turn brought writer Arna Bontemps on the promise that Langston Hughes would be there. From 1924 to 1931, while Cullen taught at the Harlem Academy, he lived in St. Nicholas Court, down the street at 746 St. Nicholas Avenue.

At one point, Nance recalled, all you had to say was "580," and people knew that you meant 580 St. Nicholas Avenue. "It served as a sort of Renaissance USO," she later wrote, "offering a couch, a meal, sympathy, and proper introductions to wicked Harlem for newcomers on the Urban League approved list."[18]

It was during these years that Langston Hughes, a regular at the salons, was making a name for himself as a poet. Hughes would distinguish himself early on with a unique style that "captured, as no other Black poet had,

Figure 48. 580 St. Nicholas Ave. Courtesy D. S. James

both the rhythmic and the human qualities of the blues."[19] Hughes was praised for his ability to use a natural vernacular to capture the mood and scenes of Harlem and its people. He was also unafraid to use free verse.

Langston Hughes had quit Columbia University after a year, held various menial jobs in New York, and traveled in Europe and the Mediterranean by working his way aboard a tramp steamer. Upon his return to the U.S., he wound up in Washington, D.C., where his mother and brother were staying. He worked briefly as an assistant for the legendary scholar and historian Dr. Carter G. Woodson, who would create Black History Month. Woodson was the second African American to receive a doctorate from Harvard. He was on the faculty of Howard University and served as dean of the College of Arts and Sciences. It was a clerical job that was prestigious but brought him no joy, so Hughes quit.

In 1924, "*Opportunity* magazine began an annual literary contest with the goal of discovering new writers and encouraging those who were already being published."[20] While in Washington, Hughes was notified that his poem "The Weary Blues" had won first place and $40, his first poetry prize.

Jessie Fauset, the editor at the *Crisis*, was also a prolific writer, and the magazine often published her work. When her first novel, *There Is Confusion*, was to be published in 1924, Regina and others suggested a gathering to mark the event. Charles Johnson agreed and invited people in publishing and several of the leading young writers of the day to a dinner at the Civic Club. The event wound up being not just a celebration of Fauset's publication, but a nod to the more seasoned writers and activists. Importantly, it was an introduction to patrons of the arts and publishers to the many new young Black writers just finding their voices.

The Civic Club, on Twelfth Street near Fifth Avenue, was described as "the only upper crust New York club without color or sex restrictions, where Afro-American intellectuals and prominent white liberals gathered."[21] Johnson anticipated about fifty guests, yet more than twice that number showed up.

Until this point so many of the books written by African Americans had dealt with civil rights or politics, and there were few creative works. Fauset and the new crop of authors brought hope of a new era in which writers would take poetry and fiction in a new direction. Their writing also showed African Americans in positive, sophisticated settings, defying the prevailing stereotypes.

The importance of the March 21, 1924, Civic Club event cannot be overstated. For the first time in the history of African Americans, a broad range of whites and Blacks—people from humble backgrounds, descendants of those once enslaved, millionaires, former busboys, publishers, businessmen, novelists, poets, philanthropists, civil rights leaders, and sociologists—came together in one place to celebrate a new era of Black literary achievement. The ground shifted.

Alfred and Blanche Knopf were not there to speak of Walter White's upcoming novel, but Frederick Lewis Allen of Harper & Brothers had brought other colleagues in publishing, including Walter Bartlett of Scribner's. Many of these same people often frequented Harlem at night, hitting the clubs and salons. But this was a very different kind of event.

Alain Locke, a professor of philosophy at Howard University, was the master of ceremonies. An upper-crust Philadelphian, he "had been educated at Harvard, the University of Berlin, and Oxford, where he was the first African American Rhodes Scholar."[22] To many he seemed aloof, with an air of superiority that rubbed many in this young crowd the wrong way.

Zora Neale Hurston had not yet arrived in New York City. But in her brutally honest manner she would one day describe Locke as "a malicious, spiteful little snot that thinks he ought to be the leading Negro because of his degrees."[23]

The evening began with W. E. B. Du Bois describing a new generation of writers who were no longer restricted by a certain style or voice. "He closed by predicting the end of the literature of apology."[24] Du Bois was followed by James Weldon Johnson, the lawyer, social critic, and author whose poem "Lift Every Voice and Sing" would one day be called the Black national anthem. Johnson had written the lyrics to the song, and his brother the music, in 1900 to be sung by school children in a celebration of Abraham Lincoln's birthday. It was years before he learned that it was being sung over and over by people all across the country.

Although the dinner had been initially planned to celebrate the publication of Fauset's book, it proved to be much more. As Ethelene Whitmire later wrote describing the evening, "Many credit the dinner with launching the Harlem Renaissance by giving African American writers and poets an opportunity to showcase their work before prospective publishers, magazine editors, and patrons."[25]

Jean Toomer, author of the novel *Cane*, declined the invitation to the banquet. Both Claude McKay and Langston Hughes were out of the country. Hughes most likely would have attended. Other young poets, Eric Waldron, Gwendolyn Bennett, and Countee Cullen, read some of their poems.

The editor of the *Century Magazine*, Carl Van Doren, said he had a feeling "that the Negroes of the country are in a remarkable strategic position with reference to the new literary age which seems to be impending."[26] Further, Van Doren said, "I have a genuine faith in the future of imaginative writing among Negroes in the United States. What American literature decidedly needs at the moment is color, music, gusto, the free expression of gay or desperate moods."[27]

Paul Kellogg, editor-in-chief of the progressive magazine *Survey Graphic*, was so impressed that he later devoted an entire issue to the output of African American artists and intellectuals. Alain Locke edited the publication, titled "Harlem: Mecca of the New Negro," which introduced the general public to Harlem Renaissance poets, writers, visual artists, and intellectuals. The issue included the work from the older guard of James Weldon Johnson, Walter White, W. E. B. Du Bois, and Puerto Rican–born book collector Arturo Alfonso Schomburg. Among the younger writers contributing poems and stories were Claude McKay, Rudolph Fisher, Langston Hughes, Countee Cullen, Georgia Johnson, and Eric Waldron. It would later be published as a book in the groundbreaking anthology *The New Negro*, which also included illustrations by Renaissance artist Aaron Douglas. For all these reasons, Fauset's book party at the Civic Club became one of the pivotal events in Harlem Renaissance history.

Nor was the evening quite over when the festivities ended. "After the Civic Club dinner, and a stop at Small's Cabaret, many of the participants wandered over to 580 for an afterparty," Ethel Ray Nance would recall decades later. "It was after this affair that a number of them went up to our apartment . . . where we usually had bacon and eggs, that was our standard food we had on hand all the time. We went up on the roof the next morning and took some pictures."[28]

Among this amazing group of young trailblazers, many of their greatest accomplishments were yet to be made. For others, their light had shone as brightly as it ever would. There were no more meaningful contributions to literature or the world at large.

Pictured in Figure 49 are some notables from the era.

A week after the Urban League's *Opportunity Magazine* Civic Club dinner, the *New York Herald Tribune* gave the era its name in noting that "America was on the edge, if not already in the midst of, what might not improperly be called a Negro renaissance."[29] From this one historic event there emerged two memorable terms that would be used thereafter to define this period in Harlem's history, "the Negro Renaissance," later to be called the Harlem Renaissance, and Harlem as a "mecca" of what was being described as the New Negro.

Jessie Redmon Fauset   Countee Cullen   Arna Bontemps   Langston Hughes   Nella Larsen

Aaron Douglas   Jean Toomer   Zora Neale Hurston   Claude McKay   Wallace Thurman

Figure 49. Harlem Renaissance Artists Photo Collage. Created by D. S. James. Public domain

Regina and Ethel's St. Nicholas Avenue apartment was far from the only salon taking place, though not all of them were of an arts nature. This was also the Roaring Twenties. And those who weren't at house parties or dinners made their way to the clubs in Central Harlem or along St. Nicholas Avenue in Hamilton Heights. Depending on which of the parties one went to, it could be an interracial crowd full of bohemian types from Greenwich Village, the top intellectuals of the day, movie stars or Broadway actors, NAACP or Urban League leaders, bon vivants or any combination thereof.

At Jessie Fauset's salons it was a more selective and sedate group, with few to no white people. The evening was very much about literature and reading poetry, and sometimes conversations were in French.

Madame C. J. Walker's daughter A'Lelia Walker held lavish parties in the spacious townhouse in Central Harlem her mother had built, and despite the elite list of guests, things could get quite wild. The elegant red brick building, located at 108–110 West 136th Street and constructed in 1915, had been designed by Vertner Woodson Tandy, the city's first licensed Black architect. A'Lelia, heiress to her mother's hairdressing fortune, was known for being as outrageous as possible; she reserved a special gathering space in the house for the Harlem Renaissance writers and labeled it "The Dark Tower."

And 580 St. Nicholas was not the only apartment building near City

College that represented a set of firsts for new occupants on the hill. The historian Michael Henry Adams has written that just a few blocks away, both 80 and 90 Edgecombe Avenue at 138th Street, completed in 1915 and designed by Gronenberg & Leuchtag, were also among the stately row houses of this period. All the first Black residents in these buildings would have been very aware that everything possible had been done to keep them out of these apartment houses. The building was still fairly new and, according to Adams, boasted features that included steam heat and private baths, electric lights, a doorman, and porters to assist tenants.

A'Lelia Walker's one-bedroom apartment at 90 Edgecombe Avenue was tiny compared to what she was accustomed to at the sprawling three-story house down the hill. Yet in it, "Princess Violette Murat, Lord and Lady Louis Mountbatten, the crown prince of Sweden, Tallulah Bankhead, Countee Cullen, and many other luminaries met here over glasses of vintage champagne and bootleg cocktails and plates of spaghetti, pigs feet, and caviar."[30]

Another Sugar Hill resident, Walter White, was heralded for his work in civil rights. A blue-eyed man with very light skin, he totally embraced his Negro heritage despite his appearance. He was "born the son of a mailman in Atlanta, Georgia, and he could have led his life comfortably within the white establishment, but chose rather to devote himself to gaining equality for African Americans."[31] In 1918, NAACP field secretary James Weldon Johnson recommended that White join the NAACP in New York as assistant secretary, a job in which he gained a reputation for investigating race riots and lynchings. This would have been an impossible assignment for a Black man in the South, but Walter White exploited his ability to pass for white and willingly moved among bigots and Klan members to gain information about their activities.

In addition to his civil rights work, White was also a writer and a philanthropist who used his influence to help others establish their reputations during this unprecedented moment in history. He entertained artists, writers, and other activists at cocktail parties and dinners, among them CBS executive William Robeson, Clarence Darrow, James Weldon Johnson, and W. E. B. Du Bois. "White proceeded to turn his apartment at 90 Edgecombe Avenue into a stock exchange for cultural commodities," wrote David Levering Lewis, "where interracial contacts and contracts were sealed over bootleg spirits and the verse or song of some Afro-American who was then the rage of New York."[32]

White once wrote to a friend that he and his wife, Gladys, had entertained a few folks: Julius Bledsoe, Paul Robeson, James Weldon Johnson,

Carl Van Vechten, and George Gershwin. Their legendary dinner parties and cocktail gatherings became sought-after invitations. He often moved behind the scenes, bringing together authors and publishers, nudging one or the other toward each other, making invaluable connections and careers.

Julius Bledsoe was a Columbia medical student when he lived as a boarder at 90 Edgecombe. But his natural talents as a singer led to a starring role on Broadway in 1927 as Joe in the Hammerstein and Kern musical *Showboat*. That same year, he became one of the first Black tenants at Colonial Parkway Apartments at 409 Edgecombe Avenue. Walter White, W. E. B. Du Bois, Thurgood Marshall, and a host of other famous Harlemites would take up residence at 409 as well, sealing its reputation as the home of the period's luminaries.

Howard University student Zora Neale Hurston arrived in New York City the year after the Civic Club Banquet. Like many new writers to the city, she found her way to 580 St. Nicholas and slept on Regina and Ethel's couch. The National Urban League's *Opportunity Magazine* hosted an awards banquet on May 1, 1925, at the Fifth Avenue Restaurant. By that year, the magazine had 10,000 subscriptions. Hurston won second prize for short story and playwriting. She and Langston Hughes met there for the first time, striking up an immediate friendship. Among the prestigious judges that Charles Johnson was able to line up was the Pulitzer Prize–winning playwright Eugene O'Neill, who would win a second Pulitzer a few years later and the Nobel Prize the following decade. O'Neill had made the Black experience the subject of a few of his theatrical works.

Hurston had a gregarious and outspoken personality that would both shock and charm people, including several influential guests at the dinner who were impressed with her. Annie Nathan Meyer, founder of Barnard College, pledged to get Hurston a scholarship at the Columbia University affiliate. Zora also caught the attention of the prolific novelist and short story writer Fannie Hurst, another of the contest judges.

It was a night to remember, as Hughes recalled, highlighted by James Weldon Johnson reading his winning poem "The Weary Blues" to the assembled guests. At the end of the evening, Carl Van Vechten congratulated Langston on his award. Hughes had been introduced to him at an NAACP benefit party in Harlem. Van Vechten asked whether the young poet had enough poems to fill a book. Hughes sent him a large batch of his poetry, which would become his first published poetry collection in 1926 by Knopf, named *The Weary Blues*. Langston Hughes is the wordsmith who would eventually live in Harlem the longest, until his death, and become its laureate.

Regina and Ethel Ray hosted a breakfast party for Langston. The iconic photo they took on their apartment building rooftop shows the gifted young artists and brilliant scholars who were the anchors of the Harlem Renaissance, the very foundation of this unique period. Some associations would last lifetimes. Others would gradually go the way of a feather in the wind, and many would end abruptly with harsh words and hurt feelings.

One wonders if they had a full grasp of the legacy they were creating. Some of them would certainly have understood that they were part of an important societal change for the Black race. What they exhibited was a sense of belonging, sophistication, joy, confidence, and poise. It was a sense that they knew they had arrived at a new place in history.

Hubert Thomas Delany, who was among those pictured, would become one of New York City's first appointed African American judges. He would also live on 144th Street, one of Sugar Hill's most historic streets among the homes built by De Forest and Mowbray, a mere glance from where the Grange once stood. Delany, who came from North Carolina, was the son of Bishop Henry T. Delany, a former slave and prominent Episcopal cleric, and Nanny J. Delany, an instructor at St. Augustine's College. He graduated from City College in 1923 and from New York University School of

Figure 50. BACK ROW (Left to Right): Ethel Ray (Nance), Langston Hughes, Helen Lanning, Pearl Fisher, Rudolph Fisher, Luella Tucker, Clarissa Scott, and Hubert Delany. FRONT ROW: Regina Anderson (Andrews), Esther Popel, Jessie Fauset, Marie Johnson, and E. Franklin Frazier. Courtesy New York Public Library

Figure 51. Left to Right: Langston Hughes, Charles S. Johnson, E. Franklin Frazier, Rudolph Fisher, and Hubert Delany (City College on Convent Avenue in background). Courtesy New York Public Library

Law in 1926, the same year he married Clarissa M. Scott, one of the writers of the period. Hubert's sisters, Sadie and Bessie Delany, would become famous in their own right for their 1993 best-selling book and subsequent Broadway play *Having Our Say: The Delany Sisters' First 100 Years*.

E. Franklin Frazier, also pictured, would become one of the twentieth century's most prominent African American sociologists. After graduating from Howard University with honors in 1916, Frazier taught at several educational institutions, including the Tuskegee Institute in Alabama. He received a master's degree from Clark University in Worcester, Mass. A student at the New York School of Social Work, which later became the Columbia University School of Social Work, Frazier would matriculate and receive his doctorate from the University of Chicago.

He made history as the first Black president of the American Sociological Association, and wrote publicly that racism was akin to insanity, which contributed to his dismissal as director of the Social Work Department at Atlanta University (later Clark Atlanta). His seminal work was the 1957 book *Black Bourgeoisie*, a critical look at the Black middle class. Some felt it pointed directly at the elitist attitudes in Sugar Hill society.

The photograph included Charles Johnson, whose role during the Harlem Renaissance and as editor of *Opportunity* cemented his place in Black history. In 1928 Johnson left New York to work at Fisk University in Nashville, Tennessee, one of the nation's leading HBCUs. There he became the first chairman of the university's new Department of Social Sciences and, in 1946, the university's first Black president.

All these people photographed that morning on the roof of 580 St. Nicholas Avenue represented history, both current and in the making.

Langston Hughes returned to D.C. after the awards dinner. A few months later in December 1925, while working as a busboy at the Wardman Park Hotel, he met the well-known poet Vachel Lindsay. Hughes cleverly managed to put copies of some of his poems on Lindsay's dining table, a bold move that paid off. The next day a newspaper article described Lindsay's discovery of a "bus boy poet," and reporters and photographers descended on the hotel to interview Hughes. Lindsay was so impressed with Hughes' poetry that he left him a handwritten letter of encouragement and a set of poetry books.

The criticism of the Black middle and upper classes had been voiced early on by poet Claude McKay. Other writers and politicians would echo the same complaint that too many prominent Black people were trying to imitate a white lifestyle. It hit home especially in Sugar Hill, where attitudes of superiority over their brethren in other parts of Harlem were not far from the surface, nor were distinctions of skin color.

Just as the Renaissance itself lasted little more than a decade, the literary salons at 580 St. Nicholas Avenue would last for only two pivotal years. Yet the gatherings made history and proved to be a source of inspiration and encouragement to major artists early in their careers.

Regina Anderson married William Andrews on April 10, 1926. The *New York Amsterdam News* covered the wedding, which took place at Jessie Fauset's apartment at 1945 Seventh Avenue, off 117th Street. It was the building where Bill also lived and where the couple made their initial home. Though the literary salons that Regina and Ethel had hosted ended, others thrived. Regina was a librarian and a playwright and stayed active in the theater world. She began to archive Black history achievements, documenting milestones in all fields. Her extensive collection would become an invaluable repository of historical facts.

True to her word, Annie Nathan Meyer raised money for Zora's scholarship, making her the first African American student at Barnard in 1926 when she transferred from Howard University. Race relations were such at the time that she could not board in campus housing. Zora needed a job with flexible hours so she could study and afford a place to live. Fannie Hurst, whom Zora had met at the awards banquet, hired her as a live-in personal secretary and chauffeur; the arrangement also developed into a friendship. The dean later organized a student loan fund for Zora so she could afford her own apartment.

In the world of college admissions, men dominated the enrollment, with many institutions adhering to a strict "no females allowed" policy. The formation in the nineteenth century of colleges just for women was a powerful statement. Many young women aspired to go to one of a prestigious group of historically all-women's colleges, the female Ivy League of sorts. The consortium gradually increased to seven from the original four. The primary goal was to join efforts in building a shared endowment fund. In 1926, the year Zora enrolled at Barnard, they were nicknamed the Seven Sisters, supposedly after the Pleiades, the seven sisters from Greek mythology. The schools were Barnard (part of Columbia), Bryn Mawr, Mount Holyoke, Radcliffe (to become part of Harvard), Smith, Vassar, and Wellesley.

Serendipity may not adequately describe the happy accident that occurred in downtown Mobile, Alabama, on St. Joseph Street on July 23, 1927. The stars aligned to bring together Jessie Fauset, Langston Hughes, and Zora Neale Hurston, culminating with a visit to Tuskegee University, one of the most respected of the Historically Black Colleges and Universities. Hurston and Hughes had originally met at the *Opportunity Magazine* Awards Dinner in New York two years before. They were both young and still early in their careers. Fauset, of course, was the woman who had first published Hughes in the *Crisis*.

Hughes wrote in his autobiography *The Big Sea* that he had barely gotten off the train from New Orleans when he ran into Zora, walking down the main street. Neither knew that they were traveling to the same place and marveled at finding each other.

Yuval Taylor wrote that "Hurston was in Mobile to interview Cudjo Lewis, a former slave born in Africa, and then planned to make her way back north, doing folklore research along the way."[33] Oluale Kossola (Cudjo Lewis) was one of the last known survivors of the slave ship Clotilda, which arrived in Mobile, Alabama, in 1860, decades after the U.S. had banned the international slave trade. Hurston was an investigator for the Association for the Study of Negro Life and History, an organization that would thrive into the twenty-first century. She chronicled his life story first in an article that later became the book *Barracoon*, a jumping point for her life's passion of cultural anthropology.

Hughes had been touring the region, trying to earn a little money from making public appearances and doing readings. Hurston invited him to join her expedition, and Hughes happily accepted. The next day, on July 24, Zora and Langston arrived at Tuskegee, Alabama, and ran into Jessie Fauset, who happened to be visiting the university. This chance meeting brought together three key figures of the Harlem Renaissance, people closely intertwined in New York and Sugar Hill.

Of the photographs taken on the trip, the one following (Figure 52) shows the three of them standing at the center of Tuskegee's campus in front of Charles Keck's statue "Lifting the Veil of Ignorance." Booker T. Washington is depicted uncloaking a newly freed slave.

Zora Neale Hurston graduated from Barnard in 1928 with a degree in anthropology, and her time at the college could not have been easy. That same year she wrote an essay titled, "How It Feels to Be Colored Me," an examination of many issues on race and her sense of self.

In it, she shared about her time at Barnard that "beside the waters of the Hudson, I feel my race. Among the thousand white persons, I am a dark rock surged upon, overswept by a creamy sea. I am surged upon and overswept. . . ." Yet of being around her own people she also wrote that "at certain times I have no race, I am me. When I set my hat at a certain angle and saunter down Seventh Avenue, Harlem City, feeling as snooty as the lions in front of the Forty Second Street Library, for instance. The cosmic

Figure 52. Jessie Redmon Fauset, Langston Hughes, Zora Neale Hurston at Tuskegee, 1927. Courtesy Langston Hughes Papers; James Weldon Johnson Collection: Yale Collection of American Literature, Beinecke Rare Book and Manuscript Library; Harold Ober Associates and the Estate of Langston Hughes

Zora emerges. I belong to no race nor time. I am the eternal feminine with its string of beads."

In 1933, Zora's early patron Fannie Hurst would write one of her most famous and seminal books, *Imitation of Life*, a poignant story about a Black woman who chooses a life passing as white and her shameful dismissal of her dark-skinned mother. The book would be made into two successful film versions: 1934 with Claudette Colbert, Louise Beavers, and Fredi Washington and the 1959 remake with Lana Turner, Sandra Dee, and Juanita Moore.

Fredi Washington (born Fredericka Carolyn Washington) began her career as a Cotton Club dancer during the 1920s. She was friends with A'Lelia Walker and frequently attended parties at Walker's Edgecombe Avenue apartment in Sugar Hill. Fredi had appeared in a 1929 short film, *Black and Tan*, with Duke Ellington and his orchestra and starred with Paul Robeson in the 1933 film *The Emperor Jones*, based on Eugene O'Neill's 1920 hit play. Fredi's most famous role, though, as the mixed-race daughter passing for white in *Imitation of Life*, was ironic because she was often subject to a form of reverse racism. Her very light skin drew criticism from many Black people in a colorism period when she was deemed not Black enough. But much like Walter White, she always embraced her heritage, identifying as a Black woman, with no attempts to pass for white. She was a civil rights activist, involved with the NAACP and one of the founding members of the Negro Actors Guild of America.

The Harlem Renaissance was in many respects a complicated period, with many of the young Black artists often at the beck and call of white patrons. It was also a time when royalty, movie matinee idols, struggling poets, civil rights legends, and elevator operators might mingle in the same room. As Langston Hughes wrote, it was not uncommon that a "colored chorus girl, amber enough to pass for a Latin American, was living in a penthouse with all her bills paid by a gentleman whose name was banker's magic on Wall Street. . . . It was the period when the Negro was in vogue."[34] It was this brief time where, at almost any upper-crust gathering in Harlem, one could name-drop easily about who was in attendance. The poet shared that if one mentioned that you had been speaking to "George," people knew you meant George Gershwin.

Some years after the Harlem Renaissance was over, in an article titled "The Two Harlems," one of its favorite sons, the writer Arna Bontemps, would describe some of what made the period so special. Bontemps wrote about the feeling of being in Harlem, among one's own people. One could argue that the real subject of "The Two Harlems" was that there existed two entirely different communities: one white and one Black.

There was the white Harlem, which, like the rest of New York, had emerged from the pastoral woodlands into a growing urban neighborhood. The second Harlem, which blossomed during and after the Great Migration, became the nation's largest Black community, a mecca for people of color around the country. Prosperous Black communities in places like Rosewood, Florida, and Tulsa, Oklahoma, had been looted and burned to the ground. Black people had been slaughtered by white mobs. That this thriving Black community in New York City had emerged, thrived, and expanded despite all attempts to keep Black people out of the grand apartment buildings and stunning brownstones, made it a place known around the country and the world.

Thousands of white people began to flock to this second Harlem, pouring money into the nightclubs, dance halls, bars, and civic groups. Harlem and Negroes were suddenly fashionable. White people wanted to take some part in African American life to know they had helped elevate them, slept with them, partied with them, or at least gotten close enough to stare at them.

In creating this space and place, the artists of the Harlem Renaissance helped inspire subsequent generations of writers. Nella Larsen, Zora Neale Hurston, Langston Hughes, Claude McKay, Countee Cullen, and Ann Petry would lay the groundwork for Ralph Ellison, Richard Wright, Lorraine Hansberry, Nikki Giovanni, James Baldwin, Maya Angelou, Alice Walker, Toni Morrison, Samm-Art Williams, Alex Hailey, Audre Lorde, and eventually Ta-Nehisi Coates, Colson Whitehead, and Isabel Wilkerson, to name but a few.

It was the sheer size of the African American presence in Harlem that made the neighborhood a celebrated destination. As Bontemps wrote in describing his arrival in Harlem in the autumn of 1924, it was also a foretaste of paradise:

> A blue haze descended at night and with it strings of fairy lights on the broad avenues. . . . I looked over the rooftops of Negrodom and tried to believe my eyes. What a city! What a world! And what a year for a colored boy to be leaving home the first time! . . . The first danger I recognized that fall, however, was that Harlem would be too wonderful for words. Unless I was careful, I would be thrilled into silence.[35]

Bontemps committed to paper in the article what countless Black people were feeling: the possibilities of what could be achieved in this beautiful haven of Black humanity and culture. He soon realized that he was one of many who were coming to Harlem with the same thoughts and intentions. He realized that the artists among them had begun to recognize themselves "as a group and to become a little self-conscious about our significance." At the same time, he recognized that to many of the white philanthropists and others who hung out in Harlem, African Americans were, as he put it, "shown off and exhibited and presented in scores of places, to all kinds of people."

"And," he added, "we heard their sighs of wonder, amazement, sometimes admiration when it was whispered or announced that here was one of the New Negroes."[36]

Langston Hughes and many of the writers of the period flitted from one party to the next, from one swank Sugar Hill residence to another, there to be guests of honor at events hosted by both the Black elite and white philanthropists and voyeurs. But they knew they were on display and that any kind of renaissance that was taking place in Harlem was likely unknown to most of the people who lived there. The average Harlem resident was not hanging out at bars and nightclubs or even reading about what was going on in the *Amsterdam News*. They were just trying to survive.

No one can say exactly when the Harlem Renaissance ended, although it was certainly around the mid-1930s. The lingering effects of the 1929 stock market crash and the Great Depression that followed dampened the party atmosphere and the philanthropy of the twenties. By 1934 or 1935 the magic was all but gone. With the Depression, people moving away or turning to other careers, and some dying, it faded away rather than coming to an abrupt halt.

Black writers had in the previous years continued to win recognition for their work. In the late 1920s "Nella Larsen wrote two well-received novels—*Quicksand*, the story of a Black girl set in the South, and *Passing*, the story of Blacks who "passed" as whites."[37] The two novels came back-to-back in 1928 and 1929, respectively. In 1930 she was awarded a Guggenheim Fellowship, the first African American woman to be so honored. Larsen's writing has been recognized as a critical lens into the complexity of Black identity and life, and *Passing* would be made into a film almost a century after its publication.

Zora and Langston had begun work on a play together called "Mule Bone." They had a falling out when Langston discovered she was attempting to produce the play with the Gilpin Players in Cleveland and had not given him author credit. He considered it a work in progress, but it caused a bitter rift, and they never reconciled, nor was it produced.

While Langston Hughes was studying at Lincoln University in the late 1920s, he had begun work on his first novel, *Not without Laughter*, which was published in 1930. During this same time, he met and befriended a couple named Joel and Amy Spingarn. Not only did he spend time at the Spingarns' country estate, but also in Hamilton Heights at their apartment at 634 St. Nicholas Avenue, in the next block from where he had attended the salons at Regina Anderson's place. In 1931 he received the Harmon Gold Award for Literature, which came with a $400 prize. George Edmund Haynes, who had helped establish the awards, sent the letter of announcement to Hughes at the Spingarns' St. Nicholas address.

Langston was still smarting over the dispute with Zora and her willingness to dismiss both their friendship and his contribution to the play they coauthored. He wired Alain Locke to help intervene. Locke responded that Hughes had the Harmon Award, so he didn't know what more he could want.

To some, "the publication at the beginning of 1932 of Thurman's last novel, *Infants of the Spring*, had already announced the end of the Harlem Renaissance."[38] What is generally considered the last great novel of this period was Zora Neale Hurston's *Jonah's Gourd Vine*, published in 1934. Two other authors of the era, Walter Thurman and Rudolph Fisher, died later that same year.

Jessie Fauset's brother, Arthur, may have offered the most succinct explanation of why the Harlem Renaissance ended as soon as it did. In 1934 he wrote in *Opportunity* that the entire movement had left the race unprepared because it was unrealistic in its expectations that "social and economic recognition will be inevitable when once the race has produced a sufficiently large number of persons who have properly qualified themselves in the arts."[39] That was clearly not the case in the 1930s, nor would it be for many decades.

Chapter 10

The Heights Identity and the Black Mecca

> History is a relentless master. It has no present, only the past rushing into the future. To try to hold fast is to be swept aside.
>
> —John F. Kennedy

Entertainment in Harlem did not have a dividing line. For all the elitism of which people in Sugar Hill were often accused, they still frequented all the popular nightclubs and dance halls in Central Harlem. The Lafayette, the Savoy, Wells, Small's, and the Cotton Club (once it was no longer segregated) were an evening out for residents of the Heights as well.

In 1933, when newly elected mayor Fiorello La Guardia railed against burlesque, his attack sounded the death knell for a form of entertainment that was already on its last legs. Hurtig & Seamons on West 125th Street was one of many theaters compelled to stop presenting burlesque shows, and the building was sold in 1933. The rich history of its earlier years, when famed acts like George Jessel and Fanny Brice performed, was about to be overshadowed by its new life. After a lavish remodeling, it reopened on January 26, 1934, under the management of Morris Sussman as the Apollo Theater. Management capitalized on the neighborhood's increasingly Black population, and the theater sought to attract local African Americans who had been banned from the premises just a few years earlier. From 1934 on, the Apollo became a legendary venue for Black entertainment and the many artists discovered there. Yet just like Buddy Holly's performance there in 1957, decades later appearing at the famed

Apollo would become a badge of honor for any artist, regardless of race or stature in the music industry.

There was a world of social distance between those who lived in the overcrowded tenements and overpriced rooming houses in Central Harlem around Lenox, Seventh, and Eighth avenues and the residences in Hamilton Heights to the northwest that sometimes took on mythical charm.

"Sugar Hill," *Ebony* magazine wrote in 1946, "the green bluff . . . is so high that all Harlem looks up to it, and would rather live in its canopied apartments than any place in America."[1] Living there was representative of the "sweet life." There were a few explanations as to why the area was called Sugar Hill: rents were higher, being on a hill meant that there were great views, there was less crime, and the neighborhood was home to grand apartment buildings and mansions that were increasingly populated by many famous and influential people. Perhaps most importantly, Sugar Hill was a sign that you had arrived and were enjoying a better kind of life.

In December 1931, a musical comedy titled *Sugar Hill* opened on Broadway and represented the neighborhood said to be the cafe au lait of the Harlem residential district. It ran for just one week.

Portions of Sugar Hill continued to open up to Black families, though some holdout apartment buildings would endure as whites-only into the late 1930s. The Garrison apartment building at 435 Convent Avenue at 149th Street was built in 1910 and designed by Neville & Bagge. The six-story, twenty-nine-unit structure was originally called Elmsworth Hall. In 1929, the building was renamed the Garrison and converted into co-ops by a Black businessman named Samuel J. Cottman, who bought it for $204,000.

The Garrison is one of the city's oldest cooperatives and is considered to be the first in Harlem. Garrison lived there until his death in 1941, and his widow remained for two more decades. Residents of the building included Henry Craft Kempton, the executive secretary of the YMCA, Adam Clayton Powell Sr., minister of the Abyssinian Baptist Church, and later his son, the future Congressman Adam Clayton Powell Jr.

In 1931, when George and Elizabeth Haynes bought the three-story townhouse at 411 Convent Avenue at 147th Street, they were settling on a picturesque, historic street lined with trees, brownstones, limestone rowhouses like theirs, a Black-owned co-op apartment building, mansions, Hamilton Grange, and City College. Their house had been designed by New York architect Henri Fouchaux, who was responsible for dozens of distinctive turn-of-the-century townhouses in Sugar Hill. One of his important buildings was the Institution for the Instruction of the Deaf and Dumb on Riverside Drive at 163rd Street. Fouchaux also built several brownstones and factory buildings throughout the city.

The Hayneses' home, built in 1901, was one of five Renaissance Revival townhouses on Convent Avenue. Almost all the townhouses in the neighborhood share the common design of three stories and a basement or "garden apartment" that opens to a small rear courtyard. For owners who kept the buildings as private dwellings, this patio was their only bit of the outdoors: a coveted patch of green. Others would rent the basement space or keep it for servants or guests. In those early, heady days of the neighborhood transforming itself into the home of wealthy African Americans, many families had live-in servants.

Bruce Haynes would grow up in the Convent Avenue house when his father, George Haynes Jr., took possession of it. In his memoir *Down the Up Staircase*, Bruce would write about his grandparents' house, noting that "the entryways to each room were built of thick mahogany. Tiled fireplaces with five-foot-tall mahogany mantelpieces and built-in mirrors graced each room on the first floor, where visitors were entertained."[2] Haynes would fondly remember the double doors, brass doorknobs, and hand-waxed oak floors in an impressive house that boasted a formal parlor, a music room with a baby grand piano, and a dining room framed by six-foot-high wood panels.

On the second floor was an expansive master bedroom and a sitting area, separated by sliding pocket doors. "Connecting the two rooms," the grandson recalled, "was an arched dressing area of dark red oak with his-and-hers mirrored closets and a six-foot-wide marble washbasin encased in wood and flanked by beveled glass medicine cabinets."[3]

George Edmund Haynes, the respected sociologist and cofounder of the National Urban League, would be visited often by his friend and mentor W. E. B. Du Bois, who lived close by. One wonders what conversations must have taken place here: discussions of literature, politics, and social welfare struggles. Haynes was still managing the Harmon Awards that had been issued to many artists of the Harlem Renaissance.

A short distance away, 555 Edgecombe Avenue, the thirteen-story Roger Morris Apartments adjacent to the Morris-Jumel Mansion, was becoming integrated. Most residents were middle-class families whose names would fade into oblivion. But for decades to come this building, nicknamed the triple nickel, became famous for the number of musicians and actors who would live there.

"In 1939 the building's owner, Albert Schwarzler, apparently refused to renew the leases of the building's white tenants, many of whom had lived there for years. Given the changing nature of the neighborhood, Schwarzler saw that his economic future lay with renting to Black tenants."[4]

Celebrated residents included Kenneth and Mamie Clark, Howard graduates who were the first African Americans to earn doctorates in psychology from Columbia University. Dr. Kenneth Clark accomplished three noteworthy firsts for an African American: becoming a tenured professor at City College and president of the American Psychological Association and being named to the New York State Board of Regents, the state's educational watchdog agency.

His wife, Mamie Phipps Clark, was also credited with major accomplishments in the field of civil rights and psychology. After working with children in an all-Black nursery school, she undertook a research study to determine how children self-identify racially. This study became the subject of her master's thesis, titled "The Development of Consciousness of Self and the Emergence of Racial Identification in Negro Pre-School Children." It was published in 1939 in the *Journal of Social Psychology* under the joint auspices of the Departments of Psychology of Columbia and Howard Universities. The work led to the famous "doll test." Given a choice, Clark's research showed, Black children chose the white doll over the black one, saying the black doll was bad. Demonstrating this, she showed that children's awareness of racial differences in their preferences for the white dolls showed how segregation negatively affects the development of Black children. This research and testimony were a critical piece of evidence presented to the United States Supreme Court during the arguments of Brown vs. Board of Education and was cited in the court's decision.

Other notable residents of 555 Edgecombe included Paul Robeson, the singer, actor, and civil rights activist best remembered for his memorable rendition of the song "Ol' Man River" in the 1936 film *Showboat*, and his wife, the anthropologist Eslanda Goode Robeson.

In addition, the building was home to world heavyweight champion Joe Louis and his wife, Rose Morgan, creator of Rose Morgan House of Beauty, which became the world's biggest African American beauty parlor. The roster of residents also included Andy Kirk, a bass sax player who led one of the hottest swing bands of the 1930s and 1940s, Andy Kirk and His Twelve Clouds of Joy; Bessie Buchanan, the first African American woman member of the New York State Assembly; and the musicians Coleman Hawkins, Johnnie Hodges, and most memorably Count Basie.

Not long after the Roger Morris building became integrated, it also became Black-owned when it was bought by the colorful evangelist "Daddy Grace," who founded the United House of Prayer for all People. Born Marcelino Manuel da Graça in the Cape Verde Islands, he became known as Charles Manuel "Sweet Daddy" Grace, or just Daddy Grace. The church had extensive real estate holdings throughout the country and internationally, as did Grace personally. In 1953 Grace also purchased the Eldorado, an iconic twin-towered apartment complex at 300 Central Park West off 90th Street overlooking the park. In future decades it would become known for its famous tenants, among them Bruce Willis, Faye Dunaway, Garrison Keillor, Sinclair Lewis, Marilyn Monroe, and Groucho Marx.

After the color barrier was broken in the late 1920s, 409 Edgecombe Avenue, the neo-Renaissance building constructed in 1916, just a few blocks from 555, also became the home of a growing number of distinguished African Americans. The two buildings became such signature addresses in Sugar Hill that each came to be referred to just by the building numbers, and "409" or "555" was all one needed to say.

Figure 53. 409 Edgecombe Avenue. Lower left corner going clockwise: W. E. B. Du Bois, Aaron Douglas, Thurgood Marshall, William Stanley Braithwaite, Billy Strayhorn, Jimmie Lunceford, Mercer Ellington, Roy Wilkins, and Walter White; NYC Landmarks Preservation Commission Facebook page

In 1929 the civil rights leader Walter White and his wife, Gladys, moved from their apartment at 90 Edgecombe Avenue into 409, and they remained there for nearly two decades. White was the executive secretary of the NAACP from 1931 until his death in 1955. There was a constant flow of important people from the world of business, politics, and entertainment who socialized regularly at the couple's apartment. White and his wife, Gladys Leah Powell, had two children, Jane and Walter Jr. Their apartment was nicknamed "The White House of Harlem" because of the prominent people they entertained. Walter White resided there until 1947, when he and Gladys divorced. His ex-wife and daughter continued to live at 409 Edgecombe until 1961.

New York State Assemblyman William T. Andrews and his wife, librarian Regina Anderson Andrews, lived in the building from 1947 until the 1960s before retiring permanently to their country house in Lake Mahopac, which they had owned as a weekend retreat since the 1940s.

Among other well-known residents were "Dr. May Edward Chinn, the first Black female intern at Harlem Hospital and for years Harlem's only Black female physician. The daughter of an escaped slave from Virginia and a Chickahominy Indian, Dr. Chinn lived at 409 from 1942 to 1957 and also had a medical office in the building."[5]

Saxophonist Jimmie Lunceford's orchestra was highly praised as a perfect swing band, and they were stiff competition for Duke Ellington, Count Basie, and Benny Goodman. He replaced Cab Calloway as the Cotton Club's house band in 1934. His band leadership came to be known as the "Lunceford Style" and influenced future bandleaders and arrangers like Tommy Dorsey. Lunceford resided at 409 from 1936 until 1942.

W. E. B. Du Bois also lived in the building from 1945 to 1950.

And the list goes on. Eunice Hunton Carter, who lived at 409 for most of the 1940s, was one of New York State's first African American judges. She was "only the second woman in the history of Smith College to receive a bachelor's and a master's degree in four years. She then went on to earn a law degree from Fordham School of Law and started her own practice."[6] Mayor Fiorello La Guardia appointed her to the Commission on Conditions in Harlem after the 1935 riots, and Special Prosecutor Thomas E. Dewey later hired her to be his assistant in a prominent mob prosecution case. "She was the only African American and only woman on the ten-member staff and was instrumental in the successful prosecution of Lucky Luciano, where she earned the title 'Lady Racketbuster.'"[7]

Aaron Douglas, the painter and graphic artist who was among the Harlem Renaissance artists of the 1920s, moved from Strivers' Row in 1932 to 409. Roy Wilkins, who for more than two decades headed the NAACP, moved into 409 with his wife, Aminda (Minnie) Badeau, in 1936.

Also in residence was Thurgood Marshall, the first African American U.S. Supreme Court Justice and one of the attorneys who successfully argued the case of Brown v. Board of Education in 1954, legally ending school segregation. It was one of twenty-nine successful cases he argued before the Supreme Court. "Marshall maintained a residence at 409 Edgecombe Avenue from about 1940 until 1957. Marshall was married to the former Vivian Burey from 1929 until her death in 1955. He married Cecilia Suyat shortly thereafter, with whom he had two sons."[8]

Many of these historic people developed close friendships and often moved between homes for dinners or parties in an unprecedented accumulation of talent and brain power in one building.

It is ironic that both 409 and 555 Edgecombe Avenue, where whites fought so hard to keep African Americans out, became owned by African Americans. In the 1930s, the West Indian native Augustine Austin had bought 409 Edgecombe Avenue. Considering that Austin had arrived in New York penniless, this was an extraordinary feat.

In 1932, a controversial figure arrived in Harlem. She was in equal parts voyeur, philanthropist, narcissist, and lover of Black men, if not Black people. Nancy Cunard made waves in Harlem and in Sugar Hill. The extremely wealthy English shipping line heiress was very verbal about her feelings that she found the notable "talented tenth" that W. E. B. Du Bois had promoted as narrow and feudal. Historian David Levering Lewis shares in his book *When Harlem Was in Vogue* that since "the Hotel Theresa had not yet dropped its ban on Afro-Americans, Cunard raised headlines and 'respectable' eyebrows in May 1932 by renting a two-room suite in a St. Nicholas Avenue hotel favored by musicians, writers, and even more questionable lodgers."[9] This may have been the Dawn Hotel at 149th and St. Nicholas, a block from the Bailey Mansion.

Cunard had already scandalized her mother and polite British society by writing a pamphlet titled "Black Man and White Ladyship." She had been having an affair with jazz pianist Henry Crowder and came to Harlem to see her lover's people firsthand. She arrived with pushy requests that the noted writers of the Harlem Renaissance contribute to an anthology she was putting together titled, "Negro." Some objected to her outrageous persona. "McKay and Eric Walrond refused to contribute unless paid, and Toomer advised everyone that he had put the issue of any Negro ancestry behind him."[10] Toomer had decided that he was simply no longer of the Negro race. It was definitely in defiance of that pesky "one-drop rule" that racists proclaimed as resolute that even one drop of Negro blood, no matter your skin color, made you a Negro.

Cunard no doubt embarrassed some of the Black intelligentsia because she was painfully honest about Harlem's snobbery around skin color. It was one of those open secrets that Black people preferred not to acknowledge, except in select company with each other: this bias within the Black race of light skin over dark. It had been drilled into African Americans as a kind of brainwashing from slavery times when the darker "field Negroes" were seen as inferior to the "light-skinned" house servants, a warped painful legacy that had lingered in many circles. Additionally, "her low opinion of the NAACP and the Renaissance was no secret. Despite various protestations, many of the writers responded and in the end Sterling Brown, Du Bois, Frazier, Locke, Schomburg, and White, among others" had contributed to the piece.[11]

There are so many stories of exceptional people who lived in Hamilton Heights and Sugar Hill that will go untold. While there was a fair share of the wealthy and upper-crust, many were just working people going about their business and raising their families in obscurity, like most people in the city. Many of these silent history-makers were instrumental in shaping Hamilton Heights, and they are worthy of their own books and tributes.

The thirty-seven-unit, six-story building at 400 Convent Avenue, directly opposite the Hayneses' limestone townhouse, was built in 1926. Many four- and five-story apartment buildings were still walk-ups. Some of the earlier buildings that were constructed had shared hallway bathrooms, so tenants did not have private bathrooms. This building boasted one-, two-, and three-bedroom layouts, an elevator, hardwood floors, full kitchens, separate dining rooms, French doors, and spacious living rooms with working gas fireplaces.

Figure 54 shows a street scene in 1948 with Black children playing on the corner at 147th Street. The building at 400 Convent Avenue also marks the approximate end of Alexander Hamilton's original property line, then overlapping to the former Bradhurst estate of his friend.

In the 1960s, the tenants' association would take over management of the building from a derelict landlord. Among its residents by the sixties would be a studio house musician who played drums in several Broadway shows, including "The Wiz" and "Hair," and a woman named Esther Brown who used her home as a private invitation-only boutique of sorts. There she displayed and sold the stunning African cloth, furniture, and clothing that she would import on her many trips to Africa in the 1960s and '70s when the "Black is beautiful" awakening sparked sojourns to the

Figure 54. 400 Convent Avenue, at 147th Street, 1948. Courtesy New York Public Library

motherland. Joe, the super, made mango wine in the rear courtyard. And on the third floor there lived a bartender of such renown that at one time he could demand what he wanted in salary as he moved from one famed Harlem nightclub to the next. The building would be converted into a co-op in the 1970s. Three decades later it would become part of the neighborhood's historic landmark designation.

Less than a mile away from the Hayneses' home the Morris-Jumel Mansion was now well established as the place "where Washington slept" and a popular tourist attraction for New Yorkers and visitors alike. Duke Ellington would refer to it as "the jewel in the crown of Sugar Hill," a quote that the museum would use in its promotional material well into the twenty-first century. Figure 55, taken in 1934, shows a striking contrast between the Morris-Jumel Mansion and the taller Roger Morris Apartments at 555 Edgecombe Avenue.

Figure 55. Morris-Jumel Mansion (white house), 1934. Courtesy of NYC Dept. of Parks & Recreation

The mansion also held particular symbolism for the actor, singer, and activist Paul Robeson, who lived at 555, a building that would one day bear his name. From his apartment Robeson mused about the connection between his ancestors and the founding of America.

"I am an American," he wrote. "From my window I gaze out upon a scene that reminds me how deep-going are the roots of my people in this land. Across the street, carefully preserved as an historic shrine, is a colonial mansion that served as a headquarters for General George Washington in 1776."[12]

Robeson recalled how at Valley Forge, his great-great grandfather Cyrus Bustill, a former slave who had purchased his freedom, became a baker. Washington reportedly thanked him for supplying bread to the starving Revolutionary Army. For the people who lived near the Morris-Jumel Mansion, it was meaningful that the building was part of Sugar Hill and the history of the Revolutionary War.

Figure 56 was taken from inside the mansion during this same period in the 1930s is most likely from the widow's walk. It shows a clear view of the Polo Grounds and a small sliver of 555 Edgecombe to the right.

In 1931, the same year the George Washington Bridge opened, there was only one house left on the Audubon property, the main family home, which still sat at its original site. Riverside Drive had been developed in front and in back of it with roads, a retaining wall to its rear, and apartment buildings surrounding the old house. The property was condemned in the mid-1920s, and the house was scheduled for demolition. Individuals

Figure 56. Polo Grounds from Morris-Jumel Mansion. Courtesy of NYC Dept. of Parks & Recreation

and community groups had been trying to save the Audubon house for more than a decade, to no avail. In November of 1931 workmen began dismantling the Mansard roof and bay window. An ornithologist named Harold W. Decker offered to pay to move the house to a site at Riverside Drive and 161st Street that had been donated by the city and to work with the Audubon Society to restore the house as a museum.

By December, the house had been cut into pieces and moved to the new location. "In the midst of fundraising efforts, the house suddenly disappeared. Most people believed that it had been lost to looters, the elements and general decay."[13]

And as the Audubon Park New York Society noted eloquently in describing Audubon's original estate, "Gone are the ancient elms and oaks that towered above dogwood and tulip trees on the hillside . . . the streams that flowed through ponds and over a waterfall before joining the river, the enclosures where deer and elk mingled."[14]

It is not a description, taken on its own, that anyone would imagine described New York City, Harlem and its heights included. Yet it is because of those paved sidewalks and smooth streets that progress is made and a city's infrastructure develops. Modernity often comes at the cost of the treasured structures of past eras.

The magnificent buildings that make up the Audubon Terrace Museum

Figure 57. Audubon House, circa 1920s. Milstein Division of U.S. History, Local History, & Genealogy, NYPL, Astor, Lenox, and Tilden Foundations

Complex are a lasting memory, in name, of Audubon's former Harlem property. There are people who have lived in the heights for generations who do not know the history of Audubon as an artist and naturalist or that the stately complex and parts of Trinity Cemetery were his former lands. The same would be true of the Audubon Ballroom, where people would dine and attend social events, weddings, and parties without possibly knowing the bird man whose name it held. Yet there are active societies and civic groups throughout the country that keep his memory alive.

But impressive buildings, literary soirees, and famous residents were not the only reason for Hamilton Heights' renown. The area was a pivotal location for the education of the city's public schoolteachers. During the nineteenth century, with the expansion of New York's public school system and the waves of immigrants, the need for teachers was great. Several institutions were formed to train prospective teachers. And when the city's Department of Education was looking for a new location for a dedicated teachers' training school, a site was suggested around 135th Street between Convent Avenue and St. Nicholas Terrace. It was surrounded by

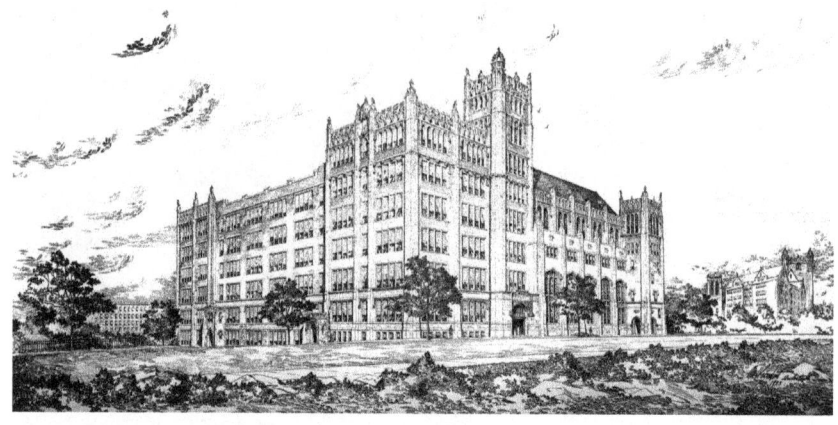

Figure 58. Teacher Training School. NYC Board of Education Archives; rendering, William H. Gompert (1923), Landmarks Preservation Commission

City College and Jasper Field, the Sacred Heart, and the Croton Aqueduct Gate House.

The New York Training School for Teachers was built between 1924 and 1926 at 443 West 135th Street. It was designed by William H. Gompert, who was both the architect and superintendent of School Buildings for the city's Board of Education. "In his nearly five years as school architect, Gompert was credited with overseeing the design and construction of some 170 new schools and additions, including DeWitt Clinton and Theodore Roosevelt High Schools in the Bronx."[15]

But this was a first of its kind: a building constructed exclusively as a training school for teachers as well as a model school for practice teaching. The five-story structure included a basement and tower designed in an abstract, Collegiate Gothic style. It opened on April 12, 1926, in an unassuming dedication in the auditorium on April 19th.

In 1930, its neighboring school City College admitted women for the first time, but only to graduate programs. It would be 1951 before the entire institution would finally become coeducational.

The name of the teaching school was changed to the New York Teachers Training College in 1931. So many things can change in such a short time, and the school was closed a few years later when it was determined that there was now a glut of teachers.

From 1936 to 1984 the imposing structure became the High School of Music & Art, established by Mayor La Guardia. Once again, the building made history, as it is believed to be one of the nation's first public high schools to specialize in the study of music, drama, and art.

The admissions procedure, which was based on competitive auditions and the evaluation of portfolios, was a novel idea at the time. The anticipated enrollment of 250 students eventually reached around 2,000 under the twenty-three-year tenure of its first principal, Benjamin Steigman. This stunning building marked a new high in educational opportunities for Harlem students, though it was open to young people throughout the city. And come they did.

The courses were planned with the hope that graduates would continue their education either at college or a conservatory of music but would leave the school first with an academic or general high school diploma. Students would study music theory and instrumental practice to offer ample opportunity for participation in chamber ensembles, orchestra, bands, and choral singing. The art courses included the study of drawing, painting, sculpture, etching, and the applied arts.

In 1935, the *New York Times* reported that "principals of elementary and junior high schools are now busily interviewing boys and girls of the 8th grade who have shown talent in music or the fine arts and who may wish to enter the city's new high school of music and arts."[16]

The article also indicated that in being the city's first school exclusively structured for gifted children, its primary goal was to encourage the artist in the students so that they could develop the richness of their personalities and talents.

"Another advantage is to develop a love for music and a love for art as well as proficiency in both these lines of expression so that music may be again established in the home and children and their parents will become more conscious of the advantage of having beautiful things in the home."[17] The students who achieved greatness in their fields of interest in the coming decades proved this new innovative model to be a success.

Though the land for another park in Harlem Heights was acquired in 1894, it did not open as a playground until 1911. The land was part of the original eighteenth-century Bradhurst family estate. With growing urbanization and green space quickly disappearing, its construction was part of a nationwide effort to ensure more organized play for city children. Originally called Colonial Park, it was bounded by 148th and 155th streets and Bradhurst and Edgecombe avenues. It was one of the first ten parks in the city to have a pool, which opened in 1936. By this time, Harlem had been a solidly Black community for some time. The park's architect

Figure 59. Youth Boxing Club, Colonial Park 1942. Courtesy of NYC Dept. of Parks & Recreation

was Aymar Embury II. The pool, along with an additional playground, basketball, volleyball courts, and roller-skating areas, was part of the Works Progress Administration. Over the next century, the park would undergo many transitions and become a true jewel of the neighborhood.

Ralph Ellison arrived in Manhattan in 1936. Born in Oklahoma in 1913, Ellison attended Tuskegee Institute in Alabama for three years before heading to New York. He was interested in sculpting and music and had hoped for a career as a classical musician. But after moving to New York, as he associated with other writers, he began to shift focus. He met Langston Hughes outside of the YMCA. A short time later he met Richard Wright, another new writer to the city, who encouraged him to consider writing full-time.

Ellison penned several essays and wrote descriptive letters to his family about life in New York, the beauty and excitement as well as the economic disparities. He found work interviewing people for the Federal Writers Project and eventually moved into a small apartment at 749 St. Nicholas Avenue, off 147th Street. It was there that he began to work on his novel *Invisible Man*.

Mississippi native Richard Wright, who had arrived in New York in 1937, just a year after Ralph Ellison, had been writing for the Federal Writers Project in Chicago. But people told him that he had a better chance of making a living as a writer in New York. His 1938 short story collection *Uncle Tom's Children* earned him a $500 prize from *Story* magazine and led to a Guggenheim Fellowship in 1939.

The stretch of St. Nicholas Avenue from 145th Street to 152nd was home to so many neighborhood bars and live jazz spots during the 1930s that there was no shortage of entertainment or places to just have a drink with familiar faces. Yet for some of the Sugar Hill elite, it was the proliferation of these night spots that was bringing down the neighborhood.

At 763 St. Nicholas Avenue there was a club called Jimmie's Chicken Shack. The chicken was good, but the music was better. It was so good that Charlie Parker washed dishes there just so he could listen to the performers. The great Art Tatum was a regular on the piano. In the early 1940s, Redd Foxx (born John Elroy Sanford), who was destined to forge his own path in comedy and TV, also washed dishes there. His coworker was a young man nicknamed Detroit Red (born Malcolm Little) who waited tables, purportedly living in a room upstairs. In the late 1950s, after a six-and-a-half-year stint in prison for larceny, the previous zoot-suit-wearing Detroit Red would emerge converted to the Muslim faith and change his name to Malcolm X.

Another bar lounge on the avenue was the Silver Dollar Café at No. 721, on the ground floor of the building that had been the Barnard School for Boys. A speakeasy during Prohibition, the place was renamed the 721 Club after Prohibition's repeal in 1933.

Starting in the 1930s, 773 St. Nicholas became the home of Sugar Hill's famous and most enduring basement jazz spot. It remained the neighborhood's favored club for almost eighty years, changing hands and names and morphing into a restaurant and homosexual safe place long before the gay rights movement. An article on the club that appeared in the *Amsterdam News* on October 19, 1935, bore the headline "Big Opening of Swank Poosepahtuck Club." It had taken its name from one of the thirteen tribes of Long Island.

By the 1930s, some 165,000 Black people were estimated to be living in Harlem, most in the area that would be called Central Harlem around Lenox, Seventh, and Eighth avenues from 110th Street to 155th. Conditions in some buildings and blocks were terrible. Rents had often been inflated beyond market price, which meant too many people sharing one apartment. It was the beginning of slum landlords in Harlem, as owners were slow to make repairs in the buildings.

Those conditions helped explain why people who could afford to live in Hamilton Heights were perceived as being of a higher class than those who lived in Central Harlem. Presumably, if you could afford the higher rents on the hill, you were of a different economic strata and social standing. But there were many stunning buildings in Central Harlem as well.

The residents of Hamilton Heights and Sugar Hill would sometimes call Central Harlem down the hill from them the Valley, which, as Isabel Wilkerson wrote in *The Warmth of Other Suns*, "accounted for most of what would be considered Harlem and was thought of as a perfectly respectable, even admirable place to live."[18] Yet the grand apartment houses built in the late 1800s and early 1900s in Hamilton Heights and Sugar Hill, rising straight up from Edgecombe Avenue, ascending Amsterdam and Broadway and then sloping down to Riverside Drive on the Hudson River, were the ones to which many aspired to live. Langston Hughes described the affluence of Sugar Hill in an essay in the *New Republic* in 1944. The cultural differences that exist in any neighborhood, no matter what race or ethnicity, certainly were apparent in Harlem. Hughes wrote:

> Don't take it for granted that all Harlem is a slum. It isn't. There are big apartment houses up on the hill, Sugar Hill, and up by City College, nice high-rent-houses with elevators and doormen, where Canada Lee lives, and W. C. Handy, and the George S. Schuylers, and the Walter Whites, where colored families send their babies to private kindergartens and their youngsters to Ethical Culture School.[19]

People were not trying to keep up with the Joneses, but rather with the Ellingtons and the Marshalls.

The arrival of huge numbers of African Americans in Harlem, and more specifically Sugar Hill, did not mean that whites disappeared from the neighborhood. While there may have been wholesale white flight from Central Harlem, the whites on the hill clung to those spacious apartments and brownstones much longer. Despite the many efforts made to keep African Americans from buying homes or renting apartments in the area, the barriers put in place continued to dissolve. Sugar Hill was a smaller part of Hamilton Heights, but the two names for the neighborhood were often used interchangeably, and where one began and the other ended varied according to whom you were speaking.

"Negro Harlem is situated in the heart of Manhattan and covers one of the most beautiful and healthful sites in the whole city," James Weldon Johnson wrote in his 1930 book *Black Manhattan*. "It is not a fringe, it is not a slum, nor is it a 'quarter' consisting of dilapidated tenements. It is a section of new-law apartment houses and handsome dwellings, with streets as well paved, as well lighted, and as well-kept as in any other part of the city."[20]

In 1938, William "Billy" Strayhorn was living in Pittsburgh when a friend took him backstage at the Stanley Theatre to meet Duke Ellington. Strayhorn played some of his music for Ellington, who promptly invited him to come to New York. The Duke scribbled down directions to his home, telling him to take the "A" train to where he lived in Sugar Hill in Harlem. Strayhorn's life changed that night. A month later, having followed Ellington's directions, he turned up and presented the famed band leader with the composition he had written: "Take the 'A' Train." Ellington hired Strayhorn immediately, and it became the band's theme song. In the decades to come, Strayhorn would write many of the band's hits.

In the 1930s, it was brave for a gay man to be open about his sexuality. Strayhorn was living his dream, being able to work for the famous Duke Ellington. The two men forged a close collaboration, with Strayhorn contributing to the band for decades as composer, pianist, lyricist, and arranger. Billy's apartment at 409 Edgecombe was not far from Ellington's long-time residence at 935 St. Nicholas Avenue, off 157th Street. Ellington lived in apartment 4A from 1939 to 1961. Strayhorn resided the longest at 315 Convent Avenue, near City College.

In the 1940s, the Great Migration was well underway and would continue to be so for three more decades. Most people making that northward journey would never know that they had been part of anything great. In the end, just the millions of their numbers alone made it historic, and that is not counting the monumental ways that this population shift transformed the country. What the ones arriving in New York City did know was that they were entering a new world, one in which they could walk with their heads held high.

The *Amsterdam News* had changed hands in 1926, and the paper struggled financially for another decade. Its fortunes improved after 1935, when it was bought by two of the country's leading Black entrepreneurs, Dr. Cielan Bethan Powell and Dr. Phillip M. H. Savory of the Powell-Savory Corporation. Powell received his medical degree from Howard University School of Medicine and focused his early career on specializing in x-ray technology. He owned his own x-ray laboratory in Harlem, where he met Dr. Savory.

Powell took over as publisher, and during his tenure, the *Amsterdam News* began to report not only local stories of import to the Black community, but national news as well. The paper, which in the 1940s moved its offices to 2340 Eighth Avenue, became the nation's most quoted source of Black news.

In 1940, the publication of Richard Wright's most acclaimed novel, *Native Son*, brought the author fame and a certain amount of financial freedom. During his brief time in New York, he would have spent time with some of the same writers of the Renaissance era. Langston Hughes was still in Harlem, as was Countee Cullen. *Native Son* was on the bestseller list for a week, and Wright made history by becoming the first African American author whose work was selected by the prestigious Book-of-the-Month Club.

Not long after the book was published, Wright left New York and lived in Mexico for several years. He then moved to Paris, where he crossed paths with another African American expatriate, James Baldwin, who considered Wright his mentor. Indeed, Wright would read early drafts of Baldwin's first novel and gave him encouraging notes. But the two had a falling-out in Paris, from which their friendship never truly recovered.

Music had become an integral part of what Harlem had come to be known for in these decades. The talented jazz pianist Mary Lou Williams used her Hamilton Heights apartment at 63 Hamilton Terrace, off 141st Street and around the corner from the Grange, as a place of solace and home for her fellow jazz musicians. It was also where they could share and explore new music. Williams' life was one of those seldom-told stories that fades into anonymity, but she led a life that contributed immeasurably to what made the neighborhood a special place. Her talent, what she contributed to the music world, and the legends that graced her Hamilton Terrace apartment are the titans of jazz, as is she.

The photographs taken by the writer-photographer William P. Gottlieb between 1938 and 1948 are during what was considered the Golden Age of Jazz. The ones in Mary Lou's apartment in Hamilton Heights showed typical gatherings with her fellow musicians. Gottlieb's collection of more than 1,600 jazz subject photographs, taken mostly while on assignment for the *Washington Post* and *DownBeat Magazine*, are in the Library of Congress.

Mary Lou Williams was "an important contributor to every aspect of jazz that developed during a career that began in the late 1920s and lasted for more than half a century."[21] She played a vital role in the Kansas City jazz scene in the late 1920s as both a writer and a pianist for Andy Kirk and His Twelve Clouds of Joy.

She was born in Atlanta, the second of eleven children, and taught herself to play piano, which led to supporting her family by playing at neighborhood parties as a child.

Figures 60 and 61. LEFT: Left to Right: Jack Teagarden, Dixie Bailey, Mary Lou Williams, Tadd Dameron, Hank Jones, Dizzy Gillespie (hidden next to pianist), and Milt Orent. RIGHT: Left to Right: Dizzy Gillespie, Tadd Dameron, Hank Jones, Mary Lou Williams, and Milt Orent. Courtesy of William P. Gottlieb/Ira and Leonore S. Gershwin Fund Collection, Library of Congress, 1947

"By the middle of the twentieth century, Williams had solidified her status as a jazz great. And in the 1940s, she mentored some of bebop's most famous innovators like Charlie Parker, Dizzy Gillespie, and Thelonious Monk."[22] Yet despite her obvious talent and being a highly respected musician, Williams never received either the fame or money that should have come her way.

Like the Harlem Renaissance, when a whole new generation of African American writers found their voices, so too was this period for music. Many of the musicians who in the decades to come would be considered legends were merely newcomers on the scene. Some were just meeting or solidifying fledgling friendships, encouraging each other's instrumental experiments, and chiming in to round out the sound. Within Mary Lou's circle she was often the sole female, and it is unfathomable what that meant in the 1940s in a male-dominated environment.

Henry Minton soon discovered that he was really on to something in 1938 when his fellow musicians started showing up at his new club, Minton's on 118th Street. They came together, separately, and invited by others to jam or listen to a new riff someone had created. In this way, Thelonious Monk on piano, Dizzy Gillespie on trumpet, Max Roach on drums, Charlie Parker on alto sax, and the more seasoned Cab Calloway all moved in the glorified air of their combined gifts. Experiments in new ways of playing and blending those sounds would create the lasting foundation of a jazz era that, if possible, would be a national landmark of music. Minton's was also where they created bebop, a form of jazz unique for its fast rhythms and

Figure 62. The Deerfield, 676 Riverside Drive (c. 1913). Courtesy Irma and Paul Milstein Division of United States History, The New York Public Library

complex chords. And in the midst of all that, Duke Ellington and Count Basie walked those same streets and mixed in their circle.

During the Swing Era, Mary Lou Williams wrote hits for Benny Goodman, Jimmie Lunceford, and Duke Ellington. "In the be-bop years in the '40s, she wrote a Dizzy Gillespie hit, "In the Land of Oo-Bla-Dee."[23] Williams found herself physically and emotionally exhausted by the 1950s and stopped performing. The jazz world was a hard place for women.

Riverside Drive development in the early twentieth century was evidenced by beautiful apartment buildings going up at a rapid pace. The Deerfield apartment building at 676 Riverside Drive at 145th Street was built in 1910, and it had 174 units. It was originally called the Dacornel, designed by George and Edward Blum, a leading architectural team at the time. Like all these elegant buildings, it was built with little expectation of being integrated. The spacious apartments, which ranged from four to seven rooms, boasted both gas and electric lighting, a female switchboard attendant to service calls via the long-distance phones in each apartment, and a liveried doorman and elevator operator.

Yet by the late 1940s, the Deerfield was owned by Dr. Charles N. Ford, an African American dentist who came to the U.S. in the 1920s. Ford was a Trinidadian native who had worked on the construction of the Panama Canal. He graduated from NYU School of Dentistry. Along with his other business ventures, Dr. Ford had a dental practice in Harlem until his retirement in 1956.

James Weldon Johnson wrote an essay in the 1920s at the height of the Great Migration questioning whether Blacks would be able to hold onto the vast land mass and beautiful architecture in Harlem. Dr. Ford and a few other Black real estate developers were trying to disprove his worry, which was prophetic. Dr. Ford became president of the Uptown Chamber of Commerce and then president of the United Mutual Benefit Association, which became the United Mutual Life Insurance Company.

The Hamilton Theatre on Broadway was still in use as a movie theater. Some neighborhood folks might never have known that it started out as a vaudeville house. What they did know was that this grand movie palace was in their neighborhood.

Figure 63 shows the crowd outside of the Hamilton at the world premiere of Louis Jordan's *Beware* in 1946. Although Astor Pictures had

Figure 63. Louis Jordan Marquis at Hamilton Theatre 1946. Public domain

multiple "world premieres" for this film, Cinema Treasures writes that this appears to be the first one.

Politics affecting Harlem had been controlled by everyone outside of Harlem for far too long. After just three years on the City Council, the charismatic Adam Clayton Powell Jr. ran for Congress. "Until this time," writes Jonathan Gill in his book on Harlem, "gerrymandering made sure that Harlem was represented in Congress by whites. It was Powell who helped Black voters realize that in 1944 a new era was upon them."[24] Powell was heavily supported financially by liberal Jews who were impressed that he opposed British rule in Palestine. Some already viewed Powell as a little over the top, and his victory all but made him reach "movie star status, with the cars, clothes, and women that went along with it."[25]

Chapter 11

Jazz Clubs, the Numbers, and Firsts

> Hurry, get on board, it's comin', listen to those rails a-thrumming all aboard. Get on the "A" train, soon you will be on Sugar Hill in Harlem.
> —Duke Ellington

The jazz clubs in Sugar Hill were distinctive in their similarity. They were generally small, crowded, and filled with smoke. Men ran in and out with hot (meaning stolen) items for sale, watches going up their arms, and items of clothing that somehow "fell off a truck" in the Garment District. The women generally had quaffed, straightened hairdos, often dyed blonde. No one wore dungarees or sneakers. People put on their best, even in these small neighborhood clubs. The patrons looked good and smelled even better.

One usually walked down a few steps to the entrance of what might have originally been a basement apartment. To one side was a long bar and stools, and to the other were tables that mostly accommodated two people, sometimes four. At the places that sold food, there would be a kitchen all the way to the back where the aromas told you that someone with soul was cooking.

No matter how small or crowded the joint, there was always a space that could accommodate a trio or quartet, although seldom more than that. And by some miracle of engineering the sound always seemed perfect. People could still talk over the music. Because these places were small, there was little or no need for amplification. Somebody was on a horn or two, and someone else might be on drums. In the small clubs that dotted Edgecombe and St. Nicholas avenues it was rare to have a singer, but it could happen. Cigarettes could be bought at a machine for twenty-five cents a pack. Occasionally, a few peanuts might appear in a bowl at the bar, an early version of Happy Hour.

It was not uncommon to see a child perched in a corner sipping a Shirley Temple, that perfect combination of ginger ale, a splash of Grenadine, and a maraschino cherry that gave kids waiting for their parents the illusion that they were having a cocktail like the adults. The bars served as an unofficial babysitter as children waited for the responsible person to pick them up and drop them home.

Numbers runners and later drug dealers often had a favorite table or stool at the end of the bar where they took bets, held court, and could see who was coming in the door. Cops made very rare appearances.

Down the hill were the bigger clubs and dance halls, places with names known throughout Manhattan that attracted larger crowds and people who wanted to see and be seen. But up on the hill, on St. Nicholas, Amsterdam, and Broadway, the clubs catered mostly to local residents. All those apartment building dwellers made their way to their favorite nightspots, where the drinks were poured liberally. In these places you were surrounded by people who wanted a nice night out with good music and a bartender or barmaid who knew your name and your drink.

Nearly all the bartenders were men, and they were typically dressed in sharp black pants, a crisp white shirt, a black tie, and an apron. These men were a combination of priest, lover, and barber, the kind of men you sobbed to on a barstool, told your secrets to, and sometimes went home with. Some of the bartenders were as popular as the bands.

This was past the Harlem Renaissance era of white voyeurs who came to Harlem to peer at the habits of the Negroes. If white people were hanging out in Harlem, it was because they had friends there or a serious appreciation for intimate clubs with great music.

Like all the city's bars, the clubs in Sugar Hill were open until four in the morning, and there were any number of after-hours joints (speakeasies) where you could keep the party going after that. One popular spot was three doors down from the police station. Some patrons stayed until dawn, and anyone who could pass for being close to eighteen could be served a drink.

By the 1940s, the talented pianist Charles Luckeyth "Luckey" Roberts and his wife, Lena, changed the name of the club at 773 St. Nicholas to Luckey's Rendezvous. The place was frequented by an impressive roster of movie stars, and it was welcoming to homosexuals; people there were at ease in being who they were. Historian Michael Henry Adams notes how classically trained waiters brought a smile to patrons, singing arias and ballads while delivering drinks. Patrons were likely to see Billie Holiday, Clifton Webb, Tallulah Bankhead, Lena Horne, Art Tatum, Duke Ellington, and Billy Strayhorn alongside the neighborhood regulars. It was not uncommon for well-known musicians to sit in and jam with the house band or to try out new music in these little clubs. The Roberts, a musical couple who lived for a time at 409 Edgecombe Avenue, also sang impromptu snatches of opera.

There were also bars and lounges along Amsterdam Avenue, although most were more neighborhood watering holes than jazz clubs. Perhaps the one that brought the most atmosphere and glamour to the neighborhood was Randolph's Shangri-la Cocktail Lounge at Amsterdam Avenue and 158th Street. The Shalimar, at 150th and Broadway, also offered an evening of elegant entertainment.

Don Raphael, the regular organist at the Shalimar, also taught classical piano during the day at the Juilliard School of Music. In 1959, *Jet* magazine wrote in a small clip that though his fans knew him as Don Raphael, the café organist becomes Ike Reid whenever he appears in Philadelphia, because that's his real name, known to his buddies.

For larger celebrations there was the Audubon Ballroom, which had opened in 1912 at Broadway and 166th Street. At the time, Blacks would have been allowed in only as servants, if that. But by the 1940s the Audubon Ballroom had become a favorite nightspot on the hill, and it was around that time that patrons could hear a sextet that included Sonny Rollins, Art Blakey, J. J. Johnson, and Miles Davis.

Despite all that was slowly changing when it came to access to clubs and public places in Harlem, Black people were still excluded from many establishments. This was clear from the New York City section of Victor Hugo Green's indispensable work *The Negro Motorist Green Book*, first published in 1936. It offered a guide to establishments owned by Blacks and those that were "Negro-friendly." It is hard to believe that a travel guide could save lives, but Green's booklet did just that. Green was born in New York on November 9, 1892. His family moved to New Jersey when he was young, and he went to work as a mailman. In 1917 he married a Virginia woman named Alma Duke, who had moved to New York. Victor Green was drafted into the Army during World War I, where he rose to the rank of sergeant. The couple moved to Harlem during the early days of the Harlem Renaissance. Green continued working as a mailman after the war, but his increasing frustration with travel restrictions in segregated areas prompted him to create a travel guidebook for African Americans.

The guide was modeled after those created for Jewish travelers, a group that had also experienced discrimination. Although a great convenience, automobile travel was often dangerous for African Americans, who didn't know where it was safe to use a restroom, get something to eat, or spend the night. In the notoriously frequent "sundown" towns, Negroes could be harassed, arrested, or worse for being out after sunset.

The first edition of *The Negro Motorist Green Book* (later renamed *The Negro Travelers' Green Book*) was initially limited to listings in New York City. But word spread, and the guide was so popular that Green went national the following year. It would be published from 1936 until the 1960s.

The standard business listings were most critical to help Black people function in a segregated world: hotels, motels, restaurants, beauty and barber shops, service stations, garages, nightclubs, resorts, and beaches. "The most high-volume listings were in cities with large populations of Black Americans, like New York, Detroit, Chicago, and Los Angeles. But the book's use was more valuable to travelers crossing smaller towns in rural areas across the South and out West."[1]

Eventually, Green moved to 938 St. Nicholas Avenue at 158th Street in Sugar Hill, across the street from Duke Ellington. The 1941 edition of *The Green Book* has his address on the cover.

Green distributed the books by mail order, to friendly businesses, and at Esso Standard Oil gas stations, as Esso was one of the rare gasoline distributors that franchised to African Americans. The 1941 edition of the guide made a distinction in Harlem's "dance halls" like the popular Savoy versus "nightclubs" like Smalls Paradise and designated the clubs in Sugar Hill as "taverns."

In addition to the well-known clubs about which there was more information available, the 1941 *Green Book* also listed the location at 773 St. Nicholas, the future Luckey's Rendezvous, as the Mayfair at the time, and the 400 Night Club was then called Jay's. Other St. Nicholas clubs listed in that edition were LaMar Cheri at 739, Eddies at 714, Millicent's at 826, and Fat Man at 450 West 155th Street.

The *Green Book* would be published until the mid-sixties, when stringent restrictions eased in terms of segregation in housing and other establishments. It was what its publisher had hoped: that one day such a guide would be unnecessary.

In 1940, the Black population of New York City was nearly 460,000, roughly 6 percent of the city's total population of about 7.4 million. "The

Figure 64. *The Negro Motorist Green Book 1941*. Public domain

city's Black population ranked first in the nation, ahead of Chicago, Philadelphia, the District of Columbia, and Baltimore."[2]

Because of the neighborhood's steadily declining white population after the Depression, as the racial demographics shifted, several Harlem churches had sold their buildings to Black congregations. In Hamilton Heights, the Lenox Presbyterian Church sold its building on West 141st at St. Nicholas Avenue to St. James Presbyterian Church in 1927. St. James had been founded in 1895 to serve its downtown African American congregation, and its history was rooted in the abolition movement and the Underground Railroad.

In 1942 the Washington Heights Baptist Church, at 420 West 145th Street and Convent Avenue, was renamed the Convent Avenue Baptist Church. That same year, half a century after its construction on Convent Avenue, St. Luke's Episcopal Church finally opened its doors to people of all races.

Changes were also affecting the area's social scene. Around 1950, the new owner of Luckey's Rendezvous at 773 St. Nicholas Avenue changed its name to the Pink Angel, and the clientele included an even more noticeable number of same-sex couples. At a time when homosexuality was still illegal, this continued to be a neighborhood club where people of all persuasions were made to feel comfortable.

Bowman's Grill at 92 St. Nicholas Place and 154th Street, a lounge that in the mid-1950s presented jazz trios and organists, became Branker's Lounge after 1958, the same year Kenny Burrell and Sonny Rollins began appearing there into the mid-1960s. The location dated back to 1892, when people stopped there after watching the horse races on the Harlem River Speedway when it was Troger's Hotel. Harlem Heights was seeped in history around every corner, perched on the hills, and in countless buildings that, through the decades, were evolving with the times.

By the 1920s a unique form of gambling called "the numbers" had become central to life in Harlem. It flourished in Sugar Hill, and the businesses up and down St. Nicholas, Amsterdam, and Broadway were either discreet or flagrant participants.

To play the numbers was simple: you placed a bet that three numbers would win that day's "lottery" of sorts. A winning number could transform a person's life. Because you could play as little as a nickel or a dime, even the poorest person could place a bet. The odds were totally against them, of course, but even a small winning bet could make a person rich overnight. A big hit could mean buying a home or a car, starting a business, or sending a child to college.

And while some form of the numbers game had been around since the nineteenth century, it got perfected in Harlem in a way that not surprisingly drew the attention of the mob, the police, and eventually the state government.

Winners traditionally paid 10 percent of their winnings to the numbers runner, who was responsible for taking bets and paying the winners. Each person in the organization took a cut from the total collections. Up and down Sugar Hill's avenues, which were increasingly filled with barber shops, beauty salons, food joints, and bars, gamblers could count on their favorite numbers runner popping in to take bets. He (they were most often men) was usually a well-known and charismatic person, quick to witticisms and able to laugh and talk his way around the neighborhood.

The runners also had astounding memories and a mind for math that might have won them awards in college or the top spot on a game show. For every hundred or so runners there was a collector whose job was to organize his crew of runners and bribe the necessary people, generally the cops. At the top of the food chain were the so-called "bankers," millionaires overseeing an illegal gambling empire, to whom the greater portion of the daily collections eventually came.

St. Croix native Casper Holstein was a former porter who amassed an incredible fortune and became one of the leading Black philanthropists of the era. It wasn't just rich white people helping to underwrite the writing prizes for the Urban League's *Opportunity* magazine. Holstein did, as well, and he also built Harlem's first Elks Lodge.

Langston Hughes would acknowledge as much: that after winning his first *Opportunity* poetry award, "in succeeding years, two other (contests) were held with funds given by Casper Holstein, a wealthy West Indian numbers banker who did good things with his money, such as educating boys and girls at colleges in the South, building decent apartment houses in Harlem, and backing literary contests to encourage colored writers."[3]

Playing the numbers was illegal, of course, but the impact of the game was not entirely negative. Unlike drugs, which were often deadly, the numbers provided jobs and income to poor people, even if it was just a small win that helped pay a bill. As the *New York Times* would write, an estimated 60 percent of the area's economic life depended on the cash flow from numbers.

> Harlem businesses for generations have been bankrolled by the cash of numbers operators. Bars, restaurants, corner groceries, apartment houses, name the business and in Harlem those who know will tell you that they have been started, or in bad times saved from bankruptcy, by the money of the numbers man.[4]

Nor was the enterprise exclusively male. A woman named Madame Stephanie St. Clair, who had been born on the French Island of Guadeloupe and lived at 409 Edgecombe Avenue, was one of the few noted female bankers. She boasted of her status as "Harlem's Policy Queen" in the 1920s and 1930s. Dutch Schultz was a famous violent gangster and nationwide bootlegger during Prohibition. In 1935, J. Edgar Hoover referred to Schultz as "Public Enemy Number One." Schultz used violence to either force African American and Latino numbers bankers out of business to come work for him or coerced them to give him a portion of their bank. St. Clair and several other Black numbers bankers joined forces to try to fight Schultz and other white racketeers who were trying to take control of the numbers business in Harlem.

On October 23, 1935, Schultz was shot at the Palace Chophouse in Newark, New Jersey. Despite their best efforts, the Black policymakers were incapable of fighting off the constant pressure from the mob, which eventually took over a significant slice of the Harlem numbers racket. While both Holstein and St. Clair moved on to other enterprises, one of St. Clair's lieutenants, Ellsworth "Bumpy" Johnson, took over her business, earning the trust of the Italian mobsters. A truce ensued, and the numbers racket continued to thrive with the mob as head banker.

There was a cyclical problem in Harlem, sadly, that riots seemed to haunt the community on a periodic basis. In March of 1935 a riot broke out in Central Harlem after a rumor spread that a boy had been badly beaten by a store clerk on 125th Street after he was accused of shoplifting. In an article about the attack in the *New York Post*, Congressman Adam Clayton Powell Jr. was quoted as saying that it was not a riot but rather an "open, unorganized protest against empty stomachs, overcrowded tenements, filthy sanitation, rotten foodstuffs, chiseling landlords and merchants, discrimination on relief, disfranchisement, and against a disinterested administration."[5]

The fact that stores allowed Black people to spend their money shopping but wouldn't hire them for anything other than menial jobs was a clear indication of what everyone in Harlem already knew. Black people had managed to integrate housing in Harlem, but equal access to jobs was still on the horizon. Although New York had no formal Jim Crow laws, there were still places where Blacks would not be served, by policy if not by law. Some stores closed rather than hire Black people, which was reminiscent of landlords who left their buildings empty rather than allow them to be integrated.

The city, meantime, finally caught up with most major cities in the country and passed rent-control laws in 1935. Some felt that La Guardia was responding to the riots in Central Harlem that year. But rent control was something that would benefit people throughout the city, regardless of race or socioeconomic status, much to the chagrin of landlords.

The drug use that was more common among musicians, primarily heroin, would steadily increase and begin to seep more into everyday lives in Harlem and destroy sections of the community wholesale. Hamilton Heights gradually saw a rise in crime, drugs, and rundown housing, just as all sections of Harlem did. But the utter devastation that cut through large swathes of dilapidated buildings in other parts of Harlem did not come to Hamilton Heights. Somehow, even if unspoken, there was still the collective awareness that this was the more elite section of Harlem. What went on down the hill was not supposed to happen in the heights.

The different reality for those in Central Harlem versus Hamilton Heights had become intolerable in some neighborhoods. On August 1,

1943, a young Negro soldier came to the assistance of a prostitute being arrested by a white police officer. It was at the Braddock Hotel, on 126th Street off Seventh Avenue. "The soldier struck the cop in the head and tried to flee but was shot in the shoulder and arrested. Within an hour, thousands of angry Harlemites had taken to the streets."[6]

The soldier's interference with an arrest and then assaulting a police officer might seem an odd spark for a riot, since the soldier was legally in the wrong. Yet seething discontent over a myriad of social ills: grievances about slum landlords, inflated store prices, and a lack of jobs did just that. Things quickly degraded into looting and violence where thousands of rioters moved through the streets in waves.

Mayor La Guardia sent an extra six thousand police officers to Harlem to quell the violence. Over a thousand stores were looted, and firemen responded to over thirty fires. In the aftermath of riots, there are almost always band aid social reforms to temporarily placate people. "The commissioner of markets and the Office of Price Administration had cited more than one hundred Harlem stores for ignoring price restrictions, and he pushed for ending racial discrimination and inadequate funding for public housing."[7]

The next year, Langston Hughes wrote about the riots in the *New Republic* and of the differences between Central Harlem and the Heights. "Most of the people on Sugar Hill were just as indignant about the riots as was Mayor La Guardia," Hughes wrote. "Some of them even said the riots put the Negro race back fifty years. But the people who live in the riot area don't make enough money really to afford the high rents and the high prices merchants and landlords charge in Harlem."[8]

Hughes pointed out that most people in Harlem don't live the life that people in Sugar Hill do, acquainted with liberal whites, attending banquets at the Astor, or lunching with movie stars at Sardi's, a famous midtown restaurant and bar favored by actors. "Indeed, the average Harlemite's impression of white folks, democracy and life in general is rather bad. Naturally, if you live on nice, tree-lined, quiet Convent Avenue, even though you are colored, it would never occur to you to riot and break windows."[9]

When former Harlem Renaissance poet Arna Bontemps returned to Harlem for a visit in 1945, after an absence of almost two decades, he wrote about the changes he saw. Notably, so many of the luminaries who had made Harlem a magical place during the Harlem Renaissance were now gone, having moved to other neighborhoods in the city or left the city entirely.

Bontemps, who by then had written several novels and children's books, found a Harlem quite different than the one he and his fellow poets were singing about in the streets at night during the 1920s. "At least one reason for avoiding the Harlem night streets in 1942," he wrote, "would have been the fear of muggers. Where poets went about singing in the days of the new awakening, now angry, frustrated boys prowled."[10]

The changes occurring in Central Harlem and Sugar Hill were not the only ones taking place. The Great Depression and World War II marked a huge shift in Italian Harlem, which also became evident in some of the housing problems in its neighboring Central Harlem. Substandard and overcrowded tenements, a majority of which had no indoor sanitary facilities or central heating, made for a brutal form of living. The majority Italian population changed for several reasons, including the gradual move to other boroughs. Also, the growing arrival of Puerto Ricans that had started slowly in the 1920s coincided with the start of the Great Migration of millions of African Americans leaving the South. As a territory of the United States, Puerto Ricans held U.S. citizenship and were not subject to the regulations of immigrants entering the country.

Starting in the 1940s, tens of thousands of Puerto Ricans started moving to the U.S., primarily to New York City, and they settled largely into an already crowded East Harlem. As with all immigration, economic struggles in Puerto Rico encouraged them to seek the chance for a better life in the U.S. By the 1950s, the neighborhood that had once been deemed Little Italy got the nickname of Spanish Harlem. The social makeup of the entire city would be influenced by the food and music of these "new" New Yorkers. In later decades, East Harlem's Historic District would encompass 111th to 120th streets between Park and Pleasant avenues, with just a few vestiges of the old Italian neighborhood in the storefronts and churches.

On a historic street in Hamilton Heights, with the first set of nineteenth-century stunning townhouses, a new history was created. On November 14, 1943, First Lady Eleanor Roosevelt visited Judge Hubert T. Delany and his wife, Willetta, at their home at 467 West 144th Street. Mrs. Roosevelt was meeting with a group of women to lend her support to the formation of the Harlem Activities Committee of the Colored Orphan Asylum. The First Lady stressed the importance of reaching out to provide opportunities for all children, regardless of race.

A year earlier, on September 24, 1942, Mayor La Guardia had performed the marriage ceremony for the Delanys. La Guardia appointed Hubert T. Delany as Justice of the Family Court, where he served from 1942 to 1955.

In the 1950s, an influential adoption nonprofit, the Spence-Chapin

Figure 65. Judge Hubert Delany to left of First Lady Eleanor Roosevelt, 1943. Public domain

Agency, would make strides to help adoption outreach to the Black community. It would appoint several Black women to its board for the first time, including Willetta Delany, Mrs. Rachel Robinson (wife of Jackie Robinson), and opera singer Marian Anderson.

Beyond being identified as a neighborhood in the Heights, the name "Sugar Hill" would come to be used by a variety of artists and businesses in coming decades. In 1949 Timmie "Oh Yeah" Rogers, a comedian, dancer, and singer, launched the first all-Black television variety show, which was called *Uptown Jubilee* and was broadcast on CBS. It was a short-lived show that ran from September 13 to October 20, 1949.

The hour-long program aired live on Tuesday nights. Each time it had a different title, first *Uptown Jubilee*, then *Harlem Jubilee*, and finally *Sugar Hill Times*. The show was hosted by Willie Bryant, and performers included Maxine Sullivan, Harry Belafonte, The Jubileers, and Don Redman and His Orchestra. It was likely the first time the name Sugar Hill had been in the national news.

The city that Alexander Hamilton loved still remembered him. On March 30, 1949, in a brief item that ran under the headline "Play on Hamilton Given," the *New York Times* reported that the Federal Union had presented the play the night before at the Barbizon-Plaza Theatre on

Central Park South. The historical drama, by Hattie Mae Pavlo, was based in part on Gertrude Atherton's 1902 critically acclaimed novel *The Conqueror*. The book purported to be the true and romantic story of Alexander Hamilton, a bestseller at the time and extensively researched. It would be cited as a reference almost a century later by author Ron Chernow in his award-winning book on Hamilton.

The stated purpose of the play, which appears to have been staged only a few times, was to detail "the important role Hamilton played in helping the growth of the original thirteen states," adding, "The script also touched on major episodes in the short but brilliant life of Hamilton."[11]

Meanwhile, the money that J. P. Morgan and George Walker had contributed for maintenance of the Grange did not stretch as far as hoped. By the 1950s, the building's shabbiness was so apparent that the Hamilton Museum on Convent Avenue was not much of an attraction. Visitors were greeted by plaster falling from the ceilings and peeling paint inside and out. Eventually, almost no one came.

This is quite unlike the description in the *New York Amsterdam News* in 1941 when St. Clair Bourne wrote of a thriving museum space that contained rooms filled with original Hamilton memorabilia. In addition to the marble bust of Hamilton by the Italian sculptor Ceracchi, there was a dress worn by Mrs. Hamilton, as well as "a collection of books which were in the family library in the Grange, [which] apparently escaped notice when the family moved away and sold the place and were discovered stored away in a closet when the American Society took over the place."[12] The books, which were published in London and Dublin in the eighteenth century, were described by Bourne as having the signatures of Eliza Hamilton and two of her sons: Philip and Alexander, with notes in the margins. The article makes clear that the importance of the Grange as a historical landmark "is not lost on Harlemites in the neighborhood who go through their daily lives with the knowledge that history was made just around the corner."

In 1951, Marguerite and Warren Blake bought the nine-bedroom Bailey House from which Marguerite would operate the M. Marshall Blake Funeral Home for decades. For many people in Sugar Hill the Bailey House had no history other than being a funeral home housed in what most people would consider a Gothic mansion.

Years after buying the building, Marguerite Blake told a reporter that she had admired the house as a teenager when she lived nearby, on West 153rd Street.

"I always wanted to own this house," she said. Then one day she and her husband noticed a "for sale" sign. After they bought it in 1951, they made few changes. "Mrs. Blake opened the M. Marshall Blake Funeral Home in the house, and Mr. Blake, who served in the Army on a demolition team and landed at Normandy, later became a detective in the New York City Police Department."[13] The house built by the Barnum & Bailey impresario had taken on a new life.

The year 1952 brought the publication of Ralph Ellison's novel *Invisible Man*, the story of an African American who moves to New York City and gets caught up in the tumultuous civil rights struggle but eventually recedes into invisibility. The book became an immediate success and earned Ellison both international fame and the National Book Award.

Later, the man who had left Tuskegee University before completing his degree, highly critical of some of the school's cliquish and bourgeois attitudes, taught at New York University. Ellison had long since left the small apartment at 147th and St. Nicholas Avenue, where he had started writing *Invisible Man*, and he and his wife now lived at 730 Riverside Drive at 150th Street. The distinguished landmarked residence had also once been home to Senator Jacob Javits and opera singer Marian Anderson. Ellison was one of those fortunate writers who lived long enough to enjoy the notoriety of a successful book.

There is a scene in the first *Godfather* movie in which the gangsters are discussing whether they should move into drugs as part of their criminal empires. Vito Corleone is against it. It is the 1940s, and one of the family heads, Don Giuseppe Zaluchi, knows it is a lucrative business with incredible financial returns. Yet he still admonishes that there must be guidelines. It is a shining example of the juxtaposition of whether life imitates art or art imitates life. Zaluchi tells those assembled what came to be reality by the time the film was released in 1972. The mob boss says that he wants to run it like a business and keep it respectable. "I don't want it near schools. I don't want it sold to children! That's an infamia. In my city, we would keep

Figure 66. Ralph Ellison, Seated in His Apartment, ca. 1972. Courtesy Library of Congress

the traffic in the dark people, the coloreds. They're animals anyway, so let them lose their souls."[14]

Illegal drugs were not piped into the suburbs, to white neighborhoods on Park Avenue or Beekman Place. That was a future drug epidemic that would be created by the billionaire Sackler family and sanctioned by doctors on prescription pads with the blessing of the FDA. These drugs, heroin and cocaine, were primarily distributed in Harlem and killed droves of Black people. It started with a trickle-down network among musicians and other bohemian crowds and spread to the average person. The resultant effects would decimate large sections of the community, without any notable city, state or federal outcry about an epidemic that needed to be stopped.

The five grand museums that Archer Huntington built in the early twentieth century on Broadway and 158th Street had become a destination for visiting schoolchildren. In her memoir about growing up in Sugar Hill, the author Terry Baker Mulligan recalled that on her first visit to the American Indian Museum in the 1950s with her third-grade class, "we filed through its carved front door, into a gallery smelling of mold, rotting wood.... I was standing across from a fully assembled animal skin teepee that stood about fifteen feet tall, with an open flap for its front door."[15]

Mulligan remembered the giant totem pole in the courtyard. And she added, "Inside, the building was crammed with artifacts, some as small and finely crafted as a topaz ring and a little girl's deerskin dress. There were rifles, tomahawks, saddles, dolls, sleds. On a larger scale, there was also a forty-foot dugout canoe."[16] Later, Mulligan's schoolgirl mind also began to wonder how they acquired the displays, which was an excellent thing to ponder. The provenance of museum acquisitions and to whom they rightfully belonged was a sensitive issue that would often be litigated around the world in future decades.

By the 1950s, Duke Ellington had cemented his place in music history. Ellington and his orchestra appeared at the Leeds Festival in England in 1958. Having impressed Queen Elizabeth with the band's performance, Ellington gained an audience with Queen Elizabeth. They exchanged enough pleasantries that it slowed down the reception line.

Ellington outlined the movements of a special composition just for Queen Elizabeth called, "The Queen's Suite." After recording it with his orchestra, he sent it to Her Majesty, but never released it publicly.

At the Morris-Jumel Mansion in those years, debate raged as to what the building's focus should be. Gladys V. Clark, the president of the Washington Headquarters Association, agreed with several members of the DAR

Figure 67. Queen Elizabeth II and Duke Ellington. Courtesy Library of Congress

who "wanted to alter the interpretation, from solely displaying artifacts to offering fully furnished rooms focusing on the various time periods of the house's history."[17] Events and functions were still very patriotic, with Washington's birthday still the highlight event of the year. Washington's encampment for eight weeks during the start of the American Revolution still overshadowed almost two centuries of other history in the house. Yet the significance of this last-standing place where Washington had slept during the Revolution was profound.

The mansion's new curator, Henry Harrison de Frise, embraced the idea of the rooms being furnished to represent certain historical periods. He and members of the Washington Headquarters Association tried to locate some of the mansion's original artifacts that had been sold at auction in 1916. We know, for instance, that one of Eliza Jumel's gowns is now part of the collection of the Museum of the City of New York.

As Mulligan wrote in her autobiography, "By the late 1950s it was apparent that parts of Harlem were in deep decline. It's no secret that underemployed, marginally educated and disillusioned citizens populated rundown sections of Harlem."[18] Despite a changing neighborhood, older residents struggled to maintain the hill's elite status. "The duality had long been there, and today's residents continue grappling with Harlem's uppity, versus its lowly image and lifestyle."[19]

In 1952, one of Sugar Hill's most illustrious residents, revered NAACP attorney Thurgood Marshall, traveled to Washington, D.C., to join his colleagues in arguing the case of Brown vs. the Board of Education before the U.S. Supreme Court. Marshall had long since solidified his reputation as a litigator in taking on civil rights cases of African Americans falsely accused of crimes. He would eventually argue thirty-two cases before the Court and win twenty-nine.

On November 28, 1953, the *New York Amsterdam News* reprinted remarks from Marshall's first public appearance since filing the briefs in Brown: "The fight to end segregation will not stop with the Supreme Court ruling in these cases," Marshall said. "We will have to go on fighting until we have broken out of the ghettos and can live where we want to."[20]

On May 17, 1954, the Supreme Court overturned *Plessy v. Ferguson*, the 1896 case that had stood as precedent where the Court held that state-mandated segregation laws didn't violate the equal protection clause of the Fourteenth Amendment. The justices unanimously affirmed Brown. In its written decision, the Court cited the work of two Sugar Hill residents, esteemed psychologists Kenneth Bancroft Clark and his wife, Mamie Phipps Clark, who designed a "doll test" to study the psychological effects of segregation on Black children.

By the 1960s, Hamilton Heights was no longer dominated by upper-crust professionals. The old timers continued to cling to fading bourgeois aspirations. Convent and Edgecombe avenues were still the favorite address of doctors and lawyers, many of whom were by now from the Caribbean. Some residents were the subject of articles in *Jet* magazine, which was something of a Social Register for African Americans.

There was both irony and hypocrisy in the people criticizing the influx of those still arriving from the South and their unsophisticated ways. For the most part, the residents doing the complaining were only the first generation whose parents had moved from the South. Twenty years before, it was their elders who had to adapt to city life. But having been born to the city and unfamiliar personally with the racism of the South, the new arrivals from southern shores seemed foreign to them. Richard Wright's statement after some of his interviews for the Works Progress Administration could not have been truer when he wrote, "Perhaps never in history has a more utterly unprepared folk wanted to go to the city."[21]

Yet the vestiges of a once implied promise lingered that living in Sugar Hill meant that a person was above the riffraff, literally and figuratively. If the neighborhood no longer held that distinction as the better sections of Harlem, what was it?

There were other celebratory accomplishments by African Americans throughout Harlem in the fifties. Whether or not these people had tenuous or strong ties to Sugar Hill, there was a shared sense of pride in these moments of Black achievement.

Four history makers had a joint book signing in 1956 at Lewis Michaux's legendary National Memorial African Bookstore on 125th Street off Seventh Avenue. Celebrated that year were the publication of Langston Hughes' *I Wonder as I Wander: An Autobiographical Journey*, Eartha Kitt's *Thursday's Child*, Henry Armstrong's *Gloves, Glory and God*, and Pauli Murray's *Proud Shoes*.

One of the four in the historic photo, Anna Pauline "Pauli" Murray, was destined to leave a powerful impact on civil rights, the law, religion, gender equality, and gender identification. Murray would become the first African American woman to be ordained as an Episcopal priest and would earn degrees from Hunter College in New York, Howard University School of Law, and Berkeley. Murray was also the first woman to earn a doctorate

Figure 68. Langston Hughes, Eartha Kitt, Henry Armstrong, Pauli Murray, Mr. Bowman, and Ralph Cooper; Book party at the National Memorial Bookstore. Schomburg Center for Research in Black Culture, Photographs and Prints Division, NYPL, Courtesy of Austin Hansen Photograph Collection

from Yale Law School, eventually teaching there and at Brandeis. A young Pauli Murray was also one of the authors who contributed to the anthology of Negro writing that Nancy Cunard published in 1934.

Murray's legal analysis aided cases argued by Thurgood Marshall and Ruth Bader Ginsburg, both future Supreme Court Justices. In a paper written while at Howard University, Murray suggested a direct challenge to the Plessy "separate but equal" doctrine. The paper was used as a resource in the *Brown v. Board of Education* briefs, which Murray found out ten years after the verdict. Ginsburg would credit Murray as coauthor on the brief in a winning landmark 1971 U.S. Supreme Court decision on gender discrimination, *Reed v. Reed*. Murray was also a founding member of the National Organization for Women (NOW), birthed at a 1966 Washington, D.C., conference on Title VII and the Equal Employment Opportunity Commission (EEOC). Murray's many achievements would finally be recognized in 2021 in a documentary titled *My Name Is Pauli Murray*.

In 1958, a young woman from South Carolina named Althea Gibson became the first African American woman to win the U.S. Open tennis championship in Forest Hills in Queens. A group of people who recognized Althea's abilities back in 1940 had gotten together and arranged for her to have her first formal tennis lessons at the Cosmopolitan Tennis Club at 441 Convent Avenue at 149th Street. The club was the place on Sugar Hill where the city's talented African Americans played.

That same year, in a bizarre episode that would not endear New York City to Martin Luther King Jr., the civil rights leader was almost killed in an attempt on his life. King's book *Stride toward Freedom: The Montgomery Story* had just been published. It was an account of efforts to desegregate public transportation in Montgomery, Alabama, and the role of Rosa Parks in that struggle. King was at Blumstein's Department Store on 125th Street for a book signing when a mentally disturbed woman named Izola Ware Curry walked in, cut to the front of the line of autograph seekers, took a letter opener from under her coat, and stabbed King in the chest. Then she fled.

"Curry was pursued by a group of ladies who had been waiting in line and was stopped by an ad salesman for the *Amsterdam News*."[22] King was taken to Harlem Hospital, which was probably as well equipped to deal with traumatic wounds as hospitals in wealthier neighborhoods. King identified the woman from his hospital bed and spent two weeks recovering.

In 1959, borrowing words from the Langston Hughes poem "Harlem," and the poem's query as to what happens to a dream deferred, Lorraine Hansberry wrote a play entitled *A Raisin in the Sun*. It opened in New

York on March 11 with a young actor named Sidney Poitier in the starring role, along with Ruby Dee, Louis Gossett, Claudia McNeill, Diana Sands, and Glynn Turman. *A Raisin in the Sun*, the first play written by an African American woman produced on Broadway, was nominated for four Tony Awards and won the New York Drama Critics Award for best play of the year.

That same year, Ella Fitzgerald and William "Count" Basie became the first African American performers to win Grammy Awards. Both had deep roots in Harlem's musical scene, and Basie had lived in Sugar Hill at 555 Edgecombe Avenue.

There was a small whirlwind of change and opportunity steadily building for African Americans in New York City and around the country. Harlem, and Hamilton Heights in particular, saw and felt its own whirlwind, the impact of which would continue to change its character, some for the good and some not.

Chapter 12

The Advent of the Sixties, Generational Changes, and the Arts

> The most effective way to destroy people is to deny and obliterate their own understanding of their history.
>
> —George Orwell

People often look at the tumultuous years of the 1960s Civil Rights Movement as if it were a sudden emergence of activism. Yet African Americans had struggled for equality from the moment the first enslaved person arrived on North American shores over three centuries before and tried to break free of their chains. By the 1960s the children born in Harlem were two and sometimes three generations away from their elders, who had made history by populating the northern section of Manhattan. Although the Great Migration ostensibly ended in 1970, it had definitely slowed by the 1960s.

The generation entering adulthood in the sixties had an easier time renting an apartment. Many of them had grown up in the beautiful and stylish brownstones in Hamilton Heights, either as renters or because their parents owned the building. Despite the fact that some of them were only separated from sharecropping, the cotton and tobacco fields, and the citrus groves of the South by one or two generations, they saw themselves solely as New Yorkers, with the world at their feet.

Richard Wright, the author of *Native Son*, and Ralph Ellison, author of *Invisible Man*, had both come to New York in the late 1930s. Like thousands of writers still reeling from the Great Depression, they were employed by the federal Works Progress Administration. Some of what they wrote about then seemed to foreshadow the reality of the sixties.

The Federal Writers Project (FWP) was part of the New Deal's Works Progress Administration (WPA) to get people working during the Great Depression. Jill Lepore writes that at its peak, the agency employed over six thousand writers, a group ranging from newspaper reporters to playwrights. From 1935 to 1939, the government hired writers to conduct interviews with crafted questions that wound up being a multifaceted cultural history. The initial set of interviews was with formerly enslaved people throughout the South in a compilation that became known as the Slave Narratives. FWP workers later interviewed everyday people with the goal of publishing anthologies on different aspects of American life. It was likely the first time that ordinary Americans were asked to speak about their lives.

Working under national folklore director Benjamin Botkin, these direct questions to everyday people took a contemporary approach that influenced oral histories. The product of these interviews is archived in the Library of Congress. In cultural terms, the Writers' Project both provided employment for a great many talented authors and sparked a new way of weaving stories into their own writing for some who were just discovering their interest in the craft as a possible profession. In addition to Wright and Ellison, some other notable interviewers were Gwendolyn Brooks, May Swenson, John Cheever, Saul Bellow, Zora Neale Hurston, and Studs Terkel.

In the case of Wright and Ellison, as with many of the other writers who took part in this program, elements of those interviews worked themselves into the books they wrote. The two authors followed the agency's script when interviewing ordinary men and women on the streets of Harlem. In 1939, while traipsing up and down the avenues and in and out of apartment buildings in Hamilton Heights, Ellison "asked an old man hanging out in Eddie's Bar, on St. Nicholas near 147th Street, 'Do you like living in New York City?'"[1]

The man replied, "Ahm in New York, but New York ain't in me. You understand? What do I mean? Listen. I'm from Jacksonville, Florida. Been in New York twenty-five years. I'm a New Yorker! Yuh understand?"[2] The man went on to explain that the streets were riddled with pimps, the numbers game cheating people out of their money, shootings and other violence and crime. He wanted to make clear that while he may have been a New Yorker from living decades in the city, he felt that he retained part of his Southern character, disassociating himself from the harsher aspects of being a Black man on the streets of Harlem. Wright worked the essence of that encounter into his opus *Invisible Man*, published in 1952.

The FWP "reinvented the interview and changed American journalism forever. The project's folklore editor, Benjamin Botkin, had a mad, beautiful vision. He wanted to turn the streets, the stockyards, and the hiring halls into literature."[3]

As part of the same program, Richard Wright wrote *12 Million Black Voices: A Folk History of the Negro in the United States* in 1941. Wright had been asked to pen the narrative to accompany photographs of Black people living in poverty during the Depression that had been taken for the Farm Security Administration by photographers such as Walker Evans, Arthur Rothstein, Marion Post Wolcott, and Gordon Parks. One of the most widely recognized black and white photos of the era was by Dorothea Lange in 1936 of the migrant mother holding her children. Wright's book *12 Million Black Voices* chronicles Black life in the United States from slavery until the 1940s.

Lepore writes that Ellison fell apart, highly emotional, when he read *12 Million Black Voices*, he wept and wrote to Wright, "God! It makes you want to write and write and write, or murder." Ellison chose to write.

It is members of the generation coming to age in the 1960s and 1970s that Wright seemed to be describing when he wrote in the 1940s that "we watch strange moods fill our children, and our hearts swell with pain. The streets, with their noise and flaring lights, the taverns, the automobiles, and the poolrooms claim them, and no voice of ours can call them back."[4]

This was the world inhabited by the children and grandchildren of formerly enslaved persons who now lived in upscale neighborhoods like Hamilton Heights and Sugar Hill, a century after slavery was abolished. A century seems like a relatively short period of time in the longer view of history because, as Lepore writes of the Great Migration, thirty years earlier "in the nineteen-thirties, about a hundred thousand people who had once been owned by other people were still alive."[5]

Decades later, one wonders if the Pulitzer Prize–winning author Isabel Wilkerson took some measure of inspiration from the interviewing methods of the Federal Writers Project and from the truths Ellison and Wright unearthed from this first generation of transplants from the South. Wilkerson would walk the paths they had, interviewing dozens of people over hundreds of hours, weaving the stories into what many consider the definitive book about the Great Migration, *The Warmth of Other Suns*. Its title is borrowed from a line in Richard Wright's autobiography *Black Boy*.

In many respects life was relatively easy for members of the newer generation, which is why they didn't realize how remarkable it was that their parents and others had created a predominantly Black neighborhood in the heart of New York City. Perhaps for this reason some began to take for granted and misuse all that had been so sacred in Sugar Hill. Graffiti began to appear on the avenues, and some apartment buildings sank into disrepair.

Add to that growing unemployment, rising school dropout rates, increasing drug use, and criminal activity as the number 1 source of income, and it is hardly surprising that sections of Central Harlem, down the hill, began to show signs of rapid deterioration. And although Hamilton Heights continued to be less affected by what was happening in other parts of Harlem, the neighborhood was not immune to the decline. For a long time, the changes were just more subtle.

As Terry Baker Mulligan wrote in her memoir, "In a crowded city, stingy with space and light, Edgecombe was Harlem's big sky country; a street blessed with a wide-open view, where the sun rose over Harlem and bathed our front windows in a three-season glow."[6] Mulligan describes looking out the window of her Edgecombe Avenue apartment as deep green leaves turned gold and then brown with the approach of autumn. It is almost possible to forget that she was living in a concrete jungle.

It was the same with many of the residents who lived on Convent Avenue or the streets just a short stroll down to the Hudson River on Riverside Drive. These were such choice locations that one felt it would be something akin to sacrilege for them to fall into urban decay.

George Edmond Haynes' grandson Bruce would reflect how his parents used to entertain regularly at their Convent Avenue limestone rowhouse, hosting bridge parties and other gatherings with drinks served in hand-painted, gold-rimmed Italian tumblers and appetizers in Waterford crystal bowls. This second generation of the National Urban League founder could still recall the "Black bourgeoisie" elite that E. Franklin Frazier and others criticized for mimicking white society. Undoubtedly, these social structures in Black communities throughout Harlem built important networks. And, by this point, what may have initially been patterned after Anglo lifestyles in the twenties and thirties could now be seen in the fifties and sixties as incorporated into middle-class Black life.

Increasingly, the author notes, women from this neighborhood could shop anywhere they wanted, not just on 125th Street. Trips to posh Fifth Avenue department stores like Saks, B. Altman, and Sterns on 42nd Street had become commonplace for the women of Sugar Hill.

During those years, Bruce Haynes wrote, "Black middle-class women would come to embody the first 'supermoms' that America produced. Not only did they cook and raise their children, just as their mothers had done before them, but also this generation of women would be the first to have professional careers in traditional middle-class occupations."[7] It is this group of Black women who would be the first to work in integrated settings where they could both demand and receive respect from their white peers, or at least make an effort to do so.

Since Harlem had become solidly Black, it had become routine to describe the neighborhood as a ghetto, the word used to describe urban African American neighborhoods across the country, regardless of the number of hard-working residents or lovely and tasteful homes.

There is a 1963 book called *Harlem: The Making of a Ghetto; Negro New York 1890–1930,* by Gilbert Osofsky, that, by its very title, gives the impression of a blanket moniker of Harlem's place in history. The book, which originated as a Ph.D. dissertation and grew from there, has a lot of very instructive sociological facts and census data about how modern-day Black Harlem came into being. It is a resource often quoted in historic landmark reports, other city and real estate documents, and works of nonfiction.

Yet, some would surmise that it leaves out the heart and spirit of many lovely neighborhoods, relegating almost all of Harlem to what his title indicates: a ghetto. The title and much of its contents minimize the beauty of well-kept, stately brownstones and beautiful apartment buildings, historical architecture, the neighborhood civic groups, professional residents, and proud homeowners that always maintained a sense of community and pride.

In the early days of New York coming into its own in the 1800s, there were pockets of ghettos throughout the city: Irish, Italian, and German. The root meaning of the word "ghetto" was a place where people of a similar race or religion were gathered. But it is Harlem, or rather Black Harlem, that was issued the stigma of being called "a ghetto" not just because of the number of African Americans that came to live there, but the negative societal symptoms as well.

If one traces the word "ghetto" to its fourteenth-century origins, we see that in 1382, after the Venetian government approved Jews living in Venice, they sectioned off a particular area after an outbreak of syphilis. The disease had no certain name, diagnosis, or treatment, but was linked to the arrival of a group of Jews from Spain.

As scholars Bruce Haynes and Ray Hutchison write, "With the act of the Venetian Senate on March 29, 1516, some 700 Jewish households were required to move into the Ghetto Nuovo, an island in Cannaregio sestieri on the northwest edge of the city, with entry controlled by two gates that were locked at sundown."[8] These isolation areas would eventually expand to two other named ghettos where the Jews would leave in the morning to work among the gentiles and then return in the evening.

"While the Ghetto developed as an urban space isolated from the outside world, it provided the Jewish community with some measure of protection."[9] The same sense of protection would be true in the Black neighborhood of Harlem and indeed similar Black areas across the country. There was a large degree of self-segregation that was simply comforting, to be among one's own people without fear of denigration.

> The example of the Jewish Ghetto in Venice connects with the racialization of urban space across many dimensions. Racialization in this instance begins with the forced relocation of a group of persons distinguished as morally different and identified by a particular ethnic feature, their religion, to a physical space that is isolated from other areas of the city.[10]

In this way, a particular area in a city where one race or ethnic group lives becomes identified as being part of a stigmatized group of people living inside a ghetto. Housing restrictions on renting to Black people in areas outside of the confined space—namely, Harlem—added to this confluence of African Americans in one dense area.

More and more, ostensibly starting in the sixties, the word "ghetto" became synonymous with rundown, crime-ridden areas of a city where there were large Black populations, and later where there were generally large groups of people of color.

In his study titled "Conditions among Negroes in the Cities," George Edmund Haynes, the sociologist and cofounder of the National Urban League, observed that "the growing Negro business and professional classes and those engaged in other than domestic and personal service find separate sections in which to dwell. Thus, the Negro ghetto is growing up."[11] Taken within the context of the early twentieth century, it would appear that the word "ghetto" at this time was the one used to signify the gathering in one location of a group of people sharing distinct characteristics.

For the writer Arna Bontemps, the idealism that he and his fellow creative artists had felt in the 1920s at the height of the Harlem Renaissance had faded by the 1940s. In his estimation, the children born of that era had turned into muggers. While this may be a generalization, Bontemps's 1945 article "The Two Harlems" acknowledges that parts of Harlem had turned into a slum, although his wording also supports the definitions of a ghetto as simply being where similar groups of people have been concentrated.

"No matter what else one may see there, Harlem remains what it has always been in essence: a Black ghetto and a slum, a clot in the American bloodstream," he wrote. "And the fruit it was bearing was the fruit of the ghetto and the slum—the fruit of compulsory group segregation based on race."[12]

With the publication of Osofsky's book on Harlem in 1963, "historians increasingly began to use the word ghetto to refer to African American communities. The Harlem of 1930, according to Osofsky, extended from East 98th Street north to West 166th Street, a generous definition that included many areas that were less than ten percent Black."[13] The fact that what was defined as Harlem started to include neighborhoods that had concentrations of Black residents became a sensitive issue. What was once all of Harlem, reaching to the northern tip of the island, was shrinking. Identifying Harlem as the sections where Black people lived reinforced the notion that the very name "Harlem" was synonymous with being a Black neighborhood, which also negated its Dutch history.

So prevalent was this assumption that areas like Hamilton Heights and Sugar Hill were painted with the same broad brush, simply because they too were in Harlem. It mattered not that the neighborhoods were beautiful, the architecture stunning, the homes well kept, and for many years the crime rate much lower than in Central Harlem. In understanding the gentrification that would follow, along with the renaming of so much of Harlem as Washington Heights, which had steadily increased since the early twentieth century, the history of how these neighborhoods came to be described as a ghetto is enlightening.

Education took a far-reaching turn in Hamilton Heights when, in 1961, the Fiorello H. LaGuardia High School of Music & Art in Hamilton Heights and the High School of Performing Arts downtown on West 46th Street merged. The two schools maintained their individual locations until a joint campus could be built. The High School of Performing Arts opened in 1948, twelve years after the creation of the High School of Music & Art in Hamilton Heights. The school was located at 120 West 46th Street, not far from Times Square. It was created as part of the Metropolitan Vocational High School, but with a focus on harnessing the students' various talents in dance, music, and/or drama with the goal of a career in one of those fields. The professionals on staff included the young Sidney Lumet in the drama department. He would go on to a luminous career as screenwriter and director for films such as *12 Angry Men*, *Dog Day Afternoon*, and *Network*.

Also in these years, former Sugar Hill resident W. E. B. Du Bois was still revered as being part of the old guard of activists and intellectuals who helped usher in a new era for Black people. He had often feuded with the management of the NAACP, the organization he had helped to create, about the direction of its approach to civil rights. The final parting of the ways came in 1948. Thanks to his radical political views, Du Bois' passport had been confiscated by the United States government several times. After many visits to Ghana, in West Africa, Du Bois moved there in 1961, where he died on August 27, 1963, at the age of ninety-three.

The next day, by great coincidence, the historic March on Washington took place. An estimated 250,000 people from across the country gathered on the National Mall in Washington, D.C., with speakers and performers facing them against a backdrop of the Lincoln Memorial. Speakers included longtime Civil Rights leaders A. Philip Randolph and Bayard Rustin, two of the original proponents of the event.

The national headquarters during the planning of the March was in Harlem at 170 West 130th Street, a building that would become a designated landmark.

Sugar Hill resident and NAACP president Roy Wilkins, John Lewis, chairman of the Student Nonviolent Coordinating Committee, and actors Ossie Davis and Ruby Dee were among the many prominent people in attendance. Marian Anderson, Joan Baez, Bob Dylan, and Mahalia Jackson sang. It was Mahalia who called out to Martin Luther King Jr. in the middle of his speech, "Tell 'em about the dream, Martin; tell 'em about the dream!"

There were few alive in the sixties who would remember Harlem before its urbanization and the building boom. Between the Major Deegan Expressway with an exit at 155th Street and the Harlem River Drive, which was completed in 1964, the waterfront around the Harlem River in Sugar Hill was no longer a pedestrian attraction, nor was the High Bridge. The river had become polluted, with many former walking paths blocked, and there was little to entice pedestrians. In the 1970s, public access to the High Bridge was discontinued. It didn't take long for community groups to spring up, petitioning the city to repair it. But that would be decades in the making.

The once elegant Hamilton Theatre on 146th and Broadway, which had been in decline for years, closed in March of 1965. Its final screenings were *Send Me No Flowers*, starring Doris Day, and *Taggart*, with Dan Duryea.

The once stunning vaudeville house–turned movie theater was no longer a place of entertainment, though the shops in the street storefronts would continue to operate.

The federal government and states have become much more cognizant of how important it is to preserve our physical landmarks and neighborhoods. What happened with John James Audubon's Harlem home on Riverside Drive, disregarding legal challenges to preserve the building, is less likely today. There are still many landmarks in Hamilton Heights, or should-be landmarks, where people were born, died, created great works of literature, art, and music, and planned significant cultural and political events, that are being remodeled, torn down, or ignored. Indeed, these are some of the criteria for national landmark status and part of the reason that Hamilton Heights and Sugar Hill, as well as so many of the incredible structures within it, would be given landmark status.

The Grange was acquired by the National Park Service on April 27, 1962. It became known as the Hamilton Grange National Memorial, and its official designation was signed into law by President John F. Kennedy. The following year, the nation would be rocked to its core when a little before noon on November 22, 1963, President Kennedy was assassinated as he rode in a motorcade through Dealey Plaza in Dallas, Texas.

For Hamilton Heights, the main business areas started roughly at 145th Street, along the avenues St. Nicholas, Amsterdam, and Broadway. On Edgecombe, St. Nicholas Place, Convent, and Riverside Drive, it was still almost exclusively residential. This was the reigning day of the small mom-and-pop stores: food markets, hair salons, barber shops, hardware stores, restaurants, bars, shoe repair shops, dry cleaners, and laundries where you still got clothes washed, folded, and returned to you in a neat pile wrapped in brown paper. Sugar Hill supported its own, and Copeland's on 145th Street, between Amsterdam and Broadway, was still thriving as the neighborhood place where "intimate, upscale soul food establishment where Stevie Wonder, Harry Belafonte, and Sammy Davis Jr. had once been regulars."[14]

The Grange was further designated a New York City landmark in August of 1967, and it remained nestled between St. Luke's Episcopal Church and an apartment building, awaiting plans as to what its future should be. A key issue was how to safely extract it from between the two buildings for a move to a suitable new location. One suggestion was to demolish several houses in the neighborhood and to move the Grange to the site where they had been located.

The National Park Service archives hold a letter dated December 4,

1967, from one local homeowners' group that was written, but we understand not mailed, to Senator Jacob E. Javits about their concerns.

> As residents of the Hamilton Grange Community, we wish to solicit your help in preventing the demolition of our homes for the purpose of creating a Memorial to Alexander Hamilton. The present site chosen by Local Planning Board #9 and the National Park Service involves the destruction of six private homes and one or two apartment dwellings, housing 42 to 84 families. This would involve the uprooting of stable "middle-class tax-paying" Negro families. The neighborhood involved has a history of being maintained at the very highest possible level, even before the First Lady's program of beautification was introduced.[15]

Fortunately for all, this plan was dropped.

Harlem had always been a place where the arts flourished. In 1964 the internationally acclaimed soprano Dorothy Maynor founded the Harlem School of the Arts (HSA) at 141st Street and St. Nicholas Avenue in the basement of the St. James Presbyterian Church, a block from Hamilton Grange. The site was located at the outer edge of what had been Hamilton's property, a close approximation to the place where he had once told Eliza they would need to build a fence to keep the cows secure.

Maynor believed that world-class training in the arts benefits both children and their families and adds an element of pride to the community. It was a time when Central Harlem was beginning to suffer severe physical blight and high levels of poverty and offered few cultural resources for its young people. She would have opened the Hamilton Heights arts school to help remedy that. Its senior choreographer was Arthur Mitchell, New York City Ballet's first Black dancer.

Dorothy Maynor was a 1933 graduate of the prestigious HBCU Hampton Institute in Virginia. She then received a scholarship to Westminster Choir School in Princeton, New Jersey. It was while performing at the Berkshire Festival in 1939 that she came to the attention of Serge Koussevitzky, the conductor of the Boston Symphony Orchestra. Koussevitzky was so impressed by Maynor's voice that he facilitated her debut at Town Hall in New York City.

In 1949 Maynor became the first African American to sing at a presidential inauguration, performing at Harry Truman's inaugural gala and again at Dwight D. Eisenhower's 1953 inauguration at the U.S. Capitol. Not far away, in 1939 the Daughters of the American Revolution had refused to let Marian Anderson sing at Constitution Hall. In response,

First Lady Eleanor Roosevelt resigned from the organization. President Roosevelt, in support of his wife's actions, arranged for Anderson to sing at the Lincoln Memorial in Washington, D.C. The world-renowned conductor Arturo Toscanini said of Anderson that she had a voice heard once in a hundred years. She would also become friends with librarian Regina Anderson Andrews and spend time at Regina's country home.

A decade after founding the Harlem School of the Arts, Dorothy Maynor became the first African American on the board of directors of the New York Metropolitan Opera.

One of the most complex individuals to emerge from mid-century Harlem was the man who would become known as Malcolm X, a highly controversial and polarizing figure who was outspoken about the need for African Americans to embrace their power and do more to control their own futures. A devout Muslim, the one-time hustler had had a public falling-out with Nation of Islam leader Elijah Muhammad, his former mentor. Malcolm had come a long way from when he worked at Jimmie's Chicken Shack on West 148th Street and St. Nicholas Avenue. Unknown to most people, he had been meeting regularly with the author Alex Haley, who was writing Malcolm's biography.

On February 21, 1965, Malcolm X was assassinated by gunmen at the Audubon Ballroom on 165th and Broadway, which would sadly become infamous because of this violent act. *The Autobiography of Malcolm X*, Haley's first book, was published the same year; Haley's widely praised work *Roots*, tracing his ancestors, would come some years later.

By the 1960s many of the clubs in Sugar Hill were closing their doors or had stopped presenting music. The 721 Club no longer offered live music and had become just a neighborhood bar called the Spot. An evening out on the Hill in the 1960s would have included stops at Sherman's BBQ at Amsterdam and 151st Street or Lin Fong's Chinese Restaurant at Broadway and 145th Street. Then one could have drinks at the Lido Bar on Amsterdam and 150th Street.

Number 773 St. Nicholas Avenue had undergone several name and management changes since it opened in 1935 as the Poosepahtuck Club. After having morphed in the 1940s from Luckey's Rendezvous to the Pink Angel, in 1965 new owner Earl Spain renamed it St. Nick's Pub, the name by which it would forever afterward be known. Legendary musicians, those with dreams of fame as well as the house band variety, would come to play at the location that had already cemented its place in Harlem history after more than three decades on Sugar Hill.

St. Nicholas Avenue had been the epitome of a "pub crawl" for decades, with the added benefit of stirring jazz. There were fewer clubs offering music by the sixties, but it continued to be great when it came to hopping from one nightspot to the next.

Right off St. Nicholas Avenue at 400 West 148th Street was the 400 Tavern, which is believed to have closed sometime in the 1970s. The neighborhood still had its share of after-hours joints, called speakeasies during prohibition. But the 400 Tavern was one of the few clubs that was not on one of the avenues, but right off it. Lundy's at 147th and St. Nicholas was another of the successful bar/nightclubs that made St. Nicholas Avenue so well-known and was owned originally by Charles Lundy. Like most of these combined restaurant jazz clubs, it was known for its delicious food, with steaks, chops, and cheesecake on the menu.

Other changes were well underway. By the 1960s, the demographics of those frequenting the Audubon Theater and Ballroom on Broadway had long since changed. African Americans had by this time laid claim to the building, hosting lavish parties there as well as "Bring Your Own Brown

Figure 69. Harlem Nightclub; Unknown Artists, circa 1970. Courtesy David "Turk" McNeil Collection

Bag" (BYOBB) dances where one paid a modest entrance fee and could bring in one's own alcoholic beverage of choice, while a band or DJ provided dance music.

A devastating event a few years later in a city a thousand miles away would overshadow these shifts in the neighborhood's character.

On April 4, 1968, when visiting Memphis in support of a sanitation workers' strike there, the Rev. Dr. Martin Luther King Jr. was fatally shot on the balcony of the Lorraine Motel while leaving the room with Ralph Abernathy and Jesse Jackson. Over the next week the country erupted in violence, with riots in more than a hundred cities. In New York Mayor John Lindsay went to Harlem, where he had been several times, and spoke directly to the throngs of Black people on 125th Street, expressing his sorrow over King's assassination. Often publicly sympathetic to civil rights issues, Lindsay was credited with averting riots in the nation's largest Black neighborhood even as other cities across the nation burned.

In a tumultuous year with rising protests over the Vietnam War, the pileup of tragedies continued. Robert Kennedy, the Democrat who was running for president that year, was an outspoken supporter for greater rights for African Americans. He would be assassinated just two months later, on June 5, 1968, while exiting through the kitchen of the Ambassador Hotel in Los Angeles, moments after winning the California primary.

During this period, the ideology of the new Black Panther Party for Self-Defense (BPP), founded in 1966 by Huey P. Newton and Bobby Seale in Oakland, California, started taking root in New York City. The more recognized formation of the New York City chapter was in 1968 and was believed to be inspired by Dr. King Jr.'s assassination.

Several branches sprang up quickly throughout the boroughs, fueled by the activism of existing movements already demanding equality in housing, jobs, and education for African Americans. The New York chapters became the strongest of the multi-city expansion of the Black Panther Party. Several meetings were held in the East Village, and then the members moved uptown to establish the Harlem chapter on 141st and Seventh Avenue (now Malcolm X Blvd). Lumumba and Afeni Shakur went to Harlem, and Sekou Oding went to the Bronx.

The concept of an organized Black militant-appearing group demanding societal changes struck fear in a lot of people, and the FBI waged war against them. But along with some more radical members, mostly there were calls for civil and human rights changes. A great deal of what the Panther Party did was to help Black communities. Among some of the programs they organized were those to help fight police brutality and the opening of drug addiction clinics, school breakfast programs, and sickle cell anemia screenings.

Organized government infiltration of the BPP and disinformation caused distrust and tension between the Oakland and New York chapters. The arrest and indictment of several New York members fractured the Panther Party. One of its early and youngest members was Jamal Joseph, just fifteen when he joined the Harlem chapter. After several years in prison and a circuitous route on a different path, Joseph would later pen a memoir, *Panther Baby*, and eventually become a Columbia University professor. Afeni Shakur would give birth in 1971 to a son: Tupac Shakur. By the mid-seventies, the Panthers' activism would begin to dwindle. Despite differing opinions on ideology and the arrests, murders, and imprisonment of several members, the party would remain active until 1982.

The changes in Hamilton Heights continued. The main public grammar school for the area that opened in 1903, P.S. 186 at 145th Street, between Amsterdam and Broadway, had become highly diverse, reflecting the neighborhood's changing demographics. Harry Belafonte and choreographer Arthur Mitchell were two of its famous alumni. Children from a variety of economic, social, and racial backgrounds attended. But by the 1960s, conditions at the Hamilton Heights school had been declining for years and became steadily worse. The crumbling building, with almost no security, invited crime and vandals. It finally closed its doors in 1975, and it would remain a vacant eyesore for decades before finding a new purpose. In 2016, after a $48 million renovation, the old school would be converted into a mixed-use apartment building for low- and middle-income New Yorkers, as well as a huge new Boys and Girls Club of Harlem. The designers would include modern upgraded features while managing to preserve some of its historic architectural and interior design characteristics.

There were no major food chains on the hill. Rather, the Food Family Market, on St. Nicholas Avenue at 147th, would remain the well-supported neighborhood grocery store in Hamilton Heights for decades, well into the twenty-first century. It would adapt to the changing tastes of demographic trends over the years and change ownership.

Crime increased throughout the neighborhood. Women were clutching their purses more tightly. St. Nicholas Avenue was lined with more "welfare moms hanging out on the stoops," as Bruce Haynes described, "and men standing outside neighborhood dives like Lundy's, which stayed open all day and all night."[16] The local bars had always attracted hardworking men and women who became regulars, but the newer patrons now included a steady stream of individuals with unsavory backgrounds.

Student unrest was the order of the day. Young people were protesting the Vietnam War and insisting that they be more involved in the curriculum and on issues of diversity. African Americans were emboldened by the active Civil Rights Movement of the 1960s to be more demanding of their rights as human beings.

In Hamilton Heights, on April 22, 1969, a group of students at City College took over Klapper Hall in a call for more diversity in student enrollment, the faculty, and the curriculum. The protestors included Black, white, and Puerto Rican activists. On May 4, after a two-week standoff and much negotiation, they agreed to vacate the premises. "The campus was electric, students in dashikis and Afros, African drum circles, assorted smoke wafting through the air. The administration had agreed to a controversial open enrollment plan, and the university's president, Dr. Buell Gallagher, had resigned."[17]

Later that summer two incredible music events took place. One would immediately become a legendary music and cultural phenomenon, and the other would be all but forgotten for almost fifty years. On the weekend of August 15–18, 1969, the Woodstock Music and Art Fair took place in Bethel, New York, on a dairy farm. An estimated 400,000 people showed up, and the inexperienced promoters probably would have been happy if 5,000 had attended. It opened with Richie Havens, had a middle section that included Joan Baez, Arlo Guthrie, the Grateful Dead, Janis Joplin, and Sly and the Family Stone, and closed with a performance by Jimi Hendrix that is the stuff of musical lore and is still talked about fifty years later.

That same summer, over the course of six weeks, from June 29 to August 24, the Third Harlem Cultural Festival was held in Mount Morris Park in Central Harlem, the same park that two Harlem kids—Richard Rodgers and Oscar Hammerstein II—both played in as children. The entire event was filmed, and then the footage was stored in closets and basements. The performers included Stevie Wonder, Nina Simone, Sly and the Family Stone, Gladys Knight & the Pips, Mahalia Jackson, B. B. King, the Fifth Dimension, and many more. It would be 2021 before the rediscovered tapes were made into an Oscar-winning documentary by musician Ahmir "Questlove" Thompson called "Summer of Soul." At the August 17th concert, Nina Simone sang "To Be Young, Gifted and Black" for the first time.

It might seem fitting that the neighborhood that had developed around Alexander Hamilton's former thirty-two acres in Harlem had become home to a string of important cultural and civic institutions—the prestigious City

College; Hamilton's alma mater, Columbia; the Harlem School of the Arts; the High School of Music & Art; the Dance Theatre of Harlem; and beautiful places of worship.

Hamilton was among the other Founding Fathers who owned people, despite the irony of having been one of those who founded the Manumission Society in New York City to help free those same people. And his former estate in Harlem wound up inhabited by their descendants, as well as hundreds of people from his Caribbean roots. As fate would have it, an annual U.S. Virgin Islands music festival, inclusive of his former St. Croix homeland, would be held for several years in Bradhurst Park, a short walk from the Grange.

The historian Eric Sloane grew up on Hamilton Terrace after World War I, a few blocks from the Grange. He revisited the neighborhood as memories about his old childhood home drew him back to New York. Sloane's 1968 book, *Mr. Daniels and the Grange*, is about the sad condition of Hamilton's former home and about its caretaker, Raleigh Henry Daniels, the old Black man who lived in the basement and was the house's only inhabitant.

The book started out as an effort to drum up support for repairing the Grange. But after Sloane met the caretaker and had several long conversations with him, the book ended up focusing much more on Daniels. Sloane admitted that while growing up he had not known that the house belonged to Hamilton.

In 1966, shortly before Sloane's visits began, Mary Ann Clark came to New York City to see her fiancé, Laurens Morgan Hamilton, the great-great grandson of Alexander Hamilton. One of the places she and her friend visited was the Grange. It was closed when they arrived, but as they were peering through the windows, Mr. Daniels came up, unlocked the house, and showed the pair around. Years later, when telling a Park Department staff member about the friendly caretaker, she said that the thing she remembered most was that although the house was so empty, the late afternoon sun was nevertheless shining brightly through the rooms.

Daniels told Sloane that he thought the Grange was a sad house. "The sadness seems to have a special meaning; perhaps I am the only one aware of that," he said. "It is as if the General wants to say something across the years, and there is no one else to listen."[18]

Knowing the caretaker was willing to make small repairs at his own expense, Sloane noted that it must have been frustrating for him to have to deal with the layers of bureaucracy of the federal Department of the

Interior. Sloane met with Daniels several times and made lovely sketches as part of his research, reimagining events and details having to do with the old house.

The role that the former St. Luke's pastor played in saving Hamilton's home became apparent during Sloane's research. "Tuttle was the savior of the Grange," he wrote. "If not for his insight, determination, and generosity it is doubtful whether the Hamilton house would be standing today."[19] The Grange may have been saved by Reverend Tuttle's efforts decades before, but it was still in a state of decline in 1967, despite now being owned by the federal government.

In 1968, a group of community activists, philanthropists, and artists, including Romare Bearden, who had attended primary school in Sugar Hill, founded the Studio Museum at 2033 Fifth Avenue off 125th Street in Harlem. The gallery was created to involve the Harlem community more with the cultural life of the city. It would thrive in its mission to focus on exhibits of African American artists, present films, and encourage and provide support to budding talent. The museum would grow in stature in the coming decades to expand its goals and present mixed media and multicultural events. Bearden's works would be exhibited many times as his fame as an artist grew to new heights. Harlem's premiere photographer, James Van der Zee, would also have his legacy preserved by the museum.

In 1969 Arthur Mitchell and Karel Shook founded the Dance Theatre of Harlem (DTH). Mitchell had begun by teaching dance in a converted garage just down the street from the Grange, at 152nd Street off Convent Avenue, and he would leave the doors open so people passing by could see what was going on.

Mitchell had made history in 1955 when he became the first Black principal dancer in the New York City Ballet. He had also been a protégé of George Balanchine, the legendary Russian-born dancer and choreographer who was the cofounder of the School of American Ballet.

By 1979 the Dance Theatre of Harlem was touring internationally. The company would carve a niche for itself, infusing classic works with new life, and would continue to break racial and political boundaries. DTH had the distinction of being the first American ballet company to perform in Russia after the fall of the Soviet Union. Throughout its fame and periods of financial struggle, the company would remain in its same Sugar Hill location, a mere block or two from the last eighteenth-century Jan Dyckman family Stone House.

The Hamilton Grange Branch of the New York Public Library, which had opened in 1907 at 503 West 145th Street, now houses multiple collections to serve an ever-growing, ethnically diverse community. The Schomburg Branch library on 135th Street where Regina Anderson once worked had served as an exemplary model for what a library could mean to a community in terms of outreach. That model was now the cornerstone of all library branches.

"The African-American population of the neighborhood continued to grow through the 1970s, when the Harlem Task Force characterized the neighborhood's population, from 142nd Street to 165th Street, as totally Black."[20]

In 1970 Charles Gordone became the first African American to win the Pulitzer Prize in Drama for his play *No Place to Be Somebody*, and one of the original stars, Marjorie Eliot, would take her own place in the history of Sugar Hill twenty years later.

In the 1970s, the city's 14.8 percent poverty rate rose to 20 percent by 1980, seven points higher than the national average. Nearly one million people moved out of Manhattan, some to Queens or the Bronx, where they could more easily afford to buy a house. Harlem, the Bowery, Hell's Kitchen, and even Times Square evidenced a city in decline. In the mid-1970s, "faced with economic stagnation, industrial decline, and the looming threat of bankruptcy, the City of New York responded by laying off city workers and cutting municipal services such as sanitation and after-school programs."[21]

Dr. Bruce Haynes quoted his grandfather George Haynes Sr.'s brilliant sociological study of 1913, written two decades before he became one of Sugar Hill's most prominent residents. It defined what had created ghettos in urban environments. And these were the societal injustices inflicted upon African Americans that led to the destruction of large sections of Harlem and eventually impacted life in the Heights.

George Haynes' analysis of the segregation of Blacks into crowded, poorly maintained housing where they were paying high rents was exacerbated by a lack of education and not having anyone to teach them about adjusting to city life. It was the foundation of what made his cofounding of the National Urban League so important. Haynes knew that if African Americans lacked training and the opportunity to get the training, they would be unqualified for better-paid occupations "by the prejudice of fellow-employees and frequently by the prejudice of employers; with a small income and the resulting low standard of living, the wonder is not that Negroes have a uniformly higher death-rate than whites in the cities and towns, but that the mortality is as small as it is and shows signs of decrease."[22]

230 · ADVENT OF THE SIXTIES

Racism created the conditions in Harlem for which the Black residents were then criticized for living in as they tried to raise families and struggle for survival. In a parallel universe, one could wonder what Harlem would have looked like a century later had it not become "Black Harlem." A harmonious community might have defied the harsh decline if whites who were living there at the beginning of the Great Migration had not moved out in fear of being near Black people, but rather welcomed their new neighbors and helped them acclimate to the city.

It was during the seventies that the Morris-Jumel Mansion began to engage in more community outreach. Given the significance of the year 1776 to the founding of the United States, it is no surprise that the 1976 bicentennial and the 200th anniversary of the Battle of Harlem Heights held special meaning for the mansion. Large crowds gathered to tour the house and see the Revolutionary War reenactors.

Carol Ward wrote how the decade saw the museum increase its educational mission focusing on more inclusivity for "families and school groups to inform the next generation about American history."[23] But while the costumed events continued in this decade, those who managed the oldest residence in New York City were coming to realize that they too must change how its history was presented.

The original downstairs kitchen at the museum was restored, and visitors could see the hearth and beehive oven as they looked when the house was built. But the subject of the enslaved people who worked in those kitchens was still not part of the conversation on tours. Despite the fact that they had helped build it, that enslaved and free Blacks had worked in the house for sixty years, there are some parts of history that many people preferred to skip. It doesn't mean it didn't happen, just that it can be an uncomfortable conversation.

"The biggest event of the 1970s for the mansion was a visit by Queen Elizabeth II and Prince Philip for the bicentennial. They came up to the museum on July 9, 1976, and the Morris-Jumel Mansion was their only stop for the day."[24] In addition to a formal receiving line to greet invited guests, some of the musicians from 555 Edgecombe across the street attended. The Queen also toured the gardens.

People responded enthusiastically to more welcoming community involvement at the museum. The *New York Amsterdam News* article "Marie Brooks Dancers entertain at Sugar Hill" would report on Muhammad Ali's visit to the Jumel Mansion in 1982. The boxer helped celebrate the first block social held by the 162nd Street Block Association. Renee Minus White wrote that though the afternoon was grey, "it didn't stop over

Figure 70. Queen Elizabeth II and Prince Philip at Morris-Jumel Mansion, 1976. Public domain

250 Black families of Sugar Hill's Jumel area from feasting on barbecue spareribs and chicken dinners."[25] It would be an affirmation of the mansion's support of events that were indicative of the neighborhood's new demographics.

In the century since its founding, Knickerbocker Hospital had become one of the main medical institutions for residents of Hamilton Heights and Sugar Hill, which meant that the majority of its patients were now people of color. The hospital had started out in 1862 as a place for the indigent, with a "no Negroes" policy. On May 31, 1959, when Billie Holiday was taken there by ambulance, she was turned away, supposedly because she was a drug addict. She was sent to Metropolitan Hospital in East Harlem, and she died there on July 17, 1959. With its dwindling donor funds, those people of color that the hospital had historically refused to serve and the large Medicaid funds that came with them was what had sustained the hospital in recent years. An investigation of Medicare and Medicaid fraud led the hospital to the brink of collapse, and it finally closed in 1971.

As the 1960s and '70s brought a greater sense of Black pride and a desire to reclaim African American heritage, the names of some major thoroughfares in Harlem were changed to reflect those feelings. In 1974 the portion of Seventh Avenue that lies in Harlem was officially renamed Adam Clayton Powell Jr. Boulevard in honor of the late pastor turned politician who had represented Harlem in Congress for more than a quarter of a century. In 1977 a large stretch of Eighth Avenue was renamed Frederick Douglass Boulevard to pay tribute to the nineteenth-century writer and abolitionist. In 1984 West 125th Street assumed the joint name of both 125th Street and Dr. Martin Luther King Jr. Boulevard. And in 1987 Lenox Avenue was rechristened Malcolm X Boulevard.

It would take two generations or more for some of the "old timers" who disagreed with renaming the boulevards to grow accustomed to the new names. Then there would come a time when no one had ever heard of Seventh, Eighth, or Lenox avenues, because time does not stand still.

Despite evident decline on some of the side streets and the major commercial streets, Edgecombe and Convent avenues were still fairly untouched and for the most part would remain so. Yet a block over from Convent on St. Nicholas Avenue, with the myriad bars still featuring numbers runners and stolen goods hawked for sale, a notorious coke dealer named Nicky Barnes openly ran his business at the Mark Four Bar. He got robbed so often that he finally changed his base of operation a few blocks away to 147th Street, closer to Broadway, which was becoming a rougher part of Hamilton Heights.

In 1977, Barnes was convicted and sentenced to two decades in prison. Frank Lucas, his biggest rival when it came to drug trafficking in Harlem, had been found guilty the year before and was already serving a long prison sentence. (Lucas's story would one day be told in the 2007 movie *American Gangster*, with actor Denzel Washington as the title character.)

The year 1977 was much more memorable to most New Yorkers for another reason. On the night of July 13th electrical power failed throughout New York City in what would be called "the great blackout." During more than twenty-four hours without power, there was widespread violence and looting, while scores of police officers did not respond to the emergency calls to report to work. And many of those who did were injured trying to subdue rioters.

The areas with the most looting were primarily the Black and Latino neighborhoods of Harlem, the South Bronx, Bedford-Stuyvesant, and Jamaica, Queens. But other neighborhoods were not immune. On Broadway in Brooklyn and in midtown, looters devastated businesses, going first after high-end items. At the Ace Pontiac Showroom on Jerome Avenue in the University Heights section of the Bronx, fifty brand new cars were stolen, driven through the showroom after a steel door and windows were smashed. When the blackout ended a day later, more than 1,600 businesses had been looted, some bankrupted and never to reopen.

There were growing changes to the racial demographics in the Hamilton Heights–Sugar Hill area and its adjoining neighborhood of Washington Heights. Ever since the 1950s New York City had had a large Latino population. For decades the newcomers were largely Puerto Ricans who had taken advantage of their American citizenship to move to the mainland. But the late 1970s and 1980s brought a huge influx of Cubans and Dominicans, especially in the area of Washington Heights, which bordered Sugar Hill.

A massive increase in the drug trade took place, with heroin and coke giving way to the cheaper derivative crack cocaine. Seemingly overnight, an array of Latin and West Indian dealers took over, and the changes to Hamilton Heights evidenced itself with a dramatic increase in both drugs and crime.

By 2002 reports by the National Drug Intelligence Center of the Department of Justice would outline the increasing number of Asian, Colombian, Dominican, Jamaican, Puerto Rican, and other ethnically diverse drug trafficking organizations (DTOs) operating in New York. The 2008 National Drug Intelligence Report would state that "Dominican organizations are based primarily in the Washington Heights section of Upper Manhattan and serve as midlevel cocaine and heroin distributors to lower-level distributors." Many of the Washington Heights neighborhoods are areas that were formerly considered Sugar Hill.

The boundaries of the original Dutch Harlem had changed dramatically over the centuries from when Harlem stretched to the northwestern tip of the island in what is now Inwood. More areas to the northwest of Hamilton Heights started to be renamed Washington Heights. And 155th Street began to regularly be noted as the dividing line between Harlem and Washington Heights. While it was generally recognized by all who lived in these neighborhoods that Washington Heights began across Broadway, somewhere starting around 165th, this boundary could change according to whom you were speaking. Yet there was never any notion, until gentrification eventually set in, that it stretched as far as St. Nicholas or Edgecombe Avenue.

At least two different twentieth-century sources noted the area beyond 155th Street as still being Harlem. Gilbert Osofsky's much-quoted 1963 book *Harlem: The Making of a Ghetto; Negro New York, 1890–1930* defined Harlem's 1930 boundaries extending to West 166th Street. And forty years later, the 1973 report by Department of Housing and Urban Development/Harlem Urban Development Corporation recorded the population from 142nd Street to 165th Street as totally Black. And since Central Harlem's southern boundary at Eighth Avenue ends at about 155th Street, the 165th Street outer border would cover the elevated sections of Hamilton Heights at St. Nicholas Avenue stretching to the Hudson.

The Harlem School of the Arts on St. Nicholas Avenue had continued to thrive in the years since Dorothy Maynor had founded it in 1964 in the basement of a church. In May of 1979 the school opened a 37,000-square-foot building at 645 St. Nicholas Avenue, adjacent to its original location, allowing it to expand significantly. From there one could see the building at 580 St. Nicholas Avenue, where the librarian Regina Anderson and her roommates had held their literary salons.

The curriculum at HSA would gradually expand to include: a Music Program with all the instruments of an orchestra and African and Latin percussion and voice; an official recognition as a Steinway Select School, offering private and group instruction in strings, woodwinds, brass, piano, guitar, percussion, and voice; and an expanded Dance Program to develop students' physical strengths and creativity, guiding them in performance skills.

Toni Morrison wrote in her second novel, *Sula*, that for generations the Black people in the book had lived in a section of Medallion, Ohio, called "the bottom," that was actually on a hill. The Black residents realized that it was the only time they got to look down on the whites living in the valley below. But at some point, the people in the valley decided that they wanted the property on the hill with its wonderful views and cool breezes so they could build a golf course.

There is a comparison one could make to what began happening in Harlem, and particularly Hamilton Heights, and those fictional characters in the Bottom. By the 1970s real estate prices in Manhattan had escalated to such a point that solidly middle-income families could not afford to buy a place to live. Even people with healthier balance sheets could not afford a co-op apartment or a brownstone in much of Downtown, Midtown, and the Upper East and West Sides around those desirable sections near Zabar's and Columbus Avenue.

However, beautiful brownstones and apartments in Hamilton Heights could be bought for a fraction of the prices they would have fetched in many other parts of the borough. There was a growing appreciation of the stunning townhouses that had been built around the turn of the twentieth century and had long been ignored by those wanting a Manhattan address.

It was Toni Morrison's fictional "Bottom" come to life. Nonetheless, the idea of moving to Harlem was not easy for many people to imagine.

With a new century approaching, large sections of Central Harlem had become destroyed, with neglected or abandoned buildings dotting many areas that had once been beautiful and well-kept. Hamilton Heights was not invulnerable, with aging rundown brownstones that were also left empty and forsaken. The sociological and economic reasons for this decline are complicated, but they had a great deal to do with slum landlords who refused to fix properties or homeowners whose financial problems made it hard for them to keep up with repairs, taxes, or a mortgage.

Yet it was this abandonment of the buildings that became the catalyst for the city and some very savvy and opportunistic developers to take a closer look at the buildings and property in Harlem that might suddenly be available.

A new era in colonization was on the horizon, as these neighborhoods slowly and then more steadily saw an increase in white people moving to Harlem. It was a brave new world and would create far-reaching societal changes.

The perception of Harlem as a haven for African Americans had dissipated somewhat. At this point Black people could, for the most part, live wherever they chose, and many chose to leave Harlem and in some cases New York City. For more than sixty years Harlem had represented a place of cultural and racial pride for African Americans, and Hamilton Heights and Sugar Hill had retained a distinction as the crème de la crème of Harlem—the Beverly Hills of Harlem, if you will.

All this would change.

Chapter 13

A Neighborhood's Changing Face

> Are the Negroes going to be able to hold Harlem? ... Can they hold this choice bit of Manhattan Island? When colored people do leave Harlem, their homes, their churches, their investments and their businesses, it will be because the land has become so valuable they can no longer afford to live on it.
>
> —James Weldon Johnson
> "Harlem: The Culture Capital," in *The New Negro: An Interpretation*, 1925

By the 1980s, some of the Hamilton Heights residents who had understood what this neighborhood meant for African Americans and had tried to preserve its history were aging or dead. Hamilton Heights and Sugar Hill remained predominantly Black districts that still clung to their glory days from the first half of the twentieth century, but people were forgetting the past.

Some of the once-handsome brownstones were abandoned because of structural problems that made them expensive to repair and maintain. Because of their age, the buildings were often beautiful to look at. But they were in desperate need of electrical upgrades to allow for more powerful appliances. And plumbing that had been state-of-the-art in the late nineteenth and early twentieth centuries was crumbling by the 1980s.

On St. Nicholas and Amsterdam avenues, more than a few people could be seen drinking from something in a brown paper bag. The drug trade, first heroin and then crack cocaine, along the avenues had also increased dramatically. You didn't have to look hard to see drug dealers and other individuals whom you wouldn't want to meet in a dark alley. The neighborhood that as recently as a decade earlier had boasted of the lack of graffiti began to see growing evidence of it. None of these problems had reached epidemic proportions, but things were clearly falling apart.

For more than two and a half centuries, from its official founding in 1658 until about 1920, Harlem had been mostly a mix of Dutch, German, Irish, and Italian families. Large pockets of Hamilton Heights and Sugar Hill were still home to a sizeable white population through the 1930s. Not all whites moved out, yet the neighborhood on the hill became predominantly Black, just as in Central Harlem. But by the 1990s the Black population in Hamilton Heights had started steadily dwindling.

A variety of social and economic forces at work in New York City in the seventies and eighties made Harlem a perfect target for gentrification. Hamilton Heights and Sugar Hill would become an epicenter of skyrocketing real estate prices.

What seemed like a symbolic marker of the changes occurred in 1981 with the death of Mary Lou Williams, one of the people who had made Hamilton Heights such a special place in the 1930s and '40s. The gifted pianist, arranger, and composer, whose opinion had been sought out by the greatest jazz musicians of the era, passed away on May 28 of that year from cancer. She was seventy-one and had been living in Durham, North Carolina, where she taught jazz history at Duke University.

Williams had welcomed musicians into her home in Hamilton Heights, but according to the extensive obituaries detailing her life, including one in the *New York Times*, she had taken that outreach to a new level, "scraping together whatever she could from royalty checks and friends (including Dizzy and Lorraine Gillespie) to take in the poor and help musicians struggling with addiction."[1] The effort stretched her thin, but she persisted.

Williams' apartment at 63 Hamilton Terrace became a haven for musicians of all stripes: those who were unknown, those on the rise, and those who were already famous. "I'd leave the door open for them if I was out," she said years later. "Tadd Dameron would come to write when he was out of inspiration, and Thelonious Monk did several of his pieces there. Bud Powell's brother, Richie, who also played piano, learned how to improvise at my house."[2] Charlie Parker and Miles Davis asked her opinion about different bands they were putting together.

Some years later, inspired by her conversion to Catholicism and intense periods of prayer, Williams composed a series of religious choral works, one of which she performed to thousands in a standing-room-only crowd in the first jazz mass ever presented at St. Patrick's Cathedral. Eventually Mary Lou accepted a position as artist in residence at Duke University in

North Carolina. But she continued to perform and promote the majesty of jazz, and her Hamilton Heights home had been one of those places where a little bit of magic happened. There is a famous 1958 picture taken by Art Kane titled, "A Day in Harlem," featuring a host of legendary jazz musicians. Mary Lou Williams is standing among them on the first row next to Thelonious Monk.

The word "gentrification" was coined in the 1960s in London by a German-British sociologist and city planner, Ruth Glass. She wrote about how the upper-class gentry or "landed gentry" of large landowners, who were a step below the nobility, were displacing poor people in London as they moved in to refurbish houses and flats in previous working-class areas. The word is widely used now, often racially and socially charged, and generally defined as the movement of upper-class (or wealthy) people into declining urban areas. The shift often brings an influx of new development to the neighborhoods, improved infrastructure, high-end stores, and other improvements. Yet it generally causes property values to increase, and it has the direct effect of driving out poorer families, many of whom have lived there for generations. And in New York City its effects were especially powerful in neighborhoods like Harlem, where changes that started in the 1980s became more noticeable roughly in the 1990s. The same thing would happen in predominantly Black neighborhoods in Brooklyn.

In 1986, researchers Richard Schaffer and Neil Smith published a study in the *Annals of the American Association of Geographers* about the history of gentrification in urban areas and the early stages of that process that were beginning to evidence itself in Harlem.

"Because gentrification in Harlem is at best in its infancy and because the area has an inordinate number of vacant and abandoned buildings, it will be difficult to use this empirical study to advance our knowledge of the effects of gentrification."[3]

They also point out that the "debate over gentrification has emerged around three main questions: the significance of the process (or its extent), the effects of gentrification, and its causes."[4]

The city took various steps to encourage redevelopment in these neighborhoods, such as making abandoned buildings available for next to nothing or the payment of back taxes. Similar programs and revitalization schemes would gradually be undertaken in other American cities such as Philadelphia, Baltimore, Atlanta, Portland, San Diego, and Washington, D.C., and gentrification would steadily take hold. In Harlem, developers invested millions of dollars into new construction and the reclamation of classic brownstones on the verge of collapse. Real estate developers purchased and tore down huge blocks of buildings to replace them with pricey condominium apartment complexes.

The Schaffer study had been conducted when signs of gentrification in Harlem were just beginning to be noticeable. The same process would happen in economically struggling areas of all New York boroughs in the coming years. Many Black families took advantage of the programs to obtain these abandoned buildings. Yet even if a middle-income family bought a property at a reasonable price, they often couldn't afford the needed improvements. Many repairs were not cosmetic, but involved major and costly structural issues that, left undone, would make the building uninhabitable. Consequently, most people able to afford to renovate or rebuild in many parts of Harlem were invariably higher income and white.

As a precursor to a 1985 auction of abandoned buildings, the city set a minimum income of $50,000. However, according to the Schaffer report, "The 1980 census data reveal that . . . in the whole of Manhattan, the number of Black households earning more than $50,000 did not exceed 1,800."[5]

The paucity of Black families able to afford to buy and rehabilitate troubled buildings in Harlem in the 1980s was only one of the forces fueling change in the neighborhood. Along with the burning question of displacement for incumbent residents, many of the issues about the gentrification of Harlem in the coming decades would stem from the concerns raised in this early report.

This truly was just the tip of the iceberg in the 1980s, as researchers identified Harlem as a target for gentrification despite it being "an international symbol of Black culture" and went on to write that "two themes dominate most contemporary images of Harlem. The first, a nostalgic image now, is the Harlem of the Harlem Renaissance or of the Black Panthers. The second theme is Harlem the ghetto, one of the largest concentrations of Black working-class and poor inhabitants in the U.S."[6] Schaffer and his team concluded that the overriding image of Harlem was one of physical dilapidation accompanied by crime, drugs, and poverty. While recognizing that the two themes may be different, they also hold a ring of truth while still describing only a part of Harlem.

Quite to the contrary, there were always lovely sections of Harlem that were well maintained with a continued sense of neighborhood pride and community. And there were always sophisticated, wealthy professionals, and upwardly mobile residents, especially in Hamilton Heights and Sugar Hill.

Many years later the celebrated Black filmmaker Spike Lee would become belligerently vocal about his opposition to gentrification. "Why does it take an influx of white New Yorkers in the South Bronx, in Harlem, in Bed Stuy, in Crown Heights for the facilities to get better?" Lee roared.[7] He also railed against the notion that the new residents were "discovering" an area that had already been populated by people of color and then changing the names of the neighborhoods to ones that suited them, rather than using names that had been in place for decades or even centuries.

It is easy for people to regard an influx of cash into a deteriorating neighborhood as a reason to replace an old history for a new one. Yet it goes without saying that it is important to remember that earlier history. Perhaps that is why, given the gentrification that swept through Hamilton Heights, there are now historical, civic, and preservation societies in the neighborhood such as the Hamilton Heights Homeowners Association. These organizations are trying to preserve the heritage of what the neighborhood has traditionally meant to African Americans, highlight its historic architecture, and adapt to an increasingly diverse populace.

Gentrification would gradually transform Harlem into what it had once been: the preferred uptown residence for wealthy people of European descent. Real estate speculators snapped up properties large and small, quickly making both rents and homeownership unaffordable for most Black people. And once a house sold for an exorbitant price, Realtors used that price as a benchmark of what other properties should cost.

The analysis in Schaffer's report on early Harlem gentrification also shared that during Jimmy Carter's presidency "the U.S. Department of Housing and Urban Development (1979, 1981) eventually acknowledged displacement as a problem but downplayed its importance; two percent was the unofficial but widely accepted approximation of annual displacement in gentrifying neighborhoods."[8]

While rents and purchase prices were escalating in the 1980s and 1990s, much of Harlem was becoming home to more white people than had been seen there since the early twentieth century.

There is a truth that must be acknowledged about the bucolic Harlem of centuries past and the urbanized twentieth-century one known worldwide. Other than the eight weeks that George Washington headquartered in Harlem Heights at the Morris Mansion on West 162nd Street in 1776, nothing of significance had happened in Harlem to make it a name or place universally known. It was not until Harlem became a predominately Black neighborhood that it was suddenly famous across the United States and, indeed, the world. It was the sheer mass of Black humanity in one location that made it a place to be known. It was the Harlem Renaissance writers, musicians, artists, luminaries of the Civil Rights Movement, creative souls that breathed legend into the Apollo, dancers at the Savoy, entertainers and gangsters at the Cotton Club, and its growing reputation as a safe haven and mecca for the huddled masses of Black people on its streets that made the name Harlem legendary. Harlem became famous because Harlem became Black.

There was also the incredulity for many Blacks that Harlem was allowed to grow as a Black enclave, unmolested. The other two best-known examples of Black community excellence and prosperity, Rosewood, Florida, and Tulsa, Oklahoma, had been violently destroyed during the 1920s with much loss of life and unprecedented property destruction. Yet here sat Harlem, a neighborhood full of beautiful buildings being populated and repopulated by Black people who were becoming homeowners and entrepreneurs.

The Great Migration had taught Black Americans that Harlem was the gathering place for a new generation of the descendants of an oppressed people, a once enslaved people. It is that same connection between Black people and the parts of Harlem that became a ghetto that turned fleeting fame into infamy. And it is that connection that prompted many people, including some of the newer residents, to want to call this section of Upper Manhattan anything but Harlem. That name had become synonymous, often unfairly so, with all the worst things that had happened in the neighborhood since Harlem became predominantly Black. The underlying sociological reasons for the decline seemed unimportant.

As gentrification began to take hold more, there was also growing discussions about the boundary between Harlem and Washington Heights. West 155th Street has become widely accepted as delineating the western edge of Harlem, despite the fact that no one living in the neighborhood for many a decade would have known that was the new dividing line in Hamilton Heights or Sugar Hill. There is a natural physical end to Central Harlem at 155th Street and Eighth Avenue at one of the junctions of the Harlem River Drive.

In 1988, writing in the *New York Times*, Suzanne Slesin noted that "before the Depression, when Hamilton Heights was a predominantly white neighborhood, it was thought of as part of Washington Heights. Since the late 1930s, when it became mostly Black, Hamilton Heights has been considered part of Harlem."[9]

That Hamilton Heights was once Washington Heights (instead of the reverse) is repeated so often by journalists, Realtors, and new residents that few have stopped to realize that such a description puts the cart before the proverbial horse. Such a statement negates Harlem's Dutch and

English beginnings dating back to the 1600s, when the Harlem flatlands and the heights had no northern borders and extended to the tip of the island. The 1710 land divisions by the Dutch sought to divide the Harlem common lands in the heights stretching from the Harlem to Hudson rivers, from approximately 131st Street to Spuyten Duyvil, and they did.

Fifty years later, Roger Morris secured land in Harlem Heights stretching beyond current day 165th Street and built his home, Mount Morris, in 1765. Founding Father Alexander Hamilton bought his property in Harlem in 1799.

As Jervis Anderson, the author of *This Was Harlem: 1900–1950*, wrote, "When some nineteenth-century New Yorkers said 'Harlem' they meant almost all of Manhattan above Eighty-sixth Street."[10] Romer and Hartman's book on Jan Dyckman and his descendants echo that statement. In every factual way, there is no part of Harlem that was once Washington Heights, as Harlem existed for two hundred years before parts of it were renamed.

A good example of differing opinions on these West Harlem boundaries can be seen in a statement made by Ralph Ellison when he appeared before Congress in 1966 about racial issues in American cities. Ellison began his testimony by saying, "I live in New York City, on Riverside Drive at 150th Street. It isn't exactly Harlem, but Harlem has a way of expanding. It goes where Negroes go, or where we go in certain numbers. So, some of us think of it as Harlem, though it is really Washington Heights."[11] Decades later the Ralph Ellison Foundation website would note that the Ellisons lived in their Riverside Drive apartment in Harlem for twenty-five years.

The ever-shifting notion of what was Harlem and what is now Washington Heights would continue. There would also be a resurrection of old names on maps that no one had paid attention to in a century or more: like Manhattanville and Carmansville, their usage increased even more with gentrification.

Crossing Broadway: Washington Heights and the Promise of New York City, a 2014 book by Robert W. Snyder, may include some of the best descriptions of the changing borders of the westernmost point in Harlem that borders Washington Heights. That basic premise is that for countless African Americans, Washington Heights was across Broadway and generally in the higher street numbers of the 170s and beyond.

Snyder writes that "the combination of diverse ethnic communities and the rough topography of Washington Heights, with its great ridges and hillside streets, encourages sharp and territorial visions of community and identity. Depending on the era, Broadway has been a boundary between white and Black, Irish and Jewish, affluent and poor, Dominican-born and American-born."[12]

As Snyder and others have written, where Harlem ends and Washington Heights begins is often a matter of perspective. Yet as to the demarcation of West Harlem (Hamilton Heights and Sugar Hill), ending at 155th Street at Edgecombe or St. Nicholas, there is no question that for African Americans who were living in that area, even in the 1970s and 1980s, one was still very much in Harlem. Look no further than the fact that one of the most historic buildings in the neighborhood—555 Edgecombe Avenue at 160th Street—is part of Sugar Hill lore. Recall that George Washington sent his missives to Congress in 1776 from his address at "the Roger Morris House in Harlem Heights." Yet both buildings are now considered in Washington Heights, several blocks from crossing Broadway.

The basic issue is that people generally don't know that all of Northern Manhattan was Harlem and then got carved up into the newer neighborhoods of Manhattanville, Morningside Heights, Carmansville, Audubon Park, Washington Heights, and Inwood. Rather than describe West Harlem as lower Washington Heights, as some people do, it would be more accurate to note that the start of Washington Heights is Upper Harlem. There is also the fact that New York City does not specifically assign official designations as to where one neighborhood ends and another begins. It is a matter of someone or some group saying over several years "this is the new boundary," and it is gradually accepted as fact.

In the 1940s, when Arna Bontemps returned to Harlem, he was critical of the changes he saw. He had always known that life in Central Harlem was quite different from that on the hill. And James Baldwin, whose writing career took off in the 1950s and 1960s, wrote primarily of the Central Harlem experience that had been his reality. But in an interview published in 1984 in the *New York Times* he echoed Bontemps' words about the two very different Harlems. When asked by the Black writer and academician Julius Lester if he had ever approached Langston Hughes, Baldwin said that while he knew of Hughes and that he didn't live far from him, it would never have occurred to him to approach the writer. He replied that not only would his shyness have stopped him, but also:

> You see, there were two Harlems. There were those who lived on Sugar Hill and there was the Hollow, where we lived. There was a great divide between the Black people on the Hill and us. I was just a ragged, funky Black shoeshine boy and was afraid of the people on

the Hill, who, for their part, didn't want to have anything to do with me. Langston, in fact, did not live on the Hill, but in my mind, he was associated with those people. So, I would never have dreamed of going and knocking on his door.[13]

The divide separating the two Harlems was both physical and metaphysical. Yet many issues as to actual borders are the product of ethnic and racial divisions in the neighborhood. As Snyder wrote, "There is an old saying that Washington Heights begins where Harlem ends. The implication is clear: Washington Heights is a white neighborhood. If African Americans dominate the streets, the neighborhood is Harlem."[14]

This nomenclature primarily comes down to race, as Snyder notes. Starting in the nineteenth century, African Americans had been forced several times to move from various parts of Manhattan that include Greenwich Village, around the old Penn Station and Central Park. They had to move somewhere. We know that some, with money, thrived in growing Black neighborhoods in Brooklyn. But many began a gradual move uptown to Harlem.

Forget the Dutch, forget the Schieffelin, Bradhurst, Hamilton, Morris, Dyckman, Rensselaer, Bussing, and Maunsell families of old who had all owned extensive Harlem estates from the 1700s until almost 1900, estates that stretched north up to 180th Street and beyond. That legacy was no longer one that had taken place in Harlem. Rather, it was now said that it took place in Upper Manhattan, Northern Manhattan, or Washington Heights.

That rich history alone prompts one to question why anyone would ever want to rename the area that at one time covered most of northern Manhattan. Why wouldn't we want to embrace and celebrate the name Harlem, a name that evokes the area's Dutch beginnings, a name that is a tribute to bravery? It is the name that embraces the African American history that made the area famous worldwide, especially the rich history of the Harlem Renaissance and its legendary inhabitants.

Then there is today's Hamilton Heights and Sugar Hill, which represent new histories being written with the rebirth of the neighborhood in the twenty-first century. In this there is renewed respect for the beautiful architecture and its wonderfully diverse population, a mix of cultures, races, and economic levels building strong and harmonious places in which to live, work, shop, worship, and be entertained.

Among the civic organizations in this part of town, the Hamilton Heights Homeowners Association is a group that holds an annual Heritage

House Tour. Local residents welcome into their homes visitors who have an interest in the area's history and architecture. Proceeds from the tours go to a restoration fund for Hamilton Grange.

Michael Henry Adams, a graduate student in historic preservation at Columbia University, was renting the basement apartment in one of those historic houses when interviewed in 1988 by Suzanne Slesin of the *New York Times*. Adams was chairman of the tour and a member of the restoration efforts. His cozy apartment was in "an 1896 Romanesque-style house on Convent Avenue that was designed by John Hauser. His landlords are Sylvia Waters, the artistic director of the Alvin Ailey Repertory Ensemble, and her husband, Chauncey F. Jones, an architect, both of whom grew up in Harlem."[15] The couple had given up their Chelsea loft five years earlier and bought the house in Hamilton Heights.

Adams' one room has served many functions since it was once the dining room of the residence. He shared how much he liked the original fireplace and the renovations that his landlords were doing. In 1988, Jacqueline Downey, president of her own construction company, still had major repairs to make on the 5,000-square-foot brownstone on West 144th Street in Hamilton Heights that she had bought five years earlier. The brownstone, built in the late 1880s, had been designed by the celebrated architect William E. Mowbray, whose buildings had helped define the character of the neighborhood. It sits on one of the most photographed streets in Hamilton Heights and is one of the city's few surviving examples of Dutch Revival architecture. Hamilton's home, the Grange, was still on its original plot of land when her brownstone was constructed.

Downey, who had bought the brownstone for $125,000 in 1983, told a reporter for the *New York Times* that her plan was to show visitors on the house tour some the building's original features, such as the gesso beadwork on the oak door frames, the staircase of American white oak that was now minus nine coats of paint, and the marble fireplace in the parlor. Downey had made her own improvements, which, according to the *Times* article, included "a black marble-lined Jacuzzi that overlooks the garden, a mirrored exercise room, a gleaming marble and mahogany galley kitchen and a dining room with under-the-floor heating."[16]

Ronald Melichar, "the director of the commercial revitalization programs for the City Office of Business Development, bought [his] 1907 Beaux Arts-style house through a city lottery for $35,000."[17] It had been converted to a rooming house, was in deplorable condition, and few of the original architectural details survived. There are people buying real estate on the hill to flip it for a profit. But there are just as many, representative of the ones that Slesin profiled, who are making Hamilton Heights their home. They have a sincere love of the neighborhood's history and the fine architecture worth preserving and restoring.

Much of the history of this neighborhood is forever lost because people generally go about living their lives in privacy. They don't stop to record what they do each day, which famous person may have visited, or which talented jazz artist might have stopped by, sung a song, or sat in with the band at one of the clubs that dotted the avenues. There was little thought that this Black mecca that had evolved at a time of great bigotry required a microscopic record-keeping. It would also have been unthinkable that it could one day be lost.

In 1930, when James Weldon Johnson wrote his classic book *Black Manhattan*, he too had embraced the narrower twentieth-century parameters of what was considered Harlem, noting the start at 110th Street covering Lenox and parts of Lexington; Eighth Avenue to West 155th Street and more northern parts of St. Nicholas to the Polo Grounds. He did write that "the heights north from One Hundred and Forty-fifth Street, known as Coogan's Bluff, are solidly Black."[18] However, Coogan's Bluff, the area at Edgecombe Avenue above the Polo Grounds, was just starting to become integrated in 1930.

But Johnson did acknowledge the huge societal shifts in the story of Harlem, writing that "in the history of New York the name Harlem has changed from Dutch to Irish to Jewish to Negro. But it is through this last change that it has gained its most widespread fame."[19] It is noteworthy that even by 1930 Johnson felt that Harlem was already worthy of analysis and a book.

The drug problems in Harlem have been the subject of countless books, newspaper articles, and sociological studies. Hamilton Heights was not immune from the problem, and as far back as 1944 Langston Hughes wrote about the accessibility of low-level drugs in Central Harlem. "In vast sections below the hill," he wrote, referring to Sugar Hill, "neighborhood amusement centers after dark are gin mills, candy stores that sell King Kong (and maybe reefers), drug stores that sell geronimoes—dope tablets—to juveniles for pepping up cokes."[20]

Over time, it became obvious that on two major avenues in Sugar Hill, St. Nicholas and Amsterdam, drugs had become part of what was available for sale, whether at bars, nightclubs, speakeasies, or corner stores that doubled as illegal numbers joints. Yet for all the changes on St. Nicholas Avenue, one patch remained mostly as it had been for centuries.

In 1980, as the illegal numbers racket continued to thrive, it was estimated that up to a billion dollars a year was generated by that gamble on three little numbers. "That's why when lawmakers in Albany proposed a similar, daily pick-three lottery that year," an article in the *New York Times* noted, "a coalition of city and state officials feared there would be a crackdown on the numbers, and tried to stop the move."[21]

Their stance was that if the traditional numbers game could get legalized, some of that revenue could continue to flow into the Black community. Essentially, the game could be legitimized, and the people working in the numbers racket could keep their jobs.

Some form of state lottery games had existed since 1964, with New Hampshire as the first state. When New York moved forward with creating the lottery in 1980, it essentially put a massive dent in illegal numbers. It may be one of the rare instances where a state, and eventually the whole country, looked at the amount of money that was earned illegally in a Black neighborhood by picking a few numbers and turned it into a legitimate, state-sanctioned billion-dollar business that could be extended to all demographics. In the coming decades, almost every state would have a version of the lottery where you picked your own numbers.

Further iterations of the legal lottery in its "pick three" numbers games would mimic the exact methodology and street language of the illegal numbers operation in that one could play the selected numbers in "straight-boxed-combo" variations.

The presence of drugs and high crime did not alter the fact that because of the beautiful buildings erected in the late 1800s and early 1900s in Hamilton Heights, the neighborhood received both national and state landmark designations. Another national preservation society, the Architectural Trust, explained the significance of Hamilton Heights by noting:

> It is a quiet residential community largely developed between 1886 and 1906, with only a few later buildings, and it retains much of its turn-of-the-century atmosphere. It is because of the tree-lined streets, with rows of low-lying houses and raised front yards that give the neighborhood a dignity unusual in an urban environment. This beautiful description of Hamilton Heights, with its long rows of three and four-story private houses and its low-rise apartment buildings, give architectural coherence to the streetscape.[22]

The distinctive Queen Anne and Romanesque buildings erected over a hundred years ago are as stunning now as they were when they were constructed. Fortunately, "the row houses in the historic district were erected just before rising land values and increasing costs made row house

Figure 71. Billy Strayhorn's Former Home, 315 Convent Ave. Courtesy D. S. James

development prohibitively expensive. Thus, they are representative of the last generation of single-family row houses erected in Manhattan."[23]

By the 1980s, Hamilton's Grange was a shadow of its former beauty, looking shabbier than ever. Eric Sloane had written in his 1968 book *Mr. Daniels and the Grange* that the faded wooden house "had assumed the color and mood of extraordinary neglect," adding, "The upper porch railing was gone and six posts of the lower porch balustrade had been used to patch a gaping hole in the lattice underneath. This old house was suffering every indignity that the city could contrive."[24]

While the Grange had been designated a National Historic Landmark in 1962, plans for the final move had not been settled. Mr. Daniels was still the caretaker in the early eighties, and many people thought that the Grange would be well on the way to being renovated by 1989, the bicentenary of Hamilton's appointment as secretary of the treasury.

A 1988 article about the house in the *New York Times* noted its sad condition. "If the Grange were anywhere else, this would be a fait accompli," Michael Henry Adams, the Columbia University graduate student in historic preservation, was quoted as saying. "The only reason it has fallen into this deplorable condition is because it is in Harlem."[25]

The house no longer looked as if it were on the verge of collapse, as it did in the 1960s, when Sloane wrote his book. "But the two great octagonal chambers, from which Hamilton and his family could once gaze to the Hudson and Harlem Rivers, are almost bare," the *Times* article noted. "In the parlor are two side chairs and in the dining room is a pianoforte."[26]

That was the total extent of the furniture. There were no window coverings at the triple-hung windows, the walls were bare, and the floorboards were devoid of rugs or carpets.

Local Harlem residents loved the old house, and any proposal over the years of moving it out of the neighborhood had always been met with strong opposition. Charles B. Rangel, the local congressman, was supportive of keeping the Grange where it was, so that it could stay next to St. Luke's and be restored in place.

"There is much more validity to keeping it in its original setting," George Dalley, Rangel's assistant, told the *Times* reporter Christopher Gray. "Putting it in a pastoral setting is too much of Disneyland."

Years ago, a petition with 10,000 signatures from people all over Harlem negated tentative plans being entertained to have Hamilton Grange leave Harlem. Angella C. Reid, deputy superintendent of Manhattan sites for the National Park Service, indicated that the most promising space was on the City College campus, an idea that had been raised in past decades. "But in order for the building to go through, they would have had to remove the arches at the college gate. It was just not feasible," Reid said.[27]

Money was another real concern, as only $475,000 has been appropriated of the $960,000 current spending limit. Reid indicated that it would likely take at least $2 million to restore and refurnish the house. The National Park Service is hopeful that a good portion of that will come from private donations.

The two merged schools, the High School of Music & Art on Convent Avenue in Hamilton Heights, founded in 1936, and the High School of Performing Arts in Midtown, founded in 1948, were finally ready to move into one location. In 1984 the schools were relocated to a new building behind Lincoln Center and were eventually christened the Fiorello H. LaGuardia High School of Music & Art and Performing Arts. A few years before, the film *Fame* became an instant mega hit, based on the midtown campus High School of Performing Arts.

The alumni from the High School of Music & Art in Hamilton Heights are a veritable who's who of the arts world. Graduates went on to work in front of and behind the scenes in film, TV, Broadway, on the concert stage, in museums, as photographers, architects, singers, composers, artists' agents, producers, and university professors. The model of admitting students through a competitive admissions process based on talent proved sound and would be repeated throughout the nation. Many of the students matriculated to Juilliard and other prestigious arts programs, where their talents continued to be nurtured.

Brock Peters, an actor, singer, and producer with a powerful bass voice, may be best remembered for his performance as the falsely accused defendant in the 1962 film *To Kill a Mockingbird,* starring Gregory Peck. Later, fans knew him from *Star Trek.* Peters' father had studied at the Sorbonne.

Early alumni of the Hamilton Heights campus also include Diahann Carroll and Billy Dee Williams, both legends. Stanley Drucker would start performing with the New York Philharmonic at age nineteen and became its principal clarinetist in 1961. Shari Lewis, a twelve-time Emmy-award-winning children's programmer and famous 1960s puppeteer, is also an early alumna. The Tony-award-winning actor Cliff Gorman was heralded for his Broadway portrayal of Lenny Bruce in *Lenny.* Among other actor alums are Hal Linden and Leslie Ann Warren.

Arthur Drexler would spend thirty-five years as the curator and director of the Department of Architecture and Design at the Museum of Modern Art. Veteran saxophone and woodwind player Mark Fineberg performed with Billy Joel, Donna Summer, Peter Frampton, Roger Daltrey, and Gladys Knight, among others. He also spent twenty years on Broadway, including performing in *Smokey Joe's Café* and *Jersey Boys.*

The television writer and producer Steven Bochco has been called one of the most important people in television. In the course of three decades, his shows *Hill Street Blues, L.A. Law,* and *NYPD Blue* transformed the medium.

Hamilton Heights alum Carole Bayer Sager had already written her first pop hit, *A Groovy Kind of Love,* while she was still a student at Music & Art. She won an Oscar in 1982 for her coauthorship of *Arthur's Theme, The Best That You Can Do* in the Dudley Moore hit film *Arthur.* Carole's partnership with her husband, Burt Bacharach, garnered a string of successes. They were a songwriting powerhouse, highlighted by the 1986 mega hit *That's What Friends Are For.*

Some of the many talented individuals who attended this groundbreaking school in Hamilton Heights knew beforehand that their path was an artistic one. And those ambitions were encouraged and finetuned in a Harlem neighborhood that had become synonymous with the awakening of geniuses. If all things happen for a reason, then how fortuitous that La Guardia suggested that the old Teachers Training School in Harlem be the setting of a school for the arts.

With the move to the Lincoln Center campus, the high school building in Hamilton Heights was being repurposed once again. It became the new home of the A. Philip Randolph Campus High School, established in 1979 as a unique educational collaboration between the Board of Education and City College. It was first located in CCNY's Goethals Hall on 140th Street and Amsterdam Avenue, from 1979 to 1983.

The school was named after the civil rights leader whom Martin Luther King Jr. had called, "truly the Dean of Negro leaders" and who had founded the Brotherhood of Sleeping Car Porters, the first successful Black trade union. It moved into the former Music and Art building in September of 1984, with a focus on a college-prep curriculum and one that marked "another" new era of education in Hamilton Heights.

The Landmarks Preservation Commission designated the former New York Training School for Teachers building as a New York City landmark in 1997.

A few blocks away, another generation had come and gone, having passed by the faded house and the imposing statue of the most prolific of our Founding Fathers. A new flurry of plans and suggestions arose from the National Park Service, civic groups, City College, and neighborhood residents as to where the Grange should go. Thirty years had now passed since Eric Sloane and Edward Anthony's book about the sad condition of Hamilton's Grange.

Christopher Gray's 1993 *New York Times* article reports on a new round of questions about what would happen to the very worn-down national landmark. The general idea that has been bounced around for almost a century is still to move the house to a more pastoral setting. "Continued deterioration brought a new push for relocation and restoration in the 1950s and 1960s. Different sites have been proposed, including the City College campus, Riverside Park, vacant land on Amsterdam Avenue and near the Cloisters."[28]

The Grange is jammed in because when St. Luke's built the church in 1892, they had it practically wrap around the old house, though they had moved the Grange to its property on Convent before construction began. Yet church wardens had probably not intended to keep the house forever, as it began to deteriorate, and would have reclaimed that lot had the house been torn down. The apartment building that abuts it was not constructed until the 1920s. Some better planning might have left more space between it and Hamilton's home, but this was not done.

The year before the article, in 1992, Georgette Nelms, Manhattan superintendent for the National Park Service, closed the landmark, as the Park Service found recent shifts in the foundation made it a safety hazard to the public. Funds to finance the move and long-overdue renovations had been another heated issue for years.

Gray writes that Representative Charles B. Rangel, the Democrat whose district takes in Hamilton Grange, secured a $1.75 million appropriation to restore the house according to the Park Service's designs. That amount is almost double what was anticipated a decade before.

Nelms confirms that the Park Service decided the house should be moved to St. Nicholas Park. Mr. Johnson, St. Luke's rector, still opposes such a move, saying, "I don't think people are interested in replicas. You don't need to put the Grange into a park to make it come alive. We see a historic link between the church and the Grange."[29] Mr. Johnson's statement could not be truer. It was the church and, more importantly, old Reverend Tuttle that had saved the Grange from demolition more than once.

Moving an old building and not damaging it takes a feat of engineering. The Grange would have to be extracted from its snug location between the church and the adjoining apartment building. Yet what a statement that this wooden house, conceived in 1799 by Alexander Hamilton and constructed by 1802, has survived where so many other homes in this neighborhood reflective of the period have been destroyed. The Grange can be moved because it outlasted all but one other, the Morris-Jumel Mansion. The other neighboring estates to which Eliza and Alexander Hamilton would have visited and dined are now just a mention in the history books, with rare images left to mark that they existed.

Chapter 14

Parlor Jazz and the Great Renovation

> By naming something, we take possession of it; by losing that name, we lose possession of it.
> —Evan T. Pritchard, *Native New Yorkers: The Legacy of the Algonquin People of New York.*

On a November day in 1987, more than two hundred people attended a ceremony at the Schomburg Center for Research in Black Culture on 135th Street and Lenox Avenue, which adjoins the library's original building. One of those present was eighty-six-year-old Regina Anderson Andrews, the pioneering librarian who had done so much during the Harlem Renaissance to help transform the library into a place for artistic expression more than half a century earlier. Regina had already made history within the New York Public Library system in 1938 when she became the first Black Supervising Branch Librarian at the 115th Street location. On this day, she was joined by dozens of other "scholars, noted writers, musicians, ministers, actors, and intellectuals. It was the start of a campaign to encourage the collection and preservation of Black cultural artifacts."[1]

Howard Dodson, director of the Schomburg, spoke of the importance that items of significance to Black culture in America and even around the world be donated to the library. Harry Belafonte, the singer, actor, and civil rights activist, was the keynote speaker. Regina had donated a treasure-trove of her extensive collection of papers, photographs, and a lifetime collection of her books and those from her grandfather Henry Simon. In future decades it would be called the Regina Andrews Photograph Collection, catalogued and archived at the Schomburg.

Two years later would be a pivotal moment for Black New Yorkers. On January 2, 1990, the city's first African American mayor, David Dinkins, would be sworn into office.

More effective policing had brought about a drop in crime. The gentrification of Harlem, along with other New York neighborhoods, was in full swing, with municipal improvements including better street lighting, repaved sidewalks, and new sewers. "The Upper Manhattan Empowerment Zone had brought $300 million in new money and almost as much in tax breaks to businesses investing in Harlem."[2] Although little of this money went into Black businesses, some Black professionals started moving back to Harlem. And they did so despite the fact that few of them could afford to buy the neighborhood's stunning brownstones, which were available at a fraction of their real value but greatly in need of costly repairs.

New York City is a metropolis so overflowing with film choices, live performances, and museums that it is sometimes hard to know where to start with all its bounty. One of its most unique private museums was in a home on one of Hamilton Heights' historic streets. It was one of those lovely brownstones that gave this neighborhood its unique character, just steps from Alexander Hamilton's Grange and the Convent Avenue entrance to City College.

Aunt Len's Doll and Toy Museum was located at 6 Hamilton Terrace, the home that Lenon Holder Hoyte (Aunt Len) and her pharmacist husband, Lewis, had bought in 1938. The Hoytes, who had been among the early Black homeowners in Hamilton Heights, were the epitome of what the neighborhood represented in those days: a welcoming place for educated Black professionals. Hoyte had earned her bachelor's degree in education from City College the year before and would go on to earn a certificate in special education from Columbia. Her husband was one of the city's few Black pharmacists.

As described in a 1994 article in the *New York Times*, the Hoyte home was "the repository for thousands of dolls along with dollhouses, glassware, vases, cherubs, tin toys and stuffed animals, stacked on the floor, crammed into glass cases and layered on all manner of tables and shelves."[3] During a forty-one-year career in education, Hoyte taught children with mental challenges, as well as giving classes in arts, craft, and puppetry.

Her interest in dolls had been sparked in 1962 when she was asked to organize a doll show for a benefit at Harlem Hospital. She founded Aunt Len's Doll and Toy Museum around 1970. "It was one of the nation's

Figure 72. Lenon Holder Hoyte. Photo courtesy Sotheby's

largest private collections of dolls and related toys, and became one of the city's most popular specialty museums during its years of operation between 1970 and 1994."[4] She also lectured at the Museum of Natural History.

Many of Hoyte's neighbors likely never knew about either the house full of dolls or its owner's passion for collecting, which began as a child. She had also opened her Hamilton Heights home to another exhibit that involved her rare international fine china pieces. In 1951, the *Amsterdam News* reported that the rarity of her collection could have graced a museum of art. "There was a touch of the professional curator in the display, which was assembled, not only with loving care and technical knowledge of size, shape, and background. Of the china, porcelain, pottery, silver, copper, pewter and glass pieces, there were famous designs of Wedgwood, Luster, Staffordshire, Dresden, and Royal Vienna."[5]

Slesin wrote of her doll collection in the *New York Times* that to enter her house "was to enter a chiaroscuro labyrinth where hundreds of pairs of glass eyes set in bisque, cloth, plastic, wood and papier-mâché stared back at visitors who progressed slowly, often sideways, always gingerly, through the narrow passageways of the crowded ground floor and basement."[6]

But by age eighty-nine, with her health failing and her husband long dead, Hoyte could no longer maintain the museum, and she closed it in 1994. Yet she had more than surpassed her life's dream of creating a museum where the children in Harlem could develop an appreciation of dolls. The Hoytes never had children, and sharing her passion for doll collecting filled some of that void.

In 1990, "soon after Mayor Edward I. Koch presented Ms. Hoyte with the Mayoral Award of Honor for Art and Culture, her genteel house and museum was broken into by thieves. At least nine dolls, including a two-foot-tall English king, considered priceless by knowledgeable collectors, were stolen. Ms. Hoyte was disconsolate."[7]

Her collection included dolls as tiny as one inch and as tall as three feet. "There were fine nineteenth-century French dolls made of bisque, an unglazed ceramic. There were rare, antique porcelain dolls and United States presidents and first ladies. There were numerous versions of Shirley Temple dolls, Barbie dolls, Betsy Wetsy dolls, and Cabbage Patch dolls."[8]

The collection was unique for many reasons but especially because of the rare Black dolls dating back to the nineteenth century. Some were rag dolls made by enslaved persons from scraps of muslin and feed bags. Others had been made by a Black handyman from Georgia named Leo Moss. One pair of his papier-mâché dolls had tears running down their cheeks. Hoyte once told reporters that these Black dolls represented the beginning of our heritage.

In 1994, when Sotheby's put the collection up for auction, the 114-page illustrated catalogue consisted of 491 lots with the priciest item, "a black Bru pressed-bisque-head bebe doll," expected to fetch up to $18,000. Thousands of others had been sold in a previous sale to dealers around the country. Lenon Hoyte died five years later, at the age of ninety-four. The Hoyte Collection Sotheby's Catalogue can now be viewed at several libraries, including the New York Public Library and the Getty Museum Library. Hers was a legacy that exemplified the many unique lives lived in Hamilton Heights.

Because the very mention of gentrification is so often thought of as white people moving into depressed ethnic neighborhoods and displacing people of color, Monique D. Taylor's 1992 journal article on Black professionals returning to Harlem, or moving there for the first time, is especially significant. Taylor begs the question that Thomas Wolfe stated as the title of his 1940 book *You Can't Go Home Again*. Countless works have been written exploring the subject of gentrification, and Taylor's article is titled, "Can You Go Home Again? Black Gentrification and the Dilemma of

Difference," published in the *Berkeley Journal of Sociology*. It explores the many complicated issues that arise and the sociological dynamics at work.

"The young, upwardly mobile, and mostly white population associated with the process of gentrification has been alternately praised and cursed for its role in recasting poor communities,"[9] Taylor wrote. Despite the benefits that gentrification may bring, such as more social services, infrastructure improvements, better policing, and a boost to the economy, it raises many valid concerns, especially the natural fear on the part of longtime residents that they will be pushed out and their culture suppressed.

The new residents often come into conflict with the existing ones, especially in matters involving neighborhood traditions and the use of public space. "Interactions between old and new, Black and white, young and old in gentrifying neighborhoods and communities have been fraught with tensions."[10]

While there is no question that there have been an influx of whites snapping up real estate bargains and other developers flipping properties, some of the new residents are what are called "buppies"—black urban professionals—who very much want to participate in the rituals that define daily life in this famous and historically Black community. They are drawn to Harlem not just because of the real estate bargains but because it offers an opportunity for them to connect with the storied history of this African American mecca. The new Black gentry are eager to embrace a racial identity that they are unable to express elsewhere.

Yet for some of the existing residents, Taylor wrote, the presence of these newcomers raises various issues, many involving class distinctions that can set more recent residents apart from their neighbors. To explore this subject, she interviewed eleven middle-class Black professionals who had moved to Harlem after 1975, and she did field work from 1988 to 1991. The idea of using the term "gentrification" to describe wealthy Blacks moving to Harlem may seem odd. But the term applies to rich people moving into poorer neighborhoods anywhere and making changes to improve them. There is no racial qualifier with the term, though more often than not the gentrifiers are white.

"The irony that Harlem's Black gentry hit on is that in a new era of race relations and even by playing by the middle-class rules that determine success—mobility through education and career—their contacts with white America reinforce their marginality as Blacks."[11]

The paradox is that the success of Black Americans in a white world has allowed them to live where they wish, which often means leaving the confines of the Black community. This is exactly what has contributed to the decimation of Harlem.

Fay Johnson, a ten-year Harlem resident, described what characterized middle-class Black professionals and their desire to live in the Black community. Despite being educated in the finest schools, articulate, working in corporate America, and able to leave one's house in Armani outfits and Ferragamo shoes, Johnson said that this cohort is also bi-cultural. They exist in a society where they have blazed the trail, not unlike their parents did, yet are still the token.

> We are sort of a transition generation. . . . We are very close to the civil rights struggle of the '60s and we were raised by parents who went through the struggles of the '40s and so our mission is clear. Essentially, we go out into the world and we exercise our intellectual and political acumen in an integrated setting and we come back and relax and let our hair down and complain and take refuge in the Black community.[12]

What W. E. B. Du Bois wrote in 1903 in his seminal work, *The Souls of Black Folk*, is applicable to what these new residents were experiencing in the twentieth century. Du Bois described the predicament as one he defined as double consciousness. "One ever feels his twoness—an American, a Negro; two souls, two thoughts, two unreconciled strivings; two warring ideals in one dark body, whose dogged strength alone keeps it from being torn asunder."[13] Future generations of African Americans would coin the term "code switching" to also identify the process by which they speak and behave differently around whites from when they are among their own people.

As Taylor points out, it is not a color line that these newcomers must confront but a class line. Those people who have been able to settle "on the well-to-do streets of Hamilton Heights, for instance, do not confront these class differences so directly. The relatively quiet, tree-lined streets of well-preserved homes remind one of the suburban amenities that usually draw people out of the city."[14] The historic, middle-class enclaves in Hamilton Heights are in direct contrast to the reality of life in other areas of the community—namely, Central and East Harlem.

George Carver, a successful magazine publisher, described his move to Harlem as a way to return to and feel a part of the community. Carver, who lives in Hamilton Terrace, takes great satisfaction in the fact that neighborhood kids see him as a man who has made it. "Harlem as a racially defined community in Manhattan and Hamilton Terrace, as a middle-class enclave within the community, function as a space within that space in which the dual identities of being middle class and Black are brought together."[15]

Carver is a role model and mentor just by living in the community. He enjoys walking down the street and having kids come off the stoop and walk him to his door. He sees them playing and might give them ten bucks to go buy Popsicles.

With all the unique architectural features and forgotten spaces in Harlem, historian Michael Henry Adams fills a critical role in identifying those places. Adams writes that "if there is any one exterior feature that defines Harlem's late-nineteenth-century row house during this age of picturesque revivalism, it is the round tower or turret. Nothing as uninhibited had ever adorned so many speculative houses."[16] The design, as he describes in his stunning book *Harlem: Lost and Found*, is borrowed from Norman barns, a style named for French architecture found in the Normandy province starting in the Middle Ages.

Adams writes that architect Theodore Minot Clark designed some of Harlem's finest round towers, varying examples of which can be seen throughout Hamilton Heights. The beautiful design is on the attached dwellings at 729–731 St. Nicholas Avenue off 146th Street, built in 1886. Clark was inspired by having seen the design firsthand. The ones shown in Figure 73, on the left, would appear to be close to the French originals, characterized by rubblestone masonry reinforced with reddish brick meant to add to the structural strength.

The majority of the facing material at 729 St. Nicholas is gray Manhattan mica schist, which was quarried on site. The towers are in a gabled roof and have striking conical roofs and aligned windows. A similar tower can be seen across the street at 740 St. Nicholas and on some stunning mansions on Convent Avenue.

Centuries ago, before music was presented in big concert halls, people had intimate gatherings in their homes with selected guests. Sometimes the artist was a new talent just starting to forge a career and sometimes one whose fame was well known. But often members of a family performed as an ensemble, or a favored daughter would sing or play on the pianoforte with the hope that she might attract the attention of a suitor. In some form or another, rich, poor, or somewhere in the middle, it has been the most intimate, yet powerful, form of performance . . . to be in someone's home listening to literary readings or musical or theatrical presentations. Even with the Harlem rent parties of the 1930s and '40s the power of live musicians in someone's apartment made for stirring entertainment.

Marjorie Eliot and her husband, Al Drears, had lived in the famed 555

Figures 73 and 74. LEFT: 729–731 St. Nicholas Avenue. RIGHT: 740 St. Nicholas Avenue. Courtesy D. S. James

Edgecombe Avenue since 1984. Al was a drummer who had worked with the pianist Mal Waldron and Dizzy Gillespie, while Marjorie taught music and performed at downtown clubs. As an actress, Marjorie was among the original cast in Charles Gordone's Pulitzer Prize-winning 1969 play *No Place to Be Somebody*.

Tragically, their son, Philip, died in 1992 due to kidney failure. Shortly thereafter, Eliot conceived of having weekly concerts on Sundays, the day he died, to help assuage her grief and pay tribute to the memory of her son, who had followed in the family tradition as an actor and music lover.

For decades 555 Edgecombe Avenue had been home to many actors and musicians, and one could often hear the music from the halls. Not surprisingly, Eliot's flyers inviting people into her cozy apartment brought an immediate and enthusiastic response. In those early days, the news was spread by word of mouth. Musicians would attend and return with other musicians and friends. Opening their home to neighbors and strangers alike, the couple created an atmosphere of warmth and artistry that was addictive. They had previously held readings and rehearsals in the apartment for years, and this was an easy transition.

The following year, in 1993, as the anniversary of her son's death approached, Eliot wanted to plan a larger affair: an entire concert dedicated to Philip. Never a shy woman, despite her petite size, she approached the staff of the Morris-Jumel Mansion, right across the street, about holding a jazz concert on its patio. And just like that, the oldest residence in Manhattan, where George Washington and British soldiers had camped out during the American Revolution, a house that for most of its history since 1765 was off limits to Blacks, became the setting for a jazz concert that featured talented and diverse musicians and drew audiences from all over the city.

Meantime, a few blocks away, the beautiful Haynes home at 411 Convent Avenue that had hosted some of the great artists and minds of the Harlem Renaissance era had long been in decay. By the 1990s, George Edmund Haynes' grandson Bruce, now living and teaching in California, had no choice but to sell it. In the packing up, he found long-lost family treasures from both his grandfather and father's time. Despite the deterioration that would cost someone a small fortune to repair, the house still had many of the original classic features that had made it so unique. Yet even with a reduced price because of its condition, it was still too costly for most. In the end, it was a video jockey and documentary filmmaker named Fab 5 Freddy who bought the home.

By the nineties, many of the vibrant jazz clubs that had dotted St. Nicholas Avenue were just a memory. In a 1997 article in the *New York Times*, the newspaper's jazz critic Ben Ratliff expressed hope that some jazz spots might be revived and new ones opened to serve a changing demographic. And one of these legendary venues got a boost from a woman on a mission to keep alive the history of the music once played up and down St. Nicholas Avenue in Hamilton Heights.

Roberta "Berta" Alloway is a seamstress by trade who grew up on the Lower East Side and would frequent jazz clubs in the Village in the sixties. After she got hooked on the music, she decided to move to Harlem in the mid-1970s and discovered that a once vibrant jazz scene was vanishing.

At first, Alloway "settled on the Mark Four, at 147th Street and St. Nicholas Avenue, rounded up the saxophonist Patience Higgins and Mr. McCloud, and before long had brought together a house band."[17] The Mark Four had for decades been an institution on St. Nicholas Avenue, a place where generously poured drinks could be had for a reasonable price, where one could enjoy good music and, at one time, spot the notorious gangster Nicky Barnes holding court.

Alloway shifted her efforts to St. Nick's Pub, two blocks away. For a time on St. Nicholas Avenue a person could hit half a dozen jazz clubs on any given night. She helped turn St. Nick's, which had been around since the 1930s, back into a bustling scene. Ratliff shared in the article that "there are different house bands five nights a week. The alto saxophonist

Figure 75. St. Nick's Pub, circa 1990s. Copyright unknown

Abraham Burton often stops by; his regular bass player, Billy Johnson, is also in one of the Wednesday-night groups."[18]

St. Nick's Pub is the kind of place where Arlene Talley, performing dual roles as barmaid and her true calling as a talented singer, will serve you a drink and is likely to sing a number with the band a few minutes later. Ratliff wrote that Monday nights are given over to the Sugar Hill Jazz Quartet that Alloway helped put together. "That's the group with Mr. McCloud, an unruffled, narrative-flow kind of bass player, and Mr. Higgins, who's as comfortable playing free abstractions as he is playing standards behind a singer." Patience Higgins was a member of the Duke Ellington Orchestra for twenty years who also toured and recorded with the Count Basie Orchestra, Aretha Franklin, Lionel Hampton, Ray Charles, Stevie Wonder, and Paquito D'Rivera. A host of horn players and more singers wait their turns to perform.

"And on most Monday nights, Esther Spain, the owner's wife, cooks fried chicken and beans for everyone in the club." And because Alloway knows the regulars, she is apt to call someone who doesn't show up on an evening to ask if everything is all right.

Although jazz is central to Harlem's history, it is not easy to promote commercially, which is one reason Alloway feels proud of her success in helping to bring it back to Harlem. She has reinvigorated this stretch of Sugar Hill. "Jazz is a peaceful thing," Alloway said. "You don't go to a jazz club and see anybody fighting. And the clubs are getting more diverse now. People are coming in from Jersey and elsewhere, because it's hip and it's comfortable. We owe this to the community."[19]

In the year 2000, the Schomburg Center for Research in Black Culture published a stunning book called *The Black New Yorkers*, an illustrated chronology of 400 years of African American history. It was also largely the culmination of a project that former librarian Regina Anderson Andrews had worked on for many years—gathering and collating photos and creating a timeline of Black history. Her singular role in the project was underscored in effusive praise:

> This book is dedicated to Regina M. Andrews, a pioneer African American librarian. She was also a socially conscious writer, author, civic leader, and activist in the struggle for truth about African American experience. . . . A pivotal figure in the development of the Harlem Renaissance, she assisted and supported many of its young writers. . . . We dedicate this book to her in recognition of her vision, her inspiration, and her commitment to telling the world about the unique and extraordinary role of Black New Yorkers in the making of America's greatest city.[20]

The editors further noted that it was Regina Andrews "who conceived of the idea of writing a chronological history of Black New York more than thirty years ago," adding, "Her draft manuscript, written in 1968 but never published, has served as an inspiration for and an important resource in the development of this book."[21]

It was a beautiful and well-deserved dedication to the woman who gave Langston Hughes and so many other Harlem writers a special spot of their own at the 135th Street library and who hosted poetry readings, dinners, and breakfast salons for them at her Hamilton Heights apartment. Her life story brings a breath of warmth and humanity to W. E. B. Du Bois, who, when she and her roommates were looking at a bare cupboard between paydays, would take them out to lovely dinners. The bigoted personnel manager who had sent her to the 135th Street branch so many decades ago could never have known what a profoundly important service he was performing for Black history.

The church that had owned the former Hamilton Theatre on Broadway since the 1960s sold it in the mid-1990s. The building had been deteriorating, the auditorium was vacant, and the marquee had been removed in

1995, which meant it lost its outward structural identity as a movie theater. The lobby was converted to retail space. For the generations of local residents who had known the place as a movie house, this was likely a sad moment.

The Hamilton Theatre's original exterior was designated a New York City landmark in 2000. There are several exterior decorative features that are not part of the landmark protection, as they were altered when RKO bought the building in 1928. Unfortunately, the application and hearings did not protect the interior as a landmark, which left the door open for demolition and any kind of remodeling future developers wanted to do.

Other changes in the neighborhood involved the M. Blake Funeral Home, which by the twenty-first century had occupied the former James Bailey Mansion at 10 St. Nicholas Place for almost fifty years. The house had been named a New York City Landmark in 1974. Most people knew it only as a funeral home, and probably even fewer knew that the mansion had been built by the legendary circus impresario.

Tragedy struck in August of 2000 when a fire started on the building's upper floors. *New York Times* reporter Christopher Gray wrote that "there was not much interior damage, but firefighters broke out many of the upper-floor windows, and the Blakes have since been living with his sister on Riverside Drive."[22] The house was by then 112 years old, and the interior was an intact Victorian mansion. Gray would be described as an architectural detective and social historian for his long-running "Cityscape" features in the *Times*.

"The doorknobs are still in place, the cut and etched glass is intact, the painted scenery on the ceiling has never been overpainted, the varnished wooden spindlework in the dining room is unbroken," Gray wrote. "Even the mace-shaped hanging pieces, attached with chains, are still whole."[23]

Architectural historian Michael Henry Adams, a great advocate for preserving Harlem's history, was quoted as saying that the Bailey-Blake house "could have been lost 100 times over by now, the Blakes are heroes for that. It deserves the kind of dramatic intervention that was made to preserve Olana, Frederic Church's spectacular house on the Hudson River in Hudson, N.Y."[24] The state bought that house.

Adams' thought was that the house would make a great museum that could focus on Harlem's architectural history and that of the circus, drawing tourists from around the country. Meantime, the house sat empty, repairs were needed, and the funeral home that had served the area for five decades was, for the time being, out of business.

Countless City College students had strolled right past the aging wooden

Figure 76. Martin Spollen Holding Wooden Mace-Shaped Ball and Chain. Courtesy D.S. James

house on 141st Street and Convent Avenue, tucked between an apartment building and the imposing brownish red stone of St. Luke's Church. The church itself was on the downturn of its life cycle and showing signs of its age. There had been complaints about the roof leaking just a couple of years after it was constructed in 1892. It would forever be a problem. Probably few of those City College students knew that this was the former home of Alexander Hamilton, despite the fact that the statue of Hamilton still stood in front of the house slightly off to the side. In a city peppered with old buildings, little about this one indicated its age.

The small college that began building on the empty lot adjacent to St. Luke's Episcopal Church and Hamilton's Grange in 1903 had probably grown to heights, in both size and prestige, beyond the imaginings of its earliest founders. The Convent Avenue entrance to City College, the Hamilton Gate, and the entrance to St. Nicholas Park down the hill are part of Hamilton's original farm. Alexander Hamilton's former acreage is now as developed as a neighborhood can get. Except for St. Nicholas Park down the hill, a grateful respite from all the concrete, there is no sign of the wooded hills, streams, and flowers that once defined this neighborhood. Yet the house still stood, in a much-changed Harlem, in a neighborhood that had long carried his name: Hamilton Heights.

Figure 77. 339 Convent Avenue. Courtesy Tom Miller

Some of the houses down the street from the Grange are quite literally mansions. The house at 339 Convent Avenue on the corner of 144th Street was the setting in 2001 for Wes Anderson's film *The Royal Tenenbaums*.

The house was completed in 1890 by developer Jacob D. Butler, who built a row of fifteen residences on Convent Avenue between West 141st and 144th streets designed by architect Adolph Hoak. Tom Miller's "Daytonian Manhattan" article fills in some of the history of the house, which also ties into St. Luke's and the Tuttle family.

"The row was a delightful blend of styles—Flemish Revival, neo-Tudor, and Romanesque Revival. The corner tower with its conical cap, carved spandrel panels, and the clustered colonnettes under a single capital, were combined with a Flemish Revival stepped gable."[25] By the 1920s, the house was owned by Charles Henry Tuttle, grandson of Rev. Isaac H. Tuttle, the longtime pastor of St. Luke's. "By the time the family moved into the Convent Avenue mansion, he had made a name for himself as a reformer. In 1927, President Calvin Coolidge appointed him as United States Attorney for the Southern District of New York."[26] Tuttle went on to earn a reputation by launching investigations into the corrupt activities of gangsters, public officials, and crime rings.

In 1930, he ran unsuccessfully against Franklin Delano Roosevelt for governor of New York and then went on to a successful career in the law. The house was later split into two residences, whereas many Harlem mansions and large houses had been divided into separate apartments or turned into rooming houses.

Miller wrote that in 2001 the "new owners were poised to restore the mansion to a single-family home. But they were stopped by motion picture director Wes Anderson, who pleaded to leave the property in its somewhat frowzy condition—at least temporarily." Anderson was set to shoot a quirky film titled *The Royal Tenenbaums*. The mansion would become famous as the family home with shots of the interior and exterior. The family proceeded with renovations after the film wrapped.

Exterior shooting from the film also has shots of an equally beautiful mansion just across the street at 336 Convent (see Figure 78).

The 336 Convent Avenue mansion has eight bedrooms and seven bathrooms and includes almost 5,000 square feet of living space. It is another of those buildings that makes you pause and marvel at it. It hosts another example of the conical cap tower indicative of many homes in Hamilton Heights. Built in the Queen Anne style, the house has a medieval feel.

In 2004, Ron Chernow wrote his bestselling book *Alexander Hamilton*.

Figure 78. 336 Convent Avenue. Courtesy D. S. James

Some people who had previously passed by the faded building may have stopped and snapped a photo. Seemingly, only a few more tourists took notice, as the number of visitors only increased by about 3,000. Yet attention had been drawn to it.

Gentrification now had a firm hold in Harlem, and that "means that demographics are changing, and Harlem is getting whiter," wrote Rose Hackman in a 2015 article in the *Guardian* titled, "What Happens When Harlem Becomes White?" For African Americans, the idea that Harlem could one day become a majority white neighborhood was almost unthinkable, yet this is what was happening.

And it is not just whites who are changing the racial makeup of Hamilton Heights. For much of the mid-twentieth century Puerto Ricans were the neighborhood's (and the city's) predominant ethnic group. Puerto Rican restaurants were everywhere, and older residents remember a time when Chinese-Spanish restaurants were common uptown, with menus that featured egg rolls and fried rice on one side of the menu and arroz con pollo and plantains on the other.

"Between 2000 and 2010, the number of Black residents fell notably, and white population share grew, particularly in central Harlem where white residents increased fivefold."[27] In one sense history is repeating itself. Harlem had started out as a place where Black residents struggled to find housing in the area in the early twentieth century, and Hamilton Heights was one of the last Harlem strongholds to resist integration. But slowly at first and then quickly the floodgates opened.

What was a major demographic shift in the city, starting in the 1970s and increasing dramatically in the 1980s, was that Dominicans surpassed Puerto Ricans as New York's dominant Latino population. A once predominantly Jewish Washington Heights continued to see such an increase in this population that it gradually became Manhattan's major Latino neighborhood. By 2000 Latinos had a stronger presence in Hamilton Heights than African Americans, and their numbers were growing.

From its early history as a country refuge for wealthy whites to its early twentieth-century one as a sanctuary for Black professionals, civic leaders, and people in the arts, Hamilton Heights is becoming a diverse neighborhood, albeit one in which the number of African Americans are quickly becoming the minority.

People have left Harlem for any number of reasons. One, of course, is the relentless pressure from landlords that often goes unchecked by authorities. Some older residents may have a myriad of other reasons for moving: needing long-term care, wanting to be closer to grandchildren, being unable to keep up with increasing property taxes, etc.

And, no surprise, real estate prices were rising. As Michael Henry Adams points out in his book *Harlem Lost and Found*, "At the Grinnell, at 800 Riverside Drive, a handsomely restored five-bedroom apartment, with two and a half baths, a large living room, dining room, entry, and kitchen, that rented for less than $1,000 monthly as late as 1985 sold in 2000 for $850,000, setting a record for real estate sales in Harlem."[28]

For all its infrastructure improvements, in many ways gentrification will always be the antithesis of anything positive. This is especially true when it comes to the people it displaces, some of whom were born in these houses or whose parents and grandparents fought the good fight to inhabit them. Historic buildings are allowed to be modernized, destroying the unique architectural characteristics from earlier periods that made them so special.

Then, of course, there are the beautifully restored homes in Sugar Hill's historic district that each have individual features that make one have a new respect for the architects of old, as just a few of the homes from Adams' book feature.

Crime had been on the increase in Hamilton Heights and Sugar Hill with a growth in the drug trade that had started in the 1980s. Statistics compiled by the online newspaper *DNAinfo* show that between 1993 and 2010, in this part of West Harlem, "major crime actually dropped 74 percent, led by an 88 percent decline in murders, an 87 percent drop in burglaries, and an 85 percent decline in car theft."[29] These statistics made West Harlem (which Manhattan Board 9 identifies as Morningside Heights, Hamilton Heights, and Manhattanville) the thirty-third safest New York neighborhood per capita out of sixty-nine neighborhoods analyzed.

But although drug-related crime continued to decrease dramatically, rapes soared from nineteen to thirty-five in 2010, an alarming 84 percent increase. That year also saw murders increasing from one to seven, and robberies up 23 percent to 253. Interestingly, property crimes declined during that period, making West Harlem one of the city's safest neighborhoods in this category—fifth citywide and number one for Manhattan. These figures would clearly indicate that during the same period of increased gentrification, crime has generally been on the decline.

Changes in a neighborhood's demographics also affect local businesses, often negatively. In July of 2007 an article in the *New York Times* noted that "Copeland's, at 547 West 145th Street, between Broadway and Amsterdam Avenue, where Harlem is known as Hamilton Heights, will

Figures 79, 80, and 81. ABOVE LEFT: 420 West 143rd Street. ABOVE RIGHT AND BOTTOM LEFT: 465 West 140th Street. Courtesy Paul Rocheleau Studio

hold its last gospel brunch at 1 p.m. on Sunday and then close its doors for good."[30]

Calvin Copeland, who had been at the location for nearly half a century, cited gentrification as a major reason for the closing. Many of the Black families who had patronized his business had moved away, and the new residents were looking for a different and lighter cuisine.

"The white people who took their place don't like or don't care for the food I cook," Copeland explained. "The transformation snuck up on me like a tornado."[31] The restaurateur, who had invested more than $250,000 of his savings in the restaurant, had fallen behind on his rent and finally had to accept defeat.

In its heyday Copeland's menu featured primarily Soul Food dishes such as Oxtails, Smothered Pork Chops, Chicken and Dumplings, Fried Chicken, Ribs, Candied Yams, Macaroni and Cheese, Peas and Rice, and Collard Greens. It was delicious, rich food, and the restaurant had been a home away from home for Black families from as far away as Philadelphia. "Black entertainers and other notables would stop by when in town," the *Times* article noted. "Desmond Tutu, the retired Anglican archbishop, ate there once, and so did Muhammad Ali and the comedian Richard Pryor."[32] Natalie Cole was a regular, and Michael Jackson came by once, though he had the food brought to his car. Yet an establishment that had been a vital part of Hamilton Heights for half a century would ultimately fade away.

This time of great change in Hamilton Heights would also be one for the country when, in 2008, Barack Obama was elected as the forty-fourth president of the United States. It was the first time that an African American had been elected to the nation's highest office. More than seven million New Yorkers had voted for the Obama-Biden ticket.

Debates about where to move the Grange finally ended in 2004 when, after extensive studies and field work, the Public Archaeology Lab (PAL), which does preservation planning and architectural history analysis, submitted a ninety-eight-page report to the National Park Service. After debates that had started almost a century before, it was decided that the best place was right down the hill in St. Nicholas Park, five hundred feet from where the house sat on Convent Avenue. The site selected was along West 141st Street at the park's northern end. From the slope one could see City College and a corner of the old St. Luke's. Yet the space was far from pristine; back in 1995, there had been evidence of drug use, homelessness, vandalism, litter, and graffiti.

Although significantly altered since it was built in 1802, the two-story wooden building is one of America's very few surviving examples of domestic architecture in the Federal style. In planning the move and the challenge involved in safely restoring it at a new location, the National Park Service researched, in meticulous detail, the house's original architecture and some of the changes that had been made over the years.

Because the original architectural plans do not exist, there are only historical documents describing aspects of its construction from 1800 to 1802. Eric Sloane and Edward Anthony made sketches of the house while doing research for their 1968 book *Mr. Daniels and the Grange*. The 2022 schematics in Figures 82–84, though not to scale, incorporate details from those sketches, the National Park Service layout, and a note to Hamilton from the original architect, John McComb Jr.

The main floor of the house contained the living area and the formal rooms, which were warmed by fireplaces topped with mantels of Italian marble. The connecting octagonal drawing room and dining room, which was considered the house's most distinctive features, form bay windows that open onto broad porches. At the Grange's original location on Amsterdam Avenue, at a time when the area was still mostly woodland, the windows would have opened onto sweeping views of the Harlem and Hudson rivers. Most of the existing interior molding and plasterwork throughout the Grange are original.

In a letter dated December 8, 1952, New York City parks commissioner Robert Moses had written to Alexander Hamilton, his great-great grandfather's namesake, who was then president of the American Scenic and Historic Preservation Society, expressing in no uncertain terms his disdain for the idea of moving the house. Moses said that the suggestion of moving the Grange to St. Nicholas Park was absurd for numerous reasons.

> It does not belong in the Park, could not be protected there, cannot and should not be operated as an ordinary city park facility and this suggestion, if publicized, would involve immediate, unfortunate and unconstructive controversy. You must therefore assume that this suggestion is impractical. . . . There remains, of course, the possibility of purchasing a suitable piece of land in the neighborhood and moving the Grange to that site. I suggest the northeast corner of St. Nicholas Avenue and West 141st Street which is vacant.[33]

Moses went on to write that the lot was available for $35,000. The estimated cost of moving and restoring the Grange at that time was between $150,000 and $175,000. Fortunately, the house being designated a historic landmark the following decade and the National Park Service assuming

Figures 82, 83, and 84. ABOVE LEFT: Grange First Floor Sketch. ABOVE RIGHT: Grange Second Floor Sketch. BOTTOM LEFT: Grange Basement Sketch. Schematics Courtesy of Nomad Concepts LLC

administration of the Grange would negate Moses's opinion, though it would take half a century.

Robert Moses is regarded as the man who did more to shape the physical design of New York City than any other figure in the twentieth century. He constructed parks, highways, bridges, playgrounds, housing, tunnels, beaches, zoos, and civic centers. In addition to his pivotal role as New York City Department of Parks commissioner from 1934 to 1960, he had almost a dozen other powerful overlapping roles, among them president of the New York 1964 World's Fair.

Yet all those additions to the infrastructure of New York City were not without controversy. His huge public works projects removed entire neighborhoods, often in low-income minority areas, destroying the traditional historic character. They displaced countless families with deep roots in those communities. In 1974, Robert Caro published his Pulitzer Prize–winning book *The Power Broker*, a highly critical biography of Robert Moses that showed another side of the brilliant urban planner.

The number of visitors to the Grange had grown steadily over the years, from 2,653 in 1983 to 41,372 in 1991, the year before it closed.

With a location identified and prepared, the National Park Service began actively working on moving the Grange to St. Nicholas Park. For starters, a foundation had to be built upon which the house would sit.

The Pennsylvania Dutch architectural firm Wolfe House & Building Movers was engaged to plan and execute the move. In 2008 the house was first braced inside to avoid movement and damage, then elevated in one piece in preparation for its journey. In a marvel of modern ingenuity and engineering, the Grange was placed on specially built stilts that held the entire building about ten feet off the ground in the middle of Convent Avenue, between 141st and 142nd streets, while traffic was routed around it. The full renovations, inside and out, would take another three years, and the porches Alexander Hamilton loved would be faithfully restored.

It took nine dollies, each with its own propulsion and braking system, to gingerly roll the house five hundred feet to St. Nicholas Park and the new foundation that had been built for it, all the time in sight of the church that had saved it. The house was then ready for its restoration.

It had taken forty-six years after its landmark designation for Hamilton's Grange to finally get its due respect. Many other important old buildings were less fortunate. The Audubon house was lost, as was Pinehurst, the Bradhurst mansion. Even the eighteenth-century Dyckman stone house at 152nd Street and St. Nicholas Avenue, an early example of Dutch architecture, was demolished in the late 1800s. To build the new often comes with destruction of what is old, with an appreciation too late for what we tore down. Almost miraculously, Hamilton's home had survived more than two centuries to make its final journey, down the hill from St. Luke's Episcopal Church to St. Nicholas Park, where it would sit on land that Hamilton had walked two centuries before.

Its greatest protector, Reverend Isaac Tuttle of St. Luke's, would have been proud. He knew that the Grange was worth saving and had spent his own money to protect it from being demolished. The only home Hamilton ever owned had been occupied by various families and used as a church, a pastor's home, and a school. Though his land had been sold off in lots to

Figures 85 and 86. TOP: Hamilton Grange Interior Braced 2008. BOTTOM: Hamilton Grange Final Move 2008. Courtesy National Park Service

real estate developers in the 1800s, his old neighborhood became home to some of New York City's most stunning and historic architecture.

And as it turned out, the developer William De Forest and his son, descendants of the original seventeenth-century Dutch settlers Henry and Isaac De Forest, the sons of Jesse the dyer from the Netherlands, also left a legacy in this part of the city—shaping the architectural character of Hamilton Heights. Over the years, apartment buildings, stores, bars, nightclubs, and churches were built on parts of Hamilton's former estate, the plans for which he hinted to Eliza in 1798.

Everywhere one looks, there is concrete, glass, and streetlights. On either side of the Grange, there are now subway stops. Given the ingenuity involved in the move of Hamilton's house and the millions of federal dollars used to renovate it, it is fitting to remember the prophetic words written in 1968 by Eric Sloane when he had just published his book *Mr. Daniels and the Grange*.

Speculating on whether the Grange would ever be shown the respect it was due, he mused,

> Perhaps hours or months or years after this book has been published the Grange will emerge from its predicament. The problems of moving an ancient building, of vacating land and demolishing buildings for such a project might be overcome, and the Grange may finally sit upon an appropriate piece of land with grass and trees.[34]

A small and steady stream of people would visit the Grange when it reopened in 2011, after a $14 million renovation that had painstakingly restored original details that had been altered over the centuries. Hamilton's family had long since donated most of the original furniture, historic relics, and paintings to the federal government, libraries, and museums.

The William G. Ward family, who purchased the Grange in 1845, bought some of the original furniture that had been left in the house when Mrs. Hamilton sold it in 1833. One of the family's descendants, Mrs. Julia Ward Stickley of Washington, D.C., wrote to the National Park Service in 1963 and advised, "We own a good deal of furniture from the Grange, original furniture. I possess the parlor sofa, my sister has four matching small chairs, and my cousin has two armchairs, plus a clock, one of two that Hamilton ordered. One was for his own home, the other was for Gen. Washington, and can be seen at Mt. Vernon to this day, its exact duplicate."[35] Most of the furniture at the Grange today consists of carefully built replicas from the period.

"The original plans or other detailed documentation, the restoration of the Grange as built depended largely on what the house itself could tell us," said Steve Laise, the chief of Cultural Resources for the National Park Service during the relocation and restoration. During a 2016 interview with Elizabeth Pochoda for the *Magazine Antiques*, Laise went on to say, "A painstaking examination conducted by the National Park Service revealed that a great many alterations had been made over time. But the

Figure 87. Grange Dining Room. Courtesy of National Park Service

eloquent voice of the remaining structure spoke clearly of Alexander Hamilton's vision."[36]

The article went on to share how the restoration team that replicated the furniture was able to examine the originals at museums or in personal collections. The pianoforte, in need of restoring, is one of the few original items owned by the Hamiltons during Alexander's lifetime, given to his daughter Angelica by her aunt and namesake, Angelica Schuyler Church. This is the daughter who never recovered from her breakdown after first her brother and then her father's murders.

A copy of the great 1792 John Trumbull portrait of Hamilton hangs in the hall, "to give visitors an immediate sense of Hamilton's grace and his aesthetic. The elongated octagonal parlor and dining room were centered on the eastwest axis, thus admitting maximum sunlight in both morning and afternoon."[37] The team also discovered that the folding dining room doors had been mirrored, reflecting the exterior light when opened, and were able to reproduce that. The paint colors were based on samples of the earliest coat uncovered after getting through the many layers applied over two centuries.

In 1896 the Hamilton family bequeathed the 1794 Ceracchi bust and the Gilbert Stuart portrait of George Washington to the New York Public Library and Astor-Lenox-Tilden Foundations. Both were put up for auction

Figure 88. Marble Bust Carved by Italian Sculptor Giuseppe Ceracchi, 1794. Public domain

in 2005 at Sotheby's and bought by the Crystal Bridges Museum of Art in Bentonville, Arkansas, for more than $8 million.

And in 2012, the first full year after the renovation, 16,358 people visited Alexander and Eliza Hamilton's Grange in an effort to capture, through preserved history and architecture, a dim but potent sense of what life had been like more than two centuries earlier in one of the most historic sections of Manhattan, on Harlem's elevated hillside in the neighborhood now called Hamilton Heights.

Chapter 15

Changing Demographics and a Revived Hamilton Heights

> If history repeats itself, and the unexpected always happens, how incapable must man be of learning from experience.
>
> George Bernard Shaw

It is no small thing to create an institution that serves as a supportive and inspirational space for young people to hone their creative gifts. By the first decade of the twenty-first century, the Harlem School of the Arts (HSA) was playing an increasingly large role in shaping the neighborhood's cultural legacy and the futures of countless performing artists. The school was now housed in an expanded state-of-the-art building on St. Nicholas Avenue and 141st Street that had opened in 1979, next door to its original location in the basement of a church. HSA had created new programs and was graduating a new "talented tenth." By the 1990s enrollment had reached 1,500, a new record.

Although the founder, Dorothy Maynor, had died in 1996 at the age of eighty-five, she left a profound legacy in terms of both her own contributions to music and the arts institution she had founded in 1964. In 2003, the President's Committee on the Arts and Humanities recognized HSA as one of the top afterschool arts and humanities-based programs in the country.

In 2012, the Harlem School of the Arts received a $6 million gift from acclaimed trumpeter Herb Alpert. St. Nicholas Avenue was transformed, as the school was able to make extensive renovations, including a modern glass façade at its entrance. Its alumni have gone on to brilliant careers in music, theater, film, and television. The talented Giancarlo Esposito, who had his film debut in Spike Lee's 1989 film *Do the Right Thing*, became famous in more recent years in the TV shows *Breaking Bad* and *Better Call Saul* as crime lord Gus Fring. Grammy-award-winning singer and accomplished actor Lenny Kravitz has shown his versatility in film and TV. His mother, Roxie Roker, is part of Black theater royalty, having begun her career downtown in the early days of the Negro Ensemble Company (NEC). She went on to win an Obie Award and a Tony nomination for her performance in *The River Niger* before her ten-year role on TV's *The Jeffersons*.

Condola Phylea Rashād has received four Tony Award nominations. The daughter of Phylicia and Ahmad Rashad and niece of Debby Allen, she would go on to star as Kate Sacker on the Showtime series *Billions*. And Caleb McLaughlin came to the public attention for his role as Lucas Sinclair on the hit Netflix Original series *Stranger Things*.

In taking its place as a landmark institution in the education and training of performers, HSA has accomplished artists in all fields come onboard

Figure 89. Harlem School of the Arts, 645 St. Nicholas Avenue. Courtesy D. S. James

as artists-in-residence. The school boasts a highly diverse student body that comes from not just Harlem but the Bronx, other parts of lower Manhattan, Washington Heights, and Inwood.

As gentrification moves across Harlem, for many it is the closing of Harlem Soul Food restaurants that is another kind of cultural death. The disappearance of mom-and-pop stores, displaced by big chain stores, was another casualty of the changing times. There was a seismic shift underway in terms of the demographics of Harlem.

Gentrification as a broader concept is not always bad. Private investment dollars that have flooded Harlem have helped rid many blocks of drugs, crime, and unscrupulous slumlords. But older residents and activists wonder: Why didn't the city clean up these neighborhoods earlier? Why was there no plan to form a path to home ownership for existing residents? Why did the city ignore decades of complaints about deplorable housing conditions? Why did large-scale police action against drug dealers only increase after the influx of new buildings and white residents?

Having a Starbucks in Harlem is nice, but some would argue that Harlem is being turned into the new Soho or Chelsea.

An extensive analysis of these gentrification trends is contained in a 2008 report published by Humanity in Action and authored by Sharon Obialo, Nienke Venema, and Marie Gørrild. The organization is a nonpartisan international nonprofit with a team of research fellows committed to advancing social justice. It helps to facilitate and promote a dialogue to understand and respond to the challenges that democratic societies face as they become increasingly diverse.

"From 2000 to 2005, 32,500 Blacks moved out and some 22,800 whites moved in to the Harlem district," the report noted. "Many argue that this displacement of Blacks from the neighborhood is a result of increased housing costs. Housing prices on the open market have soared 247 percent in the past ten years. With renovated lofts and brownstones going for anywhere between $1.5 and $4 million, one must assume that these developments are aimed at wealthy New Yorkers looking for a new home."[1] The report confirmed the fact that many longtime residents believed that they had little or no protection from the city's Division of Housing and Community Renewal. Landlords used a variety of loopholes to evict tenants. Some made unnecessary repairs that allowed them to raise the rent. Others charged fees for things like parking that had been free in the original lease.

Commenting in this 2008 study, William Allen, the Democratic district leader in Harlem, "describes a feeling of instability and frustration in the community as people slowly realize that the long-awaited improvements are not meant for them, but instead are aimed to move them out." Allen openly criticizes local government for actively deceiving communities of color, who are too trusting of their local politicians. "Many in the community cite Charles Rangel, congressmen for the 15th district and current chair of the powerful Ways and Means Committee, as well as C. Virginia Fields, former borough president, as culprits."[2]

Harlem is seen as the historic capital of African American culture, and gentrification appears to be erasing the rich history of Black culture and community. "Indeed, many Harlem residents feel that the rise of increasingly unaffordable luxury housing, lack of school improvement and limited job market demonstrates the absence of meaningful investment in the community. Instead, the money coming in is being spent on commercial development."[3]

Leading into the crisis, in the 1970s an unprecedented number of building owners defaulted on their taxes and abandoned their properties. "The city became the collective landlord for some 70% of the borough's properties," the *Humanity in Action* report noted. "And for years, buildings remained unwanted shells used as congregating points for drug deals and other nuisance activities."[4]

A major shift occurred in the 1990s when the government began allowing the transfer of city-owned property to private developers via the Third Party Transfer Program. But while the goal was to stimulate the housing market in poor neighborhoods like Harlem, gentrification continued. The price paid has been the slow but relentless eradication of Harlem's Black heritage as people who had lived in neighborhoods for generations were forced out of their homes or were unable to afford the renovated properties.

Some people believe that gentrification and displacement were the wake-up calls for longtime Harlem residents to take control of their own communities. But there is a broader question as to whether African Americans had control in the first place. Gaining access to these precious buildings was a struggle from the beginning of the Great Migration in the early twentieth century.

On St. Nicholas Place the Bailey House had sat for eight years since the fire, slowly deteriorating and suffering constant water damage. According to *Daytonian in Manhattan*, a blog about the city's history, "Finally, at the age of 87, Marguerite Blake put her dream house on the market in 2008 for $10 million. The Blakes's inability to maintain the hulking property was apparent. Water had continued to seep in through the roof. Plaster had fallen from some of the ceilings."[5] The house was still an architectural wonder, almost miragelike and out of place in the heart of this compactly built urban neighborhood. Then one remembers that the house was here before most of the rest of the structures. A writer for *New York* magazine called the forlorn mansion a modern Grey Gardens, a name that has become analogous to the deterioration of once elegant homes since the time Edie Bouvier Beale and her mother, Edith, two eccentric relatives of Jackie Kennedy Onassis, allowed their Long Island estate to fall apart around them.

It took the right kind of people to understand what the house meant and what it could once again be. And the right people proved to be Martin Spollen, a physical therapist, and his wife, Jenny, who in August of 2009 bought the "fixer-upper" for $1.4 million. (Some one-bedroom condos cost more than that.) For an 8,250-square-foot Romanesque mansion, it looked like a steal. But repairing and renovating the building would take time and an astronomical amount of money. First step: repair the roof to prevent further water damage. The rest of the work would come in stages.

That same year, five blocks away, a small but important tribute would be made on a rocky triangular site on Edgecombe Avenue and 155th Street. The New York Parks and Recreation Department responded to a request from a community group, which was endorsed by Community Board 12 in Manhattan, for the little section of green space to be named *Sugar Hill Luminaries Lawn*, a way to acknowledge the remarkable people who helped make the Triple Nickel at 555 Edgecombe Avenue famous.

In 2012 the wealthy real estate developer Ben Ashkenazy bought the old RKO Hamilton Theatre on Broadway at 146th Street, along with two adjoining lots and another property for $19 million. Although the interior had been horribly vandalized over the years and was a sad echo of its former splendor, the bones of the building remained. It has been proposed that the site be redeveloped to include luxury condos and possibly subsidized housing, a prospect that has awakened in many people memories of what the theater used to represent.

Unfortunately, some of the community protests and outrage come too late for these historic buildings. "As one of the last remaining vaudeville theaters in Harlem, the RKO Hamilton holds great historical significance for the West Harlem community," an article in the *Columbia Daily Spectator* noted. "Some older residents in the area remember when the RKO Hamilton served as a theater, while others, such as Manhattan Community Board 9 Landmarks Preservation & Parks subcommittee co-chair Anthony Carrion, recall some of the site's other historic uses."[6]

Carrion remembered as a child walking by the RKO Hamilton every

Figures 90 and 91. TOP: Hamilton Theatre Interior Stage. BOTTOM: Interior from above, circa 2021. Courtesy of David Hanzal

day when it was a children's clothing store. "I understood that it was different from other stores," he said, "because you can kind of feel that you're in the lobby of some enormous structure, but it's hard to really comprehend that all this grandeur once had occurred in the neighborhood and been allowed to deteriorate."[7]

The billionaire grocery store magnate John Catsimatidis, who grew up a few blocks away, was about ten when he watched his first movie there, a 1957 Walt Disney classic called *Old Yeller* about a boy and his beloved but doomed stray dog. "I cried and cried and cried when the dog died at the end," Catsimatidis said. "But it was the greatest theater in the world."[8]

Many residents believe that the constant mistreatment of historic sites in West Harlem is part of a much larger issue. "This site, the RKO Hamilton, is not just about preserving this property and preserving this culture and piece of history," said Daniel Marks Cohen, a member of Community Board 9, which covers the West Harlem neighborhoods of Manhattanville, Morningside Heights, and Hamilton Heights. "It is about righting a wrong that continues to be perpetuated on the people of West Harlem and Community Board 9."[9]

Meanwhile, at the Grange, an unexpected but tsunami-like cultural phenomenon turned Hamilton's former home into a bigger tourist attraction than ever and the entire neighborhood that bore his name into a destination. Lin-Manuel Miranda was already famous, along with author Quiara Alegría Hudes, for their 2005 Tony Award–winning musical *In the Heights*, which celebrated Latino heritage in Washington Heights. Miranda had read Ron Chernow's much-praised biography of Alexander Hamilton and was inspired to write a play, *Hamilton*, to tell the statesman's story to rap music, along with ingeniously choosing a diverse cast to play major historic figures. The playwright became an artist-in-residence at the Morris-Jumel Mansion and, perhaps fittingly, used Aaron Burr's old bedroom as an office.

As Miranda was quoted as saying in the online magazine *Gothamist*, "Working in the Jumel Mansion allows you the rare privilege of time travel in this incredible city."

In 2009, some years before *Hamilton*'s phenomenal success on Broadway, Miranda was invited to the White House by President Barack Obama to take part in his Evening of Poetry, Music, and the Spoken Word. He told the audience that he was working on a hip-hop album "about the life of someone I think embodies hip-hop. . . . Treasury Secretary, Alexander Hamilton." Needless to say, that got a chuckle. Miranda proceeded to sing what became one of the musical's signature songs, "Alexander Hamilton," accompanied by Cuban American composer Alex Lacamoire, who would become the show's conductor and orchestrator.

Hamilton opened in early 2015 at the Public Theater in Lower Manhattan, instantly attracted sold-out crowds, and moved that summer to Broadway, where it garnered rave reviews and became a smash hit. It won eleven Tony Awards, the second-highest total ever, after *The Producers*, by Mel Brooks. While the play makes only slight mention of the Grange, simply noting that the statesman had a place "uptown," it didn't take long for audiences to connect the dots.

Busloads of tourists suddenly wanted to visit both Hamilton's grave, which was downtown at Trinity Cemetery on Wall Street, and his former home, which was uptown in Harlem. In an article in the *Magazine Antiques* about the restoration of the house and recreating furniture pieces from the era, Elizabeth Pochoda described the play's effect on the neighborhood: "Up in Harlem, Hamilton Grange is feeling the glow. Last year there were more than thirty-five thousand visitors. In the first six months of this year [2016] they have already equaled that number."[10]

The two years before the play *Hamilton*, the Grange was averaging 20,000 to 21,000 visitors a year. In 2015, after the musical opened, that number jumped to 35,446. And the year of its runaway Tony awards in 2016, park rangers were overwhelmed by 85,348 visitors. They had to stop and recalibrate how to handle the crowds. That number held steady the following year. Interest in the Founding Father on the $10 bill only grew. Plans to replace Hamilton's face with that of Harriet Tubman, the courageous abolitionist who had escaped enslavement and returned to the South thirteen times to free others, were put on hold. How often does a Broadway play impact a decision about U.S. currency? Hamilton mania had gripped the country.

Neighborhoods evolve in stages, and it is not uncommon for modern dwellers to find it beyond belief that where they live was once a forest where wild game roamed. Even some twentieth-century additions in Hamilton Heights were beginning to disappear. But a number of them are recalled by a writer and blogger named David Ryan, author of a book titled *The Gentle Art of Wandering*, and in the course of traveling around this neighborhood he came upon some hidden gems.

Although the Polo Grounds were long gone, Ryan found his way to the John T. Brush Stairway, between 157th and 158th streets on Edgecombe Avenue, a ghostly reminder of the famous stadium. The staircase had been built in 1913 by the Giants with the hope that it would entice the residents at the top of Coogan's Bluff on Sugar Hill to attend more games by offering easier access to the ballpark just a short walk down the slope from where they lived.

In 2015, less than a mile north, the long overdue renovation of the old High Bridge had been completed and the structure reopened to the public. From the Manhattan side a person enters Highbridge Park at West 172nd Street and Amsterdam Avenue, then turns east to the staircase at the High Bridge Water Tower Terrace. The Brush Staircase was fully renovated as

Figure 92. John T. Brush stairway, prior to renovation. Courtesy David Ryan

part of this same civic improvement with dedications from representatives of the Yankees, Giants, and city officials.

New York is a walking town. In the almost forty years since the bridge had closed in 1978, the neighborhood had undergone massive changes that included a lower crime rate. A new generation, as well as a lot of longtime residents, welcomed this old bridge that was new again.

In his 2017 book *Magnetic City* the architectural critic Justin Davidson wrote, "The most romantic bridge in New York reaches from cliff top to cliff top, joining two neighborhoods forged by dreams and disappointment. On a damp, tropical day, I've ridden my bike to High Bridge, a disused aqueduct in Washington Heights, dominated on its Manhattan side by a stone water tower that looks out over the Harlem River like a medieval fortification."[11]

The bridge, he continued, is a link between two splendid areas of the city that had once been grand and poetic but became less so as drugs, racial hostility, and urban decline took their toll. The two neighborhoods, "Edgecombe Avenue and the Grand Concourse, two roughly parallel ridge roads on opposite sides of the river, were both nobly built; both saw

Figure 93. The High Bridge circa 2017. Courtesy NYC Parks and Recreation

their populations turn over and their architecture degrade. Both have now started to recover their old prosperity, though at dramatically different rates, and always at a cost."[12]

The High Bridge that the poet Edgar Allan Poe used to enjoy strolling across is now a National Historic Landmark, as is the Croton Aqueduct.

The designations of historic landmark buildings and locations are not as extensive in Harlem as they could be, a criticism noted by many historians and local civic groups. It leaves important structures open to demolition and remodeling that could destroy unique features. In Hamilton Heights, there is no marker on St. Nicholas Avenue to indicate the block where Norman Rockwell lived and drew his early sketches as a boy or the apartment building down the street from the Rockwells where Ralph Ellison lived for several years as he began to write *Invisible Man*. The building on 144th Street in Hamilton Heights where George Gershwin wrote "Swanee" has no marker as of yet; but there is a plaque in Central Harlem on 110th Street and Cathedral Drive in front of the building where he wrote "Rhapsody in Blue"—not a landmark, but at least it is noted. The home of George Haynes on Convent Avenue, the cofounder of the National Urban League, holds no indication of its importance either. Nor does the old Troger's Hotel at 92 St. Nicholas Place, built around

1892, a building that served the clientele from the newly opened Harlem Speedway and became a leading jazz club for decades. As of this writing, it is a take-out chicken eatery. Even St. Luke's Episcopal Church, which was built in 1892, does not have landmark status, though it is within the Hamilton Heights–Sugar Hill Landmark District.

The fortunes of the Morris-Jumel Mansion underwent a significant upswing in 2013 because of the discovery of a remarkable document in the museum's archives.

In an excerpt from *Rare Books Uncovered: True Stories of Fantastic Finds in Unlikely Places*, published in *Smithsonian Magazine*, Rebecca Rego Barry wrote, "Once in a very long while, a rare book or manuscript discovery is so remarkable that it makes national headlines."[13] An intern named Emilie Gruchow, she continued, had discovered, "in an unlikely place, a document of monumental historic value, and a small museum in strained circumstances was about to gain lots of positive media attention and a bundle of cash." The document, titled "The Twelve United Colonies, by their Delegates in Congress, to the inhabitants of Great Britain," had been written by Robert R. Livingston, who, along with Thomas Jefferson, John Adams, Benjamin Franklin, and Roger Sherman, had been assigned to write the Declaration of Independence in 1776.

Gruchow, an archive intern at the museum, was working in the attic at the time. She had been asked to recatalogue seventeenth- and eighteenth-century manuscripts stored in file cabinets, and she knew that a hot attic was not the best place for historic documents.

She was reading one paper, the book noted, when she found others, "which were interleaved with fragments of another document. They were not in order, so I started reading fragments one by one until I got to the fourth or fifth leaf, which had the opening passage on one side."[14] Then she realized the words were familiar. Her previous classes many years before as a student of American history jogged her memory that she had read a letter addressed "To the Inhabitants of Great Britain" in a college class. The intern was holding an original 1775 draft of an urgent plea by the Second Continental Congress intended to be sent directly to the people of Great Britain.

In a steamy attic on 162nd Street in Sugar Hill, where George Washington had camped out, was what was described as "an appeal not to King George, but to the British people, for reconciliation, and a last-ditch effort to avoid war by touting 'the glorious achievements of our common ancestors.'"

Gruchow brought the document to the museum's curator, Jasmine

Helm, and its director, Carol S. Ward. Both thought that it looked legitimate and concurred that it was an original, genuine, and immensely significant Revolutionary-era document. The Morris-Jumel Museum was in possession of a valuable piece of American history, both for its historic and financial value. Barry wrote that "it's no secret that historical house museums—landmarks or not—struggle both for funding and for visitors. The Morris-Jumel is no different, and the expense to maintain it can be onerous."[15]

Before Gruchow's discovery, scholars did not believe that such an original manuscript, an appeal to the British people, existed. While the Continental Congress had directed delegates Robert R. Livingston, Richard Henry Lee, and Edmund Pendleton to write the letter, it was unsigned. The board voted to sell the document, and several experts determined that it could fetch up to $400,000.

The auctioneer Leigh Keno from the PBS television show *Antiques Roadshow*, who was slated to conduct the auction, described seeing the manuscript as one of the most exciting moments of his career.

"It is extremely rare in the field of historical American Colonial documents for new discoveries of this importance to turn up," Keno said. "When reading the draft, with its many changes in place, one gets a sense of what was going through the minds of our Founding Fathers. It really is a national treasure."[16]

On January 26, 2014, Keno Auctions put the item up for sale, and bidding was intense until Keno hit the final gavel at $912,500. Gruchow's work that day in the hot attic had garnered nearly $1 million for a document that had gone unnoticed for possibly a century.

"This auction quadruples the size of our endowment and ensures that the mansion can serve the public for generations to come," the museum's director, Carol Ward, said. Brian Hendelson, a New Jersey private collector who won the bid, was quoted as saying after the auction, "The only thing I can compare this to would be to own the original draft of the Declaration of Independence." Hendelson allowed the New-York Historical Society to put the document on public exhibit.

When people move to a new city, town, or neighborhood, they are only "the newcomers" for a given period. Then they settle in, become part of the fabric of the place, fall in and out of love, raise their children, bury their dead, join committees, and find their favorite coffee shop, restaurant, place of worship, or nightclub. As the decades progress, those "new" residents who began to gentrify Harlem are now entrenched and part of its history.

Journalists still find the changing demographics and marvels of the heights of Harlem newsworthy. In a 2016 article in the *New York Times*, Julie Besonen raves that "from river vistas to the neo-Gothic splendor of the City College of New York, Hamilton Heights provides compelling sights around nearly every corner. On Amsterdam Avenue and 153rd Street, for instance, a mural of birds and a giant image of John James Audubon cover the facade of a building."[17] The mural is very close to Audubon's former property, and the famous ornithologist is buried at Trinity Church Cemetery on Broadway and West 155th Street, just a few blocks away.

In recent years, the U.S. has struggled mightily with the names on buildings, societies, monuments, schools, sports teams, and other symbols that salute people who held African Americans in bondage, embraced and promoted highly racist ideologies, or degraded Native Americans. We would have to rip out the core of the country to set it all right. Our first president and the man who wrote the Declaration of Independence both enslaved people. Thomas Jefferson had several children by one of those he enslaved, Sally Hemmings. Documentation seems to confirm that Alexander Hamilton owned a few, and he married into a slaveholding family. How do we revere those men's contributions and balance the evil that was slavery? Yet a balance must be struck.

Audubon has not escaped that criticism as one who bought and sold Black bodies. By the time he settled in Harlem, slavery had just ended a few years before in the state. Yet arguments are now raised as to whether the Audubon Society should change its name because of his history. Some board members embrace this, while others strongly oppose it.

For the last century, this neighborhood, which was once the home of those who owned enslaved people, came to be heavily populated by their descendants. One Hamilton Heights resident that Besonen interviewed in 2016 remarked, "When I moved here 17 years ago, I saw mostly African-Americans and Dominicans, and now it's more multicultural."

Judith Insell, a professional musician and a member of Manhattan Community Board 9, which includes Hamilton Heights confirmed that the neighborhood is still composed of music makers too, saying, "I've noticed a lot of young musicians with instruments on their backs all over the place."[18]

In 2015, Barry Katz bought a two-bedroom condo on Riverside Drive and 146th Street. "Selling his one-bedroom fifth-floor walk-up in the West Village (he declined to disclose the price), he paid $260,000 less for a space in Hamilton Heights that was twice as big, with an elevator and eight windows facing Riverside Park and the Hudson River."[19] Katz told Besonen that he could sit and look out all day long.

We spoke to a Heights' resident, Jasmine Baulkman, who went to school in Spanish Harlem on 116th Street and Pleasant Avenue. She now lives in Hamilton Heights on 140th Street between Broadway and Riverside Drive. Baulkman appreciates the variety of commerce in the neighborhood and said, "There are bars, there are restaurants, the Harlem Cigar Bar, some speakeasies, and some fancier coffee shops. And these places have come in the past ten years, and obviously it has caused a different mix of people to move in as well."

The answer to what the neighborhood is like today is in many ways complicated and in others quite simple: it is a microcosm of the larger melting pot that is New York City. Or is it more of the mosaic, that picture made up of small parts, that David Dinkins spoke of during his 1990 inaugural address as mayor of New York City when he said, "I see New York as a gorgeous mosaic of race and religious faith, of national origin and sexual orientation."

It is not uncommon to sit in a small nightclub and hear a singer or musician who makes you wonder why the person never won a Grammy. Or you might pick up a used book on a whim, finish it, and marvel that it was on the dollar pile; that this well-written, poignant, masterful use of words and story was only a dollar away from being recycled.

Then there are those brilliant writers who create one masterpiece and are done. In juxtaposition, there are prolific authors who produce a constant flow of books on a regular basis. Yet some wordsmiths, Harper Lee, Emily Brontë, Margaret Mitchell, J. D. Salinger, and Sylvia Plath, to name a few, give us one great novel in their lifetimes. The celebrated writer Ralph Ellison is among the latter. He died in 1994 and is buried at Trinity Cemetery, not far from his former home at 730 Riverside Drive at 150th Street.

A tribute to Ellison by the late sculptor Elizabeth Catlett, which stands on Riverside Drive, depicts in both spirit and execution the protagonist of Ellison's 1952 novel *Invisible Man*. The monument is near what was one of Ellison's favorite spots to relax, on the benches of the traffic island on Riverside Drive near his home.

The fifteen-foot-high, ten-foot-wide bronze monolith features a hollow silhouette of a man. Two granite panels are inscribed with Ellison quotes and biographical material. The Riverside Park Fund and a neighborhood group, the Ralph Ellison Memorial Committee, helped build momentum and raise funds for the venture. It was a collaboration with a city-funded relandscaping project. Many of the people who helped raise money for the monument knew Ellison personally. In 2021, the lovely area would be renamed Ralph Ellison Plaza in his honor.

Figure 94. Invisible Man Statue; Ralph Ellison tribute, Riverside Drive Park. Courtesy NYC Parks and Recreation

A few blocks away, in Sugar Hill, the celebrated St. Nick's Pub, which had been offering live music since the 1930s, closed in 2011. Federal agents raided the place and finally shut it down after several warnings to the owner about an expired liquor license. The old St. Nick's Pub sign at 773 St. Nicholas served as a sad reminder of better days when one could barely get in the door. Local residents still held out hope that the club would reopen, despite having been shuttered for years.

But St. Nick's, which had been Harlem's oldest nightclub and which had made entertainment in Sugar Hill famous, met a tragic end in 2018. During filming of the Edward Norton and Bruce Willis movie *Motherless Brooklyn*, the building caught fire. The flames destroyed the historic location, sadly taking the life of Michael Davidson, a firefighter who had been injured battling the blaze and died days later. A life was lost and a huge part of Sugar Hill's musical history destroyed. A general sense of outrage permeated the neighborhood that more precautions had not been taken to protect the legendary location. Ironically, St. Nick's was standing in as the film location for another famous Harlem club—the Red Rooster.

In January of 2017 the Schomburg Center was named a National Historic Landmark by the National Park Service in recognition of its vast collection of materials exploring the history and culture of people of African descent. It had been designated a New York City landmark in 1981.

Figure 95. Former 400 Tavern off 148th and St. Nicholas. Courtesy D. S. James

Only a few signs remain from the clubs that had once been the neighborhood's lifeblood. The faded signs for Lundy's and the 400 Tavern Club are worn, rusted reminders of a time when more than a half-dozen nightspots dotted this section of St. Nicholas Avenue, a time when the music rang out in Hamilton Heights every night.

It is hardly surprising that Hamilton Heights and Sugar Hill have been designated New York Historic Landmark Districts. Although they would qualify just because of the architecture, the neighborhood's legacy has been burnished by the historic figures who lived here, created great works of art, or helped bring about transformative social justice issues while in the neighborhood.

The Tsion Cafe, which serves Ethiopian and Mediterranean food, opened in 2014 at 763 St. Nicholas Avenue at 148th Street in what was previously Jimmie's Chicken Shack. When the Tsion opened, it was the only step-down nightclub left on the avenue, keeping the old neighborhood spirit alive with jazz on the weekends. Perhaps one day this spot that once employed Malcolm X, Redd Foxx, and Charlie Parker—three legends of African American history in social revolution, comedy, TV, and jazz—will have a plaque "legends worked here."

A few blocks away at Trinity Church Cemetery and Mausoleum in Hamilton Heights, the changing city had developed so much that the cemetery grounds represented more green space than most of the environs around it. Audubon's Minnie's Land and Richard Carman's Carmansville were but a memory.

The cemetery has provided the final resting place for many influential New Yorkers and just as many less famous people. Politicians, artists, land barons, musicians, writers, and architects, many of whom helped shape New York, Hamilton Heights, and Sugar Hill, are here. Its first interment

Figure 96. Tsion Café.
Courtesy D. S. James

was in 1843, and the naturalist John James Audubon was buried not long after in 1851. Eliza Jumel, as well as the eighteenth-century real estate baron John Jacob Astor and several of his family members, are here. His great-grandson, John Jacob Astor IV, was interred here after his body was recovered from the North Atlantic after the sinking of the Titanic.

The Bradhursts, who owned neighboring estates to the Morris family, also have an adjoining crypt with Eliza Jumel. And then there is Alfred Tennyson Dickens, Charles Dickens's son, who died while in New York doing marketing for his father. Ralph Ellison, the author of *Invisible Man*, keeps final company with Clement Clarke Moore, the author of "A Visit from St. Nicholas." An annual reading of Moore's celebrated poem takes place at his grave every Christmas Eve.

There is something to be said about statistics, surveys, and national census reports . . . and then there is reality. If you walk the streets of Harlem and Hamilton Heights in particular, despite the Census numbers, you will find no shortage of people of color.

The Pew Research Center writes of the 2020 Census, "Those who have not responded to the census so far, according to the survey, are disproportionately likely to be from groups the census has struggled to count accurately in previous decennial census collections, including the Black and Hispanic populations."[20] The study also indicates that four-in-ten who haven't yet filled out a U.S. Census say they wouldn't answer the door for a census worker.

The 2021 census data summarized by censusreporter.org for Manhattan District 9 indicates a racial breakdown of: Latinos at 40 percent; Whites at 26 percent; Blacks at 18 percent; Asians at 10 percent, and Other races 6 percent. They are numbers that no African American resident of Harlem who has lived there for any length of time would have believed possible: that Blacks now rank third in the racial makeup of who populates this section of Harlem.

Perhaps more importantly than what the numbers record is the reality. The number of people walking these neighborhoods and going in and out of dwellings would prompt one to question the statistics. There are still a lot of African Americans here, and the problem, of course, is that many Black people are resistant to filling out the census. There is a "big brother is watching" attitude, a feeling that the census is an invasion of one's privacy. Yet not being counted harms communities in terms of services and representation in Washington, D.C. It skews the numbers in a way that has far-reaching effects.

Large portions of Amsterdam Avenue and Broadway, the major

commercial thoroughfares, are still throwbacks to what they were like in the 1970s or '80s with a myriad of businesses in between apartment buildings. Although St. Nicholas has its fair share of businesses, the street is still primarily residential. Most shops fill local needs—the dry cleaners, a supermarket, a hair salon or two, a convenience store, the Citibank branch at 145th Street, the odd bar or café, and a smattering of restaurants. There is a wonderful diverse group of individuals to be found, with a cacophony of languages and accents, as well as a few people that, at a glance, you would not want to meet late at night alone.

Then there is Edgecombe, narrow, lined with trees and magnificent apartment buildings, facing the Harlem River. That leaves Convent Avenue, which has become quite analogous to Central Harlem's Strivers' Row in terms of the relative sanctity of still being one of the most well-preserved, beautiful streets in all of Harlem. All these avenues—Edgecombe, St. Nicholas, Amsterdam, Broadway, and Riverside Drive—are part of Hamilton Heights, part of Sugar Hill. Yet Convent Avenue continues to be the street that is somehow shown the most respect in terms of going unmolested by outward property defacement.

City College has become the main campus of the now sprawling CUNY system and its only urban campus. The majestic buildings rival those of any university in the country. The list of alumni includes ten Nobel Prize and three Pulitzer Prize winners, one each of a Turing Award winner and a Fields Medalist, and three Rhodes Scholars. The Fields Medal is only awarded every four years and is regarded as one of the highest honors a mathematician can receive. The Turing Award, of a similar distinction, is in the field of computing. It is named in honor of Alan Turing, the Brit who helped break the German Enigma machine encryption code during World War II. Turing's brilliance, contributions to the war, and to the world of computing did not keep him from being unjustly persecuted for being homosexual, which led to his suicide.

Celebrated CCNY alumni also include Colin Powell, Tony Curtis, Henry Kissinger, New York City mayor Ed Koch, United States Supreme Court justice Felix Frankfurter, Ira Gershwin, and Jonas Salk, who created the polio vaccine.

The college's Hamilton Heights campus had the nation's first student government and, in Delta Sigma Phi, the first national fraternity that ignored religion, race, color, or creed as determinants for admission. In 1907 City College started the first degree-granting evening program in its School of Education.

Another institution that is helping to contribute to educational excellence in Hamilton Heights is Harlem Academy, a private school that in 2020 broke ground for its new campus at 655 St. Nicholas Avenue at 142nd Street and officially opened at the end of 2021. The COVID-19 pandemic slowed down construction and the opening. Head of school Vincent Dotoli shared with us his sentiments that they "want to address a critical lack of educational options for promising students in Harlem, Washington Heights, and the Bronx. It is humbling to plant our roots here in Hamilton Heights, home to so many inspiring writers, activists, and artists over the years, and to know the school will play a role in opening a door to opportunity for future leaders."

The school, which was founded in 2004 and is located a block from the Grange, provides full scholarships to needy students. "We intentionally built Harlem Academy's permanent home in this wonderfully diverse and vibrant community," Dotoli said. "We see the city as an extension of our classrooms, and we're tremendously fortunate to be within walking distance of historical sites, beautiful parks, and renowned arts and academic institutions."

One could ponder that the real estate prices in Hamilton Heights are obscene and possibly part of a housing bubble that is unsustainable. A house is only worth what someone is willing to pay for it. Some of the $2 million dollar brownstones often reported about in the newspapers are still just a block away from where you can find graffiti scrawled on buildings and a crime rate that is not insignificant.

It takes one back to Suzanne Slesin's 1988 *New York Times* article, still early in the gentrification process, when she remarked that brownstones in Hamilton Heights ranged from $250,000 to $425,000, with some homeowners having gotten a steal at $125,000. Now, $425,000 is about the price of a studio or one-bedroom, one-bath co-op.

Not every building was the home of someone famous. Most were not. Behind and in between the buildings are small moments of further grace: tile-lined patios and gardens. Within these buildings are also interesting and unusual characters that give the neighborhood life.

One of them is Kurt Thometz. He is incredibly knowledgeable about Black history and those who wrote about it. He has been quoted several times describing himself as being a white guy from Minnesota who was raised to be racist and anti-Semitic. His life was changed, he has said, after he read Stokely Carmichael's autobiography, whereupon he immersed himself in African American culture and literature.

Jim Dwyer of the *New York Times* wrote that in between working for various bookstores after moving to New York in the 1970s, "Mr. Thometz has tended the serious private libraries of Brooke Astor and Diana Vreeland, Leonard Lauder, Felix Rohatyn and various Newhouses, and others of such staggering wealth."[21]

Thometz felt an incredible sense of history when in 2004 he bought the brownstone directly opposite the Morris-Jumel Mansion and around the corner from 555 Edgecombe Avenue. After he unpacked his 10,000 books, it seemed a natural transition to open Jumel Terrace Books. The window has one word on it: word. It is an homage to his autistic son and to the first time he used a word on purpose. He was letting his dad know that he realized he had skipped a word while reading him his favorite book. So, his son said "word."

In the bookstore's heyday, Thometz could point to any nook or shelf and tell a visitor, "Eighteenth century over there. On this shelf, slavery, many oral histories; sports, jazz, street literature, narcotics, black military history. Bound volumes of Muhammad Speaks. Vinyl records of speeches by Malcolm X and Eldridge Cleaver. A signed Langston Hughes volume. Bruce Davidson's photos of 100th Street."[22] The collection had a special focus on Harlem history, slavery, Reconstruction, Jim Crow, civil rights, Black Power, and Africa.

Before the bookstore closed in 2015, the collection had grown to more than 15,000 volumes. He next turned the bookstore–garden apartment in Sugar Hill into a bibliophile's dream, a unique Bed & Breakfast where you could sleep surrounded by thousands of books.

When we spoke in 2022, Thometz discussed how COVID shut down the B&B. The next life of the apartment has been as an in-demand location space for movies and photo shoots. He told us that recently *Glamour* was shooting Amanda Gorman, the young poet from President Biden's inauguration, for the cover.

"What I am doing with the place now is photoshoots and films. We've had *Gucci*. I had HBO here recently doing a Tawana Brawley documentary. I've had *Vogue* and *Elle*," Thometz said. Some of the photo shoots utilize the apartment and the lovely, tiled backyard.

It is a small world. Thometz remarked that one of the many friends he made in Sugar Hill over the years was Fab Five Freddy, who asked him to come look at the former Haynes home on Convent Avenue when he was considering buying it in the 1990s. The bookseller and his wife became frequent visitors at the documentarian's home, the same one W. E. B. Du Bois visited in the 1930s.

A few blocks away, at 1942 Amsterdam Avenue, there is another independent bookstore that has beat the odds and kept its doors open in an era

Figures 97 and 98. TOP: Jumel Terrace Books Airbnb. Courtesy of Lisa Kato. BOTTOM: Jumel Terrace Books Patio. Courtesy Kurt Thometz

when online shopping has shuttered most brick-and-mortar bookstores. Janifer P. Wilson founded Sister's Uptown Bookstore and Cultural Center in 2000. Post-pandemic, they have reopened for in-person shopping and events. As noted on its website, the bookstore provides "resources for members of the community to nurture their minds, hearts and souls with present and past works of gifted African American authors and other great authors and intellectuals including masters of spoken word."

Then, as now, one never knows whether the man or woman one passes by in the neighborhood is on his or her way to a clerical job, to sell insurance, clean someone's house, record new music, attend college, teach, or help us mail our packages. Neighborhoods are full of people with countless stories: some that get revived, some never told, and some that make it into books, songs, the big screen, or our small handheld devices. And the buildings with their ornate carvings, cornices, carved demons, and angels hold those people and their collective dreams and fears. It is the duty of storytellers to help record some of those names and memorialize places and events.

Here is a harsh truth. Out of 363 years in Harlem's history after being colonized by the Dutch, only about seventy years, or approximately 19 percent of that time, was associated with the name Harlem as an African American neighborhood. Black people held this choice piece of Manhattan for seventy years, during which time Harlem was becoming Black, was mostly Black, and sections, for a time, were all Black . . . a time when *Harlem was in vogue*, as poets and historians have termed its status.

How powerful is it that those seventy years dominate one's immediate reaction to the name and place that is Harlem? Those years were so culturally and socially significant, the good and the bad, the trailblazing and the mundane, that the fact that Harlem was a Black neighborhood is what became paramount in the minds of people all over the world. It was the creation of a Black mecca in Harlem that made it world famous, that gave it a mystical aura. Yet it was a wisp of time in the overall history of Manhattan, Harlem and these heights that were first the land of the Lenape, then the Dutch, British, and finally an American Harlem that has been home to half dozen or more races, religions, and ethnic groups now has a new story being rewritten daily.

Chapter 16

Bailey House, Jazz, and the Renaissance Remix

> Wherever you live, you owe it to yourself to know the history of the land you live in and who lived there before.... The spirit of the people before you is still there in some sense, so it is appropriate and necessary to do a spiritual and moral 'title search' wherever you live.
>
> —Evan T. Pritchard
> *Native New Yorkers: The Legacy of the Algonquin People of New York*

The Bailey House, the 1888 mansion that Martin and Jenny Spollen bought in 2009, had been much improved by 2021. The couple, who live in a brownstone down the street, had spent twelve years slowly renovating it. Without their appreciation for the stunning house and its historic importance, it may have continued to decay. Strolling past the apartment buildings that line St. Nicholas Avenue, one can look across at this castle and wonder if it is a mirage. It is so perfect and stately that it seems out of place in New York City. Yet it was in this place first, before most of what now surrounds it. The neighborhood grew around the house; indeed, there is an 1890 picture of a family bundled up on a snowy day in their horse-drawn carriage in front of the mansion. The Bailey House wraps around the corner of 150th and St. Nicholas Place, a short street just seven blocks long that is an offshoot of St. Nicholas Avenue and a block north of Edgecombe Avenue and the Harlem River.

If a house can be loved back into its former glory, that is what the Spollens are doing to the Bailey House, the Romanesque mansion they had bought from Marguerite and Warren Blake. It is no small undertaking to

Figure 99. James A. and Ruth M. Bailey House. Courtesy Tom Miller

renovate a 133-year-old house that has suffered extensive damage from age, fire, and a leaky roof. It was exacerbated by the Blake's dogs, who had caused the kind of damage that makes some landlords say, "No pets." It takes vision, respect, a lot of love, and a substantial amount of physical and financial investment to take on such a project. It also takes patience. The Spollens searched deep to instill their own spirit into refinishing the house while paying close attention to getting the historical aspects of its restoration accurate. They consulted with conservationists and museum staff to help them match the period details.

    At their gracious invitation to tour their home in 2021, we started with the first basement, a huge space where the servants used to live, which has been converted to a workshop. "When we bought it," Martin says, "this floor was so rotted that you could fall through it to the sub-basement. So, we replaced all the joists here and reset everything to its correct level." Pointing to his father's bandsaw, he added, "He bought it used, and it dated from 1899. Now it's part of our functional workshop for doing our restoration work in this area."

Figure 100. Basement Workshop.
Courtesy D. S. James

Martin Spollen can point to any wall, staircase, floor covering, lighting fixture, window frame, or doorway and recite its history, tell you its provenance as original or refinished, and give you a good idea of how it was damaged and repaired. In the twelve years since the couple bought the house, they and their team of resident workers, both family members who have learned the art of restoration and the occasional professionals they bring in, are still hard at work fixing up the house.

He indicated where there was a bathroom that they removed to make more room for the workshop. This is a huge space, with multiple rooms that had once been used as a dining room, staff living room, main kitchen area, bedrooms, and another large bathroom.

He pointed to the dumbwaiter and shaft where, after the food was cooked in the main kitchen down the hall, servants would have placed the food in the dumbwaiter to send up to the butler's pantry for serving the family. There are many old buildings that still have the inside cabling for dumbwaiters, with the doors sealed.

Martin said that it would be great to excavate the sub-basement because the 1890 *Scientific American* article wrote that they believe the house to be built on bedrock. "So, to go deeper would be to go through the Manhattan schist," Martin said. Schist is the second-oldest of New York City's bedrocks, about 450 million years old. It is right behind Fordham gneiss, the billion-year old rock foundation formed during the fusion of ancient mountain-building that created super continents.

We asked if all the beauty is commonplace now. "We appreciate it and as we gradually make progress, that's obviously gratifying," Martin said. "We look at ourselves as custodians of the house. Nobody ever owns anything forever. So, we just want to be the custodians of it, and we are trying to be as detailed as possible."

While there is much that is beautiful, Martin is quick to point out damage yet to be repaired: flaked wallpaper on one wall, a chipped ceiling above one staircase, an exposed beam in the ceiling of another room. The couple's commitment to keeping the renovation as authentic as possible prompted them to create their own set of museum-quality workshops. The Spollens have the ability to follow museum drawings that show various periods from the time the house was built to make accurate repairs to damaged banisters, latticework, cornices, and archways.

On the first floor, Martin pointed to the windows and said, "Most of the stained-glass we've had restored. This is Belcher glass, a company that was not around for very long, but left stunning, one-of-a-kind, distinctive stained glass to mark their heyday in the 1880s. They found a way to make

Figure 101. Martin Spollen at Open Stained-Glass Window. Courtesy D. S. James

these stained-glass windows in mass production, but they sag over time. Some were quite deteriorated, and some just needed a little touching up." Martin was referring to Belcher's innovative method of pouring molten lead between two panes of glass to create a solid panel of glass and metal. The result concentrated the light causing brilliant reflections that changed as the natural lighting did throughout the day. One thinks of stained-glass windows as fixed. But another unique feature is that they open, as with any other window.

The Spollens are fortunate to be able to concentrate on the accuracy of the restoration, which is their main focus, rather than on a date they might occupy the house. There is one room that has a gold and white scheme: James Bailey's former office. In here there are pictures of Bailey with the Barnum & Bailey Circus marketing.

Rounding a corner on the ground floor, you come to an inglenook, one of those enchanting little sitting areas built around a fireplace. You enter through a beautiful latticework arch into a space with a stained-glass

Figure 102. Bailey's Former Office. Courtesy D. S. James

window above an elaborately carved decorative fireplace. You can picture yourself retiring there with your favorite book, pouring something comforting to drink, and hoping that no one finds you for hours.

It is hard not to sound repetitive while marveling at every beautiful and unique new detail. But it is that kind of house, worthy of awe up each staircase, around every bend, and in various alcoves and corners.

Leading to the living room are finely tooled intricate Celtic patterns in the pocket doors that speak to Bailey's Irish heritage, since he was born "McGinnis."

On the opposite side are several detailed patterns in the glittering finished wood. Jenny pressed on the inside door frame to show how they slid out. The same idea holds true of the traditional pocket shutters that Martin opened at the front windows facing the porch, where the hidden panel then popped open to allow one to pull up the shutters. He proudly announced that Jenny also refinished these.

As you approach the first set of stairs to the second floor, it's impossible

Figure 103. First Floor Carved Wooden Door. Courtesy D. S. James

Figure 104. Newell Post Finial at Base of Stairway. Courtesy D. S. James

not to admire the beautiful designs on the banister highlighted by an intricately carved Newell post finial at the base of the banister. CBS Sunday Morning would do an entire segment on these distinctive finials, and in visiting the Spollen home historian Michael Henry Adams would discuss this exact one. A few steps away is intricate latticework on the arch leading to a hall.

Upstairs, Martin pointed to two of the smaller bedrooms, indicating what he believed to be the original linoleum. There is a massive, very old bathtub that seems to be original to the house. In an indication of just how much the couple is committed to authenticity, Martin pointed to valley rafters (main beams that support a corner in a room), three out of the five of which they replaced. "We couldn't find anything like that in a lumber yard here," he said, "so we had trees cut in Vermont, hemlock trees, and these were milled specially for the house."

As to where all this refinishing talent comes from, Martin said, "We hired a first-rate company to help us with the mantel, and it was very expensive. We had them agree to teach us the methods while they were doing it so we could learn. They agreed, and we learned a lot, especially Jenny." They've had twelve years to become very knowledgeable about restoration and finishing, and it shows. Martin is grateful that the Blakes did not make any major changes to the original architectural character of the house.

For that alone, there is a huge debt of gratitude to be paid to the Blakes. They were the longest owners of the home, over sixty years. There are others who would have gutted the interior, obliterated the unique historic features, and turned it into something modern and forgettable. The Blakes had already owned the mansion for twenty-two years by the time they supported the application for the New York historic landmark designation.

The stairways are narrow and steep and have the dizzying effect reminiscent of an M. C. Escher drawing. Throughout our climb, Martin pointed to work still to be done.

The rounded curves, differing angles, and shades of wood in the room below the widow's walk are a showstopper. If ever there was a space to take one's breath away, this is it. It is empty, and, in a way, one feels it should

Figure 105. Three Sets of Interior Staircases. Courtesy D. S. James

stay that way. This is a room where all that is needed is one's imagination. It feels like you should pray or meditate, or both at once. Window coverings would be an insult and deflect from the outside light casting beautiful shadows on the walls and flooring. And to say the views are majestic does not do justice to the views or the word "majestic." The conical stone turret room is right outside the multicolored dormer window, which has tiny alternating squares of blue, pink, red, and lavender framing its arch. Two other landmark buildings can be seen from Figures 106 and 107. This was worth the climb. All that was left to see of this magnificent house was the widow's walk that tops the mansion, which we did not tackle.

The house was electrified when it was built, and electricity was still fairly new then. Many homes still had gas lighting and would take decades to upgrade.

Martin commented that Sugar Hill never saw the level of deterioration that other parts of Harlem did, with rows of buildings that had been damaged or boarded up. He remembers Sugar Hill being an attractive neighborhood when they first moved here, and the houses on Hamilton Terrace looking pretty much the way they do now. But Jenny remarked that when they first bought the house there were bullet holes in the windows.

"You would see a couple of houses boarded up," Martin said. "There

Figure 106. Outer View of the Conical Stone Turret Room Outside, of the Dormer Window. Courtesy D. S. James

Figure 107. Interior Dormer Window Room. Courtesy D. S. James

was an apartment building on 152nd Street, say between Convent and Amsterdam. There was an interesting opening in that block because the water system from the Croton Reservoir was right under there. There were two apartment buildings totally boarded up."

And of the work the couple has done and what they hope to do going forward, Jenny remarked, "You think we own the house, but the house owns us." It is a magnificent historic structure, inside and out, that was built in the 1880s with incredible care for detail and craftsmanship. It is now being restored in the same manner.

Not far away, on a cold day in the winter of 2020 at the celebrated 555 Edgecombe Avenue, a journalist named Julyssa Lopez was in Apartment 3F, hard at work. Lopez, who was preparing an article for the BBC, took note of the crowd of about forty people outside of the door, on which was posted a note that read, "Music: 3:30." An older couple from the Upper West Side stood next to three students from France. A woman from Denmark had brought her mother and her two children. A couple exiting from the elevator announced, "We're here for Marjorie." A man nearby added, "Everyone's here for Marjorie."[1]

Marjorie Eliot, a woman now in her eighties, has kept the music going in her apartment for twenty-eight years. The Sunday concerts, started all those years ago as a tribute to the son she had lost, are now listed on countless websites suggesting, "What to do in New York." She has been written up on blogs, magazines, and newspapers, including the *New York Times*, *National Geographic,* and on this day, a second *BBC Travel Magazine* article. A month later, COVID-19 would shut down half the world. But not on this day.

"Over the years, the event, known as Parlor Jazz, has become an immutable Harlem tradition that has drawn audiences from across the world," Lopez later wrote. "When the door opens, a lively, chattering wave of strangers rush into Eliot's home like family."[2] The journalist went on to describe how guests gather on the folding chairs in her living room or cluster in the kitchen or the hallway. There is very little space between audience and entertainers, which makes the small setting and the music more powerful.

"Even if someone doesn't speak the language, they get the emotional weight of it," Eliot told Lopez. "[This event] has kept me from wallowing in sadness." In the years since she started the concerts in 1992, they continued, though Eliot has lost two more sons and then her husband, Al, in 2011. Her youngest son, Rudel Drears, still performs with her and alternates between singing and playing the piano. "Ours was a jazz house," Eliot said. "My sons could play all kinds of things, but they grew up hearing this music."

Though the roster of band members changes occasionally, it generally includes the same folks: saxophonist Sedric Choukroun and trumpet players Nicholas Mauro and Koichi Yoshihara. The drummer Will Glass, from the Jazz Foundation of America, recently performed here.

"Parlor Jazz is a profound summation of Eliot's life's work," Lopez wrote in her article. "They're reminiscent of after-hours meet-ups that took place in people's homes before and after the Harlem Renaissance, similar to how the famed brownstone of pianist Mary Lou Williams became a salon-style gathering place for jazz musicians in the 1950s and '60s."[3]

Eliot hopes the music will always continue.

The Grange was still closed in the fall of 2021 because of the pandemic, but Deputy Superintendent Lorena E. B. Harris arranged for an interview with its Lead Park Ranger, Vladimir Merzlyakov. He started with the National Park Service in 2012, just a year after the museum had reopened to the public after the renovation. The number of visitors in 2018 was 66,216, and the number rose slightly to 71,247 in 2019, the year before the pandemic.

Unsurprisingly, interest in the Grange soared after the play *Hamilton* opened at the Public Theater in January 2015, when there was a 75 percent increase in visitors. "And then when it went to Broadway," Merzlyakov said, "we went up about 145 percent. All of a sudden we were bombarded with visitors, and we were not prepared for that." The park management made plans for how to accommodate the unprecedented increase.

People enter and are greeted by rangers via the basement area, which is not historically accurate after two moves. Post-renovation, it now holds the visitors center where guests can watch a short film, get more information about the Grange, access restrooms, and visit the gift shop. These are the modern features added for visitor comfort that are separate from the main floor.

The exterior has been restored to look the way it did when Hamilton built the house in 1802. The portion of the house that the public visits, on the first floor, had been painstakingly renovated with the help of historians and museum archivists. The period furniture was accurately reproduced based on descriptions from Hamilton's records and on photographs and drawings made available by owners of the originals. The pianoforte in the parlor, shown in Figure 108, is one of the few authentic pieces from the Hamilton era and dates to about 1795. Made in London, it was a gift from Eliza's sister, Angelica Schuyler Church, to her niece and namesake Angelica Hamilton.

Since there was no dumbwaiter in the house, Merzlyakov stated that it was likely that there was a second everyday dining area downstairs. The upstairs dining room was probably reserved for entertaining or special occasions. The second floor is not accessible to visitors. These were the family bedrooms, though there is no evidence regarding to whom each one was assigned. The area is now used for administrative offices. Merzlyakov said the house would have had to be altered too much, disrupting the historical accuracy, to make the kind of changes for safely moving tourists up and down the stairs.

"We get people from all over the world, not just the United States. We would have groups coming from Spain, England, Sweden, South Africa, all different races and age groups. The most frequent questions we get are how much is original, why did he build his home here, what caused the duel to happen, what happened to his wife, and what happened to the house after he passed."

Figure 108. Hamilton Sitting Room and Pianoforte. National Park Service

The musical had put into the limelight both one of America's most important and undervalued Founding Fathers and the home in Harlem that he helped design. And it wasn't just the Grange that would grow in popularity and see tens of thousands of visitors annually. People wanted to be closer to what was left of the real Hamilton, and the cemetery at Trinity Church Wall Street was inundated with visitors at the graves of Hamilton and his wife. The couple's eldest son, Philip, and Eliza's sister, Angelica, are also buried there.

Hamilton's epitaph reads, "The Corporation of Trinity Church has erected this Monument in Testimony of their Respect for the Patriot of incorruptible Integrity, the Soldier of Approved Valor, the Statesman of Consummate Wisdom, Whose Talents and Virtues will be admired by Grateful Posterity Long after this Marble shall have mouldered into Dust."

Two centuries after Hamilton's death, in its report making the Grange a city landmark, the New York City Landmarks Preservation Commission would sum up succinctly the extraordinary role Hamilton played in the founding of the United States.

Figure 109. Tomb of Alexander Hamilton, Trinity Churchyard, circa 1915. Public domain

During the Revolutionary War, he served as secretary and aide-de-camp to General Washington with the rank of lieutenant colonel. Later, he commanded a regiment under General Lafayette. In 1798, he was appointed Inspector-General of the Army. A brilliant lawyer, he served in the Continental Congress of 1782 and of 1788. A member of the New York State Legislature in 1787, he was appointed Secretary of the Treasury in 1789. He is credited with proposing a national bank in 1791 and the mint in 1792, and he advocated the excise tax on spirits. With some friends, he founded the *New York Evening Post* in 1801. He left a rich legacy of political writings, many Federalist papers, to his country and to posterity.[4]

Everything in humankind is built upon what has come before. The truth is often unkind, but the majority of the writers whose names make up the list of those active in the Harlem Renaissance period are only familiar to scholars. Very few created a body of work that would be regarded in the decades or century to come as writing that would later stand the test of time. But that is because writing evolves, and the same can be said about many of the writers of earlier centuries, race, social standing, or geographical demographics notwithstanding. Writing evolves, and so do writers.

The period is often overshadowed, though, by the written word and not enough acknowledgment given to the other artists making history during this time. In addition to the scribes, there were sculptors, painters, actors, singers, and playwrights, all of whom were contributing bodies of work during the Harlem Renaissance. Among them were painters Gwendolyn Bennett and Aaron Douglas, sketch artist Winold Reiss, and sculptor Augusta Savage. Jacob Lawrence's paintings came just at the end of the Harlem Renaissance, though he was inspired by the artists of the period. His sixty-panel epic Great Migration Series, commissioned in 1940 with a Rosenwald Foundation grant, has left a lasting legacy of the historic movement of which his parents were part.

A revived appreciation had grown around the artistry of one of the legends of Harlem's most brilliant short era as a mecca, the photographer James Van der Zee. His widow, Donna Mussenden Van der Zee, and the Studio Museum in Harlem would maintain his archive for decades. Van der Zee had captured many images of the Harlem Renaissance. In 2021, the Met would assume stewardship of his entire collection of over 20,000 prints, 30,000 negatives, and other material in collaboration with the Studio Museum and Mrs. Van der Zee with a goal to conserve, digitize, and provide public access to the photographer's entire catalogue.

There are many more writers of this period whose names are not spoken of as often, yet they made distinctive contributions to the field. Ann Petry's novel *The Street*, published in 1946, was highly acclaimed and was the first novel by an African American to sell over a million copies.

There are the poetry, novels, and short stories of Dorothy West, who was very much creating during the Harlem Renaissance and published in the Urban League's *Opportunity*. West tied with Zora Neale Hurston for second prize in *Opportunity's* 1926 contest. The story she wrote, "The Typewriter," earned her a trip to New York City. In 1927, she became an extra for several years in the original stage production of Gershwin's opera "Porgy and Bess." Settling back in her family's home in Martha's Vineyard, she published her first novel, *The Living Is Easy*, in 1948. Well received critically, it was also a modest financial success. In 1995, at age eighty-eight, she wrote her best-known novel, *The Wedding*, adapted for TV in 1998 starring Halle Berry. With her death that same year, Dorothy West is generally thought to be the last of the Harlem Renaissance writers.

Key among those authors whose works became memorable are Langston

Hughes, Countee Cullen, Claude McKay, James Weldon Johnson, and Zora Neale Hurston. Well after the Renaissance was over, exceptional work was produced in Richard Wright's 1940 *Native Son*, Ralph Ellison's 1952 novel *Invisible Man*, and Lorraine Hansberry's 1959 play "A Raisin in the Sun." The greater majority of those highlighted from this time would leave New York. But Ellison lived in Sugar Hill and Hughes in Central Harlem until their deaths. Countee Cullen also remained in New York City.

For a generation of authors who came later, the artists of the Harlem Renaissance offered a road map showing a new way to write. In her novel *Women of the Harlem Renaissance*, Cheryl Wall writes that "this new generation of women, in particular, had this earlier generation of women as artistic models and cautionary tales. Their literary legatees critique, revise, and extend the themes, forms, and metaphors that they employed in their poetry and fiction."[5]

As for the brilliant and often outrageous Zora Neale Hurston, who slept on the couch in the apartment shared by Regina Anderson and Ethel Ray Nance in Sugar Hill, her work has gone on to be read and praised by a new generation. She dropped out of memory for decades, lived in poverty, and in the 1950s, shortly before her death, once again worked as a maid. Her works resurfaced in the 1970s, almost fifteen years after her death. They have since been reissued several times over and taught in colleges. One of Hurston's most acclaimed novels, *Their Eyes Were Watching God*, was made into a television movie in 2005 starring Halle Berry and produced by Oprah Winfrey.

If one first reads the most heralded Black female authors of the latter part of the twentieth century and then reads Hurston for the first time, it may not overstep the mark to think, *Aah, that's where they got it from. She was their inspiration and a kind of godmother.*

In a 1995 *Washington Post* article, David Nicholson writes about Zora and the resurgence of her work. He discusses the 1975 *Ms.* magazine article by Alice Walker titled, "In Search of Zora Neale Hurston," in which Walker talks about rediscovering the writer and her search for her grave. After Walker's article appeared, the interest in Hurston's writing became even greater. In 1979 the Feminist Press published a collection of Hurston's works with an introduction by Walker. "It speaks to me," Walker wrote of *Their Eyes Were Watching God*, "as no novel, past or present, has ever done."[6]

Nicholson wrote that "with those words, she canonized Hurston as the patron saint of Black women writers."

Alice Walker, the first African American woman to win the Pulitzer

Prize for fiction for her 1982 epistolary novel *The Color Purple*, had made it her mission to find Hurston's grave in the Garden of the Heavenly Rest Cemetery in Fort Pierce, Florida, where the writer was buried. Upon finding the unmarked grave, Walker had a headstone placed on it that reads, "Zora Neale Hurston: A Genius of the South. 1901–1960. Novelist, Folklorist, Anthropologist."

Today Hurston is praised as a singular talent with a unique voice. Toni Morrison called Hurston one of the greatest writers of our time. Journalist David Nicholson wrote in 1995 that, "completing the apotheosis begun 20 years ago by Walker's article, the Library of America has published a collection of Hurston's work, making her the first Black woman writer so honored."[7] The first African American Barnard College alum, a 1928 graduate of one the Seven Sisters at Columbia University, had certainly made her alma mater proud. The university now has regular forums celebrating Hurston's legacy and body of work.

From her 1927 trip to Alabama, when Zora ran into Langston Hughes, her later visit to interview eighty-six-year-old Oluale Kossola (Cudjo Lewis), has now resulted in the publication of her nonfiction book titled *Barracoon: The Story of the Last "Black Cargo."* "Barracoon" is the Spanish word for the barracks or enclosure where the enslaved were held. The West African Kossola is a survivor of the *Clotilda*, the last illegal slaver that is known to have transported humans across the Atlantic. Hurston published part of Kossola's story shortly after the 1927 trip in an article titled "Cudjo's Own Story of the Last African Slaver" for the *Journal of Negro History*. But her fuller manuscript was only recently published. Hurston's earlier attempts at publishing it were repeatedly rejected, largely because of her insistence at writing in Kossola's authentic dialect.

"Descendant," a 2022 Netflix documentary, would memorialize the often-sad history of Kossola's people and Africa Town, the community he helped found in Alabama. The documentary includes details of the 2019 discovery of the wreckage of the *Clotilda*. As such, Zora's body of work lives on in an even more powerful way.

Hurston's works were not the only writings from the Harlem Renaissance to be newly recognized long after their publication. Nella Larsen's 1929 novel *Passing* was made into a film in 2021 and had its premiere at the Sundance Film Festival. The novel deals with a topic not widely discussed, that of light-skinned African Americans who moved into Anglo society passing for white. The set designer did not need a Hollywood re-creation of Harlem's classic brownstones. The movie was filmed in Harlem, with some scenes shot near the famous Strivers' Row.

Figure 110. The Morris-Jumel Mansion

In 2021, when Shiloh Holley, then director of the Morris-Jumel Mansion, offered a private tour of the oldest surviving residence in Manhattan, it was an opportunity not to be missed.

One feels the complex layers of the past embodied in both the building and Sugar Hill. It's hard to imagine any thoughtful person visiting the museum and not taking a deep breath and thinking, "I am standing in a house that enslaved people helped build, where they slept and toiled, where George Washington settled in after his first Revolutionary War victory in the Battle of Harlem Heights, where he slept, conferred with Alexander Hamilton and his generals, issued directives to employ his troops up and down what is now St. Nicholas, Convent and Amsterdam Avenues to guard against the enemy, a place British troops occupied for another three years." This is the house where President George Washington dined with his secretary of the treasury, Alexander Hamilton.

All of that washes over you. One is standing in a house that is at the very foundation of the birth of the United States, with all those multifaceted layers of history in play.

In conducting the tour, Shiloh noted various features of the home,

Figure 111. Grey Settee and Slipper Chair. Courtesy D. S. James

which has been renovated inside and out many times since it became a museum in 1907. There is a lovely couch with two very small chairs that are a mystery.

"Yes, those were for children," Shiloh clarified, responding to my query about them. "They are called slipper chairs. So, the two children who are depicted in the portrait in the hallway with Eliza Jumel would have used these."

The curators have taken care to replicate furniture, carpets, and wallpaper. "One thing about the wallpaper," Shiloh noted, "is that we try as much as we can to get close to or draw inspiration from primary source documents. In this case, there was a letter when Eliza Jumel was writing to her husband, Stephen, in France asking for marble wallpaper, and she also asked for cloud wallpaper for the backroom, which we interpreted as the bathroom." Since it is a documented period design, Shiloh explained that they were able to look in other museums to match it.

There are two features in the house that represented innovative designs for the period and came to set a standard for countless homes built afterward. The Morris-Jumel dining room represents one of the first instances in which a room was designated just for dining. Shiloh explained that the house was built at a time when there was "a transition from rooms being quite flexible spaces where the function of the room would change depending on the season and the time of day, to rooms having more fixed uses." The Morris-Jumel dining room, therefore, is one of the first instances in which there was a room that was designated just for dining.

"And then there is the serving alcove, which was another innovation at the time. This is a closet now. Originally, this would have led to the kitchen and the domestic staff, which was paid labor during the Jumel era." The alcove would have allowed the staff to bring her food in without disturbing the flow of the rest of the room. Eliza owned the house during the period when slavery ended in New York City. So, she likely had both enslaved and free people of color servicing the house at various times.

On the way to the kitchen, which is downstairs, Shiloh points out a section of the wall that has exposed beam. It may seem odd to have a stretch of an unfinished wall in a museum. But the current administration

Figure 112. Dining Room Alcove. Courtesy D. S. James

Figure 113. Interior Wall Beam. Courtesy D. S. James

realizes that it must face certain deeply troubling facts that the home's first managers, the Daughters of the American Revolution, did not care to acknowledge.

"We think that the home was actually constructed by hired and enslaved laborers," Shiloh said. "They likely rented day laborers who were enslaved to actually build the house. So, we are going through an assessment to reprioritize the stories that we tell here. And we are planning on using this (exposed beam) to tell more about the home's construction which we are inferring is done by enslaved laborers."

What this beam signifies is that with all the cosmetic changes to this house, the original interior structure remains. Underneath the replicas and refashioned wallpaper, this piece of wood and others along this wall or inside this house were handled by enslaved persons. At its core, the house still holds the DNA of stolen people.

When we reach the kitchen, Shiloh points out different features. "And this is our eighteenth-century kitchen, original to the building's construction," she continued. A photograph from the Carol Ward book about the house shows William Henry Shelton, the mansion's first museum director, pointing to a massive hole that he had chopped in the side of the wall to expose the original hearth.

Figure 114. Eighteenth-Century Kitchen. Courtesy D. S. James.

"The Earle family, when they occupied it in the 1890s, built a separate exterior kitchen. But this was a functioning kitchen up to that point." The Morris family were enslavers, Shiloh added, "so they did have a few people part of their household who were enslaved who probably lived here or in outbuildings."

The kitchen is outfitted with period items like the wooden molds for candle-making and the antique cooking tools hanging in the fireplace. She spoke of Anne Northup, the wife of Solomon, who penned the book *Twelve Years a Slave*. It is good that they speak truths about this history today. Because history should be told, as the pleasant and ugly parts make a whole story and a whole nation. It should be the truth or nothing at all.

Upstairs, the room thought to be Washington's war room has various items laid out as if the president were about to draw up new battle plans.

On the stairs to the third floor, which is not part of the normal public tour, the wood is old and flaking, as one would expect of a 256-year-old building. Parts of it should look old, chipped, and in need of repair. This is likely where the celebrated 1775 document was found. From here one can see spectacular views that must have been even more breathtaking two centuries ago when the area was mostly undeveloped.

Figure 115. Left to Right: Rudel Drears, Service Chouckroan, Nicholas Mauro, Marjorie Eliot at Piano. Courtesy D. S. James

Finally, Shiloh mentioned the wonderful woman who lives across the street, Marjorie Eliot, who holds her annual jazz concert on the patio. Clearly, this is a museum that has moved with the times.

There are ways to keep history alive, to hold onto the spirit of a place. At 555 Edgecombe Avenue, for example, Marjorie Eliot is still holding intimate jazz parlor soirées in her apartment as she has been for three decades. In 2019, when the Jazz Journalists Association named twenty-two activists, advocates, and abettors of jazz in twenty American cities as Jazz Heroes, Marjorie Eliot was one of those honored.

I attended the first live concert in Marjorie's living room as the pandemic appeared to be on its downward spiral in the fall of 2021. For the previous year, the Sunday soirees had been streamed online. Everyone was vaccinated and masked up, and there were very few of us. The cozy apartment made one think of all the talented souls who lived in 555, a roster that includes the legendary singer Paul Robeson, Count Basie, and Andy Kirk. Marjorie Eliot was keeping both the music and the vibe alive. Members of the audience were mesmerized.

In the best of all worlds, one has quality musicians, great acoustics, and ambience. Those three don't always come together, and you sometimes settle for one or two. Yet at this thirty-year-running event, it is the ambience that is overwhelming and grabs at you even more than the music, though that is good. The small living room resounds with the history of all that music has ever been and how it can move people and unite them. Marjorie's parlor is the embodiment of all the talented people who lived in 555.

The crowd that day included the actress Barbara Montgomery, who lives a few floors up. In 1974 Barbara won an Obie Award for her role in the Off-Broadway production of *My Sister, My Sister*. She is a brilliant actress with numerous stage, film, and TV credits, including the 1989 TV miniseries *The Women of Brewster Place*, which featured an A-list of African American actors, including Mary Alice, Oprah Winfrey, Lynn Whitfield, and veteran actor Moses Gunn. She starred in NBC's *Amen* with Sherman Helmsley for four years.

Barbara has lived in the building for seventeen years. "An actress friend, Elaine Graham, introduced me to the building," she said. "There are still several people in the industry here. There's a couple of dancers. There was a makeup artist, who just moved." Barbara reflected on the longevity of

Figure 116. Actress Barbara Montgomery. Courtesy Barbara Montgomery

people in the building, sharing that her next-door neighbor has lived here forty years. "There are some people who were born in this building and still live here."

Marjorie is well into her eighties now, frail and strong all at once, and shows no signs of stopping. A few months after the concert, she shared memories of the Sunday event that has now become a Sugar Hill staple, along with memories of her building and the neighborhood.

She still loves to explore the streets and avenues that she knows so well. "I walk on Convent. It's so beautiful, just fantastic. Convent and Strivers' Row are like another part of New York. The people living there on the side streets of Convent take care of everything, and they have their own little cooperatives."

She mentions that Joe Louis and his wife, Rose Morgan, once lived on the tenth floor. Marjorie went on to say how people who lived in the building knew each other. "They came and they stayed and passed the apartments on to family. There were people who lived here a very long time. And you could hear the music from the street."

Marjorie recalls some of the clubs on St. Nicholas Avenue: the Mark Four, the Gold Brick, and, of course, St. Nick's Pub. But now, she said, "One day melds into another and presents another challenge, but then you look back and think of the people who have touched your life and are critical to who you are, and it's a pretty thing."

In thinking of 555 and what makes the building so special, Marjorie talked about the 1980s, when she moved in.

"You know, when coming into the building, when we moved here, it had an elevator operator, twenty-four-hour doorman, and a staff," she said. "Coming in, musicians would be going out to their gigs. You think of all the folks who lived here, and that's what I still feel. Andy Kirk lived in 14B. Sonny Rollins would come to see Mr. Kirk. I still feel the love and energy from all those souls who were here. And you think about when they weren't wanted here, and I connect."

Andy Kirk was the famed bass player who led a popular band in the 1940s and sometimes employed Mary Lou Williams. Sonny Rollins is the acclaimed tenor sax player who was mentored by Thelonious Monk. Miles Davis wrote that Rollins was a legend, that he was one of his earliest fans and often hung out with him and his Sugar Hill crowd. In 2011, Rollins was awarded the Medal of Arts by President Barack Obama.

Marjorie also said that for a building like 555 Edgecombe that was always the pride of Sugar Hill, that Washington Heights keeps creeping further down into Harlem. Sugar Hill extended to streets in the 160s, she said, and she tells me there were demonstrations about the boundary changes. It is causing a divisiveness that she does not think is good for the neighborhood.

She is aware that some of what she leaves behind is another part of the building's history, in this case a legacy. "Where I am living now, with the concerts at the Jumel Mansion, we were not even allowed in there at one time, even though Africans built that. I think of that." The twenty-ninth outdoor concert was performed at the mansion in 2021.

For Marjorie, those concerts are also a celebration of the Africans who built the Morris-Jumel Mansion but could not enter the yard. She reflected on how her children would skate on the grounds. As for the fact that so many of the talented jazz musicians who electrified the clubs in Harlem never got the accolades they deserved, "that's the musician's life," she said. "Most musicians are not going to get the awards and the press, but they were all virtuosos. They knew what they were doing, and they connected."

Figure 117. Morris-Jumel Annual Jazz Concert, circa 2013. Photo by Koichi Yoshihara. Courtesy Marjorie Eliot

Figure 118. Marjorie Eliot at Piano. Courtesy Marjorie Eliot

When one thinks of how historical places of importance can evolve with the times and adapt to a neighborhood's changing demographics, the jazz concert held at the entrance of the Morris-Jumel Mansion may be a stellar example. Once a year, Marjorie and a group of musicians gather at the Morris-Jumel Mansion for a concert there. Marjorie and the jazz concert she conceived embodies Duke Ellington's words that the mansion is "the jewel in the crown of Sugar Hill."

Anyone wondering whether the magic of Sugar Hill's music scene has faded need only look as far as 555 Edgecombe Avenue, the famous "triple nickel," and on Sunday afternoon ring the buzzer for Apartment 3F.

The gentrification in just this section of Manhattan and the renaming of neighborhoods are a reminder that few speak of the Indigenous people of New York City. In the biggest demographic change of all, they are gone from what was their land hundreds of years before Hudson scoped out the area for his Dutch employers.

The Indigenous population is gone because the people who colonized New York (and all of the United States) knew, as Isabel Wilkerson wrote in her book *Caste*, that "if they were to convert this wilderness and civilize it to their liking, they decided they would need to conquer, enslave, or remove the people already on it and transport those they deemed lesser beings to tame and work the land to extract the wealth that lay in the rich soil and shorelines."⁸ In that one statement Wilkerson speaks to the erasure of the Native Americans from their former lands and the enslavement of Africans to work that land.

The debatable lines over which street or avenue means you have now moved into a different neighborhood clouds a more profound change no longer spoken of: that all this land belonged to the native people, despite their inherent belief systems as to whether anyone can actually own land.

For this historic neighborhood, another important musical event was the Fifth Annual Sugar Hill Jazz Festival, held on September 25, 2021. The *Amsterdam News* reported that "Harlem's rich musical and spoken word history was honored and celebrated by the heritage-preservation organization, While We Are Still Here."⁹ The concert was held on the Sugar Hill Luminaries Lawn at 155th Street and Edgecombe Avenue.

"Karen D. Taylor, founder and executive director of While We Are Still Here, organized this year's festival to pay tribute to two local artists who achieved national and global fame," the article continued. The artists, the Mizell Brothers and Gil Scott-Heron, both lived for a time at 555 Edgecombe Avenue.

While We Are Still Here is one of those critical arts nonprofits that is dedicated to gathering and sharing the vast history of Harlem. It has gone to great lengths to chronicle the cultural legacy of two of Sugar Hill's most famous buildings and its occupants at 409 and 555 Edgecombe Avenue. The article stated how the organization "has been in the forefront of spearheading high-quality programming in the arts and humanities throughout the community."

Behind both the stunning and plain facades in Hamilton Heights, as with all neighborhoods, are the people. There are some who step outside and go about their business unnoticed, and they may be off to change the world, attend classes, or just run to the post office. And then there are those who step outside, and you can't help but notice them.

Lana Turner is the latter, and a fixture in Harlem, a woman who is known for, among other things, her love of both her neighborhood and fashion. In an article in *Curbed: NY*, Wendy Goodman described Turner as a "real-estate broker, professional organizer, swing dancer, Bill Cunningham muse, and vintage-clothing collector."¹⁰ Bill Cunningham is the legendary photographer who for decades chronicled fashion for the *New York Times*.

Turner knew where she wanted to live when she started apartment hunting in 1970. When several apartments in her current building on Convent Avenue were available, she nabbed the one that had the most light and a view of the Hudson River.

As she thought about how to make the space her own, "the one thing Turner was determined to do was strip the paint off all the original woodwork and the painted-over glass panes in the French doors and transoms. It took her three years, going room by room and listening to Aretha Franklin all the while, to complete the job."[11]

Along the way, her fashion collections continued to grow, and a major part of every room was adapted to accommodate her hundreds of dresses, shoes, hats, gloves, and boxes of jewelry. "I could live in this apartment forever and never go out," Turner said, "because everything I love is here."[12]

The fashion icon has been the subject of many newspaper and magazine articles, including in the *New Yorker*, describing her remarkable collections of gowns, hats, and gloves. Her collection includes a gown originally designed by Geoffrey Holder for his wife, Carmen de Lavallade, that Turner deconstructed to fit herself.

Hamilton Heights and Sugar Hill have had so many secret passions that unfold: doll collections that fill a Sotheby's catalogue, a woman with a fashion collection that *Vogue* would envy, and history-making politicians and church leaders, as well as little boys playing stickball and little girls playing jacks.

In 2020, just when it seemed that the homes on the hill had reached the height of the price market, 72 Hamilton Terrace went on sale for $5.5 million.

The townhouse at 144th Street had been built in 1920, designed by Neville & Bagge as a single-family home. The structure, which is slightly under 5,000 square feet, is made of gray brick and terra cotta with a crested mansard roof and Renaissance details.

The jeweler Charles Goldsmith and his family lived in the house until at least the 1940s, and in 1974 it was declared a New York City landmark. In 2003, a fire all but gutted the building, which had been the home of the Nazareth Deliverance Spiritual Church for more than fifteen years. A developer bought the building in 2013 and spent several years completely renovating it. Many of the original features were saved, and the new owners added a basement recreation room, two wet bars, a wood-paneled library, and several fireplaces. There are four bedrooms, five bathrooms, a landscaped backyard, and a roof deck. In 2021, the mansion set a Harlem real estate record when it was sold for $5.1 million.

The six-bedroom, six-bath, 6,000-square-foot home at 339 Convent

Figure 119. 72 Hamilton Terrace. Courtesy D. S. James

Avenue that was used as a location site for *The Royal Tenenbaums* in 2001 was listed for $3.2 million. The homes in Hamilton Heights were being shown a new appreciation and were garnering record-breaking prices.

In Harlem, as throughout the city and the country, countless businesses did not survive the pandemic, which lingered for over two years, the worst of which finally lessened by the end of 2021. It was heartening to see new businesses spring into life throughout Hamilton Heights and some doors that had been shuttered open again. One can only hope that they will thrive in a post-pandemic world where many people are still skittish about public gatherings.

Berta Alloway, meantime, the jazz lover who brought new life back to St. Nick's Pub before it closed, has continued to make and promote music. Ralph Ellison Memorial Park on Riverside Drive is reviving its outdoor jazz concerts. The park's namesake, who had a passion for music, would likely approve.

In 2021 Big Apple Jazz Tours noted on its blog: "Berta Alloway continues to present great bands with surprise guests sitting-in every Sunday between 2–5 p.m. at Ralph Ellison Memorial Park at 150th Street and

Figure 120. Riverside Park Jazz Concert. Courtesy Gordon Polatnick, Big Apple Jazz Tours

Riverside Drive. Trumpeter and Vocalist Michael Young is there with Soul Guard every Saturday from 2–5 also with an open policy to join the jam." The artists will change, obviously, but there is music to be made and fans eager to hear it.

In 2020 the Jazz Journalists Association on its Facebook page praised Alloway's twenty-plus years of continuous jazz programming in Harlem. Reflecting on her contributions at the former legendary St. Nick's Pub, the organization wrote that Alloway "continued earning her stripes by hosting an impressive, Harlem-centric array of artists including vocalists Vanessa Rubin and Ghanniya Green; tap dancers Savion Glover and Buster Brown . . . even Wynton Marsalis showed up to play in the wee hours."

Gordon Polatnick, founder of Big Apple Jazz Tours, doesn't live in Hamilton Heights or Sugar Hill. But one night he finally took to heart Duke Ellington and Billy Strayhorn's famous song, "Take the A Train," a line of which goes, *"You must take the A train, to go to Sugar Hill, way up in Harlem."* Since Polatnick took that same train home, he decided to get off one night before continuing to Inwood, on the northern tip of Manhattan.

Gordon loves jazz, and music is the great equalizer among human beings. "I was doing the jazz tours from 1997," Gordon said, "and I already felt fairly established in my knowledge of jazz history and the jazz scene. I decided that I was going to take a left turn and open up a place of my own." He opened a jazz club in Central Harlem on West 131st Street and Seventh Avenue (Adam Clayton Powell Boulevard) and named it Big Apple Jazz and EZ's Woodshed. It lasted for a couple of years before he returned his focus to the jazz tours.

Gordon then arranged a plan to take people to three different clubs on a single night so he could show them the real underground scene. The clubs were mostly in Greenwich Village. Then a friend asked him why he wasn't including the real jam sessions in Harlem.

"And, honestly, just being a white guy, and the brainwashing I underwent growing up in New York," Gordon said, "I didn't know that I was invited to the jazz clubs in Harlem. So, getting off the train in the middle of the night to go to a small club didn't even seem like a natural choice. It took about a year for me to say, well, let me just check it out."

His friend lived in Sugar Hill and had been telling him to check out Monday nights at St. Nick's Pub on St. Nicholas Avenue. Gordon finally did so. "And that night, I never left," he said. "I just stayed all night long until they closed the place. I ran into some people at the bar and a guy who was a big jazz fan, befriended me and said, 'Let's go look for some more music.'"

What happened next was the genesis of a jazz listing Gordon created on his website, bigapplejazz.com. He and his new friend went from spot to spot only to find out that a club was not open that night or had shut down entirely. From that experience, Gordon started gathering listings of who was playing where and when and what the over charges were. He turned his love of the music into businesses, with tours that now included St. Nick's Pub, and his listings became an invaluable resource for other jazz lovers.

In 1950 the *New York Age* newspaper, established in 1887, published an article celebrating fifty years of Harlem as a Black community. They asked several residents why they lived in Harlem. An unemployed man who was originally from Daytona Beach, Florida, and had lived in Harlem for seventeen years replied, "What a question! I can't find anywhere else to live, and if I could, I don't think I'd want to live there. I wouldn't know how I'd feel living any place else. There's something in Harlem that gets in one's blood. It gets there and stays, it never leaves."[13] He may have been speaking a forever truth for many people about the power of Harlem to

Figure 121. Interior St. Nick's Pub, circa 2000. Photo Courtesy Gordon Polatnick, Big Apple Jazz Tours

become part of one's DNA. Even if you do leave physically, the spirit of it remains in you.

Langston Hughes's ashes are buried in the Schomburg Center under a medallion in the foyer titled *Rivers*. The library is located near the 135th Street subway stop that Hughes exited after his first exhilarating subway ride in the 1920s. This is the library where Regina Anderson secured a private place for him and other Harlem Renaissance authors to write, a library that is now a New York City and federal historic landmark. True to his assertion that he would rather live in Harlem than anywhere else, the poet stayed in his Lenox Avenue apartment building long after the neighborhood had crumbled around him.

In addition to leaving a large body of poetry, Hughes wrote eleven plays and several works of prose, including the well-known *Simple* books.

The words surrounding the mural are taken from Hughes's poem "The Negro Speaks of Rivers," written in 1919 when he was just seventeen. He was on a train crossing the Mississippi on his way to visit his father in Mexico. It begins, "I've known rivers: I've known rivers ancient as the world and older than the flow of human blood in human veins."

When in Mexico, Hughes's father asked him what he wanted to be in terms of a career. His father wanted to steer his son toward engineering. Hughes replied that perhaps he would be a writer. His father wanted to know whether writers made any money, indicating that he had never heard of a colored writer supporting himself. Langston Hughes responded by mentioning Alexandre Dumas, the French writer whose works include the novels *The Three Musketeers* and *The Count of Monte Cristo*.

"Yes," his father replied, "but he was in Paris, where they don't care about color."

In his 1940 autobiography, *The Big Sea*, Hughes no longer doubted where his career path lay. And despite all the part-time jobs he had to take in his youth to stay afloat, his perseverance paid off because his writing supported him.

He saw that "shortly poetry became bread; prose, shelter and raiment. Words turned into songs, plays, scenarios, articles and stories. Literature is a big sea full of many fish. I let down my nets and pulled. I'm still pulling."[14]

There are stories in these hills, the true ones we bring to light, the legendary tall tales, and those that authors have taken inspiration from to create incredible works of fiction. They all help the public remember the generations of people that have made Hamilton Heights and Sugar Hill so special.

Chapter 17

Where It Leads

> The soul of the city was always my subject. And it was a roiling soul, twisting and turning over on itself, forming and re-forming, gathering into itself and opening out again like a blown cloud.
>
> —E. L. Doctorow
> *The Waterworks*

Even if you know just a smattering of Manhattan history, if you walk through Hamilton Heights and the hilly lands occupied by the original inhabitants, the Lenape of the Algonquin Nation, the ghosts of all those who have walked these hills before you call out.

In the mid-seventeenth century, we know that the area came to be called Jochem Pieters Hills, honoring the Dutchman from Holstein who was murdered by the native people and did not live long enough to fully appreciate the beautiful setting with its breathtaking views. But when he was making the journey to America in 1639 with his friend Jonas Bronck, the two men did bring with them Holstein cattle with their distinctive black and white markings.

In selecting a site on which to build a house, Bronck chose property that was close to the land his friend owned but on the other side of the narrow Harlem River. His legacy lives on throughout the borough, although few New Yorkers know that this area was once called Bronck's Land and then just the Broncks before it was officially named the Bronx.

These hills have always been prominent in the names that have been used to designate this part of Manhattan: "the island of many hills," Jochem Pieters Hills, Harlem Heights, Hamilton Heights, Sugar Hill, and the newer neighborhoods carved from Harlem Heights: Washington Heights and Inwood.

More than many parts of New York City, these neighborhoods are rich with history. Here is Duke Ellington's old building at 935 St. Nicholas Avenue, now a New York City landmark. Ellington's scribbled directions to his house, when his meeting Billy Strayhorn led to the hit song "Take the 'A' Train," are now in the Smithsonian. A great deal of music was created in this nondescript apartment building, and there is no telling how many memorable people passed through its doors.

Victor Hugo Green lived across the street, and his travel guide, *The Green Book*, would have helped visitors to Harlem find some of the good spots to listen to music and find essential services. More importantly, it helped African Americans find safe places where they could secure food and lodging while traveling at a time when segregation was rampant throughout the country.

There is a special place for children to explore their creative sides—the Sugar Hill Children's Museum of Art & Storytelling—developed by the Broadway Housing Community (BHC). The museum is located on the first two floors of 898 St. Nicholas Avenue at 155th Street; it has a goal of educating children from ages three to eight in the community in the arts and providing pre-K classes. The creative space is the mixed-use part of an affordable housing complex on Sugar Hill that has been controversial from its initial design inception through final construction. The thirteen-story austere gray cantilevered cube structure is the creation of renowned Ghanaian architect David Adjaye, who also designed the National Museum of African American History & Culture in Washington, D.C. The building seemed to many residents and architectural historians a dramatic stylistic clash compared to the century-old characteristic style of buildings that has made Hamilton Heights and Sugar Hill a historic landmark neighborhood. Still, the museum is a stimulating space for families, many facing financial challenges, to share in cultural programs, often held by professional authors and artists.

Walk a block south to Edgecombe Avenue ("Edgecombe" is the Dutch name for the edge of a cliff), and you will quickly come to the landmark apartment buildings at 409 and 555 that overlook the Harlem River and the old Polo Grounds location; 555 was home to so many talented musicians and actors, not to mention one boxing champ and the memorable Sunday musical salons that take place in a woman named Marjorie's parlor. It's almost impossible to believe that in just one building, at 409, there lived W. E. B. Du Bois, the grandfather of the civil rights movement; Walter White, who traveled to the South to investigate lynchings on behalf of the NAACP; and Thurgood Marshall, who would have been reviewing his notes in preparation for arguing the profoundly important case of Brown v. Board of Education before the United States Supreme Court. It doesn't take much of a leap of the imagination to envision the tenants from these two buildings going back and forth between them, sharing laughter, ideas, and cocktails.

On 152nd Street and St. Nicholas Avenue, the old Kingsbridge Road, where Jan Dyckman's son Gerrit built a stone house around 1710, there now sits a row of symmetrical and splendid apartment buildings. A couple of blocks away and you are in front of the 1888 James A. Bailey Mansion, which is being painstakingly restored by Martin and Jenny Spollen. Although Bailey and his family spent so little time there, the circus impresario sprinkled a little Barnum & Bailey fairy dust money, and behold this castle appeared, still standing strong 134 years later.

When you walk past the apartment building at 789 St. Nicholas Avenue, you feel as if you should be holding a copy of one of the hundreds of issues of the *Saturday Evening Post* that featured covers by Norman Rockwell. This is the spot, not the building, where his family lived. This one was erected a few years after they moved. How wonderful that the person who grew up on this block and played on these streets later pondered in his memoir that he hoped local racism had lessened. How prophetic, and what a measure of the man to go from that hope to one day painting a picture of a little Black girl, Ruby Bridges, being escorted by federal marshals into an all-white elementary school in New Orleans in 1960. The title of the painting is "The Problem We All Live With." How tragic that she needed the escort. Bridges later sat on the board of the Norman Rockwell Museum. In 2011, the museum made a short-term loan of the painting to the White House, and Ruby Bridges viewed it with President Barack Obama.

In 2015 the British newspaper the *Guardian* published an article that ran under the headline, "What will happen when Harlem becomes white?" What, indeed? If history truly repeats itself, Harlem is now returning to what it was a century ago. And the wealthy will once again own impressive properties and mansions that are financially out of reach for many people. The question becomes the answer, since Harlem is now well on its way to becoming white and much of its transformative African American history possibly erased.

At 749 St. Nicholas Avenue off 147th Street there stands an unassuming apartment building with no marker to indicate that the celebrated African American novelist Ralph Ellison lived here in the 1940s while he was writing *Invisible Man*. Hamilton Heights is dotted with such structures, or the ghost of them, buildings where history was made but that have since burned down, been torn down, or modernized to the point where their original character is lost, along with any traces of the memorable people and events associated with them.

At 645 St. Nicholas Avenue at 141st Street there stands the handsome Herb Alpert Harlem School of the Arts. It is on the last of Hamilton's old property, across the street from St. Nicholas Park. The school is just three blocks from 580 St. Nicholas, Regina Andrews and Ethel Nance's old apartment building. Up and down these few streets, Harlem Renaissance artists walked over to their place to share their thoughts, their writing, and have a bit to eat or drink. And one morning they took a historic photo, not realizing that they were preserving a once-in-a-lifetime portrait of Harlem Renaissance greatness.

In centuries past, this thoroughfare of St. Nicholas Avenue was named the King's Way, then Kingsbridge, all king titles in homage to King George, who lost the colonies when the U.S. won independence, and then lost his mind for good, becoming Mad King George. And then, finally, it was named the Avenue St. Nicholas. In many ways, this avenue in Hamilton Heights shows the true versatility of any urban street. In the eighteenth and nineteenth centuries it was where the rich raced their horse-drawn carriages. And then it gradually became the home of orchestra leaders, authors, librarians, actresses, gangsters, schools, and jazz clubs frequented by local residents and movie stars, a street where the music rang out all night.

On 145th Street, the major north-south thoroughfare between Hamilton Heights and Central Harlem, there is one of the steepest climbs in the neighborhood, in Manhattan truthfully. It makes one understand why this area was called Harlem Heights. Up that steep hill, toward Broadway, is the Hamilton Branch of the New York Public Library, another landmark. Broadway itself, that broad thoroughfare that started as a trail that the Native Americans walked in pre-colonial times, twists and turns through the length of Manhattan. A street named because of its width, first by the Dutch as *Brede Wegh* (Broad Way), and then the Anglicized version the British gave it: Broadway. Parts of it became the Bloomingdale Road and the Old Post Road and were altered with the progress of that 1811 street grid. Across the world the word "Broadway" brings to mind not a street but the legend, glamour, and magic of New York Theatre. Names truly do have power.

On 146th Street and Broadway, the Hamilton Theatre is crumbling. Yet many of the intricate exterior features are still noticeable in this incredible space where vaudeville acts performed in a grand setting, where the first silent moving pictures were shown in New York City, and where the newly formed and now defunct RKO showed its new films here in Hamilton Heights.

At the peak of Broadway there is a clear view down to what was called, in past centuries, Mahicanituk, the Algonquin name for the river that flows both ways; the North River; Henry Hudson's River; and finally, just the Hudson River. And on Riverside Drive where the bird man, John James Audubon, built his wife an estate and nicknamed it "Minnie's Land," all his family's houses are sadly gone.

What is it about waterways, about rivers, lakes, and oceans that make us want to stare and dream and ponder on all those ripples? How grand that in Hamilton Heights and Sugar Hill one can walk between two of them, the Hudson and the Harlem rivers, in minutes.

Back down on Convent Avenue you find a street that could fill a book. The convent at its eastern end is what gave it its name in the nineteenth century. The avenue was lengthened to allow for revisions to the street grid. Great and ordinary people loved, created new life, and lost some, formulated revolutionary ideas, created beautiful music, nurtured loved ones on their final journey, gave birth, dazzled the fashion world, wrote social science treatises, mapped out theatrical events, reflected on the sermons to be given at historic churches, galvanized the world of dance, and walked beside the giants of early twentieth-century Black intelligentsia. All on this one tree-lined avenue named after a long-gone convent.

There is a lovely little garden here on Convent Avenue that is too small to be called a park. It is Convent Garden, and in a neighborhood that was once nothing but trees, flowers, brooks, and wild game, it is refreshing to see this small patch of green on this street.

The garden is part of the old Pinehurst estate, the eighteenth-century mansion of the Bradhurst family that sold Hamilton part of his land. It later became the site of a gas station and, after that, an empty lot littered with trash. Now the plot of land has come full circle and become a thing of beauty. Thanks to community activists, this spot has returned to what it was several hundred years ago: an expanse of grass, trees, and flowers and a restful place for the eye.

Continue down the street and we pass 339 Convent, the mansion that was the location setting for the 2001 film *The Royal Tenenbaums*. Just a few doors away, at 315 Convent Avenue, is the peach-colored townhouse that was the home of the celebrated jazzman Billy Strayhorn. It is just minutes away from that final patch of land.

And on the next block, tucked away next to St. Luke's Episcopal Church, is the empty place where Hamilton's house used to be but is now just rocks and grass, with the imposing statue of Hamilton still looking out at the avenue. It is almost as if he is still looking over what was once his estate. One hopes that someone will remember Reverend Isaac Tuttle, the man who saved Hamilton's old home from demolition. It is a stunning church, though it is now tented, and one can only see snippets of it. This might be its declining days. The church put it up for sale in the fall of 2022 for $12 million. St. Luke's does not have landmark status, surprisingly, though it is within the historic landmark neighborhood. It is hard to imagine that the church that saved Hamilton Grange from destruction could be destroyed, that St. Luke's could no longer be St. Luke's. A pending sale in 2023 notes plans to convert it to a school. That is an outcome that would honor the legacy of this important house of worship.

The descendants of the Walloon family of Jesse De Forest, the master fabric dyer from Leiden in the Netherlands, has left a deep imprint in Manhattan, and especially in this part of Harlem. William De Forest and his son wound up owning a large part of Hamilton's estate and his house. They had a profound impact in the late nineteenth century on the development of the neighborhood, creating its distinctive look leading to its landmark status. The De Forest legacy and that of the other Walloon families is honored by a ten-foot monument in Battery Park in downtown New York City.

The name Bradhurst is memorialized on a boulevard just down the hill and on a park. Jan Dyckman's Hamilton Heights properties became part of the Roger Morris estate. But his name rings out at the farthest reaches of Manhattan on numerous buildings and streets in Inwood, where he received his earliest Harlem land patents.

One of the grand arched entrances to City College is right here, the Hamilton Gate. Turn the corner south at the college with the church right behind you, and head down 141st Street toward St. Nicholas Park. Turn right, enter the park, and there it is. It all leads here. With a bit of imagination one can infer that this could be the patch of land where Alexander Hamilton wrote to his wife, Eliza, about building a fence so the cows would not wander too far. It is the patch of land at the end of where his original property line finished on the old Kingsbridge Road, now St. Nicholas Avenue, now St. Nicholas Park.

It is on this land that Hamilton's former house sits. The Grange is at its final destination. Focus on this patch of land around the house that has been so carefully restored. Ignore the tall buildings, directional signs, streetlights at the corners, the cars, the busy and often loud nature of modern twenty-first-century life. All around and outside of this one patch of land there exists the modernity that was part of why Eliza and Alexander's home had to keep being moved.

The forward motion of progress in an urban environment will not be stopped, not even for the man who built the U.S. banking system and advised our first president during the American Revolution. Look only there where the Grange sits with thirteen newly planted gum trees representative of the thirteen original colonies for which Hamilton fought beside George Washington and so many other brave men and women to create the United States of America.

No doubt, the old caretaker Mr. Daniels would have been pleased. It is the neighborhood that now bears Hamilton's name in honor of the place he called home and what he did for our country. Beyond this spot on which his house now sits is the rest of Harlem, though in somewhat less acreage than in Hamilton's day.

This house and the former acres were the *sweet project* of which Alexander Hamilton hinted to his dear Eliza. It was the project that turned into their country home. The setting is so far removed from what it was like in 1799 when Hamilton purchased the property, except perhaps what surrounds the house, this bit of earth that mimics the rural environment of centuries past. So, it all leads here.

In the final declaration of Hamilton Grange as a federal memorial, Part 9 of the Congressional Public law 106-387 appendix reads, "No obelisk, monument, or classical temple along the national mall has been constructed to honor the man who more than any other designed the Government of the United States, Hamilton should at least be remembered by restoring his home in a sylvan setting." It is a tribute worthy of the man.

Figures 122 and 123. LEFT: Hamilton Grange National Memorial, St. Nicholas Park at 141st Street, Harlem. Built by Alexander Hamilton in 1800–1802. Courtesy National Park Service.
RIGHT: Alexander Hamilton. Public Domain

Afterword

Note about the Location of Hamilton Heights and Sugar Hill

Throughout this book, I have identified places as being in Hamilton Heights (HH) and Sugar Hill (SH) in West Harlem that go beyond the often-cited description of Harlem ending at 155th Street. I thought an afterword clarifying this geographical point might be helpful.

The Hamilton Heights and Sugar Hill boundaries have shifted many times over the past century. The area around Alexander Hamilton's former home the Grange only started being called *Hamilton Heights* in the 1930s when the American Scenic and Historic Preservation Society took over ownership of his home. It is likely that at that time HH might have referred to just a dozen or so blocks immediately surrounding 140th to 148th streets from St. Nicholas to Amsterdam, the estimated parameters of Hamilton's original property lines. But there is no official New York City designation of HH, as with other neighborhoods in the city.

Sugar Hill lore has it that the name was adopted for the elevated neighborhood rising above Edgecombe Avenue after African Americans started moving into some of the grand apartment buildings on the hill in the 1920s and were said to be living "the sweet life." Some histories suggest that the term "Sugar Hill" was used before then. So, the name "Sugar Hill" was in use for the neighborhood before Hamilton Heights became a designation. It is often said that Sugar Hill is "within" Hamilton Heights; but it may be more accurate to say the reverse. Some say Sugar Hill is a "state of mind" and the boundaries change according to whom you are conversing. There were apartment buildings at 90 Edgecombe and 138th Street, where A'Lelia

Walker and Walter White lived, that were considered Sugar Hill. And the landmark "Triple Nickel" Paul Robeson Building at 555 Edgecombe Avenue at 162nd Street (with the Morris-Jumel Mansion across the street) was always identified as being the very epitome and "crown" of Sugar Hill.

For most of the twentieth century the combined neighborhoods were defined by residents who lived there as "about" 135th Street at Edgecombe Avenue and the Harlem River to approximately 165th Street at the Hudson River. So, despite the geographic drop to the Hudson, many people still thought of it as Sugar Hill (and/or Hamilton Heights).

In the mid-nineteenth century, some people started to refer to parts of the Hamilton Heights neighborhood as Washington Heights (WH). But that definition of WH starting anywhere around 135th Street did not stick and was not widely referenced to in my estimation, experience living in the neighborhood, or from my research.

In the late twentieth century, the two neighborhoods (HH and SH) became defined by many as the area from 135th Street to 155th Street and from Edgecombe Avenue at the Harlem River to the Hudson River. This is also the defined area listed in *The Encyclopedia of New York City*. By this definition, everything west of 155th Street was considered Washington Heights, and farther west as Inwood.

But for decades, if not a century, Washington Heights was generally considered to start at Broadway. Then, in the early twenty-first century, it started being defined as more southerly to St. Nicholas Avenue. There is even a section of Washington Heights that is now being called Hudson Heights.

Realtors have had broad sway in redefining where the neighborhoods begin and end for commercial reasons, and they simply rename them as they see fit. And if a newspaper or magazine taps into those newly cited boundaries, it gives the redefined area more credibility. (A powerful example of the impact of marketing by Realtors and land developers is the world-famous Hollywood sign in Los Angeles that was erected there to sell more property; the original sign read "Hollywoodland.") As gentrification increased in Harlem and property values skyrocketed, defining neighborhood boundaries—and names—became even more important. For whichever groups wanted to say Harlem ended at Amsterdam, Realtors and media bragged of the deals in Hamilton Heights with those river views of the Hudson. So that supports HH and SH reaching the river. Newer civic groups, journalists, community activists, and residents continually debate the boundaries. But the more it was put into print that Harlem ended at 155th Street, the more it was accepted as fact, which it is not.

Some authors and historians familiar with the 1811 Street Grid will use the fact that the commissioners originally only laid out 155 streets to be paved, stopping at 155th Street as a way to support that as the official end of Harlem. That too is part of a false narrative. The commissioners noted in their documentation that they were only planning to pave 155 streets because they thought it would be another century before the land in the rest of Harlem, beyond those first 155 blocks, would be developed. In no way was it a determinant that Harlem ended at 155th Street, because at that time it extended to Spuyten Duyvil (Inwood).

There are references in 1930 in James Weldon Johnson's book *Black Manhattan* stating that Harlem ends at 155th Street and St. Nicholas. Yet he then notes, without defining the neighborhood as Sugar Hill, that the Coogan's Bluff (Edgecombe Avenue) area above 145th Street is solidly Black—not entirely accurate in 1930.

Gilbert Osofsky's 1963 book *Harlem: The Making of a Ghetto; Negro New York, 1890–1930* is cited by scholars and authors and in numerous historic landmark reports. Osofsky defined Harlem's 1930 boundaries as from East 98th Street north to West 166th Street. The eastern border of 98th Street would have included East Harlem, which was a heavily Italian neighborhood at the turn of the twentieth century. It then became predominantly Puerto Rican by the mid-twentieth century (and called Spanish Harlem), and now has a mix of Latino cultures.

The 1973 report on Harlem housing by the Department of Housing and Urban Development (HUD)/Harlem Urban Development Corporation noted that from 142nd Street to 165th Street the neighborhood was totally Black. Both Osofsky's and the HUD report description of the HH-SH outer boundaries are more accurate.

And while the accepted, quoted, often cited, and written about borders of Hamilton Heights and Sugar Hill are often defined as from 135th Street to 155th Street, I think these noted sources show that it is a matter of opinion, but not a fact. In checking with the New York City Archives, I've been advised more than once that Manhattan "neighborhoods" do not have an official city-defined mapped street designation. It is more a matter of what is said, written, and traditionally accepted. Gentrification has added to the notion that Harlem ends at 155th Street because there are some newer residents who love the real estate and river views but prefer to embrace any name for the neighborhood rather than its original proud Dutch one—Harlem.

Added to this identification of the neighborhood's boundaries is the historic landmark designation of parts of Hamilton Heights and Sugar Hill by the New York Landmarks Preservation Commission. The historic landmark borders include very specific streets and buildings and do not purport to define what is HH-SH as a neighborhood in its entirety; just that parts of it have been included within the historic landmark neighborhood designation. Yet there are people who take that landmark designation to mean that all of HH-SH is a historic landmark. Or, the reverse, that only the blocks defined as the landmark are Hamilton Heights and Sugar Hill.

The central issue remains that once enough people write that Harlem ends at 155th Street, it is accepted as such. They write that Washington Heights now comes down to Edgecombe Avenue (not across Broadway, as generally accepted for many generations), and gradually that statement is accepted if no one questions it. There are other cities around the country that have pockets of smaller "neighborhoods" within them that are actually incorporated as their own little city within the greater city.

All this is a further clarification of why I identify places beyond 155th Street, like the Audubon Estate, Carmansville, homes on Riverside Drive, Trinity Cemetery and Mausoleum (its website identifies it as being in Hamilton Heights), the Huntington Museums, the Morris-Jumel Mansion, and the Paul Robeson Building at 555 Edgecombe Avenue as being in Hamilton Heights and/or Sugar Hill.

The Morris-Jumel Mansion has the quote on its website from Duke Ellington where he says that the house is "the jewel in the crown of Sugar Hill." There are many jewels in Sugar Hill, as I hope readers have now seen, and the Morris-Jumel Mansion is one of the brightest.

Davida Siwisa James

Addendum A

Excerpted Ordinances and Land Patents Establishing and Reaffirming Harlem

No. XVIII 1658 Ordinance Establishing the Town of Harlem

A: Ordinance 1
Of the Director General and Council of New Netherland for establishing a New Village *at the end* of Manhattan Island. Passed 4 March, 1658.

The Director General and Council of New Netherland hereby give notice, that for the further promotion of agriculture, for the security of this Island and the Cattle pasturing thereon, as well as for the greater recreation and amusement of this City of Amsterdam in New Netherland, they have resolved to form a New Village or Settlement *at the end of the Island*, and about the land of Jochem Pietersen, deceased, and those which adjoin thereto. In order that the lovers of Agriculture may be encouraged thereto, the aforesaid proposed new Village aforesaid is favored by the Director General and Council with the following Privileges. First, each of the inhabitants thereof shall receive by lot, in full ownership 18, 20 . . . 24 morgens of arable Land, six to eight morgens of Valley, and be exempt from Tenths for fifteen years commencing next May, on condition that he pay within the course of three years, in instalments, Eight guilders for each morgen of Tillage land for the behoof of the interested, or their creditors, who are now or formerly were driven from the aforesaid Lands, and have suffered great loss thereon.

Secondly, in order to prevent similar damage from calamities or expulsions, the Director General and Council promise the Inhabitants of the aforesaid Village to protect and maintain them with all their Power, and, when notified and required, to assist them with 12 to 15 Soldiers on the monthly pay of the Company, the Village providing quarters and rations; This whenever the Inhabitants may petition therefor.

Thirdly, when the aforesaid Village has 20 to 25 Families, the Director General and Council will favor it with an Inferior Court of Justice; and, for that purpose, a double number is to be nominated out of the most discreet and proper persons, for the first time by the Inhabitants and afterward by the Magistrates thereof, and presented annually to the Director General and Council, to elect a single number therefrom.

Fourthly, the Director General and Council promise to employ all possible means that the Inhabitants of the aforesaid Village, when it has the abovementioned number of Families, will be accommodated with a good, pious orthodox Minister, toward whose maintenance the Director General and Council promise to pay half the Salary; the other half to be supplied by the Inhabitants in the best and easiest manner, with the advice of the Magistrates of the aforesaid Village, at the most convenient time.

Fifthly, the Director General and Council will assist the Inhabitants of the aforesaid Village, whenever it will best suit their convenience, to construct, with the Company's Negroes, a good wagon road from this place to the Village aforesaid, so that people can travel hither and thither on horseback and with a wagon.

Sixthly, in order that the advancement of the aforesaid Village may be the sooner and better promoted, the Director General and Council have resolved and determined not to establish, or allow to be established, any new Villages or settlements before and until the aforesaid Village be brought into existence; certainly not until the aforesaid number of Inhabitants is completed.

Seventhly, for the better and greater promotion of neighborly correspondence with the English of the North, the Director General and Council will at a more convenient time, authorize a Ferry and a suitable Scow near the aforesaid Village, in order to convey over Cattle and Horses, and favor the aforesaid Village with a Cattle and Horse Market.

Eighthly, whoever are inclined to settle themselves, there or to take up Bouweries by servants there, shall be bound to enter their names at once or within a short time at the office of the Secretary of the Director General and Council, and to begin immediately with others to place on the land one able-bodied person provided with proper arms, or in default thereof to be deprived of his right. Thus done at the Assembly of the Director General and Council holden in Fort Amsterdam in New Netherland the 4 March, 1658.[1]

British Land Patents and Charters

After the British took control of New Amsterdam in 1664, a series of confirming land patents and charters were issued, not just in Harlem but throughout the territories. Each one of the Harlem grants expanded upon the original land confirming titles as far as Spuyten Duyvil.

Nicolls Patent	May 1666
	Reaffirmed Stuyvesant's 1658 Harlem incorporation and land grants
Nicolls Patent II	October 1667
Dongan Charter	March 7, 1686

Addendum B

Photos Past and Present

Figure 124. Hamilton Bank, 1905, 1707–9 (Amsterdam Avenue). Photo Byron Company collection. Courtesy Museum of the City of New York. 93.1.1.876

Figure 125. Oma Shop, 1707–9 Amsterdam Ave. Author collection

Figure 126. Old Stone House 152nd and Kingsbridge Road, circa 1710. Public domain

Figure 127. 152nd St. Nicholas Looking from Convent 2021. Courtesy D. S. James

Figure 128. Harlem River Speedway circa 1895. Public domain

Figure 129. Harlem River Drive circa 2015. Public domain

Figure 130. 148th and St. Nicholas Subway Stop, 1930. Courtesy New York Transit Museum and NY Historical Society

Figure 131. 148th and St. Nicholas Subway Stop, 2022. Courtesy D. S. James

Acknowledgments

I would like to thank my father, David "Turk" McNeil, posthumously, for instilling his love of Sugar Hill in me. Our apartment at 555 Edgecombe Avenue, the landmark "Triple Nickel" Paul Robeson Building, and later on Convent Avenue set the stage for my love of this neighborhood. From its rivers to the architecture, the Gothic buildings at City College, and the jazz clubs on St. Nicholas Avenue, I felt I was graced with living in a special place, even before I knew its true history. I am grateful that one of the first things he said to me when we moved farther uptown was, "This is Sugar Hill, in a section of Harlem called Hamilton Heights." He wanted me to know that we had moved up in the world from our Morningside Heights digs.

I am forever grateful to Sister Fidelitas, my high school English teacher at Mount St. John Academy in Gladstone, New Jersey, who told me when I was fourteen that I should consider being a writer. Another English teacher, my first husband, Sipo Moses Siwisa, saved me, sent me on a tale of two cities, and told me I could achieve anything. I hope this would make him proud. I also owe a debt of gratitude to Barbara Kennedy, my first agent at my former literary agency, McIntosh & Otis in New York City. She took me on as a client in 1997 and, in so doing, put me in the company of literary legends. Barbara was Lorraine Hansbury's production assistant on the Broadway play "A Raisin in the Sun."

Fredric Nachbaur, the director of Fordham University Press, believed that a book on Hamilton Heights and Sugar Hill would be a good addition to Fordham's Empire State Editions imprint. I will always appreciate the unwavering support he provided me throughout this process. Thanks also to Fordham's Will Cerbone, Kem Crimmins, and Kate O'Brien-Nicholson.

When scouring through historical records, one can have no better allies than librarians, researchers, and archivists willing to answer questions, provide photos or documents, and point one in the right direction. I hope that I've remembered everyone by name. If not, you know who you are, and I thank you!

Sincere thanks to Julia Robbins, Rossy Mendez, Katie Ehrlich, and Ken Cobb at the New York City Municipal Library and Archives; Michael Mery, Antony Toussaint, Auburn Nelson, A. J. Muhammad, and Tom Lisanti at the Schomburg Center for Research in Black Culture; and Lauren Robinson at the Museum of the City of New York.

Elaine Rocheleau allowed me to use the beautiful photographs taken by her husband, Paul Rocheleau, which appeared in Michael Adams' book *Harlem: Lost and Found*. In what one would call a "table book" of some heft, Adams beautifully documents the rich history of Harlem with facts and stunning photos that boggle the mind. It is a treasure for anyone who loves New York City.

Rebekah Burgess of the New York City Department of Parks and Recreation found great photographs of the Morris-Jumel Mansion and city parks. My thanks also to Natalia Sciarini, librarian for Collection Management, Yale University Beinecke Access Services; Christopher T. Apostle of Sotheby's; and Sasha Sealey at the New York City Landmarks Preservations Commission.

When I made a research trip to New York City in September of 2021, in the "almost" waning days of the COVID pandemic, Hamilton Grange had not yet reopened. I appreciate that Shirley McKinney and Lorena E. B. Harris of the U.S. National Park Service helped connect me with Senior Park Ranger for the Grange Vladimir Merzlyakov. Shiloh Holley, the former director of the Morris-Jumel Mansion Museum, was most gracious in giving me a private tour of the house. Special thanks also to Marissa Maggs at Trinity Church Wall Street Archives for photos and documents.

I am grateful for the kindness of Terry Baker Mulligan, author of the memoir *Sugar Hill: Where the Sun Rose over Harlem*, Professor Bruce Haynes, author of *Down the Up Staircase*, and Evan T. Pritchard, author of *Native New Yorkers: The Legacy of the Algonquin People of New York*.

There are no words to express my gratitude to the very gracious Martin and Jenny Spollen for the privilege of inviting me into their home, the James A. and Ruth M. Bailey House, and taking me on an extensive tour.

ACKNOWLEDGMENTS · 357

My sincere thanks to all the wonderful and supportive friends who have always encouraged my efforts at being a writer and provided feedback on early versions of this book and my other titles. In particular, thank you to Que Gatlin and Colleen Anderson, Imani Leonard, retired university professor James Booker in Mankato, Minnesota, and to Jacleen Janzer for her early edits. Thanks also to my dear friend Mary Rain who aided my research. I also extend a nod to Constance Rosenblum for her edits and suggestions.

As I neared the end of writing this book, I lost a dear friend, the gifted Caribbean playwright David Edgecombe, a native of Montserrat. Some losses, despite the inevitability, hit you deeply. David was a theater visionary, brilliant and funny. He loved the concept of this book and was quite encouraging that I proceed with it.

Finally, to my brilliant screenwriter son, David Hudson Obayuwana, and my husband, Robelto James: you are both at the very center of my heart, dearer to me than I can express. David, it was very special to me having mother-son bonding time as I talked about the challenges of tackling 400 years of New York's history and you shared your progress on your various screenplays. Rob, you suffered through my frayed nerves, days glued to my laptop, and too many food deliveries during my research and writing. Thanks always for your love and support.

NOTES

1. Dutch Beginnings and Native Americans

1. Michael Kimmelman, "When Manhattan Was Mannahatta: A Stroll through the Centuries," *New York Times*, May 13, 2020, https://www.nytimes.com/2020/05/13/arts/design/manhattan-virtual-tour-virus.html.
2. James Riker, *History of Harlem (New York): Its Origins and Early Annals* (self-published, 1881; rev. ed.: New Harlem, 1904), 34.
3. Riker, *History of Harlem*, 87.
4. Evan T. Pritchard, *Native New Yorkers: The Legacy of the Algonquin People of New York* (San Francisco/Tulsa: Council Oak, 2002), Kindle loc. 116.
5. "The Different Views on Land," National Museum of the American Indian, *Smithsonian*, https://americanindian.si.edu/nk360/manhattan/different-views-land/different-views-land.cshtml.
6. Mike Wallace and Edwin G. Burrows, *Gotham: A History of New York City to 1898* (New York: Oxford University Press, 1999), xiv.

2. The Making of Harlem Heights

1. Adriaen Van der Donck, *A Description of New Netherland*, ed. Charles T. Gehring and William A. Starna, trans. Diederik Willem (original Dutch, 1655, repr. 1656, 1841, 1896, 1968) (repr. with new trans.: Lincoln: University of Nebraska Press, 2008), Kindle loc. 68.
2. Van der Donck, *Description of New Netherland*, Kindle loc. 174.
3. Eugene DeFriest Bétit, *Manhattan's Walloon Settlers: Jesse DeForest's Legacy* (West Conshohocken, Pa.: Infinity, 2017), Kindle loc., 27–28.
4. Jonathan Gill, *Harlem: The Four Hundred Year History from Dutch Village to Capital of Black America* (New York: Grove, 2011), 41.
5. Lynn B. E. Jencks, "Heroism or Collusion: Everardus Bogardus's Ministry to Enslaved Africans," *De Halve Maen: Journal of the Holland Society of New York* (Fall 2008).

6. Jerrold Seymann, "Colonial Charters, Patents and Grants to the Communities Comprising the City of New York," New York State Charters; New York, N.Y. Charters (New York: Board of Statutory Consolidation, 1939), 48.

7. Mike Wallace and Edwin G. Burrows, *Gotham: A History of New York City to 1898* (New York: Oxford University Press, 1999), 32.

8. James Riker, *History of Harlem (New York): Its Origins and Early Annals* (Self-Published, 1881; rev. ed.: New Harlem, 1904), 135.

9. Gill, *Harlem*, 29.

10. Riker, *History of Harlem*, 142.

11. "Peter Stuyvesant," *New Netherland Institute*, https://www.newnetherlandinstitute.org/history-and-heritage/dutch_americans/peter-stuyvesant/.

12. "Peter Stuyvesant," *New Netherland Institute*.

13. Wallace and Burrows, *Gotham*, 46.

14. Riker, *History of Harlem*, 173.

15. Dorothea H. Romer and Helen B. Hartman, *Jan Dyckman of Harlem and His Descendants* (New York: J. A. Thompson, 1981), 5.

16. Wallace and Burrows, *Gotham*, 75.

17. Carl Horton Pierce, *New Harlem: Past and Present* (New York: New Harlem, 1909), 28–29.

18. Wallace and Burrows, *Gotham*, 91.

19. John W. Pirsson, *The Dutch Grants, Harlem Patents and Tidal Creeks: The Law Applicable to Those Subjects Examined and Stated* (New York: L. K. Strouse, 1889), loc. 2464.

3. Harlem Land Grants, Mount Morris, and a Revolution

1. James D. Folts, "The Westward Migration of the Munsee Indians in the Eighteenth Century," New York State Archives, Lecture, Albany, N.Y., March 10, 2001, 1.

2. Evan T. Pritchard, *Native New Yorkers: The Legacy of the Algonquin People of New York* (San Francisco/Tulsa: Council Oak, 2002), Kindle loc. 4038.

3. James Riker, *History of Harlem (New York): Its Origins and Early Annals* (self-published, 1881; rev. ed.: New Harlem, 1904), 815.

4. Riker, *History of Harlem*, 820.

5. Allan McLane Hamilton, *The Intimate Life of Alexander Hamilton* (New York: Charles Scribner's Sons, 1910), 10.

6. Pritchard, *Native New Yorkers*, 125.

7. A. M. Hamilton, *Intimate Life*, 21.

8. Ibid., 22.

9. "The Siwanoy Nation—A History," Tribal Council of the Siwanoy Nation, https://www.siwanoynation.org/tribal-history.

10. Augustus Maunsell Bradhurst, *My Forefathers, Their History from Records and Traditions* (London: De La More Press, 1910; National Archives, 2008). https://archive.org/details/myforefatherstheoobrad/page/20/mode/2up, loc. 795–96.

11. William Henry Shelton, *The Jumel Mansion: Being a Full History of the House on Harlem Heights Built by Roger Morris before the Revolution; Together with Some Account of Its More Notable Occupants* (Boston and New York: Houghton Mifflin, 1916), 89.

12. "American Revolutionary War 1775 to 1783," www.revolutionarywar.us.
13. George Washington, "From G. Washington to J. Hancock, Sept. 18, 1776," *Washington Papers: Revolutionary War Series*, National Archives.
"From George Washington to John Hancock," September 18, 1776, archives.gov.
14. Ron Chernow, *Alexander Hamilton* (New York: Penguin, 2004), 81.
15. Shelton, *Jumel Mansion*, 84.
16. Ibid., 85.
17. Chernow, *Hamilton*, 83.
18. Bradhurst, *My Forefathers*, Kindle loc. 770.
19. "The American Revolution: A Timeline of George Washington's Military and Political Career during the American Revolution, 1774–1783," *Library of Congress*, https://www.loc.gov/collections/george-washington-papers/articles-and-essays/timeline/the-american-revolution/.

4. The Grange and the Duel

1. Richard Howe, "A Little Pre-History of The Manhattan Grid." *Gotham Center for New York City History*, https://www.gothamcenter.org/blog/a-little-pre-history-of-the-manhattan-grid
2. William Henry Shelton, *The Jumel Mansion: Being a Full History of the House on Harlem Heights Built by Roger Morris before the Revolution; Together with Some Account of Its More Notable Occupants* (Boston and New York: Houghton Mifflin, 1916), 136.
3. Mike Wallace and Edwin G. Burrows, *Gotham: A History of New York City to 1898* (New York: Oxford University Press, 1999), 285.
4. Mike Wallace, *Greater Gotham: A History of New York City from 1898 to 1919* (New York: Oxford University Press, 2017), 845.
5. Ron Chernow, *Alexander Hamilton* (New York: Penguin, 2004), 288.
6. U.S. Department of the Treasury, "History of the U.S. Treasury," https://home.treasury.gov/about/history/history-overview/history-of-the-treasury#second_link.
7. Shelton, *Jumel Mansion*, 136.
8. Chernow, *Hamilton*, 535.
9. "From Alexander Hamilton to Elizabeth Hamilton, Phila., Nov. 19, 1798," *Founders Online*, National Archives, https://founders.archives.gov/documents/Hamilton/01-22-02-0154.
10. Allan McLane Hamilton, *The Intimate Life of Alexander Hamilton* (New York: Charles Scribner's Sons, 1910), 296.
11. A. M. Hamilton, *Intimate Life*, 297.
12. Augustus Maunsell Bradhurst, *My Forefathers: Their History from Records and Traditions* (London: De La More, 1910), Kindle loc, 1192–97, https://archive.org/details/myforefatherstheoobrad/page/20/mode/2up.
13. A. M. Hamilton, *Intimate Life*, 299.
14. "From A. Hamilton (and others) to NYC Mayor Richard Varick, Sept. 10, 1800," *Hamilton Papers*: Petition to the Mayor and Corporation of the City of New York . . . (archives.gov).
15. A. M. Hamilton, *Intimate Life*, 301.
16. "From Alexander Hamilton to Elizabeth Hamilton, N.Y., Oct. 14, 1803," *Founders Online*, National Archives. https://founders.archives.gov/documents/Hamilton/01-26-02-0001-0125.
17. A. M. Hamilton, *Intimate Life*, 310.

18. "From Alexander Hamilton to Elizabeth Hamilton, 7–11 May 1804," *Founders Online*, National Archives. https://founders.archives.gov/documents/Hamilton/01-26-02-0001-0193.

19. Chernow, *Hamilton*, 693.

20. "From Alexander Hamilton to Elizabeth Hamilton, 4 July 1804," *Founders Online*, National Archives. https://founders.archives.gov/documents/Hamilton/01-26-02-0001-0248.

21. A. M. Hamilton, *Intimate Life*, 352.

22. Ibid., 354.

23. Ibid., 205.

24. Jessie Serfilippi, "As Odious and Immoral a Thing: Alexander Hamilton's Hidden History as an Enslaver" (Albany, N.Y.: Schuyler Mansion State Historic Site, New York State Office of Parks, Recreation, and Historic Preservation, 2020), 7.

25. Jessie Serfilippi, "As Odious and Immoral. . . ," 26.

26. A. M. Hamilton, *Intimate Life*, 368.

5. The Jumels, the Street Grid, and Audubon

1. Carol Ward, *Morris-Jumel Mansion*, Images of America (Charleston, S.C.: Arcadia, 2015), 16.

2. William Henry Shelton, *The Jumel Mansion: Being a Full History of the House on Harlem Heights Built by Roger Morris before the Revolution; Together with Some Account of Its More Notable Occupants* (Boston and New York: Houghton Mifflin, 1916), 144.

3. Shelton, *Jumel Mansion*, 152.

4. Gerard Koeppel, *City on a Grid: How New York Became New York* (Boston: Da Capo Press, 2015), 125.

5. Koeppel, *City on a Grid*, xvii.

6. Richard Howe, "A Little Pre-History of the Manhattan Grid," *Gotham Center for New York City History*, https://www.gothamcenter.org/blog/a-little-pre-history-of-the-manhattan-grid.

7. Keith Williams, "Tracing 350 Years of Harlem's Ever-Shifting Boundaries," *Forgotten New York*, August 2015, https://forgotten-ny.com/2015/02/hamilton-heights-to-harlem-manhattan/.

8. Mike Wallace, *Greater Gotham: A History of New York City from 1898 to 1919* (New York: Oxford University Press, 2017), 846.

9. Shelton, *Jumel Mansion*, 113.

10. Williams, "Tracing 350 Years."

11. Kenneth Jackson, ed., *The Encyclopedia of New York City* (New Haven: Yale University Press, 1995), Kindle loc. 33743.

12. Jackson, *Encyclopedia*, Kindle loc. 33746.

13. Shelton, *Jumel Mansion*, 172.

14. "A Walk through the Audubon Park Historic District," Audubon Park Historic Society, http://www.audubonparkny.com/audubonparkintroduction-1001.html.

15. James A. Hamilton, *Reminiscences of James A. Hamilton: Or, Men And Events, at Home and Abroad, during Three Quarters of a Century* (New York: Charles Scribner, 1869), 65.

16. Ibid.

17. "The Croton Aqueduct," Hudson River Maritime Museum, April 23, 2020, http://hrmm.org.

18. "Croton Aqueduct."

19. Dolkart, "Hamilton Heights/Sugar Hill Northwest Historic District, Borough of Manhattan Designation Report" (New York City Landmarks Preservation Commission, 2002), 10.

20. "The High Bridge," *New York City Department of Parks and Recreation*, https://www.nycgovparks.org/park-features/highbridge-park/planyc

21. David Fiske, "Solomon Northup's Family In New York City," *Gotham Center for New York City History*, January 23, 2018. https://www.gothamcenter.org/blog/solomon-northups-family-in-new-york-city.

22. Michael Markowitz, "The Sewer System," *Gotham Gazette Magazine*, October 20, 2003, https://www.gothamgazette.com/environment/2005-the-sewer-system.

23. Isabel Wilkerson, *The Warmth of Other Suns: The Epic Story of America's Great Migration* (New York: Random House, 2010), 248.

24. Matthew Spady, *The Neighborhood Manhattan Forgot: Audubon Park and the Families Who Shaped It* (New York: Fordham University Press, 2020), 152.

25. Shelton, *Jumel Mansion*, 197.

26. Ibid., 215.

27. Ibid., 217.

28. Ibid., 221.

29. "The Greatest Grid: The Master Plan of Manhattan 1811-Now," *Museum of the City of New York*. https://thegreatestgrid.mcny.org/greatest-grid/north-of-central-park/281#map.

6. The Bailey Mansion, St. Luke's, and a Building Boom

1. "The Ninth Avenue Elevated-Polo Grounds Shuttle," *New York Subway*, nycsubway.org: The 9th Avenue Elevated-Polo Grounds Shuttle.

2. Jonathan Gill, *Harlem: The Four Hundred Year History from Dutch Village to Capital of Black America* (New York: Grove, 2011), 111.

3. Ibid.

4. Ibid.

5. "Bradhurst Urban Renewal Area: Archaeological/Historical Sensitivity Evaluation, Harlem, City of New York," prepared for the New York City Department of Housing Preservation and Development by Greenhouse Consultants Incorporated, August 1994; rev. February 1995, 26, in Pirsson, *Dutch Grants*.

6. Eugene DeFriest Bétit, *Manhattan's Walloon Settlers: Jesse De Forest's Legacy* (Conshohocken, Pa.: Infinity, 2017), 91–92.

7. Michael Henry Adams (author) and Paul Rocheleau (photographer), *Harlem: Lost and Found* (New York: Monacelli, 2001), 94.

8. Adams, *Harlem: Lost and Found*, 95.

9. Kristen Heitert, "Phase IA Sensitivity Assessment Literature Search and Phase IB Archaeological Field Investigation Hamilton Grange National Memorial Site and St. Nicholas Park," *Public Archaeology Laboratory (PAL)*; prepared for National Park Service-Denver Service Center, 59, http://s-media.nyc.gov/agencies/lpc/arch_reports/509.pdf.

10. Carol S. Ward, *Morris-Jumel Mansion*, Images of America (Charleston, S.C.: Arcadia, 2015), 25.

11. Christopher Gray, "Streetscapes/150th Street and St. Nicholas Place; 1888 Mansion Built by the Bailey of Barnum & Bailey," *New York Times*, April 8, 2001.

12. Walter Greason, "T. Thomas Fortune (1856–1928)," *Blackpast.org*, January 18, 2007, https://www.blackpast.org/african-american-history/fortune-t-thomas-1856-1928/.

13. Gregory Wessner, "Manhattan's Master Plan: Why NYC Looks the Way it Does," *Metro Focus*, December 9, 2011, https://www.thirteen.org/metrofocus/2011/12/is-the-grid-locked-reimagining-manhattans-master-plan/.

14. H. Croswell Tuttle, *History of Saint Luke's Church in the City of New York 1820–1920* (New York: Appeal, 1926), 217.

15. Tuttle, *History of Saint Luke's*, 218.

16. Ibid., 219.

17. Ibid., 228.

18. Ibid., 255.

19. Andrew S. Dolkart, "Hamilton Heights/Sugar Hill Northwest Historic District, Borough of Manhattan Designation Report," New York City Landmarks Preservation Commission, 002, 8.

20. Tuttle, *History of Saint Luke's*, 280.

21. "The Greatest Grid...," *Museum of the City of New York*, https://thegreatestgrid.mcny.org/greatest-grid/north-of-central-park/281#map.

22. I. N. Phelps Stokes et al. *The Iconography of Manhattan Island 1498–1909*, vol. 3 (New York: Robert H. Dodd, 1915), Kindle loc. 35703.

23. Tuttle, *History of Saint Luke's*, 282.

24. Stokes, *Iconography*, Kindle loc. 35813.

25. Norman Rockwell, *My Adventures as an Illustrator* (Harry N. Abrams, 1988; repr. by Norman Rockwell and Tom Rockwell, New York: Abbeville, 2019), 36.

26. Rockwell, *My Adventures*, 36.

27. Ibid.

28. Ibid.

29. Ibid., 44.

30. Adams, *Harlem: Lost and Found*, 69.

7. The Great Migration and the Morris Museum

1. Isabel Wilkerson, "The Long-Lasting Legacy of the Great Migration," *Smithsonian Magazine*, September 2016.

2. John Mollenkopf, "The Evolution of New York City's Black Neighborhoods," *Metropolitics.org*, May 9, 2017.

3. Adeel Hassan, "Philip A. Payton Jr.—A Real Estate Magnate Who Turned Harlem into a Black Mecca," *New York Times*, January 31, 2019, https://www.nytimes.com/interactive/2019/obituaries/philip-a-payton-jr-overlooked.html.

4. Mike Wallace, *Greater Gotham: A History of New York City from 1898 to 1919* (New York: Oxford University Press, 2017), 846.

5. Wilkerson, "Long-Lasting Legacy."

6. Sydney C. Van Nort, *The City College of New York* (Charleston, S.C.: Arcadia, 2007), Kindle loc. 157.

7. Van Nort, *City College*, Kindle loc. 188.

8. Ibid., 207.

9. Jeffrey S. Gurock, *The Jews of Harlem: The Rise, Decline, and Revival of a Jewish Community* (New York: New York University Press, 2016), 36.

10. Hassan, "Philip A. Payton Jr."

11. Ibid.
12. Ibid.
13. "Black Business in the Gilded Age: Afro-American Realty Company," *Edwardian Promenade*, February 25, 2011, https://www.edwardianpromenade.com/business/black-business-in-the-gilded-age-afro-american-realty-company/.
14. William Henry Shelton, *The Jumel Mansion: Being a Full History of the House on Harlem Heights Built by Roger Morris before the Revolution; Together with Some Account of Its More Notable Occupants* (Boston and New York: Houghton Mifflin, 1916), vi.
15. Carol S. Ward, *Morris-Jumel Mansion* (Charleston, S.C.: Arcadia, 2015), 28.
16. Ward, *Morris-Jumel*, 34.
17. Andrew S. Dolkart, "555 Edgecombe Avenue-Roger Morris Apartments Landmark Report," *New York Landmarks Preservation Commission*, June 15, 1993, 5.
18. Elisa Urbanelli, "409 Edgecombe Apartments (Colonial Parkway Apartments)," *New York Landmarks Preservation Commission*, June 15, 1993, 5.
19. H. Croswell Tuttle, *History of Saint Luke's Church in the City of New York 1820–1920* (New York: Appeal, 1926), 338.
20. Tuttle, *History of Saint Luke's*, 398.
21. Wallace, *Greater Gotham*, 852.
22. James Weldon Johnson, *Black Manhattan* (New York: Knopf, 1930; repr. New York: Da Capo, 1991; 2020 Kindle version New York: IG), 126.
23. Johnson, *Black Manhattan*, 126.

8. The Hamilton Museum and the Hamilton Theatre

1. Donald G. Presa, "Hamilton Theater," *New York City Landmarks Preservation Commission*, February 8, 2000, 5.
2. Presa, "Hamilton Theater," 5.
3. Wendy Rae Waszut-Barrett, "Tales from a Scenic Artist and Scholar: Moss and Brill's New Theatre, 1913," in *Historic Stage Services: Tales from a Scenic Artist and Scholar*, Part 840 (New York: Moss and Brill's New Theatre, 1913), Drypigment.net.
4. Eric Sloane and Edward Anthony, *Mr. Daniels and the Grange* (Ramsey, N.J.: Funk & Wagnalls, 1968), 112.
5. Allan McLane Hamilton, *The Intimate Life of Alexander Hamilton* (New York: Charles Scribner's Sons, 1910), 54.
6. "Hamilton Grange Saved by Society," *American Scenic and Historic Preservation Society* II, no. 3–4 (1930): 57.
7. Sydney Van Nort, "Dr. Albert Einstein's Visit to City College," *CCNY Libraries News and Events*, April 29th, 2021, CCNY Libraries News & Events—LibGuides at City College Libraries (cuny.edu).
8. Van Nort, "Dr. Albert Einstein's Visit."
9. Ibid.
10. Isabel Wilkerson, *The Warmth of Other Suns: The Epic Story of America's Great Migration* (New York: Random House, 2010), 249.
11. Jeffrey S. Gurock, *The Jews of Harlem: The Rise, Decline, and Revival of a Jewish Community* (New York: New York University Press, 2016), 173.
12. "Duke Ellington," *All About Jazz*, March 20, 2021, https://www.allaboutjazz.com/musicians/duke-ellington.

13. "Duke Ellington Biography," *PBS American Masters*, December 12, 2002, https://www.pbs.org/wnet/americanmasters/duke-ellington-about-duke-ellington/586/.

9. The Harlem Renaissance

1. James Weldon Johnson, *Black Manhattan* (originally published New York: Knopf, 1930; repr. New York: Da Capo, 1991; 2020 Kindle version New York: IG), 3.

2. David Levering Lewis, *When Harlem Was in Vogue* (New York: Alfred A. Knopf, 1981), 103.

3. Bruce D. Haynes and Syma Solovitch, *Down the Up Staircase: Three Generations of a Harlem Family* (New York: Columbia University Press, 2017), 36.

4. Haynes and Solovitch, *Down the Up Staircase*, 59.

5. Ibid., 57.

6. Langston Hughes, *The Big Sea* (New York: Hill & Wang, 1940), 55.

7. Hughes, *Big Sea*, 55.

8. Ibid., 218.

9. Cheryl Wall, *Women of the Harlem Renaissance* (Bloomington: Indiana University Press, 1995), 41.

10. Hughes, *Big Sea*, 218.

11. Ethelene Whitmire, *Regina Anderson Andrews: Harlem Renaissance Librarian* (Urbana-Champaign: University of Illinois Press, 2014), 15.

12. Whitmire, *Regina Anderson Andrews*, 34.

13. Ibid., 35.

14. Lewis, *When Harlem Was in Vogue*, 51.

15. Jervis Anderson, *This Was Harlem, 1900–1950* (New York: Farrar, Straus and Giroux and Noonday, 1981), 197.

16. Johnson, *Black Manhattan*, 234.

17. Whitmire, *Regina Anderson Andrews*, 41.

18. Lewis, *When Harlem Was in Vogue*, 127.

19. Ibid.

20. Anderson, *This Was Harlem*, 204.

21. Lewis, *When Harlem Was in Vogue*, 90.

22. Anderson, *This Was Harlem*, 201.

23. Ibid.

24. Lewis, *When Harlem Was in Vogue*, 93.

25. Whitmire, *Regina Anderson Andrews*, 45.

26. David Levering Lewis, *The Portable Harlem Renaissance Reader* (New York: Viking Penguin, 1994), 93.

27. Lewis, *Portable Harlem Renaissance Reader*, 93.

28. Anne Allen Shockley, "Ethel Ray Nance, interview recording, San Francisco, Nov. 18, 1970; and Nashville, Tenn., Dec. 23, 1970," Black Oral History Collection, Fisk University, Nashville, 14.

29. Lewis, *When Harlem Was in Vogue*, xxi.

30. Michael Henry Adams (author), and Paul Rocheleau (photographer), *Harlem: Lost and Found* (New York: Monacelli, 2001), 256.

31. Eliza Urbanelli, "409 Edgecombe Apartments (Colonial Parkway Apartments)," *New York Landmarks Preservation Commission*, June 15, 1993," 14.

32. Lewis, *When Harlem Was in Vogue*, 136.
33. Yuval Taylor, "In the Company of Good Things: Tailing Zora Neale Hurston and Langston Hughes across the South," *Oxford American: A Magazine of the South* 93, August 4, 2016, https://main.oxfordamerican.org/magazine/item/937-in-the-company-of-good-things.
34. Hughes, *Big Sea*, 227.
35. Arna Bontemps, "The Two Harlems," *American Scholar* 14, no. 2 (Spring 1945): 167–73, Phi Beta Kappa Society, JSTOR, https://www.jstor.org/stable/41206482, 168.
36. Bontemps, "Two Harlems," 168.
37. Johnson, *Black Manhattan*, 235.
38. Lewis, *Portable Harlem Renaissance Reader*, xxxviii.
39. Ibid., xxxix.

10. The Heights Identity and the Black Mecca

1. "Sugar Hill: All Harlem Looks Up to 'Folks on the Hill,'" *Ebony*, November 1946, 5.
2. Bruce D. Haynes and Syma Solovitch, *Down the Up Staircase: Three Generations of a Harlem Family* (New York: Columbia University Press, 2017), 61.
3. Haynes and Solovitch, *Down the Up Staircase*, 15.
4. Andrew S. Dolkart, "Hamilton Heights/Sugar Hill Northwest Historic District, Borough of Manhattan Designation Report" (New York City Landmarks Preservation Commission, 2002), 5.
5. Eliza Urbanelli, "409 Edgecombe Apartments (Colonial Parkway Apartments)," *New York Landmarks Preservation Commission*, June 15, 1993, 10.
6. "Eunice Hunton Carter," *Historical Society of the New York Courts*, October 27, 2021, https://history.nycourts.gov/eunice-hunton-carter/.
7. "Eunice Hunton Carter," *Historical Society*.
8. Urbanelli, "409 Edgecombe Apartments," 12.
9. David Levering Lewis, *When Harlem Was in Vogue* (New York: Alfred A. Knopf, 1981), 302.
10. Lewis, *When Harlem Was in Vogue*, 303.
11. Ibid.
12. Paul Robeson, *Here I Stand* (Boston: Beacon Press, 1958), 10.
13. Audubon Park: 765 Riverside Drive (audubonparkny.com).
14. The Audubon Park Historic Society, http://www.audubonparkny.com/AudubonParkBriefHistory.html#anchor_142.
15. Jay Shockley, "New York Training School for Teachers/New York Model School (Later High School of Music & Art)," *New York City Landmarks Preservation Commission*, June 24, 1997, 4.
16. Howard A. Shiebler, "New High School of Arts: Talented Pupils Are Being Selected for Classes Opening in February," *New York Times*, Dec. 29, 1935.
17. Shiebler, "New High School of Arts."
18. Isabel Wilkerson, *The Warmth of Other Suns: The Epic Story of America's Great Migration* (New York: Random House, 2010), 242.
19. Langston Hughes, "Down Under in Harlem," *New Republic*, March 27, 1944, https://newrepublic.com/article/90505/down-under-in-harlem.
20. Weldon Johnson, *Black Manhattan* (originally published New York: Knopf, 1930; repr.: New York: Da Capo Press, 1991; 2020 Kindle version New York: IG), 122.

21. John. S. Williams, "Mary Lou Williams, a Jazz Great, Dies," *New York Times*, May 30, 1981.

22. Jenny Gathright, "Mary Lou Williams, Missionary of Jazz," *National Public Radio* (NPR), September 11, 2019.

23. Williams, "Mary Lou Williams."

24. Jonathan Gill, *Harlem: The Four Hundred Year History from Dutch Village to Capital of Black America* (New York: Grove, 2011), 345.

25. Gill, *Harlem*, 346.

11. Jazz Clubs, the Numbers, and Firsts

1. "Green Book Properties Listed in the National Register of Historic Places," National Park Service, https://www.nps.gov/articles/green-book-properties-listed-in-the-national-register-of-historic-places.htm.

2. Howard Dodson and Christopher Moore, eds., *The Black New Yorkers: 400 Years of African American History; The Schomburg Illustrated Chronology*, foreword Maya Angelou (Hoboken, N.J.: Wiley and Sons, 2000), 248.

3. Langston Hughes, *The Big Sea* (New York: Hill & Wang, 1940), 214.

4. Fred J. Cook, "The Black Mafia Moves into the Numbers Racket," *New York Times*, April 4, 1971.

5. Jonathan Gill, *Harlem: The Four Hundred Year History from Dutch Village to Capital of Black America* (New York: Grove, 2011), 311.

6. Gill, *Harlem*, 334.

7. Ibid., 336.

8. Langston Hughes, "Down Under in Harlem," *New Republic*, March 27, 1944, 404–5, https://newrepublic.com/article/90505/down-under-in-harlem.

9. Hughes, "Down Under in Harlem."

10. Arna Bontemps, "The Two Harlems," *American Scholar* 14, no. 2 (Spring 1945): 170, Phi Beta Kappa Society, *JSTOR*, https://www.jstor.org/stable/41206482.

11. "Play on Hamilton Given: Federal Union Presents Drama at the Barbizon-Plaza," *New York Times*, March 30, 1949, https://www.nytimes.com/1949/03/30/archives/play-on-hamilton-given-federal-union-presents-drama-at-the.html.

12. St. Clair Bourne, "Alexander Hamilton was a Harlemite! Home He Built in 1801 on Convent Avenue Site Now Historic Landmark," *New York Amsterdam News*, September 20, 1941 (NYPL Archives).

13. Christopher Gray, "Streetscapes/150th Street and St. Nicholas Place; 1888 Mansion Built by the Bailey of Barnum & Bailey," *New York Times*, April 8, 2001.

14. Frances Ford Coppola, director, *The Godfather*, Paramount Pictures, 1972.

15. Terry Baker Mulligan, *Sugar Hill: Where the Sun Rose Over Harlem* (St. Louis: Impulse, 2012), 50.

16. Mulligan, *Sugar Hill*, 51.

17. Carol S. Ward, *Morris-Jumel Mansion*, Images of America (Charleston, S.C.: Arcadia, 2015), 47.

18. Mulligan, *Sugar Hill*, 217.

19. Ibid.

20. "Says More Support Will Be Needed," *New York Amsterdam News*, November 28, 1953, 33, NYPL.

NOTES TO PAGES 208–31 · 369

21. Jill Lepore, "The Uprooted: Chronicling the Great Migration," *New Yorker*, August 30, 2010, https://www.newyorker.com/magazine/2010/09/06/the-uprooted.

22. Gill, *Harlem*, 379.

12. The Advent of the Sixties, Generational Changes, and the Arts

1. Jill Lepore, "The Uprooted: Chronicling the Great Migration," *New Yorker*, August 30, 2010, https://www.newyorker.com/magazine/2010/09/06/the-uprooted.

2. Lepore, "The Uprooted."

3. Ibid.

4. Ibid.

5. Ibid.

6. Terry Baker Mulligan, *Sugar Hill: Where the Sun Rose Over Harlem* (St. Louis: Impulse, 2012), 24.

7. Bruce D. Haynes and Syma Solovitch, *Down the Up Staircase: Three Generations of a Harlem Family* (New York: Columbia University Press, 2017), 27.

8. Bruce Haynes and Ray Hutchison, "Symposium on the Ghettos: The Ghetto-Origins, History and Discourse," *Sage Publications: City & Community Research Journal* 7, no. 4 (2008): 347, https://www.researchgate.net/publication/230106923_The_Ghetto_Origins_History_Discourse.

9. Haynes and Hutchison, "Symposium on the Ghettos," 347.

10. Ibid., 349.

11. Ibid., 350.

12. Arna Bontemps, "The Two Harlems," *American Scholar* 14, no. 2 (Spring 1945): 170, Phi Beta Kappa Society, *JSTOR*, https://www.jstor.org/stable/41206482.

13. Haynes and Hutchison, "Symposium on the Ghettos," 351.

14. Haynes and Solovitch, *Down the Up Staircase*, 31.

15. National Parks Service: Manhattan Historic Site Archives: American Scenic & Historic Preservation Society Collection, 12-4-1967; HAGR 900.0069, Hamilton Grange Collections—NPS (mhsarchive.org).

16. Haynes and Solovitch, *Down the Up Staircase*, 83.

17. Ibid., 103.

18. Eric Sloane and Edward Anthony, *Mr. Daniels and the Grange* (Ramsey, N.J.: Funk & Wagnalls, 1968), 16.

19. Sloane and Anthony, *Mr. Daniels and the Grange*, 112.

20. "A Profile of the Harlem Area: Findings of the Harlem Task Force, 1973," *Harlem Urban Development Corporation* (New York: The Corporation, 1973), 28–29.

21. "Blackout: NYC in Chaos," *PBS: American Experience*, https://www.pbs.org/wgbh/americanexperience/features/blackout-gallery/.

22. Haynes, *Down the Up Staircase*, 119.

23. Carol S. Ward, *Morris-Jumel Mansion*, Images of America (Charleston, S.C.: Arcadia, 2015), 62.

24. Ward, *Morris-Jumel Mansion*, 67.

25. Renee Minus White. "Marie Brooks Dancers entertain at Sugar Hill," *New York Amsterdam News*, September 25, 1982 (NYPL archives).

13. A Neighborhood's Changing Face

1. Jenny Gathright, "Mary Lou Williams, Missionary of Jazz," *National Public Radio (NPR)*, September 11, 2019.
2. Gathright, "Mary Lou Williams."
3. Richard Schaffer and Neil Smith, "The Gentrification of Harlem?," *Taylor & Francis, Ltd.*, on behalf of the Annals of the American Association of Geographers 76, no. 3 (September 1986): 350, JSTOR: https://www.jstor.org/stable/2562585.
4. Schaffer and Smith, "Gentrification," 347.
5. Ibid., 358
6. Ibid., 351.
7. Richard Florida, "How Gentrifiers Change the Definition of a Neighborhood," Bloomberg City Lab Online, https://www.bloomberg.com/news/articles/2015-03-06/when-asked-to-define-their-neighborhood-researchers-found-big-differences-between-black-and-white-residents-in-south-philly.
8. Schaffer and Smith, "Gentrification," 349.
9. Suzanne Slesin, "New Residents, New Life in Hamilton Hts," *New York Times*, May 19, 1988.
10. Jervis Anderson, *This Was Harlem, 1900–1950* (New York: Farrar, Straus and Giroux and Noonday, 1981), 59.
11. Anderson, *This Was Harlem*, 61.
12. Robert W. Snyder, *Crossing Broadway: Washington Heights and the Promise of New York City* (Ithaca, N.Y.: Cornell University Press, 2019), 6.
13. Julius Lester, "James Baldwin-Reflections of a Maverick," *New York Times*, May 27, 1984, Book Review Desk, https://archive.nytimes.com/www.nytimes.com/books/98/03/29/specials/baldwin-reflections.html?source=post_page.
14. Snyder, *Crossing Broadway*, 33.
15. Slesin, "New Residents," 1988.
16. Ibid.
17. Ibid.
18. James Weldon Johnson, *Black Manhattan* (originally published New York: Knopf, 1930; repr. New York: Da Capo Press, 1991; 2020 Kindle version New York: IG), 123.
19. Johnson, *Black Manhattan*, 3.
20. Langston Hughes, "Down Under in Harlem," *New Republic*, March 27, 1944, 404–5, https://newrepublic.com/article/90505/down-under-in-harlem.
21. Bridgett M. Davis, "The Daily Lottery Was Originally a Harlem Game. Then Albany Wanted In. The Numbers Were a Sprawling, Black-Run Business for Decades," *New York Times*, February 27, 2019.
22. Hamilton Heights 1974 Historic Landmark Designation, 35, https://architecturaltrust.org/easements/about-the-trust/trust-protected-communities/historic-districts-in-new-york/hamilton-heights-historic-district/.
23. Ibid.
24. Eric Sloane and Edward Anthony, *Mr. Daniels and the Grange* (Ramsey, N.J.: Funk & Wagnalls, 1968), 112.
25. David W. Dunlap, "Hamilton Grange Needs Furniture (and $2 Million)," *New York Times*, 1988, nytimes.com.

26. Dunlap, "Hamilton Grange Needs Furniture."

27. Ibid.

28. Christopher Gray, "Streetscapes: Hamilton Grange; A Move to Move a Historic House," *New York Times*, March. 21, 1993, https://www.nytimes.com/1993/03/21/realestate/streetscapes-hamilton-grange-a-move-to-move-a-historic-house.html.

29. Gray, "Streetscapes: Hamilton Grange."

14. Parlor Jazz and the Great Renovation

1. Ethelene Whitmire, *Regina Anderson Andrews: Harlem Renaissance Librarian* (Urbana-Champaign: University of Illinois Press, 2014), 116.

2. Bruce D. Haynes and Syma Solovitch, *Down the Up Staircase: Three Generations of a Harlem Family* (New York: Columbia University Press, 2017), 166.

3. Suzanne Slesin, "A Dream in Harlem Ends at the Gavel," *New York Times*, December 15, 1994, https://www.nytimes.com/1994/12/15/garden/a-dream-in-harlem-ends-at-the-gavel.html.

4. "Lenon Hoyte Biography (1905–1999)," *Jrank*, https://biography.jrank.org/pages/2522/Hoyte-Lenon.html#ixzz7DZcSF4jX.

5. "Rare Collection of Art Exhibited: Mrs. Hoyte Shows Antique Pitchers from Many Lands," *New York Amsterdam News*, February 10, 1951 (NYPL Archives).

6. Slesin, "Dream in Harlem."

7. William H. Honan, "Lenon Hoyte, 94, Who Offered Her Love of Dolls to the World," *New York Times Obituary*, September 9, 1999, https://www.nytimes.com/1999/09/09/nyregion/lenon-hoyte-94-who-offered-her-love-of-dolls-to-the-world.html?searchResultPosition=1.

8. "Hoyte Biography."

9. Monique M. Taylor, "Can You Go Home Again? Black Gentrification and the Dilemma of Difference," *Berkeley Journal of Sociology* 37 (1992): 102.

10. Taylor, "Can You Go Home Again?," 102.

11. Ibid., 108.

12. Ibid., 109.

13. W. E. B. Du Bois, *The Souls of Black Folk* (Chicago: A. C. McClurg, 1903), 14.

14. Taylor, "Can You Go Home Again?," 114.

15. Ibid., 113.

16. Michael Henry Adams (author), and Paul Rocheleau (photographer), *Harlem: Lost and Found* (New York: Monacelli, 2001), 109.

17. Ben Ratliff, "Syncopated Homecoming: Jazz Swings Back Uptown," *New York Times*, April 18, 1997, https://www.nytimes.com/1997/04/18/arts/syncopated-homecoming-jazz-swings-back-uptown.html.

18. Ratliff, "Syncopated Homecoming."

19. Ibid.

20. Howard Dodson and Christopher Moore, *The Black New Yorkers: 400 Years of African American History; The Schomburg Illustrated Chronology* (Hoboken, N.J.: Wiley and Sons, 2000), Dedication.

21. Ibid., 451.

22. Christopher Gray, "Streetscapes/150th Street and St. Nicholas Place; 1888 Mansion Built by the Bailey of Barnum & Bailey," *New York Times*, 2001.

23. Gray, "150th Street and St Nicholas."

24. Ibid.
25. Tom Miller, "The Chas. H. Tuttle Mansion—No. 339 Convent Ave," *Daytonian in Manhattan* (blog), http://daytoninmanhattan.blogspot.com/2016/11/the-chas-h-tuttle-mansion-no-339.html.
26. Miller, "The Chas. H. Tuttle Mansion."
27. Rose Hackman, "What Happens When Harlem Becomes White?," *Guardian*, May 13, 2015, https://www.theguardian.com/us-news/2015/may/13/harlem-gentrification-new-york-race-black-white.
28. Adams and Rocheleau, *Harlem: Lost and Found*, 258.
29. DNA Info: West Harlem, Hamilton Heights, and Sugar Hill, https://www.dnainfo.com/new-york/crime-safety-report/manhattan/west-harlem/.
30. Fernanda Santos, "Harlem Mainstay Survived Riots, but Falls to Renewal," *New York Times*, July 23, 2007, https://www.nytimes.com/2007/07/23/nyregion/23copelands.html?searchResultPosition=2.
31. Santos, "Harlem Mainstay."
32. Ibid.
33. National Park Service: Manhattan Historic Site Archives, Hamilton Grange Collections—NPS (mhsarchive.org).
34. Eric Sloane and Edward Anthony, *Mr. Daniels and the Grange* (Ramsey, N.J.: Funk & Wagnalls, 1968), 20.
35. Katherine B. Menz, "Historic Furnishings Report," *National Park Service*, 15.
36. Elizabeth Pochoda, "Treasury Notes," *Magazine Antiques*, July/August 2016.
37. Pochoda, "Treasury Notes."

15. Changing Demographics and a Revived Hamilton Heights

1. Sharon Obialo, Nienke Venema, and Marie Gørrild, "Gentrification and Displacement in Harlem: How the Harlem Community Lost Its Voice en Route to Progress," *Humanity in Action*, New York, 2008, https://humanityinaction.org/knowledge_detail/gentrification-and-displacement-in-harlem-how-the-harlem-community-lost-its-voice-en-route-to-progress/.
2. Obialo et al., "Gentrification and Displacement."
3. Ibid.
4. Ibid.
5. Tom Miller, "The James Bailey House—10 St. Nicholas Place," *Daytonian in Manhattan* (blog), 2019, http://daytoninmanhattan.blogspot.com/2019/05/the-james-bailey-house-10-st-nicholas.html.
6. Lucy Brenner, "At the RKO Hamilton Theater, Development and Historic Preservation Go Head-to-Head," *Columbia Spectator*, February 11, 2021, https://www.columbiaspectator.com/news/2021/02/12/at-the-rko-hamilton-theater-development-and-historic-preservation-go-head-to-head/.
7. Brenner, "At the RKO Hamilton Theater."
8. Douglas Feiden, "Harlem's RKO Hamilton Theater Is One of NYC's Forgotten Architectural Gems," *New York Daily News*, April 1, 2013.
9. Brenner, "At the RKO Hamilton Theater."
10. Elizabeth Pochoda, "Treasury Notes," *Magazine Antiques*, July/August 2016, https://www.themagazineantiques.com/article/treasury-notes/.

11. Justin Davidson, *Magnetic City: A Walking Companion to New York* (New York: Random House, 2017), 188.
12. Davidson, *Magnetic City*, 189.
13. Rebecca Rego Barry, "An Intern Saved a Museum by Finding This Revolutionary War Treasure in the Attic," *Smithsonian Magazine*, December 1, 2015, https://www.smithsonianmag.com/history/found-attic-rare-document-revolutionary-war-saved-museum-brink-financial-ruin-180957411/; excerpted from Barry's book *Rare Books Uncovered: True Stories of Fantastic Finds in Unlikely Places* (Minneapolis: Voyageur, 2018).
14. Barry, "An Intern Saved a Museum."
15. Ibid.
16. Ibid.
17. Julie Besonen, "Hamilton Heights: Harlem Enclave with River Views," *New York Times*, Feb. 3, 2016, https://www.nytimes.com/2016/02/07/realestate/hamilton-heights-harlem-enclave-with-river-views.html.
18. Besonen, "Hamilton Heights."
19. Ibid.
20. D'Vera Cohn, "Four-in-Ten Who Haven't Yet Filled out U.S. Census Say They Wouldn't Answer the Door for a Census Worker," *Pew Research Center*, July 28, 2020, https://www.pewresearch.org/fact-tank/2020/07/28/four-in-ten-who-havent-yet-filled-out-u-s-census-say-they-wouldnt-answer-the-door-for-a-census-worker/.
21. Jim Dwyer, "Making a Home, and a Haven for Books," *New York Times*, August 11, 2007, https://www.nytimes.com/2007/08/11/nyregion/11about.html?searchResultPosition=10.
22. Dwyer, "Making a Home."

16. Bailey House, Jazz, and the Renaissance Remix

1. Julyssa Lopez, "New York's Last Great Jazz Parlour," *BBC Travel: Untold Stories*, February 2020, https://www.bbc.com/travel/bespoke/untold-america/new-york-test/.
2. Lopez, "New York's Last Great Jazz Parlour."
3. Ibid.
4. New York City Landmarks Preservation Commission, "Hamilton Grange, 287 Convent Avenue," August 2, 1967.
5. Cheryl Wall, *Women of the Harlem Renaissance* (Bloomington: Indiana University Press, 1995), 204.
6. David Nicholson, "The Mark of Zora," *Washington Post*, March 5, 1995, https://www.washingtonpost.com/archive/entertainment/books/1995/03/05/the-mark-of-zora/fa4c327f-8fcd-4375-aa64-4852f3d9171b/.
7. Nicholson, "Mark of Zora."
8. Isabel Wilkerson, *Caste: The Origins of Our Discontent* (New York: Random House, 2020), 22.
9. "Hundreds Celebrate at 5th Sugar Hill Music Fest," *Amsterdam News*, October 14, 2021, https://amsterdamnews.com/news/2021/10/14/hundreds-celebrate-5th-sugar-hill-music-fest/.
10. Wendy Goodman, "A Harlem Prewar Apartment Stripped to Its Original State," *New York: Curbed Magazine,* October 9, 2020. https://www.curbed.com/2020/10/a-harlem-prewar-apartment-stripped-to-its-original-state.html.
11. Goodman, "Harlem Prewar Apartment."

12. Ibid.

13. Jervis Anderson, *This Was Harlem, 1900–1950* (New York: Farrar, Straus and Giroux and Noonday, 1981), 349.

14. Langston Hughes, *The Big Sea* (New York: Hill & Wang, 1940), 335.

Addendum A: Excerpted Ordinances and Land Patents Establishing and Reaffirming Harlem

1. James Riker, *History of Harlem (New York): Its Origins and Early Annals* (self-published, 1881; Rev. ed.: New Harlem Publishing, 1904).

SELECTED BIBLIOGRAPHY

Adams, Michael Henry. "Harlem Style and Taste Blog." https://mrmhadams.typepad.com/blog/harlem/.

Adams, Michael Henry. Style and Taste Blog: "Harlem's St. Nicholas Place and the Remarkable Rebirth of the Bailey-Blake-Spollen House!" https://mrmhadams.typepad.com/blog/2012/08/my-entry.html.

Adams, Michael Henry (author), and Paul Rocheleau (photographer). *Harlem: Lost and Found.* New York: Monacelli, 2001.

"The American Revolution: A Timeline of George Washington's Military and Political Career during the American Revolution, 1774–1783." *Library of Congress.* https://www.loc.gov/collections/george-washington-papers/articles-and-essays/timeline/the-american-revolution/.

"American Revolutionary War 1775 to 1783." http://www.revolutionarywar.us.

Anderson, Jervis. *This Was Harlem, 1900–1950.* New York: Farrar, Straus and Giroux and Noonday, 1981.

Andrews, Regina. Regina Andrews Papers. Schomburg Center for Research in Black Culture. New York Public Library. Regina Anderson, librarian.

Andrews, Regina, and Jean Blackwell Hutson. *An Interview with Regina Anderson Andrews.* Schomburg Center for Research in Black Culture. New York Public Library, 1986.

Barry, Rebecca Rego. "An Intern Saved a Museum by Finding This Revolutionary War Treasure in the Attic." *Smithsonian Magazine,* December 1, 2015. Excerpted from Barry's book *Rare Books Uncovered: True Stories of Fantastic Finds in Unlikely Places* (Minneapolis: Voyageur, 2018). https://www.smithsonianmag.com/history/found-attic-rare-document-revolutionary-war-saved-museum-brink-financial-ruin-180957411/.

"The Battle of Harlem Heights: September 16, 1776, at Harlem, New York." *Revolutionary War U.S.* https://revolutionarywar.us/year-1776/battle-harlem-heights/.

Bétit, Eugene DeFriest. *Manhattan's Walloon Settlers: Jesse De Forest's Legacy.* Conshohocken, Pa.: Infinity, 2017.

"Black Business in the Gilded Age: Afro-American Realty Company." Edwardian Promenade, February 25, 2011. https://www.edwardianpromenade.com/business/black-business-in-the-gilded-age-afro-american-realty-company/.

"Blackout: NYC in Chaos." *PBS, American Experience*. https://www.pbs.org/wgbh/americanexperience/features/blackout-gallery/.

Bliven, Bruce Jr. "Battle of Harlem Heights." *New Yorker*, November 12, 1955. https://archives.newyorker.com/newyorker/1955-11-12/flipbook/100.

Bontemps, Arna, ed. *The Harlem Renaissance Remembered*. New York: Dodd, Mead, 1972.

Bontemps, Arna. "The Two Harlems." *American Scholar* 14, no. 2 (Spring 1945): 167–73. Phi Beta Kappa Society. *JSTOR*, https://www.jstor.org/stable/41206482.

Bradhurst, Augustus Maunsell. *My Forefathers: Their History from Records and Traditions*. London: De La More, 1910; National Archives, 2008. https://archive.org/details/myforefathersthe00brad/page/20/mode/2up.

"Bradhurst Urban Renewal Area: Archaeological/Historical Sensitivity Evaluation, Harlem, City of New York." Prepared for the New York City Department of Housing Preservation and Development by Greenhouse Consultants. August 1994. Revised February 1995.

Burroughs, John. *John James Audubon*. Boston: Small, Maynard and Company, 1902.

Chernow, Ron. *Alexander Hamilton*. New York: Penguin, 2004.

Cohn, D'Vera. "Four in Ten Who Haven't Yet Filled out U.S. Census Say They Wouldn't Answer the Door for a Census Worker." Pew Research Center, July 28, 2020. https://www.pewresearch.org/fact-tank/2020/07/28/four-in-ten-who-havent-yet-filled-out-u-s-census-say-they-wouldnt-answer-the-door-for-a-census-worker/.

Connolly, Colleen. "The True Native New Yorkers Can Never Truly Reclaim Their Homeland." *Smithsonian Magazine*, October 5, 2018. https://www.smithsonianmag.com/history/true-native-new-yorkers-can-never-truly-reclaim-their-homeland-180970472/.

"The Croton Aqueduct." Hudson River Maritime Museum, April 23, 2020. http://hrmm.org.

Davidson, Justin. *Magnetic City: A Walking Companion to New York*. New York: Random House, 2017.

De Laet, Johannes. *The History of the New World or Description of the West Indies*. Printed in 1625. Library of Congress digital.

DNA Info: West Harlem, Hamilton Heights, and Sugar Hill. https://www.dnainfo.com/new-york/crime-safety-report/manhattan/west-harlem/.

Dodson, Howard, and Christopher Moore, eds. *The Black New Yorkers: 400 Years of African American History; The Schomburg Illustrated Chronology*; Foreword by Maya Angelou. Hoboken, N.J.: Wiley and Sons, 2000.

Dolkart, Andrew S. "555 Edgecombe Avenue—Roger Morris Apartments Landmark Report." *New York Landmarks Preservation Commission*, June 15, 1993.

———. "Hamilton Heights/Sugar Hill Northwest Historic District, Borough of Manhattan Designation Report." New York City Landmarks Preservation Commission, 2002.

Du Bois, W. E. B. *The Souls of Black Folk*. Chicago: A. C. McClurg, 1903.

"Duke Ellington." *All About Jazz*, March 20, 2021. https://www.allaboutjazz.com/musicians/duke-ellington.

"Duke Ellington Biography." *PBS American Masters*, December 12, 2002.

Durn, Sarah. "Stephanie St. Clair, Harlem's 'Numbers Queen' Dominated the Gambling Underground and Made Millions." Smithsonianmag.com, May 21, 2021.

"Eunice Hunton Carter." *Historical Society of the New York Courts*, October 27, 2021. https://history.nycourts.gov/eunice-hunton-carter/.

Fiske, David. "Solomon Northup's Family In New York City." *Gotham Center for New York City History*. https://www.gothamcenter.org/blog/solomon-northups-family-in-new-york-city. January 23, 2018.
Florida, Richard. "How Gentrifiers Change the Definition of a Neighborhood." *Bloomberg City Lab Online*. https://www.bloomberg.com/news/articles/2015-03-06/when-asked-to-define-their-neighborhood-researchers-found-big-differences-between-black-and-white-residents-in-south-philly.
Garrett, Debbie Behan. "Lenon Holder Hoyte: Educator, Philanthropist, Doll Museum Founder." *Ebony-Essence of Dolls in Black*, March 6, 2018.
Gathright, Jenny. "Mary Lou Williams, Missionary of Jazz." *National Public Radio (NPR)*, September 11, 2019.
Gehring, Charles T., trans., ed. "New York Historical Manuscripts: Dutch Volumes GG, HH & II Land Papers." Baltimore and New York: Baltimore Genealogical Publishing and Holland Society of New York, 1980.
"General Management Plan Environmental Impact Statement: Manhattan Sites: Hamilton Grange National Memorial (NY)." National Park Service, U.S. Department of the Interior, Denver Service Center, 1995.
"General Orders, 16 September 1776." *Founders Online, National Archives*, https://founders.archives.gov/documents/Washington/03-06-02-0250. [Original source: The Papers of George Washington, Revolutionary War Series, vol. 6, 13 August 1776–20 October 1776, ed.]
Gill, Jonathan. *Harlem: The Four Hundred Year History from Dutch Village to Capital of Black America*. New York: Grove, 2011.
Goodman, Wendy. "A Harlem Prewar Apartment Stripped to Its Original State." New York: *Curbed Magazine*, October 9, 2020.
"Gottlieb's Life and Work." *Library of Congress: Biographies; Gottlieb's Life and Work*. loc.gov.
"The Greatest Grid: The Master Plan of Manhattan 1811-Now." *Museum of the City of New York*. https://thegreatestgrid.mcny.org/greatest-grid/north-of-central-park/281#map.
"Green Book Properties Listed in the National Register of Historic Places." National Park Service. https://www.nps.gov/articles/green-book-properties-listed-in-the-national-register-of-historic-places.htm.
Gurock, Jeffrey S. *The Jews of Harlem: The Rise, Decline, and Revival of a Jewish Community*. New York: New York University Press, 2016.
Hamilton, Alexander. Alexander Hamilton Papers. Library of Congress. https://www.loc.gov/collections/alexander-hamilton-papers/about-this-collection/.
Hamilton, Allan McLane. *The Intimate Life of Alexander Hamilton*. New York: Charles Scribner's Sons, 1910.
"Hamilton Grange National Memorial Administrative Records, 1897–1999." *National Park Service*. U.S. Department of the Interior. http://www.mhsarchive.org/FullImages/HAGR901-Finding-Aid-2011.pdf.
Hamilton, James A. *Reminiscences of James A. Hamilton: Or, Men and Events, at Home and Abroad, during Three Quarters of a Century*. New York: Charles Scribner, 1869.
Haynes, Bruce D., and Syma Solovitch. *Down the Up Staircase: Three Generations of a Harlem Family*. New York: Columbia University Press, 2017.
Haynes, Bruce, and Ray Hutchison. "Symposium on the Ghettos: The Ghetto-Origins, History and Discourse." *City & Community Research Journal* 7, no. 4 (2008): 347–52. https://www.researchgate.net/publication/230106923_The_Ghetto_Origins_History_Discourse.

"The High Bridge." *New York City Department of Parks and Recreation.* https://www.nycgovparks.org/park-features/highbridge-park/planyc.

Howe, Richard. "A Little Pre-History of the Manhattan Grid." *Gotham Center for New York City History.* https://www.gothamcenter.org/blog/a-little-pre-history-of-the-manhattan-grid.

Hughes, Langston. *The Big Sea.* New York: Hill & Wang, 1940.

———. "Down Under in Harlem." *New Republic,* March 27, 1944, 404–5. https://newrepublic.com/article/90505/down-under-in-harlem.

Jackson, Kenneth, ed. *The Encyclopedia of New York City.* New Haven: Yale University Press, 1995.

Jencks, Lynn B. E. "Heroism or Collusion: Everardus Bogardus's Ministry to Enslaved Africans." *De Halve Maen: Journal of the Holland Society of New York* (Fall 2008).

Johnson, Abby Ann Arthur, and Ronald M. Johnson. "Forgotten Pages: Black Literary Magazines in the 1920s." *Journal of American Studies* 8, no. 3 (December 1974): 363–82. Cambridge: Cambridge University Press. JSTOR: https://www.jstor.org/stable/27553130.

Johnson, James Weldon. *Black Manhattan.* Originally published New York: Knopf, 1930. Reprint New York: Da Capo Press, 1991; 2020 Kindle version New York: IG.

———. "Harlem: The Culture Capital." In *National Humanities Center Resource Toolbox: The Making of African American Identity.* Vol. III. 1917–68. (Excerpts). Originally published by Alain Locke, ed., in *The New Negro: An Interpretation.* Garden City, N.Y., 1925.

Jonathan, Jonah. "Selected Observations from the Harlem Jazz Scene." Master's thesis. Newark, N.J.: Newark Rutgers, the State University of New Jersey, 2015.

Koeppel, Gerard. *City on a Grid: How New York Became New York.* Boston: Da Capo Press, 2015.

"Lenon Hoyte Biography (1905–1999)." *Jrank.* https://biography.jrank.org/pages/2522/Hoyte-Lenon.html#ixzz7DZcSF4jX.

Lepore, Jill. "The Uprooted: Chronicling the Great Migration." *New Yorker,* August 30, 2010. https://www.newyorker.com/magazine/2010/09/06/the-uprooted

Lewis, David Levering. *The Portable Harlem Renaissance Reader.* New York: Viking Penguin, 1994.

———. *When Harlem Was in Vogue.* New York: Alfred A. Knopf, 1981.

Locke, Alain. "Harlem: Mecca of the New Negro." *Survey Graphic,* March 1925. National Humanities Center Resource Toolbox: The Making of African American Identity. Vol. III, 1917–68.

Lopez, Julyssa. "New York's Last Great Jazz Parlour." *BBC Travel: Untold Stories,* February 2020. https://www.bbc.com/travel/bespoke/untold-america/new-york-test/.

McCarthy, Andy. "Class Act: Researching New York City Schools with Local History Collections." *New York Public Library,* Milstein Division of U.S. History, Local History & Genealogy, October 20, 2014. https://www.nypl.org/blog/2014/10/20/researching-nyc-schools.

Menz, Katherine B. "Historic Furnishings Report." *National Park Service,* 1986.

Michaud, Jon. "Walking the Heights." *New Yorker,* January 16, 2015.

Miller, Tom. "The Chas. H. Tuttle Mansion—No. 339 Convent Ave." *Daytonian in Manhattan* (blog). http://daytoninmanhattan.blogspot.com/2016/11/the-chas-h-tuttle-mansion-no-339.html.

———. "The James Bailey House—10 St. Nicholas Place." *Daytonian in Manhattan* (blog). 2019. http://daytoninmanhattan.blogspot.com/2019/05/the-james-bailey-house-10-st-nicholas.html.

Mulligan, Terry Baker. *Sugar Hill: Where the Sun Rose Over Harlem.* St. Louis: Impulse, 2012.

National Museum of the American Indian. "The Different Views on Land." *Smithsonian.* https://americanindian.si.edu/nk360/manhattan/different-views-land/different-views-land.cshtml.

National Park Service: Manhattan Historic Site Archives. Hamilton Grange Collections—NPS (mhsarchive.org).

"A New African American Identity: The Harlem Renaissance." *National Museum of African American History and Culture.* Washington, D.C. https://nmaahc.si.edu/blog-post/new-african-american-identity-harlem-renaissance.

New Netherland Institute. https://www.newnetherlandinstitute.org/.

New York City Landmarks Preservation Commission. "Hamilton Grange, 287 Convent Avenue." August 2, 1967.

"New York City Transit—History and Chronology." *New York City Business Centres,* March 20, 2014. https://wwbcn.com/new-york-city-transit-history-chronology/.

"New York City Subway Opens." History.com, A&E Networks, November 24, 2009. https://www.history.com/this-day-in-history/new-york-city-subway-opens.

"The Ninth Avenue Elevated-Polo Grounds Shuttle." *New York Subway.* nycsubway.org: The 9th Avenue Elevated-Polo Grounds Shuttle.

Obialo, Sharon, Nienke Venema, and Marie Gørrild. "Gentrification and Displacement in Harlem: How the Harlem Community Lost Its Voice en Route to Progress." *Humanity in Action,* New York, 2008. https://www.humanityinaction.org/knowledge_detail/gentrification-and-displacement-in-harlem-how-the-harlem-community-lost-its-voice-en-route-to-progress/.

Osofsky, Gilbert. *Harlem: The Making of a Ghetto; Negro New York, 1890–1930.* New York: Harper and Row, 1963.

Pierce, Carl Horton. *New Harlem: Past and Present.* New York: New Harlem, 1909.

Pirsson, John W. *The Dutch Grants, Harlem Patents and Tidal Creeks: The Law Applicable to Those Subjects Examined and Stated.* New York: L. K. Strouse, 1889.

Pochoda, Elizabeth. "Treasury Notes." *Magazine Antiques,* July/August 2016. https://www.themagazineantiques.com/article/treasury-notes/.

"Polo Grounds." https://www.ballparksofbaseball.com/ballparks/polo-grounds/.

Postal, Matthew A. "Hamilton Heights and Sugar Hill Historic District Report." *New York City Landmarks Preservation Commission,* June 27, 2000. http://neighborhoodpreservationcenter.org/db/bb_files/2000HamiltonHeightsSugarHill.pdf.

Presa, Donald G. "Hamilton Theater." *New York City Landmarks Preservation Commission,* February 8, 2000.

Pritchard, Evan T. *Native New Yorkers: The Legacy of the Algonquin People of New York.* San Francisco/Tulsa: Council Oaks Books, LLC, 2002.

"A Profile of the Harlem Area: Findings of the Harlem Task Force, 1973." *Harlem Urban Development Corporation.* New York: The Corporation, 1973.

Riker, James. *History of Harlem (New York): Its Origins and Early Annals.* Self-Published, 1881. Rev. ed.: New Harlem, 1904.

Robeson, Paul. *Here I Stand.* Boston: Beacon Press, 1958.

Rockwell, Norman. *My Adventures as an Illustrator.* New York: Harry N. Abrams, 1988. Republished by Norman Rockwell and Tom Rockwell. New York: Abbeville Press, 2019.

Romer, H. Dorothea, and Helen B. Hartman. *Jan Dyckman of Harlem and His Descendants.* New York: J. A. Thompson, 1981.

Ryan, David. "The Gentle Art of Wandering: A 'Step Street' Walk in New York City (Blog)." https://www.gentleartofwandering.com/a-step-street-walk-in-new-york-city/.

Sacks, Marcy S. *Before Harlem: The Black Experience in New York City before World War I*. Philadelphia: University of Pennsylvania Press, 2006. https://www.upenn.edu/pennpress/book/toc/14294_toc.html.

Sanderson, Eric W., and Markley Boyer. *Mannahatta: A Natural History of New York City*. New York: Abrams, 2009.

Schaffer, Richard, and Neil Smith. "The Gentrification of Harlem?" *Taylor & Francis, Ltd.* on behalf of the *Annals of the American Association of Geographers* 76, no. 3 (September 1986): 347–65. JSTOR: https://www.jstor.org/stable/2562585.

Serfilippi, Jessie. "As Odious and Immoral a Thing: Alexander Hamilton's Hidden History as an Enslaver." Albany, N.Y.: Schuyler Mansion State Historic Site, New York State Office of Parks, Recreation, and Historic Preservation, 2020.

Seymann, Jerrold. "Colonial Charters, Patents and Grants to the Communities Comprising the City of New York." New York State Charters; New York, N.Y. Charters. New York: Board of Statutory Consolidation, 1939.

Shelton, William Henry. *The Jumel Mansion: Being a Full History of the House on Harlem Heights Built by Roger Morris before the Revolution. Together With Some Account of Its More Notable Occupants*. Boston and New York: Houghton Mifflin, 1916.

Shockley, Anne Allen. "Ethel Ray Nance, interview recording, San Francisco, Nov. 18, 1970; and Nashville, Tenn., Dec. 23, 1970." Black Oral History Collection, Fisk University, Nashville, 14.

Shockley, Jay. "New York Training School for Teachers/New York Model School (Later High School of Music and Art)." *New York City Landmarks Preservation Commission*, June 24, 1997.

Shorto, Russell. *The Island at the Center of the World: The Epic Story of Dutch Manhattan and the Forgotten Colony That Shaped America*. New York: Doubleday, 2004.

"The Siwanoy Nation—A History." *Tribal Council of the Siwanoy Nation*. https://www.siwanoynation.org/tribal-history.

Sloane, Eric, and Edward Anthony. *Mr. Daniels and the Grange*. Ramsey, N.J.: Funk & Wagnalls, 1968.

Small, Matthew. "Harlem's Hidden History: The Real Little Italy Was Uptown." https://medium.com, July 17, 2016.

Snyder, Robert W. *Crossing Broadway: Washington Heights and the Promise of New York City*. Ithaca, N.Y.: Cornell University Press, 2019.

Spady, Matthew. *The Neighborhood Manhattan Forgot: Audubon Park and the Families Who Shaped It*. New York: Fordham University Press, 2020.

Stokes, I. N. Phelps, et al. *The Iconography of Manhattan Island 1498–1909*. Vol. 3. New York: Robert H. Dodd, 1915.

Taylor, Monique M. "Can You Go Home Again? Black Gentrification and the Dilemma of Difference." *Berkeley Journal of Sociology* 37 (1992): 101–28. Regents of the University of California.

Taylor, Yuval. "In the Company of Good Things: Tailing Zora Neale Hurston and Langston Hughes Across the South." *Oxford American: A Magazine of the South* 93, August 4, 2016. https://main.oxfordamerican.org/magazine/item/937-in-the-company-of-good-things.

"Timmie Rogers (1914–2006)." *Black Past*. https://www.blackpast.org/african-american-history/rogers-timmie-1914-2006/.

Tuttle, H. Croswell. *History of Saint Luke's Church in the City of New York 1820–1920*. New York: Appeal, 1926.

"Uptown Manhattan Trinity Cemetery & Mausoleum." *Trinity Church Wall Street*. https://www.trinitywallstreet.org/cemetery-mausoleum.

Urbanelli, Elisa. "409 Edgecombe Apartments (Colonial Parkway Apartments)." *New York Landmarks Preservation Commission*, June 15, 1993.

U.S. Department of the Treasury. "History of the Treasury." https://home.treasury.gov/about/history/history-overview/history-of-the-treasury#second_link.

Van der Donck, Adriaen. *A Description of New Netherland*. Edited by Charles T. Gehring and William A. Starna. Translated by Diederik Willem. Lincoln: University of Nebraska Press, 2008. Original Dutch publication, 1655. Reprinted 1656, 1841, 1896, 1968.

Van Nort, Sydney C. *The City College of New York*. Charleston, S.C.: Arcadia, 2007.

———. "Dr. Albert Einstein's Visit to City College." *CCNY Libraries News and Events*, April 29, 2021.

Wall, Cheryl. *Women of the Harlem Renaissance*. Bloomington: Indiana University Press, 1995.

Wallace, Mike. *Greater Gotham: A History of New York City from 1898–1919*. New York: Oxford University Press, 2017.

Wallace, Mike, and Edwin G. Burrows. *Gotham: A History of New York City to 1898*. New York: Oxford University Press, 1999.

Walsh, Kevin. *Forgotten New York: Views of a Lost Metropolis*. New York: Collins, 2006.

Ward, Carol S. *Morris-Jumel Mansion. Images of America*. Charleston, S.C.: Arcadia, 2015.

Washington, George. "Washington Papers: Revolutionary War Series." National Archives.

Waszut-Barrett, Wendy Rae. "Tales from a Scenic Artist and Scholar: Moss and Brill's New Theatre, 1913." *Historic Stage Services: Tales from a Scenic Artist and Scholar*. New York: Moss and Brill's New Theatre, 1913. Drypigment.net.

Wessner, Gregory. "Manhattan's Master Plan: Why NYC Looks the Way It Does." *Metro Focus*, December 9, 2011.

Whitmire, Ethelene. *Regina Anderson Andrews, Harlem Renaissance Librarian*. Urbana-Champaign: University of Illinois Press, 2014.

Wilkerson, Isabel. *Caste: The Origins of Our Discontent*. New York: Random House, 2020.

———. "The Long-Lasting Legacy of the Great Migration." *Smithsonian Magazine*, September 2016.

———. *The Warmth of Other Suns: The Epic Story of America's Great Migration*. New York: Random House, 2010.

Williams, Keith. "Tracing 350 Years of Harlem's Ever-Shifting Boundaries." *Forgotten New York*. August 2015. https://forgotten-ny.com/2015/02/hamilton-heights-to-harlem-manhattan/.

INDEX

abolition of slavery, 38, 40, 60–61, 67, 69, 214
Adams, John, 27, 289
Adams, Michael Henry, 79, 159, 195, 245, 249, 259, 264, 269, 308, 356; on 51 Hamilton Terrace, 98–99
Adjaye, David, 337
Africa, 6, 177–78 164
African Americans, Black people and, 12, 40, 162, 215, 239, 254, 271, 345; children, 51, 69, 144–45, 173, 177, 178, 184, 208; culture, 134–36, 239, 253, 263, 282, 298–99, 316; FWP addressing, 212–14; Great Migration by, 95, 102–6, 202, 212, 214, 230, 241, 282; in Harlem demographics, 236–37, 268, 281, 296, 301; history, 120, 135, 155, 162–63, 263, 298; intelligentsia, 143, 177, 340; middle-class, 141, 162–63, 215–16, 257–59; professionals, 110–11, 140–41, 254–58, 268; as the "Talented Tenth," 143, 148, 176, 279; women, 6, 120, 139, 149, 175, 203, 210–11, 215–16, 253–56, 255. *See also* enslaved people; segregation, racial; *specific African Americans*
African Free School, 40, 67
Afro-American Realty Company, 110

agriculture, 13–14, 25, 60, 124, 349
Aitkens, Charles, 39, 63
Alabama, 120–21, 162, 164–65, 184, 318
Alexander Hamilton (Chernow), 35
Algonquin Nation, 1, 3, 5, 23, 253, 302, 336, 340
Ali, Muhammad, 230–31, 271
Allen, William, 280–81
Alloway, Berta, 261–63, 331–32
Alpert, Herb, 279
American Renaissance architecture, 102
American Revolution. *See* Revolutionary War
American Scenic and Historic Preservation Society, 92, 126, 129–30, 272, 345
Amiaga Photographers, Inc., 80
Amsterdam Avenue, 271–72, 296–97, 319, 353
Amsterdam News, 119, 187–88, 255, 328
Anderson, James H., 119
Anderson, Jervis, 242
Anderson, Marian, 203, 205, 219, 221–22
Anderson, Wes, 266–67
Andrews, Regina (Regina Anderson), 175, 222, 229, 234, 254, 263, 314, 337, 339; during the Harlem Renaissance, 149–55, 160–61, *161*, 163, 253

Andrews, William T., 153, 163, 175
Anglo-Dutch wars, 19–20
d'Angola, Paul, 6
Annals of the American Association of Geographers (Schaffer, Smith), 238
Anthony, Edward, 272
Antiques Roadshow (television show), 290
Antony, Domingo, 12
A. Philip Randolph Campus High School, 251
Apollo Theater, x, 127, 170–71
architecture, 78, 236, 245–48, 259, 260, 265–66, 270, 294; of the Bailey House, 84, 302–11, *303, 304, 305, 306, 307, 308, 309, 310, 311*; City College, 106–8, *107*; Dutch, 4, 10–11, 25, 79–80, *80*, 274; of the Hamilton Grange, 45–46, *46*, 271–78, *273, 275, 276, 277, 278*, 312–14, *314*; Hamilton Theater, 127–28, *128*, 264; of the Morris-Jumel Mansion, *319*, 319–24, *320, 321, 322, 323, 324*; of Mount Morris, 26–27, *27*; of the RKO Hamilton, 284, *284*; of 72 Hamilton Terrace, 330–31, *331*. *See also specific architects*
Armstrong, Henry, 209, *209*
art, 73, 81, 148–49, 221, 228, 277–78, *278*; Harlem Renaissance, 157, 175–76, 261, 316–17, 339; by Rockwell, 96–97, 338
Arthur (film), 250
Arthur, Chester A., 61–62
Ashkenazy, Ben, 283
assassinations, 61–62, 220, 222, 224
Astor, John Jacob, 55–56, 60–61, 296
Astor, John Jacob, IV, 296
Atherton, Gertrude, 204
Audubon, John James, 25, 63, 291, 295–96, 340
Audubon, Lucy, 63, 68–70
Audubon estate, 63, 68, 70, 179–81, *181*, 220, 295, 340
Audubon Terrace (Audubon Terrace Historic District), 102, *103*, 180–81
Audubon Theater and Ballroom, *122*, 122–23, 181, 195, 222–23
Aunt Len's Doll and Toy Museum, 254–56, *255*

Austin, Augustine, 176
The Autobiography of Malcolm X (Haley), 222

Bacharach, Burt, 250
Backer, George W., 98
Bailey, James A., 83, 97, 306
Bailey House, 302–11, *303, 304, 306, 307, 308, 309, 310, 311*, 338; deterioration of the, 264, 265, 282–83; purchased by the Blakes, 204–5; stained-glass windows, 83–84, 85, 305, 305–6
Baker, George F., Jr., 129
Baldwin, James, 188, 243–44
Baldwin, Ruth Standish, 125
Ballanchine, George, 228
Ballou, Freelove, 56, 72
Ballou, Reuben, 56, 74
bank (central), 41, 315, 342
Bank of Harlem, 112
bankruptcy, 65, 229
baptisms, 11, 47
Barbizon-Plaza Theatre, 203–4
Barnard College, 160, 163–65, 318
Barnard School for Boys, 97–98, *98*, 185
Barnes, Nicky, 232
Barnum & Bailey Circus, 83, 306, 338
Barracoon (Hurston), 164, 318
Barry, Rebecca Rego, 289
Barrymore, Ethel, 128
baseball (Polo Grounds), 90, 93, *101*, 101–2, 179, *181*, 286
Basie, Count, 211, 324
Battle of Brandywine (1777), 36
Battle of Harlem Heights, 32, 33, 34, 230, 319
Baulkman, Jasmine, 291–92
Bayard, William, Jr., 50–51
Bearden, Romare, 81, 148–49, 228
Bedford-Stuyvesant, Brooklyn, 18, 105, 240
Belafonte, Harry, 225, 253
Belcher, Henry F., (glass company), 83, 305–6
Bellow, Saul, 213
Benedict, Jesse, 70
Bennett, Gwendolyn, 316

INDEX · 385

Berkeley Journal of Sociology, 256–57
Bernard Shaw, George, 279
Berrian, John, 39
Berry, Halle, 317
Besonen, Julie, 291
Bethel, New York, 226
Better Call Saul (television show), 280
Beware (film), *191*, 191–92
B. F. Keith's Hamilton Theatre. *See* Hamilton Theatre
BHC. *See* Broadway Housing Community
Big Apple Jazz Tours, 331–32, *334*
The Big Sea (Hughes), 146, 164, 335
Billions (television show), 280
Birds of America (Audubon), 63
Black and Tan (short film), 166
Black bourgeoisie, 162, 215
Black Bourgeoisie (Frazier), 162
Black Boy (Wright), 214
Black Harlem, 95, 105, 166–67, 216, 230
Black Legal Rights Association, 61–62
Black Manhattan (Johnson), 120, 186–87, 246, 347
Black mecca, Harlem as a, 139–40, 246, 301
The Black New Yorkers (Schomburg Center for Research in Black Culture), 263
Black Panther Party, 224–25, 239
Blake, Marguerite, 204–5, 264, 282, 302–3, 309
Blake, Warren, 204–5, 264, 302–3, 309
Bledsoe, Julius, 160
Bloomingdale Road, 43, 45, 59, 339
Bochco, Steven, 250
Bogardus, Everadus, 11, 14
Bontemps, Arna, 100, 147, 153–54, *158*, 166–68, 201–2, 217–18, 243
Botkin, Benjamin, 213–14
boundaries, 9, 346–48; Harlem, 23–24, 58, 233–34, 241–46, 347; of Sugar Hill, 140–41, 326–27
Bowen, Elizabeth "Betsey" (Eliza Jumel), 56
Bowen, George Washington, 56, 72–74
Bowen, Mary, 57
Bowman's Grill, 198
Boys and Girls Club of Harlem, 225

Bradhurst, Augustus Maunsell, 40
Bradhurst, John Maunsell, 36
Bradhurst, Samuel, 31
Bradhurst, Samuel, II, 31
Bradhurst, Samuel, III, I, 30–31, 36, 39–42, 44–45, 50
Braithwaite, William Stanley, *174*
Brathwaite, Fred. *See* Fab 5 Freddy
Brede Wegh (Broadway), 339
Brevoort, John Hendricks van, 24
Bridges, Ruby, 338
Brill, Solomon, 127
British Army, 29, 32–37
British colonists, 18–20, 28, 30, 31–35, 339, 351
British loyalists, 26, 28, 39, 55, 57–58, 113
Broadway (road, Manhattan), 59, 242, 296–97, 339–40, 346
Broadway Housing Community (BHC), 337
Bronck, Jonas, 13–14, 336
Bronck, Peter Jonassen, 14
Bronx, New York City, 13–15, 102, 182, 232–33, 281, 336
Brooklyn, 18, 105, 136, 240
Brooks, Gwendolyn, 213
Brothers, Mizell, 328
Brown, Esther, 177–78
Brown, Louis, 133
Brown vs. the Board of Education, 176, 208, 210, 338
Bruynvisch (slave ship), 60
Buchanan, Bessie, 173
Burey, Vivian, 176
Burr, Aaron, 36–37, 47–51, *51*, 62, 285
Burton, Abraham, 261–62
Bussing, Arent Harmans, 5, 18, 24
Bustill, Cyrus, 179
Butler, Jacob, 87

Calloway, Cab, 175, 189
Canarsee Native Americans, 5
Canassatego (Chief of the Onondaga Nation), 22
Cane (Toomer), 152, 156
"Can You Go Home Again?" (Taylor, M.), 256–57

Carman, Richard, 63, 75, 295
Carmansville, 62–63, 65, 243, 295
Carmichael, Stokely, 298
Carnegie, Andrew, 112
Caro, Robert, 274
Carrion, Anthony, 283–84
Carroll, Diahann, 250
Carter, Eunice Hunton, 175
Carter, Jimmy, 240
Carver, George, 258–59
Caste (Wilkerson), 327
Catlett, Elizabeth, 292
Catsimatidis, John, 285–86
cattle, 12–13, 25, 336, 349–50
cemetery, 318; Trinity Church Cemetery, 25, 114, 291, 295–96; at Trinity Church Wall Street, 66, 286, 314–15, *315*
Census, U.S., 216, 239, 296
Central Harlem, 70, 185–86, 215, 221, 235, 243, 246, 297, 317, 339; Du Bois in, 143; Hamilton Heights compared to, 200–201; real estate development, 102, 106, 110; theater projects in, 126–27; Third Harlem Cultural Festival in, 226; Walker, A'Lelia, in, 158
Central Park, Manhattan, 74–75, 92, 100
Century Magazine, 156–57
Ceracchi, Giuseppe, 204, 277–78, *278*
Chapman, John Jay, 38
Charles II (King), 18
Chase, Mary Bowen, 67, 74
Chase, Nelson, 72, 74
Cheever, John, 213
Chernow, Ron, 35, 40–41, 204, 267, 285
children, 6, 11, 14, 31, 51–52, 56–57, 320, 337; Black, 51, 69, 144–45, 173, 177, *178*, *184*, 208; education for, 59, 67
Chinn, May Edward, 175
cholera, 60, 68
Choukroun, Sedric, 312, *324*
Christian IV (King), 12
Church, Angelica Schuyler, 50–52, 277, 313
Church, Frederic, 264
Church, John B., 42–43, 50, 53
Church of England, 22
Church of the Intercession, 72, 114, *114*

City College of New York, xii, 68, 106–8, *107*, 182, 226–27, 249, 251, 254, 291, 297, 341; Einstein at, 131–32, *132*
Civic Club, 155–57
civil rights, 144, 159, 208, 219, 337–38
Civil Rights Movement, 159, 205, 212, 219, 224–25, 240–41, 337–38
Civil War, U.S., 69–71, 79, 90
Clark, Gladys V., 206–7
Clark, Kenneth Bancroft, 173, 208
Clark, Mamie Phipps, 173, 208
class, 57; upper, 106, 110, 143, 163, 238; working, 62, 106, 115, 238–39. *See also* middle-class
Clinton, George, 36, 40
Clotilda (slave ship), 164, 318
Cohen, Daniel Marks, 285
College of the Sacred Heart, 68, 81–82
Colonial Park (Jackie Robinson Park), 183–84, *184*
Colonial Parkway Apartments. *See* 409 Edgecombe Avenue
colonization, European, 1–2, 5–76, 327, 349–51. *See also* Dutch colonists
The Color Purple (Walker, Alice), 317–18
Columbia College, 39, 51, 78, *See also* King's College; Columbia University
Columbia Daily Spectator (newspaper), 283
Columbia University, 26, 94, 120, 125–26, 130–131, 155, 160, 162, 173, 225, 226–27, 245, 254, 318. *See also* Columbia College; King's College)
Columbus, Christopher, 2
Community Board 9, Manhattan, 283–85, 291
Congo, Simon, 6
Congress, U.S., 192, 242–43
Congressional Public law 106-387, U.S., 343
Congreve, Charles, 24
Connecticut, 32, 102
The Conqueror (Atherton), 204
Continental Army, U.S., 31–37
Continental Congress, U.S., 31, 289–90, 315

INDEX · 387

Convent Avenue, Hamilton Heights, 28, 75, 82, 266, *266*, 297, 326, 330, 340–41; City College on, 107, *107*
Convent Avenue Baptist Church, 197
Coogan's Bluff, Harlem Heights, 101, 118, 246, 286
Coolidge, Calvin, 266
Cooper, Charles D., 49
Cooper, Myles, 30
Copeland, Calvin, 271
corruption, 15, 77, 266
Cortlandt, Philip Van, 39
Cotting, Amos, 81, 87–99
Cottman, Samuel J., 171
Cotton Club, 126, 134, 166, 170, 175
COVID-19 pandemic, 298–99, 312–13, 324, 331
crack cocaine, 233, 236
crime, 12, 217, 225, 256, 269; drugs and, 247, 300
crime rate, 218, 287, 298
Crisis (magazine), 144, 147–48
Crossing Broadway (Snyder), 242
Croton Aqueduct, 64–65, 68, 107, 182, 287–88
Croton River, 64–65
Crowder, Henry, 176
Crystal Bridges Museum, 277–78
Cullen, Countee, 153–54, *158*, 316–17
Cunard, Nancy, 176–77
Cunningham, Bill, 329
Curacao, 15–16
Curry, Izola Ware, 210
Curtis, Tony, 297

Dalley, George, 249
Dameron, Tadd, 189, 237
Dance Theatre of Harlem (DTH), xii, 228
Daniels, Raleigh Henry (Grange caretaker), 227–28, 248, 272, 276, 342
Daughters of the American Revolution, 87, 95, 113, 221, 321–22
David's Fly (now Manhattanville), 21
Davidson, Justin, 287
Davidson, Michael, 293
Davis, Miles, 326

Davis, Ossie, 219
Davis, Theodore, 64
"A Day in Harlem," 238
Daytonian in Manhattan (blog), 282
"Daytonian Manhattan" (Miller), 266–67
deaths, 11, 14, 31, 32, 151, 230–31, 241, 260, 293, 317; assassinations, 61–62, 220, 222, 224; cholera, 60, 68; De Forest, Jesse, 10; of Dyckman, J., 25; of Hamilton, A., 50–51, 53–54, 57, 59, 62–64, 314; of Jumel, E., 71–74; of Jumel, S., 62; King, Jr., 224; of Pieters, 16, 18; of Schultz, 199–200; of Washington, G., 44; of Williams, 237
debts, 41, 53–54, 68–69
Decker, Harold W., 180
Declaration of Independence, U.S., 289–90
Dee, Ruby, 219
The Deerfield (676 Riverside Drive), *190*
De Forest, Gertrude, 10–12
De Forest, Henrick, 4, 10–12
De Forest, Isaac, 4, 10–11, 14–15, 78–79, 275
De Forest, Jean, 3–4
De Forest, Jesse, 3–4, 10, 78, 80, 275, 341
De Forest, Robert W., 81
De Forest, William, 78–81, 87, 147, 275, 341
De Forest, William, Jr., 79, 81
De Halve Maen (ship), 3
Delany, Bessie, 162
Delany, Sadie, 162
Delany, Hubert T., *161*, 161–62, *162*, 202, 203
Delany, Willetta, 203
Delaware Tribe of Indians (Delaware Nation), 29
Delta Sigma Phi, City College, 297
demographics, 76, 104–10, 115, 149, 261, 301, 327; of African Americans in Harlem, 236–37, 268, 281, 296, 301; gentrification and, 237, 268–69, 290–91; racial, 132–33, 185–86, 197–98, 233; of white people in Harlem, 119–20, 237, 281, 296; around World War 1, 133

Department of Housing and Urban Development (HUD), U.S., 233–34, 240, 347
Department of Parks, New York City, 273
"Descendant" (documentary), 318
Description of New Netherland (Van der Donck), 9
Dewey, Thomas E., 175
DeWitt, Simeon, 58
Dickens, Charles, 296
Dickens, Tennyson, 296
Dinkins, David, 254, 292
discrimination, racial, 61–62, 96, 104, 106, 108–10, 195–96, 200–201
Division of Housing and Community Renewal, New York City, 281
doctors, Black, 71, 175
Doctorow, E.L., 336
Dodson, Howard, 253
Dolkart, Andrew S., 65
doll test, 173, 208. *See also* Clark, Mamie Phipps
Dominicans, 233, 268, 291
Dongan, Thomas, 20–21, 351
"Don't You Want to Be Free?" (play), 125
Do the Right Thing (film), 280
Dotoli, Vincent, 298
Douglas, Aaron, 157, *158*, *174*, 175–76, 316
Downey, Jacqueline, 245
Down the Up Staircase (Haynes, B.), 172
Draft Riots, New York City, 69–70
Drears, Al, 259–60
Drears, Rudel, 312, *324*
Drexler, Arthur, 250
Drucker, Stanley, 250
drugs, 194, 199, 205–6, 231–33, 236–37, 246–47, 269; crime and, 200
DTH. *See* Dance Theatre of Harlem
Duane, James, 40
Du Bois, W. E. B., 172, *174*, 175–76, 219, 258, 263, 299, 337–38; at Fisk University, 121; during Harlem Renaissance, 143–46, 156
Duke, Alma, 195
Duke of York, 18–20
Duke University, 237–38

Dumas, Alexandre, 335
Dutch colonists, 1–5, 7, 301; administration of, 6–8, 9, 11–12, 14–17; British colonists and, 18–21; murder of, 14, 16, 18; property ownership of, 12–18; slavery practiced by, 11–12, 16, 27
Dutch East India Company, 1–3
Dutch Revival architecture, 245
Dutch West India Company, 3–7, 12, 14–16, 18
Dwyer, Jim, 298
Dyckman, Gerrit, 24–25, 338
Dyckman, Jan, 5, 18, 20, 24, 27, 66, 338, 341

Eacker, George, 50
Earle, Ferdinand, 82, 94–96
Earle, Lillie, 82, 95, 113
East Harlem, 70, 92, 136, 202, 231, 258, 347
East Indies, 12
East River, 14, 18
Ebony magazine, 171
Edgecombe Avenue, Sugar Hill, 101, *140*, 215, 297, 337–38, 345–46, 348; John T. Brush Stairway on, 286–87, *287*
education, schools and, 106–107, 218–19, 226, 249–51, 254, 282, 297–98; African Free School, 40, 67; of Andrews, R., 149–50; college admissions in, 163–64; dropout rates, 215; of Dutch colonists, 25, 31; Haynes, G., on, 125–26, 144; HBCUs, 126, 144, 149, 162, 221; private, 59, 297–98; public, 59, 67, 69, 181, 225; segregation and, 338. *See also specific schools*
Eendracht (ship), 3
EEOC. *See* Equal Employment Opportunity Commission
1811 Street Grid, 100, 339, 347
Eight Men (Dutch colonist council), 14–15
Einstein, Albert, 131–32, *132*
Eisenhower, Dwight D., 221
the Eldorado, 174
electricity, electric lighting and, 77, 118, 190, 310
elevated train line, 76–77, 90

Eliot, Marjorie, 259–61, 311–12, *324*, 324–29, *328*, *329*
Elizabeth II (Queen), 206, *207*, 230, *231*
Ellington, Duke, 178, 187, 190, 193, 196, 262, 327, 332, 337, 348; moving to Sugar Hill, 133–34; Queen Elizabeth II and, 206, *207*
Ellington, Mercer, *174*
Ellison, Ralph, *205*, 212–14, 242, 288, 292, *293*, 296, 317, 338–39; at Tuskegee Institute, 184
Emancipation Proclamation, U.S., 60, 69, 84
Embury, Aymar, II, 183–84
The Emperor Jones (film), 166
enslaved people, 6, 11–12, 16, *17*, 27, 38, 40, 60, 256, 318–19, 327; FWP addressing, 213–14; kept by Hamilton, A., 53–54, 291; at the Morris-Jumel Mansion, 230, 321–23; in New Amsterdam, 16, *17*
Equal Employment Opportunity Commission (EEOC), U.S., 210
Ercole, Alcide, *72*, *73*
Esposito, Giancarlo, 280
Their Eyes Were Watching God (Hurston), 317

Fab 5 Freddy, 261, 299 (Fred Brathwaite)
Fame (film), 249
Fauset, Jessie Redmon, 147–48, 155, 158, *158*, *161*, 163–65, *165*, *169*
Federalist papers, 39, 315
Federalist style architecture, 40, 44–45, 271–72
Federal Writers Project (FWP), WPA, 184–85, 213–14
Fields, C. Virginia, 282
51 Hamilton Terrace, 98–99
The Final Judgement (silent film), 128
Fineberg, Mark, 250
Fiorello H. LaGuardia High School of Music & Art and Performing Arts, 218–19, 249, 251
Fire of Troy (vessel), 12
fires, 15, 65, 69, 81–82, 264, 282, 293
Fisher, Pearl, *161*
Fisher, Rudolph, *161*, *162*

Fiske, David, 66
Fisk University, 121, 135–36, 147–48, 162
555 Edgecombe Avenue, xi, 172, 243, 283, 311, 326–28, 337–38, 355; construction of, 115–16, *116*, *117*; Morris-Jumel Mansion and, 178–79, *179*; Parlor Jazz event at, 259–61, 312, *324*, 324–26
580 St. Nicholas Avenue, 149, 152–54, *154*, 158–59, *161*, 161–62, *162*, 339
Fletcher, Benjamin, 22
Florida, 241, 318, 333
Folts, James D., 23
Ford, Charles N., 190–91
Fordham gneiss (bedrock), 305
Fort Orange (now Albany), 1, 4–5, 9
Fortune, T. Thomas, 84
Fouchaux, Henri, 171–72
400 Convent Avenue, 177, *178*
400 Tavern Club, 196, 223, *294*, *294*
409 Edgecombe Avenue, 101, 117–18, *118*, 160, *174*, 174–76, 187, 199, 329, 337–38
411 Convent Avenue, 171–72, 261, 299
Fourteenth Amendment, U.S. Constitution, 208
Fox, William, 122
Foxx, Redd (John Elroy Sanford), 185, 295
France, 1, 3, 188, 259, 320
Francisco, John, 6
Frankfurter, Felix, 297
Franklin, Benjamin, 22, 37, 289
Fraunces, Samuel, 36–37
Fraunces Tavern, Manhattan, 36–37, 49
Frazier, E. Franklin, *161*, 162, *162*, 215
free formerly enslaved people, 16, 38, 54, 60, 66–67, 69, 164, 179, 103, 213–14, 321
Freeman, Elizabeth Northup, 73
French and Indian War, 26–27
Frise, Henry Harrison de, 206–7
Fulton, Robert, 66
FWP. *See* Federal Writers Project

Gallagher, Buell, 226
gambling, illegal, 198–200, 246–47
Garden of the Heavenly Rest Cemetery, Florida, 318
Garfield, James, 61–62

the Garrison (co-ops), Sugar Hill, 171
gas lighting, 77, 190, 310
genocide of Native Americans, 2, 14, 28
The Gentle Art of Wandering (Ryan), 286
gentrification in Harlem, 218, 238, 241–42, 271, 281–82, 298, 327, 346–47; demographics and, 237, 268–69, 290–91; Lee, S., on, 239–40; white people and, 171, 239–40, 256–58, 268–69
George (King), 225, 289, 339
George II (King), 25–26
George Washington Bowen vs. Nelson Chase, 72–74
German (language), 7
Germany, 3, 5–6
Gershwin, George, 136, 160, 166, 288, 316
Gershwin, Ira, 297
Ghana, 219
"ghettos," 216–18
Giants (baseball team), 101–2
Gibson, Althea, 210
Gill, Jonathan, 11, 14, 192
Gillespie, Dizzy, 189, 189–90, 237, 260
Ginsburg, Ruth Bader, 210
Glass, Ruth, 238
Glass, Will, 312
Glassie, Henry, 55
Glover, Savion, 332
Godfather (movie), 205–6
Goldsmith, Charles, 330
Gompert, William H., 182
Goodhue, Bertram Grosvenor, 114
Goodman, Benny, 190
Goodman, Wendy, 329
Gordone, Charles, 229, 260
Gorman, Cliff, 250
Gothic architecture, 4, 107, 107–8, 114, 182
Gottlieb, William P., 188, 189
Grace, Charles Manuel "Sweet Daddy," 173–74
Graham, Elaine, 325
Grammy Awards, 211
Gray, Christopher, 249, 251, 264
Graydon, Alexander, 35
Great Depression, U.S., 105, 168, 197, 202, 212–14

Great Fire of New York, 65
Great Migration, U.S., 95, 102–6, 121, 124, 202, 212, 214, 230, 241, 282; Harlem Renaissance following, 141, 167
Great Migration Series (paintings; Jacob Lawrence), *104*, 316
Green, Andrew Haswell, 92, 129
Green, Victor Hugo, 195–97, *197*, 337
The Green Book (Green), 196,*197*, 197–98, 337
Grinnell, George Bird, 69
Grinnell, William, 134
Gruchow, Emilie, 289–90
Guardian (newspaper), 268, 338
Guggenheim Fellowship, 168, 185

Hackman, Rose, 268
The Hague, 4, 17
Haley, Alex, 222
Hamilton (musical), 285–86, 313–14
Hamilton, Alexander, 23, 26, 34, 39, 41, 43–44, 203–4, 227, 277; duel with Burr, 47–51, *51*; estate of, 341–42, *342*; in Harlem, 30, 42–43, 242; in New Jersey, 29–30; as Secretary of the Treasury, 40–41, 87, 248, 315, 319; slaves kept by, 53–54, 291; tomb of, 314–15, *315*; Washington, G., and, 35–36, 40, 42, 46–47, 87–88, 315. *See also* Hamilton Grange
Hamilton, Alexander, Jr., 57, 62
Hamilton, Allan M., 30, 43, 53, 129
Hamilton, Eliza, 42, 47–54, 59, 63–64, 341–42
Hamilton, John Church, 63–64
Hamilton, Laurens Morgan, 227
Hamilton, Philip, 50
Hamilton Bank, 112, 353
Hamilton Free School, 59, 69
Hamilton Grange, *46*, 63–64, 67–68, 81, 265, 285–86, 345; American Scenic and Historic Preservation Society and, 126, 129–30; Daniels as the caretaker of, 227–28, 248, 272, 276, 342; deterioration of the, 91–92, 248–49, 251–52; Hamilton, A., developing, 43–49, 53; as a landmark, 204, 220, 251–52, 272–73;

National Park Service acquiring, 220–21; original furniture, *129*, 129–30, *130*; pianoforte in, 249, 259, 277, 313, *314*; relocation and reconstruction of the, 251–52, 271–78, *273*, *275*, *276*, *277*, *278*, *324*, 341–43; St. Luke's and, 86–89, *88*, *89*, 90–91, *91*, 94, 118–19
Hamilton Heights, Harlem, 8, 8–11, 9–11, 126–29, 136, 201, 265, 336–37, 345–48, *345–438*; City College moving to, *107*, 107–8; during the Civil Rights Movement, 225–26; Croton Aqueduct and, 64–66; demographics, 268, 291–92; drugs in, 200, 232–33; gentrification in, 241–42, 269, 271; property values in, 330–31; real estate development in, 78–80, 245–46; Rockwell, N., in, 95–97
Hamilton Heights and Sugar Hill (combined neighborhoods), 13, 233, 236, 244, 294, 345–48
Hamilton Heights Homeowners Association, 240, 244–45
Hamilton John C., 53
Hamilton Louisa Lee Schuyler, 129
Hamilton Terrace, 79, 87, 98, 128–29, 188, 227, 237, 258–59, 310; 51 Hamilton Terrace, 98–99; 72 Hamilton Terrace, 330–31, *331*
Hamilton Theatre, 126–28, *127*, *128*, *137*, *191*, 219–20, 264, 340; sold to RKO Pictures, 136–38, 164
Hammerstein, Oscar, 70–71, 126
Hammerstein II, Oscar, 126, 226
Hancock, John, 32–34
Hansberry, Lorraine, 139, 210–11, 317
Hansen, Austin, 142
Hanzal, David, *284*
Harlem. *See specific topics*
Harlem: Lost and Found (Adams), 259
Harlem: The Four Hundred Year History from Dutch Village to Capital of Black America (Gill), 11, 14
Harlem: The Making of a Ghetto; Negro New York 1890–1930 (Osofsky), 216, 218, 233–34, 347
"Harlem" (poem), 210–11
Harlem Academy, 297–98
Harlem Common Lands, 24, 242
Harlem Creek (Muscoota), 10, 20
Harlem Cultural Festival, Third, 226
Harlem Gas and Light Company, 77
Harlem Heights, 32, *33*, 35, 75, 78–79, 230, 319, 336–37
Harlem Hospital, 175
Harlem: Lost and Found (Adams, M.), 269
Harlem Opera House, 70–71
Harlem Renaissance, 122, *151*, 166–69, 239–41, 261, 312, 315–18, 334, 339; Andrews, R., during, 149–55, 160–61, *161*, 163, 253; Du Bois during, 143–48, 156; following World War I, 139–40; Hughes during, 145–47, 154–55, 160–61, *161*, *162*, 163–65, *165*, 166–69; literature, 139, 144–48, 151–57, 160, 201–2, 316–18, 334; WPA and, 141–42
Harlem River, 13, 336–37, 340, 346
Harlem River Drive, 118, 219, 241, *354*
Harlem River Speedway, 96, 118, 198, 289, *354*
Harlem School of the Arts (HSA), 221–22, 226–27, 234, 279–81, *280*
Harlem Shadows (*Spring in New Hampshire*) (McKay), 151–52
Harlem Urban Development Corporation, 233–34, 347
Harmon Foundation Awards, 144, 169, 172
Harmon, William E., 144
Harris, Lorena E. B., 312
Harris, Townsend, 106
Harvey, Charles T., 76
Hassan, Adeel, 109
Hauser, John, 245
Haynes, Bruce, 120, *146*, 172, 215–17, 225, 229
Haynes, Elizabeth Ross, 120, 144–45, *146*, 171
Haynes, George Edmund, 120, 144, *145*, 169, 171–72, 215, 217, 229, 261, 298; on education, 125–26; on the Great Migration, 121, 124
HBCUs. *See* Historically Black Colleges and Universities
Helm, Jasmine, 289–90
Hemings, Sally, 291

Hendelson, Brian, 290
Herb Alpert Harlem School of the Arts, 339
heroin, 233, 236
Higgins, Patience, 262
High Bridge, 65–66, *66*, 219, 286–88, *288*
Highbridge Park, 65, 286
High School of Music & Art (Hamilton Heights), 182–83, 218–19, 226–27, 249–51
High School of Performing Arts (Midtown), 218–19, 249
Historically Black Colleges and Universities (HBCUs), 126, 144, 149, 162, 164, 221
history, Black, 120, 135, 155, 162–63, 263, 298
History of Harlem: (New York): Its Origins and Early Annals (Riker), 3, 9, 13, 17, 23
A History of New York (Irving), 71
The History of St. Luke's Church in the City of New York 1820–1920 (Tuttle), 86–87
The History of the New World or Description of the West Indies (Laet), 5
Hoak, Adolph, 266
Holiday, Billie, xiv, 195, 231
Holley, Shiloh, 319–24
Holstein, Casper, 199–200
homeownership, 86, 106, 115, 120, 240–41, 254
homosexuality, 185, 198
Hoover, J. Edgar, 199
horse-drawn carriages, 61, 76–77, 111, 302, 339
Hosack, David, 50
housing, Harlem, 185–86, 202, 217, 225, 247–48, 337, 347; discrimination, 108–10; gentrification and, 239–40, 268–69, 281–82
Howe, Richard, 38
Howe, William, 32
Hoyte, Lenon Holder, 254–56, *255*
HSA. *See* Harlem School of the Arts
HUD. *See* Department of Housing and Urban Development
Hudde, Andreis, 12

Hudes, Quiara Alegría, 285
Hudson, Henry, 1, 340
Hudson Heights, Manhattan, 346
Hudson River, 18, 25, 340, 346
Hudson River Railroad Company, 68, 71
Hughes, Langston, *158*, 209, *209*, 243–44, 246, 263, 316–18, 334–35; during the Harlem Renaissance, 145–47, 154–55, 160–61, *161*, *162*, 163–65, *165*, 166–69; in the *New Republic*, 201; *Opportunity* featuring, 199; on Sugar Hill, 186
Hull, David, 56, 73
Huntington, Archer, 2–6, 102
Huntington, Charles Pratt, 102
Huntington, Collis, 102
Hurst, Fannie, 166
Hurston, Zora Neale, 144, 156, *158*, 160, 163–66, *165*, 167, 168–69, 213, 316–18
Hurtig & Seamons theater, 127, 170
Hutchison, Ray, 216–17

If We Must Die (McKay), 151
illegitimate birth, 26, 56–57, 63, 72
Imitation of Life (Hurst), 166
immigration, immigrants and, 16, 69–71, 92–93, 98, 132
independence, U.S., 37–38, 339
Indigenous people. *See* Native Americans
Infants of the Spring (Thurman), 169
infrastructure, 64, 68, 77, 180, 238, 257, 269, 273–74
Insell, Judith, 291
integration, racial, 136, 146, 172–74, 200
intelligentsia, Black, 143, 177, 340
Interborough Rapid Transit Company (IRT), 111–12
interracial relationships, 12, 176
In the Heights (musical), 285
"In the Land of Oo-Bla-Dee" (song), 190
Invisible Man (Ellison), 205, 212–14, 288, 292, 293, 296, 317, 339
Inwood, Manhattan, 243, 281, 336–37, 341; Spuyten Duyvil as, 15, 18, 20–21, 23–24, 26–27, 58, 61, 242, 347, 351
Irish immigrants, 69–70
IRT. *See* Interborough Rapid Transit Company

Irving, Washington, 71
Islam, 185, 222
Italian Americans, 70, 92, 202
Italy, 70, 216–17

Jackson, Mahalia, 219
Jackson, Michael, 271
James (Duke of York), 18–20
James A. Bailey Mansion, 83, 264, 338
Jan Dyckman of Harlem and His Descendants (Romer), 18
Jansen, Lawrence, 24
Javits, Jacob E., 205, 221
Jay, John, 37, 40
jazz, x, 222–23, 262–63, 327, 332, 332–33; Big Apple Jazz Tours, 331–32, *334*; jazz clubs, 193–98, 221–24, 261–63; performed by Eliot, 259–61, 311–12, *324*, 324–29, *328*, *329*; Williams, M., supporting, 188–90, 237–38. *See also specific jazz clubs*
Jazz Journalists Association, 324, 332
The Jazz Singer (film), 137
Jefferson, Thomas, 289, 291
Jencks, Lynn, 11
Jennings, Elizabeth, 61–62
Jennings, Thomas L., 61
Jennings v. Third Ave. Railroad Co., 62
Jet magazine, 195, 208
Jewish people, 70–71, 108, 133, 192, 196, 216–17
The Jews of Harlem (Gurock), 133
Jim Crow laws, 104–5, 200
Jimmie's Chicken Shack, 185, 222, 294
Jochem Pieters Hills, 13, 20–21, 23–24, 140, 336–37
Johnson, Billy, 261–62
Johnson, Charles S., 135–36, 147, 152, 162, *162*
Johnson, Fay, 258
Johnson, James Weldon, 120, 142, 152, 155–56, 160, 186–87, 191, 236, 246, 316–17, 347
Johnson, Marie, *161*
John T. Brush Stairway, 286–87, *287*
Jonah's Gourd Vine (Hurston), 169
Jones, James Earl, 125

Jones, Robert Earl, 125
Jordan, Louis, 191–92
Jordan, Philip D., 76
Joseph, Jamal, 225
Journal of Negro History, 318
Juilliard School of Music, 195, 250
Jumel, Eliza, 56–57, 62, 66–67, 73, 112–13, 296, 320–21; death of, 71–73. *See also* Bowen, Elizabeth "Betsey"
Jumel, Stephen, 56–57
Jumel Terrace Books, 299

Kane, Art, 238
Kasner, Edward, 131
Kato, Lisa, *300*
Katz, Barry, 291
Keck, Charles, 165
Keister, George, 127
Kellogg, Paul, 157
Kempton, Henry Craft, 171
Kennedy, John F., 137, 170, 220
Kennedy, Joseph, 137
Kennedy, Robert, 224
Kennedy Onassis, Jacqueline, 124, 283
Keno, Leigh, 290
Kent, James, 47–48
Kieft, Willem, 11–12, 14–15
Kiersen, John, 24
King, Martin Luther, Jr., 210, 219, 251
Kingsbridge Road (now St. Nicholas Avenue), 13, 26, 43, 47, 59, 338–39, 341, 354
King's College, 25–26, 30, 39. *See also* Columbia College, Columbia University
King's Way (road), 23–24, 339
Kirk, Andy, 173, 324, 326
Kissinger, Henry, 297
Kitt, Eartha, 209
the Knick, 71
Knickerbocker, 71 (sports teams, hotel, magazine)
Knickerbocker Hospital, 71, 231
Knowles, Charles, 34
Knox, Hugh, 29–30
Koch, Ed, 297
Koehler, Victor Hugo, 126–27
Koeppel, Gerard, 59

Kortright, Bastiaen, 24
Kossola, Oluale (Cudjo Lewis), 164, 318
Koussevitzky, Serge, 221
Ku Klux Klan, 144, 159
Kuyter, Jochem Pietersen. *See* Pieters, Jochem

Lafayette Theater, 126–27
La Guardia, Fiorello H., 170, 175, 182, 200–202, 249, 251
Laise, Steve, 276–77
Lamb, Thomas W., 122, 126–27
land grants, 5–8, 10, 12, 15–16, 19–20, 22
landmarks, New York City, 64, 247, 288–90, 310, 314, 337–41, 346–48, 346–48; Fraunces Tavern as a, 37; Hamilton Grange as a, 29, 204, 220, 251–52, 272–73; HSA as a, 280–81; James Bailey Mansion as a, 164; Schomburg Center as a, 334; 72 Hamilton Terrace as a, 330; for Strivers' Row, 111
land patents, 12, 20, 341, 349–51
Lange, Dorothea, 214
languages, 7, 23, 108, 131
Lanning, Helen, 161
Larsen, Nella, 147, 158, 168, 318
Latino people, 233, 268, 296
Lawrence, Hannah, 44
Lawrence, Jacob, 104, 316. *See also* Great Migration Series
Ledyard, Isaac, 39
Lee, Richard Henry, 290
Lee, Spike, 239–40, 280
LeGuen, Louis, 48–49
Leiden, Netherlands, 3–4, 78, 80, 341
Lenape Confederacy, 1, 5, 7–8, 23, 28–29, 301, 336 (also Lenape)
Lenox Presbyterian Church, 197
Lepore, Jill, 213–14
Lester, Julius, 243
Levine, John Michael, 26
Lewis, Cudjo (Kossola, Oluale)
Lewis, David Levering, 143, 159, 176
Lewis, John, 219
Lewis, Shari, 250
"Lift Every Voice and Sing" (Johnson), 156
"light-skinned" people, 152, 177, 318

Lincoln, Abraham, 90, 146
Lindsay, John, 224
Lindsay, Vachel, 163
literature, Harlem Renaissance, 139, 144–48, 151–57, 160, 201–2, 316–18, 334
The Living Is Easy (Hurston), 316
Little, Malcolm. *See* Malcolm X
Livingston, Robert R., 289–90
Livingston, William, 29–30
Locke, Alain, 147, 156–57, 169
Lopez, Julyssa, 311–12
Louis, Joe, 173, 326
loyalists, British, 26, 28, 39, 55, 57–58, 113
Lucas, Frank, 232
Luckey's Rendezvous (club), 194–98, 222
Lumet, Sidney, 218–19
Lunceford, Jimmie, 174, 175, 190
Lundy, Charles, 223
Lundy's (club), 223, 225, 294
lynchings, 70, 102–5, 159, 338

Macomb's Bridge (Bronx), 102
"Macy's Thanksgiving Day Parade" ("Macy's Christmas Parade"), 132–33
Magazine Antiques, 276–77, 286
Magnetic City (Davidson), 287
Mahicanituk (river), 3, 340
Malcolm X (Malcolm Little), 123, 185, 222, 295
Manhattan, 3–8, 18–19, 336–37, 349–51; schist, 259, 304–5; street grid implemented in, 57–59, 74–75, 81–82, 85–86, 92. *See also specific topics*
Manhattan Elevated Railroad Company, 90
Manhattan Hospital, 71
Manhattanville, 21, 25, 44, 71, 100, 242–43, 269, 285
Mannahatta (Sanderson), 2
Manumission Society, New York, 40, 47, 53, 227
March on Washington, 219
Mark Four Bar (Mark IV), 232, 261
Markowitz, Michael, 68
marriage, 11, 26, 30–31, 60, 202
Marsalis, Wynton, 332
Marshall, Thurgood, 101, 174, 176, 208, 210, 338

Mason, John, 61
Maunsell, John, 26–28
Maunsell Place (Pinehurst Mansion), 28, 39–40, 44, 48, 82, 274, 340
Mauro, Nicholas, 312, 324
Mayflower (ship), 4, 57
Maynor, Dorothy, 221–22, 234, 279
McClellan, George, 111
McComb, John, 44, 88, 272
McHenry, James, 54
McKay, Claude, 151–52, *158*, 163, 316–17
McKim, Mead & White (architecture firm), 112
McLaughlin, Caleb, 280
McNeil, David "Turk", ix, 223, 355
Melichar, Ronald, 245
Merzlyakov, Vladimir, 312–13
Messenger (magazine), 144
Metropolitan Hospital, 231
Mexico, 146, 148, 188, 335
Mey, Cornelis Jacobson, 5–6
Meyer, Adolph, 5, 18, 20, 23
Meyer, Annie Nathan, 160, 163
Mezes, Sidney E., 132
middle-class, 62, 78, 96, 110, 147, 151, 172; Black, 141, 162–63, 215–16, 257–59
Mi'kmaq people. *See* Algonquin Nation
Miller, Tom, 266–67, *303*
"Minnie's Land" (Audubon estate), 63, 68, 70, 179–80, 220, 295, 340
Minton's (club), xiv, 189–90
Minuit, Peter, 6–9
Miranda, Lin-Manuel, xiii, 285
Mitchell, Arthur, 221, 225, 228
mixed-race people, 36–37, 135, 149–50, 166
Mohican tribe, 5
Mollenkopf, John, 105
Monk, Thelonious, xiv, 189, 237–38, 326
Montagne, Jean de la, 4, 10–12, 15, 24
Montgomery, Alabama, 210
Montgomery, Barbara, 325, 325–26
Moore, Clement Clarke, xv, 27, 296
Morgan, J. P., 129, 130, 204
Morgan, Rose, 326
Morningside Heights, 10, 94, 243, 269, 285
Morris, Henry Gage, 56

Morris, Mary Philipse, 26–27, 32, 55, 113
Morris, Roger, 26–27, 32–33, 52, 58, 113–14, 242
Morris-Jumel Mansion, 72–74, 231, *231*, 252, 285, 289–90, 348; architecture of the, *319*, 319–24, *320*, *321*, *322*, *323*, *324*; Battle of Harlem Heights anniversary at, 230; Eliot performing at the, 260–61, 327, *328*; enslaved people at the, 230, 321–23; New York City managing, 95, 112–13; Northup, A., at, 66–67; renovations of the, 82, 320; Washington Headquarters Association and, 206–7
Morrison, Toni, 234–35, 318
Morse, Samuel F. B., 63
Moses, Robert, 272–74
Moss, Benjamin S., 127
Motherless Brooklyn (movie), 293
Mount Morris. *See* Roger Morris estate
movie halls, 126–28, 136–38
Mowbray, Anthony, 78–80
Mowbray, William E., 80, 245
Mr. Daniels and the Grange (Sloane, Anthony), 227, 248, 272
Muhammad, Elijah, 222
Mulligan, Terry Baker, 206, 215
Munsee (Native Americans), 1, 5, 7, 23, 29
murders, 18, 61–62, 151, 269, 336; of Native Americans, 14, 16, 28
Murray, Anna Pauline "Pauli", 209, 209–10
Museum of Modern Art, 250
Museum of the American Indian, Smithsonian, 7, 102
music, 221–24, 223, 226, 250, 262, 291, 293–94, 337; drugs and, 200, 206; education, 182–83; by Eliot, 259–61, 311–12, 324, 324–29, *328*, *329*; by Ellington, D., 133–34; by Gershwin, 136, 288; by Williams, 237–38. *See also* jazz; *specific musicians*
My Name Is Pauli Murray (documentary), 210
My Sister, My Sister (play), 325

NAACP. *See* National Association for the Advancement of Colored People

Nagel, Jan, 20
Nagel, John, 24
Nail, John E., 110
names and naming of New York, 1, 9–10, 231–32, 242, 253, 339; in Hamilton Heights, 128–29; Sugar Hill in, 345–46
Nance, Ethel Ray, 152–54, 158, 160, *161*, 317, 339
National Association for the Advancement of Colored People (NAACP), 105, 140, 159, 176, 219, 338
National Historic Landmarks, U.S., 220, 248–49, 251, 288, 293
National Memorial African Bookstore, 209, *209*
National Museum of African American History & Culture, 337
National Organization for Women (NOW), 210
National Park Service, U.S., 220–21, 249, 251–52, 271–74, 276–77; National Historic Landmarks, 248, 288, 293
National Urban League, 121, 125, 134, 152, 172, 215, 217, 229, 288, 316
Nation of Islam, 222
Native Americans, 1–3, 9, 92–93, 291, 327, 336, 339; displacement of, 13–14, 23, 28–29, 81; Dutch colonists and, 7, 13–16, 18; land of, 7–8, 22–23, 30
Native New Yorkers: The Legacy of the Algonquin People of New York (Pritchard), 1, 23, 28–29, 253, 302
Native Son (Wright), 188, 212, 317
Nazareth Deliverance Spiritual Church, 330
NEC. *See* Negro Ensemble Company
The Negro at Work in New York City (Haynes, G.), 125
Negro Ensemble Company (NEC), 280
The Negro Motorist Green Book (Green), 195–97, *197*
Negro Renaissance. *See* Harlem Renaissance
"The Negro Speaks of Rivers" (Hughes), 334
Nelms, Georgette, 252
Netherlands, 3–5, 16, 241, 341. *See also* Dutch colonists

New Amsterdam, 1, 4–5, 10, 13, 80–81, 349–51; administration of, 6–8, 9, 11–12, 14–16; British takeover of, 18–19; slavery in, 16–17, *17*
New Haarlem, 17–20, 40
New Jersey, 29–30, 38, 50, 63, 102, 147, 195, 199–200
The New Negro (Locke), 157
New Netherland, 1, 4, 7, 9–10, 12, 15, 17–18, 79, 349
New Republic, 186, 201
Newton, Huey P., 224
New York (magazine), 283
New York Age (newspaper), 84–85, 108, 333
New York Amsterdam News, 163, 204, 208, 230
New York and Harlem Railroad, 61
New York City. *See specific topics*
New York City Ballet, 228
New Yorker Staats Zeitung (newspaper), 108
New York Evening Post (newspaper), 49, 315
New York Freeman, 84–85
New York Globe, 84–85
New York Herald Tribune, 157
New York Landmarks Preservation Commission, 347–48
New-York Packet (newspaper), 39
New York Post, 200
New York Public Library, 112, 149–51, *151*, 228–29, 253, 277, 339; Schomburg Center for Research in Black Culture, 134–35, 163, 229, 253–54, 334
New York State Archives, 12, 23
New York Times, 2, 78, 241, 254, 261, 291, 298–99, 329; Baldwin in the, 243; on gentrification, 269, 271; on the Hamilton Grange, 248–49, 251–52; on James Bailey Mansion fire, 264; on the lottery, 246–47; on Manhattan Hospital, 71; on Payton, Jr., 108–9; on real estate, 245–46; on school admissions, 183; on Williams, 237
New York Yankees, 101–2
Nicholson, David, 317–18
Nicolls, Richard, 18–19

INDEX · 397

Nicolls Patent (1666), 20–21
Nieuw Nederland (ship), 3, 5–6
Nigger Heaven (Vechten), 153
Ninham-Wampage (Wampage II), 30
90 Edgecombe Avenue, 159–60, 175
Nomad Concepts LLC, 273
No Place to Be Somebody (play), 229, 260
Nort, Sydney Van, 106, 131
North Carolina, 237–38
Northup, Anne, 66–67, 73–74, 323
Northup, Solomon, 67, 323
Norton, Edward, 293
Norwood, Cornelia, 39
Not without Laughter (Hughes), 169
NOW. *See* National Organization for Women

Obama, Barack, 271, 285, 338
Oblienis, Hendrick van, 24
Oblienis, Peter van, 24
Old Post Road, 339
Old Stone House (St. Nicholas Avenue), 24–25, 274, 354
Old Yeller (movie), 284–85
Oma Shop, 353
O'Neill, Eugene, 160
Onondaga Nation, 22
Opportunity (National Urban League magazine), 144, 147, 152–53, 155, 169, 199, 316
Order of the Patentees of the Township of New Haarlem (1691), 40
Orwell, George, 212
Osofsky, Gilbert, 216, 218, 233–34, 347
Oswarld, Richard, 36, 233–34
Otterspoor, New Amsterdam, 16–17
Ovington, Mary White, 105
Owen, Chandler, 144

Page, Harvey L., 79
Panama Canal, 190–91
Panic of 1873, 78, 106
Panther Baby (Joseph), 225
Paris, France, 36, 37, 57, 148, 188, 335
Parker, Charlie, 185, 189, 237, 295
Parker, Henry C., 110
Parkinson, Leonard, 56

Parks, Rosa, 210
Parlor Jazz (event), 555 Edgecombe Avenue, 311–12, *324*, 324–25
Parsons, Samuel, Jr., 100–101
Passing (Larsen), 168, 318
passing for white, skin color and, 159–60, 166, 168, 318
Pavlo, Hattie Mae, 203–4
Payton, Philip A., Jr., 108–11, *109*
Pearson, Isaac, 64
Pell, Thomas, 30–31
Pendleton, Edmund, 290
Pendleton, Nathaniel, 50, 53
Perry, Oliver "Doc," 133
Peters, Brock, 250
Petry, Ann, 316
Philadelphia, Pennsylvania, ix, 42–44, 63, 133, 156, 195, 197, 271
"The Philadelphia Negro" (Du Bois), 121
Philipse, Frederick, 32
Philipse, Frederick, III, 26
Philipse, Mary. *See* Morris, Mary Philipse
photography, 80, 179, 188, 209, 214, 238, 316; during Harlem Renaissance, 142, *161, 162, 165*
pianoforte (instrument), 249, 259, 277, 313, *314*
Pieters, Jochem (Jochem Pietersen Kuyter), 12–16, 18, 23, 349
Pinehurst estate (Maunsell Place), Hamilton Heights, 28, 39–40, 44, 48, 82, 274, 340
Pink Angel Bar, 197–98
Plessy v. Ferguson, 208, 210
Pochoda, Elizabeth, 276–77, 286
Poe, Edgar Allan, 288
Poitier, Sidney, 211
Polatnick, Gordon, 332–33, *334*
police, 132, 201, 205, 224–25, 232, 254
Polo Grounds, 90, 93, *101*, 101–2, 179, *181*, 286
Popel, Esther, *161*
"Porgy and Bess" (opera), 316
Portuguese, Anthony, 6
Post, George B., 106–7
Potter, Cornelis De, 16
poverty, 53, 70, 214, 221, 317
Powell, Adam Clayton, Jr., 171, 192, 200

Powell, Cielan Bethan, 187
Powell, Colin, 297
Powell, Gladys Leah, 175
Powell-Savory Corporation, 187
power, 18, 41, 77, 222, 229; of Moses, 273; of Stuyvesant, 15
The Power Broker (Caro), 274
prejudice, racial, 96, 110, 149
Prince Philip, duke of Edinburgh, 230–31
Pritchard, Evan T., 1, 23, 28–29, 253, 302
private schools, 59, 97–98, 98, 297–98
"The Problem We All Live With" (Rockwell painting), 338
Prohibition era, 134, 185, 199, 223
property: ownership, 12, 38–39, 254; rights, 5–8, 11, 19
property values, 22, 109, 120, 238, 330–31, 346; gentrification and, 237–38, 281, 298
Pryor, Richard, 271
public schools, 59, 67, 69, 181, 225
Public Theater, Manhattan, 285, 313
public transportation, 61–62, 76–77, 90; subway system as, 105, 109, 111–12, 134, 135, 187, 193, 332, 337
Puerto Ricans, 135, 202, 233, 268, 347
Pyle, Howard, 17

Quakers, 40, 44
Quicksand (Larsen), 168

race, 38, 69–70, 165–66, 242, 244, 256–58, 297; demographics and, 132–33, 185–86, 197–98, 233; gentrification and, 256–58; mixed-race people and, 36–37, 135, 149–50, 166; skin color and, 105, 149–50, 152, 166, 177, 318
racism, 37, 70, 108–10, 208, 230, 291, 298, 338; Frazier on, 162; Great Migration in response to, 102–4; reverse, 166; of Taylor, J., 119–20
Radio-Keith-Orpheum (RKO Pictures), 283–85; Hamilton Theatre sold to, 136–38, 264
railroads, 61, 90, 102; Hudson River Railroad Company, 68, 71
A Raisin in the Sun (play), 210–11, 317

Ralph Ellison Memorial Park, Riverside Drive, 331–32
Randolph, A. Philip, 144, 219
Rangel, Charles, 249, 252, 282
Raphael, Don, 195
Rashad, Condola Phylea, 280
Ratliff, Ben, 261–62
real estate market, developers and, 62, 191, 235, 245–46, 282–84, 298, 330, 346; Astor, John Jacob, and, 60–61; Central Harlem, 106, 110; De Forest, W., and, 78–80; following the Great Migration, 107–10; gentrification and, 238–42; Grace and, 173–74; post–Revolutionary War, 38–45, 55–56
the Red Rooster, 293
"the red summer," 151
Reed, Samuel B., 83
Reed v. Reed, 210
Regina Anderson Andrews (Whitmire), 149
Reid, Angella C., 249
Reiss, Winold, 316
religion, 3, 15, 22, 68, 97. *See also specific religions*
Renaissance Revival architecture, 127, 127–28, 172
renovations, 225, 245–46, 279–80, 286–87; of the Bailey House, 283, 305; Hamilton Grange, 251–52, 274–78, 312–13; of the Morris-Jumel Mansion, 82, 320
Rensselaerswyck (ship), 10
rent-control laws, 200
rent parties, Harlem, 149, 259
Renwick, James, Jr., 66
restoration, 269; Bailey House, 283, 302–10; of the Hamilton Grange, 245, 252, 271–78, 286, 312–13; of the Roger Morris house, 57
reverse racism, 166
revitalization programs, 238–39, 245
Revolutionary War, 31–37, 38–39, 44, 49, 55, 95, 179, 230, 240, 261, 342; Hamilton, A., and, 41, 315, 319
Reynolds, Maria, 42
Reynolds Pamphlet (Hamilton, A.), 42
"Rhapsody in Blue" (song), 136, 288

rights, 9, 40, 67–68; of African Americans, 61–62; civil, 144, 159, 208, 219, 337–38; property, 5–8, 11, 19
Riker, James, 3, 9, 13, 17, 23
The River Niger (play), 280
Riverside Drive (Manhattan), 179, 190, 242, 297, 331–32, 340
RKO Pictures. *See* Radio-Keith-Orpheum
Roberts, Charles Luckeyth "Luckey," 194–95
Robeson, Eslanda Goode, 173
Robeson, Paul, 173, 179, 324
Rocheleau, Paul, 270, 356
Rockwell, Norman, 95–97, 288, 338
Rockwell, William, 62
Rodenburg, Lucas, 16
Rodgers & Hammerstein, 126
Rodgers, Richard, 226
Roger Morris Apartments. *See* 555 Edgecombe Avenue
Roger Morris estate, 26–28, 31–35, 39–41, 44, 55, 115, 242–43, 341; Astor, John Jacob, and, 60–61; Jumel, S., purchase of, 57. *See also* Morris-Jumel Mansion
Rogers, Timmie "Oh Yeah," 203
Rollins, Sonny, 326
Romer, Dorothea H., 18
Roosevelt, Eleanor, 202–3, 221–22
Roosevelt, Franklin Delano, 222, 266–67
Roosevelt, Theodore, 69
Rose, Ernestine, 134, 150–51, *151*
Rose Morgan House of Beauty, 173
Rosenwald Foundation Grant, 316
Rosenwald, Julius, 144
Rosewood, Florida, 241
row houses, 83, 106, 159, 247–48, *248*
The Royal Tenenbaums (film), 266–67, 330–31, 340
Russia, 151–52
Rustin, Bayard, 219
Rutherfurd, John, 58
Ryan, David, 286

Sager, Carole Bayer, 250
Salk, Jonas, 297
Sanderson, Eric W., 2
sanitation, 68, 200, 202

Sarnoff, David, 137
Savage, Augusta, 316
Savory, Phillip M. H., 187
Schaffer, Richard, 238–40
Schaghen, Peter, 7
Schieffelin, Jacob, 25, 43–44
schist, Manhattan (bedrock), 259, 304–5
Schomburg, Arturo Alfonso, 134–36, 157, 177
Schomburg Center for Research in Black Culture, New York Public Library, 134–35, 163, 229, 253–54, 334
Schultz, Dutch (gangster), 199
Schuyler, Elizabeth, 40 (see also Eliza Hamilton)
Schuyler, Philip, 40, 45–46, 129
Schwartz & Gross (architecture firm), 115, 117
Scott, Clarissa, *161*
Scott-Heron, Gil, 328
Seale, Bobby, 224
Seamon's Music Hall, 127
Secretary of the Treasury, Hamilton, A., as, 40–42, 87, 248, 315, 319
segregation, racial, 61–62, 106, 121, 195–96, 200, 210, 229, 337; "ghettos" and, 216–18; Marshall addressing, 208; during the Prohibition era, 134; school, 69, 176, 338
self-segregation, 217
Serfilippi, Jessie, 53
72 Hamilton Terrace, 330–31, *331*
721 Club, 185, 222
730 Riverside Drive, 205, 292
749 St. Nicholas Avenue, 184, 338–39
773 St. Nicholas Avenue, 196–98, 222
Seymann, Jerrold, 11
Shakur, Afeni, 224–25
Shakur, Tupac, 225
sharecropping, 104, 124, 212
Shaw, George Bernard, 279
Shelton, William Henry, 31–32, 34, 71–72, 74, 112–13, 322
Sherman, Roger, 289
Sherman's Creek, 20
Shook, Karel, 228
Showboat (musical/film), 160, 173

silent films, 128, 340
Silver Dollar Café, 185
Simon, Henry, 253
Simone, Nina, xiv, 139, 226
Sister's Uptown Bookstore and Cultural Center, 301
63 Hamilton Terrace, Hamilton Heights, 188, 237
676 Riverside Drive (The Deerfield), 190
skin color, 105, 149–50, 152, 159, 163, 166, 177, 318; "light-skinned" people and, 152, 177, 318; passing for white and, 159–60, 166, 168, 318
Slave Narratives, Federal Writers Project (FWP), 213
slavery, 38–40, 53–54, 67, 291, 321–23; Dutch colonists practicing, 11–12, 16, 27; Federal Writers Project (FWP) addressing, 213–14. *See also* enslaved Africans
slave trade, 16, 27, 164
Slesin, Suzanne, 241, 245–46, 255, 298
Sloane, Eric, 227–28, 248–49, 251, 272, 276
smallpox, 31
Smith, John Howard, 72
Smith, Neil, 238
Smith College, 175
Snyder, Robert W., 242–44
Society of the Cincinnati, 49
Society of the Sacred Heart, 68
sociology, 120–21, 124, 141, 143–44, 162, 229, 241
Sons of Liberty, 29, 36–37
Sorbonne, 148, 250
Sotheby's, 255, 256, 278, 330, 356
soul food, 220, 271, 281
The Souls of Black Folk (Du Bois), 121, 258
South (rural), U.S., 102–5, 121, 125, 141, 159
Soviet Union, 228
Spain, 6, 17, 216
Spain, Earl, 222
Spain, Esther, 262
Spanish Harlem, 70, 136, 202, 291–92, 347

Spanish War, 4
speakeasies, 97, 134, 185, 194, 223, 246, 292
Spence-Chapin Agency, 202–3
Spollen, Jenny, 283, 302–3, 307, 309, 311, 338
Spollen, Martin, 265, 283, 302–5, 305, 307–11, 338
Spring in New Hampshire (*Harlem Shadows*) (McKay), 151–52
Spuyten Duyvil (Inwood), 15, 18, 20–21, 23–24, 26–27, 58, 61, 242, 347, 351
St. Anne's Church, 93–94
St. Clair, Stephanie, 199–200
St. James Presbyterian Church, 197, 221
St. Luke's Episcopal Church, 68, 93–94, 197, 220, 247, 265–66, 289, 341; Hamilton Grange and, 86–89, 88, 89–91, 91, 94, 118–19, 129
St. Nicholas Avenue, Hamilton Heights, 12, 26, 43, 47, 59, 338–39, 345–47, 354; drugs and, 247; Eliot on, 326; HSA on, 279–80; land patents around, 20; music and jazz clubs on, 158, 185, 193–98, 221–24, 261–63; during the Revolutionary War, 319; in street grid system, 74–75
St. Nicholas Park (Manhattan), 100–101, 126, 152, 265, 271–72, 274, 339; Hamilton Grange moved to, 252, 271–74, 341–43, 342
St. Nick's Pub, Sugar Hill, 222, 261–62, 262, 293, 326, 331–33, 334
St. Patrick's Cathedral, 66, 237
stained-glass windows, 56, 83–84, 85, 305, 305–6
Stamp Act of 1765, 29
statue, Alexander Hamilton, 130–31, 131, 251, 265, 341
Steigman, Benjamin, 183
Stevens, Ebenezer, 43
Stickley, Julia Ward, 276
Stoutenburgh, Isaac, 39
Stowe, Harriet Beecher, 69
Stranger Things (Netflix series), 280
Strayhorn, Billy, 174, 187, 332, 337, 340–41
The Street (Petry), 316

INDEX · 401

street grid, New York City, 57–59, 74–75, 81–82, 85–86, 92; 1811 Street Grid, 100, 339, 347
Stride toward Freedom (King Jr.), 210
Strivers' Row, 110–11, 287
Stuart, Gilbert, 277–78
Student Nonviolent Coordinating Committee, 219
Studio Museum, Harlem, 228, 316
Stuyvesant, Peter, 15–19
subway system, 105, 109, 111–12, 134, *135*, 187, 193, 332, 337
Sugar Hill (musical), 171
Sugar Hill, Harlem, 171, 186, 193–94, 219, 243–44, 245–348; drugs in, 246; Eliot on, 326–27; Ellington, D., moving to, 133–34; following World War I, 139–41; Harlem Renaissance and, 143–44, 163. *See specific streets, buildings*
Sugar Hill Children's Museum of Art & Storytelling, BHC, 337
Sugar Hill Jazz Festival, Fifth Annual (2021), 328
Sugar Hill Luminaries Lawn, 283, 328
sugar trade, 16
Sula (Morrison), 234
Summer of Soul (documentary), 226
Supreme Court, Brooklyn, 62
Supreme Court, U.S., 72, 74, 102, 173, 176, 208, 210, 297, 338
Survey Graphic magazine, 157
Suyat, Cecilia, 176
"Swanee" (song), 126, 288
Swing Era, 190
Swits, Claes Cornelissen, 14
syphilis, 216–17

Tackamack (Sachem), 13
"Take the A Train" (song), 332
"Talented Tenth" (Du Bois concept), 143, 148, 176, 279
Talley, Arlene, 262
Tatum, Art, 185
taxes, 20, 29, 238, 282, 315
Tayler, John, 49
Taylor, John G., 119
Taylor, Karen D., 328

Taylor, Monique D., 256–58
Taylor, Yuval, 164
Teachers Training College, 68
telegraph, 63
Terkel, Studs, 213
That's What Friends Are For (song), 250
There Is Confusion (Fauset), 155
This Was Harlem (Anderson, J.), 242
Thometz, Kurt, 298–99
Thompson, Ahmir"Questlove," 226
315 Convent Avenue, 187, *248*, 340–41
336 Convent Avenue mansion, 266–67, *267*
339 Convent Avenue, 266, *266*
Thurman, Wallace, *158*, 169
Titanic, 296
To Kill a Mockingbird (film), 250
Toomer, Jean, 152–53, 156, *158*, 176
topography, 24, 58–59, 92, 100–101, 242
Toscanini, Arturo, 222
tourism, 178, 278, 285–86
Town of Harlem Corporation, 23–24, 77–78
Townsend Harris Hall, 126
trade, 13, 16, 18; drug, 232–33, 236–37, 269; slave, 16, 27, 164
Training School for Teachers, New York, 182, *182–83*
Treasury Department, U.S., 40–42, 87, *248*, 315, 319
Treaty of Paris, 36–37
Trinity Church Cemetery and Mausoleum (Hamilton Heights), 25–26, 68, 114, 291, 295–96
Trinity Church Wall Street, 22, 47, 52, 86; Cemetery, 66, 286, 314–15, *315*
"Triple Nickel" Paul Robeson Building. *See* 555 Edgecombe Avenue
Troger's Hotel, 93, *93*, 289
Truman, Harry, 221
Trumbull, John, 277
Tsion Cafe, 294–95, *295*
Tubman, Harriet, 286
Tucker, Luella, *161*
Tulsa, Oklahoma, 241
Turing, Alan, 297
Turner, Lana, 329–30
Tuskegee Institute, 162, 164–65, *165*, 184

Tuttle, Charles Henry, 266
Tuttle, Henry Croswell, 87
Tuttle, Isaac (Reverend), 87, 90–92, 94, 228, 252, 266, 274, 341
Tuttle, Penelope T. Sturges Cook (Mrs. H. Croswell Tuttle), 86–87
Tutu, Desmond, 271
Tweed, William Magear "Boss," 77
12 Million Black Voices (Wright), 214
Twelve Years a Slave (Northup, S.), 67, 323
"The Two Harlems" (Bontemps), 166–68
"Two Million Negro Women at Work" (Haynes, E.), 120

Unalachtigo (Native Americans), 7
Unami (Native Americans), 1, 5, 7
Uncle Tom's Cabin (Stowe), 69
Uncle Tom's Children (Wright), 185
Underground Railroad, 69
Union Army, 69–71, 179
United House of Prayer for all People, 174
United Mutual Benefit Association, 191
United States (U.S.): Census, 216, 239, 296; Civil Rights Movement, 159, 205, 212, 219, 224–25, 240–41, 337–38; Civil War, 69–71, 79, 90; Congress, 192, 242–43; Emancipation Proclamation, 60, 84; HUD, 233–34, 240, 347; independence, 37, 38, 339; National Historic Landmarks, 220, 248–49, 251, 288, 293; Prohibition era, 134, 185, 199, 223; Supreme Court, 72, 74, 102, 173, 176, 208, 210, 297, 338; Treasury Department, 40–42, 87, 248, 315, 319. *See also* National Park Service, U.S.
Unsung Heroes (Haynes, E.), 144–45
upper-class, 106, 110, 143, 163, 238
Uptown Chamber of Commerce, 191
Uptown Jubilee (television show), 203
urbanization, 80, 103–5, 183, 219
U.S. *See* United States

vaccines, 71
Van der Donck, Adriaen, 9–10
Van der Zee, Donna Mussenden, 316
Van der Zee, James, 142, 316

Van Doren, Carl, 156–57
Van Kuelen, Matthys Jansen
Van Rensselaer, Kiliaen, 9–10
Van Rensselaer, Maunsell, 83
Van Rensselaer House, 83
Van Twiller, Wouter, 9, 12
Van Vechten, Carl, 153, 160
vaudeville, 126–28, 136–37, 340
Verhulst, Willem, 6
Vermont Telegraph, 65
Verrazzano, Giovanni da, 1
Verveelen, Johannes, 20
Vespucci, Amerigo, 2
Vietnam War, 224, 226
violence, 19–20, 124, 199–201 123, 222, 241; between Dutch colonists and Native Americans, 14–16, 18, 28
Virginia, 4, 11, 36, 47
"A Visit from St. Nicholas" (Moore), 27, 296

Waldron, Jonathan, 24
Waldron, Mal, 260
Waldron, Samuel, 24
Walker, A'Lelia, 158–59, 166, 345–46
Walker, Alice, 139, 317–18
Walker, George, 204
Wall, Cheryl, 317
Walloon (now Belgium), 3–5, 341
Wampage I (Chief), 30
Wampage II, 30
war, 14–15, 19–20, 202; French and Indian War, 26–27; U.S. Civil War, 69–70; Vietnam War, 224, 226; World War I, 114, 133, 136, 139–41, 227. *See also* Revolutionary War
Ward, Carol, 82, 113, 230, 289–90, 322
Ward, William G., 67–68, 78, 276
The Warmth of Other Suns (Wilkerson), 70, 186, 214
Washington, Booker T., 121, 144, 165
Washington, D.C., 64, 67, 133, 155, 208, 219, 337
Washington, Fredi, 166
Washington, George, 26, 31–32, 37, 44, 51–52, 57, 114, 207, 240, 261, 277–78, 289, 319, 323; Continental Army led by,

31–37; Hamilton, A., and, 35–36, 40-42, 46–47, 87–88, 315
Washington Heights, Manhattan, x, 233, 241–44, 281, 326, 336–37, 346, 348; street grid impacting, 58–59 75
Washington Heights Athenaeum, 78
Washington Heights Baptist Church, 197
Washington Theatre (Hamilton Heights), 126
Waters, Ethel, 152–53
Waters, Sylvia, 245
The Waterworks (Doctorow), 336
Watkins, John, 26–28
Watkins, Samuel, 41–42
"The Weary Blues" (Johnson, J.), 160
The Wedding (West), 316
Weeks, Ezra, 44
Welch, Alexander McMillan, 88
Wessner, Gregory, 85–86
West, Dorothy, 316, 317
Westchester County, New York, 30, 64–65
West Harlem, 30, 70, 242–43, 285, 345. *See also specific neighborhoods*
West Indies, 15, 26, 36–37
Westphalia (now Germany), 5–6
Wetzel, Rheinhard A., 131
When Harlem Was in Vogue (Levering), 143, 176
While We Are Still Here (organization), 328–29
White, Walter, 159–60, 166, 174, 175, 338, 345–46
white flight, 109 120, 186
White House, 142, 285, 338
white people, 22, 116, 167, 176–77, 197, 206, 244, 298–99; gentrification and, 171, 239–40, 256–58, 268–69; Great Migration and, 105–6, 110, 121, 124–25; in Harlem demographics, 119–20, 237, 281, 296
Whitmire, Ethelene, 149–51

Wickquasgeck (Native Americans), 2, 5, 14, 59
Wilkerson, Isabel, 70, 103, 214, 327
Wilkins, Roy, 174, 176, 219
Williams, Billy Dee, 250
Williams, Mary Lou, 188–90, 189, 190, 237–38, 312, 326
Willis, Bruce, 293
Wilson, Janifer P., 301
Wilson, Woodrow, 121
Winfrey, Oprah, 317, 325
Wolcott, Oliver, 54
Wolfe, Thomas, 256
Wolfe House & Building Movers, 274
women, 86–87, 163–64, 182; Black, 6, 120, 139, 149, 175, 203, 210–11, 215–16, 253–56, 255; of the Harlem Renaissance, 66–67, 149–53, 317–18
The Women of Brewster Place (television series), 325
Women of the Harlem Renaissance (Wall), 317
Woodson, Carter G., 155
Woodstock Music and Art Fair, 226
working-class, 62, 106, 115, 238–39
Works Progress Administration (WPA), New Deal, 141–42, 184, 208, 212–14
World War I, 114, 133, 136, 139–41, 227
World War II, 202
WPA. *See* Works Progress Administration
Wright, Richard, 184–85, 188, 208, 212–14, 317

Yankee Stadium, 102
yellow fever, 42, 60
Yorktown, Virginia, 36
Yoshihara, Koichi, 312, 328
You Can't Go Home Again (Wolfe), 256
Young, Michael, 332

Zegendael (Pieters' farm), 13, 16–17

Davida Siwisa James was born in Philadelphia, Pennsylvania. As a child, she lived alternately in her hometown and in the Morningside Heights section of Harlem in Manhattan. As an adult, she lived in Sugar Hill in West Harlem, St. Thomas, U.S. Virgin Islands, and Los Angeles, California.

She holds a bachelor's degree in English from the University of California, Los Angeles, and attended Penn State Dickinson Law in Carlisle, Pennsylvania. Her works include the memoir *The South Africa of His Heart; Senior Services for the Financially Challenged*; and *Life in Brief: A Collection of Short Stories, Essays, and Poems*. She lives in Los Angeles, California, with her husband, Robelto. Her son, David Hudson Obayuwana, is a screenwriter.

SELECT TITLES FROM EMPIRE STATE EDITIONS

William Seraile, *Angels of Mercy: White Women and the History of New York's Colored Orphan Asylum*

Daniel Campo, *The Accidental Playground: Brooklyn Waterfront Narratives of the Undesigned and Unplanned*

Joseph B. Raskin, *The Routes Not Taken: A Trip Through New York City's Unbuilt Subway System*

Phillip Deery, *Red Apple: Communism and McCarthyism in Cold War New York*

North Brother Island: The Last Unknown Place in New York City. Photographs by Christopher Payne, A History by Randall Mason, Essay by Robert Sullivan

Stephen Miller, *Walking New York: Reflections of American Writers from Walt Whitman to Teju Cole*

Tom Glynn, *Reading Publics: New York City's Public Libraries, 1754–1911*

Craig Saper, *The Amazing Adventures of Bob Brown: A Real-Life Zelig Who Wrote His Way Through the 20th Century*

R. Scott Hanson, *City of Gods: Religious Freedom, Immigration, and Pluralism in Flushing, Queens*. Foreword by Martin E. Marty

Dorothy Day and the Catholic Worker: The Miracle of Our Continuance. Edited, with an Introduction and Additional Text by Kate Hennessy, Photographs by Vivian Cherry, Text by Dorothy Day

Mark Naison and Bob Gumbs, *Before the Fires: An Oral History of African American Life in the Bronx from the 1930s to the 1960s*

Robert Weldon Whalen, *Murder, Inc., and the Moral Life: Gangsters and Gangbusters in La Guardia's New York*

Joanne Witty and Henrik Krogius, *Brooklyn Bridge Park: A Dying Waterfront Transformed*

Sharon Egretta Sutton, *When Ivory Towers Were Black: A Story about Race in America's Cities and Universities*

Pamela Hanlon, *A Wordly Affair: New York, the United Nations, and the Story Behind Their Unlikely Bond*

Britt Haas, *Fighting Authoritarianism: American Youth Activism in the 1930s*

David J. Goodwin, *Left Bank of the Hudson: Jersey City and the Artists of 111 1st Street*. Foreword by DW Gibson

Nandini Bagchee, *Counter Institution: Activist Estates of the Lower East Side*

Susan Celia Greenfield (ed.), *Sacred Shelter: Thirteen Journeys of Homelessness and Healing*

Elizabeth Macaulay-Lewis and Matthew M. McGowan (eds.), *Classical New York: Discovering Greece and Rome in Gotham*

Susan Opotow and Zachary Baron Shemtob (eds.), *New York after 9/11*

Andrew Feffer, *Bad Faith: Teachers, Liberalism, and the Origins of McCarthyism*

Colin Davey with Thomas A. Lesser, *The American Museum of Natural History and How It Got That Way*. Forewords by Neil deGrasse Tyson and Kermit Roosevelt III

Lolita Buckner Inniss, *The Princeton Fugitive Slave: The Trials of James Collins Johnson*

Angel Garcia, *The Kingdom Began in Puerto Rico: Neil Connolly's Priesthood in the South Bronx*

Jim Mackin, *Notable New Yorkers of Manhattan's Upper West Side: Bloomingdale–Morningside Heights*

Matthew Spady, *The Neighborhood Manhattan Forgot: Audubon Park and the Families Who Shaped It*

Marilyn S. Greenwald and Yun Li, *Eunice Hunton Carter: A Lifelong Fight for Social Justice*

Jeffrey A. Kroessler, *Sunnyside Gardens: Planning and Preservation in a Historic Garden Suburb*

Elizabeth Macaulay-Lewis, *Antiquity in Gotham: The Ancient Architecture of New York City*

Ron Howell, *King Al: How Sharpton Took the Throne*

Phil Rosenzweig, *"12 Angry Men": Reginald Rose and the Making of an American Classic*

Jean Arrington with Cynthia S. LaValle, *From Factories to Palaces: Architect Charles B. J. Snyder and the New York City Public Schools*. Foreword by Peg Breen

Boukary Sawadogo, *Africans in Harlem: An Untold New York Story*

Alvin Eng, *Our Laundry, Our Town: My Chinese American Life from Flushing to the Downtown Stage and Beyond*

Stephanie Azzarone, *Heaven on the Hudson: Mansions, Monuments, and Marvels of Riverside Park*

Ron Goldberg, *Boy with the Bullhorn: A Memoir and History of ACT UP New York*. Foreword by Dan Barry

Peter Quinn, *Cross Bronx: A Writing Life*

Mark Bulik, *Ambush at Central Park: When the IRA Came to New York*

Matt Dallos, *In the Adirondacks: Dispatches from the Largest Park in the Lower 48*

Brandon Dean Lamson, *Caged: A Teacher's Journey Through Rikers, or How I Beheaded the Minotaur*

Raj Tawney, *Colorful Palate: Savored Stories from a Mixed Life*

Edward Cahill, *Disorderly Men*

Joseph Heathcott, *Global Queens: An Urban Mosaic*

Francis R. Kowsky with Lucille Gordon, *Hell on Color, Sweet on Song: Jacob Wrey Mould and the Artful Beauty of Central Park*

Jill Jonnes, *South Bronx Rising: The Rise, Fall, and Resurrection of an American City*, Third Edition

Barbara G. Mensch, *A Falling-Off Place: The Transformation of Lower Manhattan*

David J. Goodwin, *Midnight Rambles: H. P. Lovecraft in Gotham*

Felipe Luciano, *Flesh and Spirit: Confessions of a Young Lord*

Maximo G. Martinez, *Sojourners in the Capital of the World: Garifuna Immigrants*

Jennifer Baum, *Just City: Growing Up on the Upper West Side When Housing Was a Human Righ*

Annik LaFarge, *On the High Line: The Definitive Guide*, Third Edition. Foreword by Rick Dark

Marie Carter, *Mortimer and the Witches: A History of Nineteenth-Century Fortune Tellers*

Alice Sparberg Alexiou, *Devil's Mile: The Rich, Gritty History of the Bowery*. Foreword by Peter Quinn

Carey Kasten and Brenna Moore, *Mutuality in El Barrio: Stories of the Little Sisters of the Assumption Family Health Service*. Foreword by Norma Benítez Sánchez

Kimberly A. Orcutt, *The American Art-Union: Utopia and Skepticism in the Antebellum Era*

For a complete list, visit www.fordhampress.com/empire-state-editions.

www.ingramcontent.com/pod-product-compliance
Lightning Source LLC
Jackson TN
JSHW022326300825
90255JS00001B/1